The Green Banking Transition Manual

Rodrigo Zeidan

The Green Banking Transition Manual

Navigating the Sustainable Finance Landscape

palgrave
macmillan

Rodrigo Zeidan
NYU Shanghai
Shanghai, China

ISBN 978-981-96-2851-3 ISBN 978-981-96-2852-0 (eBook)
https://doi.org/10.1007/978-981-96-2852-0

Cover credit: enjoynz

This Palgrave Macmillan imprint is published by the registered company Springer Nature Singapore Pte Ltd.
The registered company address is: 152 Beach Road, #21-01/04 Gateway East, Singapore 189721, Singapore

Foreword

Good bankers are experts in assessing the risk-reward calculus for their investments. In a rapidly changing world, that calculus is changing. Everything from geopolitical risk to cybersecurity to climate change must now be assessed by the smart investor to protect their returns. Most regulators across the world are responding to increased levels of risk by requiring more transparency and reporting by both corporates and investors on climate and sustainability-linked impacts.

This is a relatively new world for bankers and they have not always gotten it right. ESG products such as ETFs have been created with insufficient rigor or transparency, leading to concerns about green-washing. In addition, while studies demonstrate that many sustainability investments perform at par or in some cases outperform conventional investing products, some bankers have launched ESG products that have not performed well—often, upon further scrutiny—because they do not understand the value-drivers behind sustainability value creation.

Dr. Rodrigo Zeidan's book provides bankers with the tools they need to develop sustainable finance products that reduce risk and improve the upside—across a variety of asset classes. Zeidan's hands-on work with the banking sector, as well as his research at NYU, delivers useful insights and strategies for the reader. Bankers will come away with a better understanding of how they can manage climate risks and develop new sustainable finance products that will pass muster with regulators and investors.

Our research at NYU Stern Center for Sustainable Business, where Dr. Zeidan is a Senior Scholar, focuses on understanding the business case for sustainability. Working with different industry verticals, we find that embedded sustainability core to business strategy drives better management and performance—ranging from reducing operational inefficiencies to innovation and growth, to sales and marketing benefits, and to risk mitigation.

Bankers have the opportunity to deploy capital to help companies be better performing through sustainability and the ability to help fund the low-carbon transition at the speed and scale needed. This not only creates business opportunities but it will help create a better world for this and future generations.

New York, USA

Tensie Whelan
Distinguished Professor
of Practice, NYU Stern,
and Founding Director NYU
Stern Center for Sustainable
Business

Acknowledgments

People optimize different things. Some people want to make as much money as possible. I maximize freedom. I aim to make enough money to spend my time as I please within the constraints of being a professor. Achieving this goal requires the support of several colleagues and mentors, as well as institutional backing.

My intellectual trajectory owes to many great professors, co-authors, colleagues, and students. However, I will concentrate on the colleagues who gave me their valuable time to improve this book. Marti Subrahmanyam is the type of remarkable person that one meets once or twice in their life. I ingrained some of his lessons so profoundly that once I repeated one of his lessons back to him before quickly realizing he was the source of that wisdom. If I must steal, I might as well steal from the best.

Tensie Whelan, former head of the Rainforest Alliance and now the Center for Sustainable Business director at NYU Stern, continues to support my work. I hope I can reciprocate more in the future. Now at Schulich, Olaf Weber believed in my work and invited me to become Associate Editor at the Journal of Sustainable Finance & Investment. Seye Onabolu, from Sona Analytics, bought the idea of the Sustainability Credit Score System, and together, we developed the Sona Sustainability Credit Score System. Building solutions is much more challenging than claiming that something must be done.

I must thank NYU's GRI program for funding research trips to Florence and Prague, where I spent time writing this book. I didn't realize I had strong willpower until I had to force myself to work instead of exploring more of these beautiful cities.

I am also indebted to the HiTime Fund at NYU Shanghai. This fund provides research funds that allow me the flexibility to concentrate on research when my teaching duties are over.

Contents

List of Figures

List of Tables

CHAPTER 1

Introduction

Commercial and investment banks move slowly. Financial regulation exists to prevent systemic risks and events such as the great financial crisis, from which the world is still recovering almost two decades later. After the deregulation of the early 2000s, we now live in a robust regulatory environment. Thus, a manual on green banking must consider regulatory pressure and constraints in establishing the steps banks must take if they aim to green their operations.

This book aims to detail most of the steps for greening banks without fundamentally changing their business model. This manual is not written by a naïve financial economist. Banks have little internal incentive to move away from business as usual. Not because they are blood-sucking institutions, capitalist predators that don't care about the environment. It is much simpler than that. Organizational inertia is a powerful force; it is Newton's First Law applied to the business world: an organization in motion under business-as-usual conditions will continue in this trajectory unless an external force acts upon it.

The book's structure is straightforward. It starts with explaining the primary profit and capital adequacy indicators to establish the conditions for feasible sustainability initiatives. It then presents the primary methods for incorporating environmental and social indicators in capital requirement and value-at-risk estimations. The first chapter also describes the

R. Zeidan, *The Green Banking Transition Manual*,
https://doi.org/10.1007/978-981-96-2852-0_1

limitations of the principles for responsible investing and corporate governance models that integrate environmental concerns into institutions' hierarchical structures.

The following chapter focuses on sustainable lending. The central idea is that banks can broaden credit risk models to consider ESG and other nonfinancial indicators. This integration can increase profits while reducing systemic risks if banks create sustainability-related ratings that complement regular credit risk ratings, allowing institutions to funnel more resources via lower interest rates or better credit access to more sustainable companies and restricting credit to vulnerable firms. The methodology is described in great detail as it is partly based on an open platform where analysts can already generate nonfinancial credit scores for companies of all sizes.

Subsequently, the focus is on ESG investing, a controversial but fundamental area in wealth management. Several lawsuits in the United States have recently jeopardized integrating ESG indicators into regular portfolio management. For instance, a few American Airlines employees filed suits claiming that the firms managing their pensions violated their fiduciary duty by ESG screening companies into their portfolios. American courts have extended these to a class action suit comprising 100,000 American Airlines employees. Such litigation may define the boundaries of ESG investing in America. However, in Europe, some funds are being targeted precisely because they don't consider these indicators in their investment strategies. Depositors claim that ignoring climate change risks is also a violation of fiduciary duty. Regardless of these litigations, banks cannot ignore incorporating nonfinancial indicators into portfolio selection, even if they ultimately choose to refrain from actively using them. The chapter describes several approaches to such integration, from exclusion criteria and divestment strategies to an ESG-adjusted Capital Asset Pricing Model (CAPM) approach. It also explains why asset managers don't accelerate ESG investing, how banks incorporate green bonds in their portfolios, and how to incorporate nonfinancial information into valuation models.

Finally, the last chapter deals with green central banking, from theoretical arguments on the costs and benefits of allowing these institutions to extend their mandates to methodologies for greening stress testing, the primary supervisory tool for estimating systemic risks.

Of course, there is always the possibility that financial institutions are proactive and shake things up by adapting their operations to climate

Table 1.1 How external pressure can move financial institutions from business as usual

	External pressure		
	Supply-side/Market	*Regulation*	*Demand-side/ Ideological*
Benefits	Potentially efficient; Self-reinforcing	Potentially immediate; Customizable to local environments	Potentially efficient; Self-reinforcing
Costs	Coordination costly; Outside lag	Inside lag; Potentially inefficient	Coordination costly; Outside lag

change risks and other sustainability dimensions. Even if that is the case, the current tome is helpful because it provides a roadmap for such adaptation. However, pressure for banks to evolve will likely come from the companies' environment. Below, we have a straightforward classification of the types of external pressure that can influence companies.

External pressure can come from competitors, consumers, and regulators, as shown in Table 1.1. Market-oriented reforms can be economically efficient and are self-reinforcing, but they can take a long time. Take, for instance, the dissemination of ESG indicators. They were created twenty years ago, and we still have hundreds of standards floating around. ESG indicators may or may not be the best way forward, but it is clear that it is taking too long for a single standard to emerge. I refer to this as outside lag or the time a new initiative takes to be adopted by most market agents.

Regulation can have immediate effects, of course, bypassing outside lag entirely. Of course, blunt force regulation is rarely enforced, but it is always an option for regulators. For example, forty-six countries signed the Montreal Protocol on Substances That Deplete the Ozone Layer in September 1987; it went into effect in 1989, and 198 countries and territories eventually ratified it. The phasing out of most substances was so swift that the ozone layer should recover almost entirely in a couple more decades. Of course, such broad international agreements are rare.

Sustainable finance is a complex process in which stakeholders, companies, and regulators push and pull toward new standards and changes in financial institutions' practices. Institutions aiming to keep the status quo can usually afford to do it or postpone any fundamental changes. A former student working for a large German cooperative bank in 2017 evaluated the sustainability reports of German financial institutions. He found that less than one-third of German banks, public and private, even had sustainability reports in 2009. By 2015, virtually all institutions had been publishing shining reports about their environmental initiatives. Most of these reports were greenwashing, including the one published by the bank he worked for, as he knew that the institution didn't do much other than pay lip service to such initiatives.

Much digital ink has been spilled about how financial institutions should behave. I don't aim to contribute to this significant but frustrating debate. I aim to present a guide for institutions that want to take actual steps toward combining economic and environmental performance (defined broadly, as it includes social indicators as well). However, I do present a nuanced debate about "Green Central Banking." As we can see from Table 1.1, regulatory pressure can be transformative, given that it requires institutions to change quickly. Still, we shouldn't expect central banks to commit fully to a green transition. These are conservative institutions with a clear mandate of financial stability. Yet regulatory innovations can accelerate decarbonization faster than market initiatives.

Given that this tome is a mix of technical and theoretical manuals, we first establish the primary constraints that financial institutions face. Arguments about banks' green transitions should be grounded on the realities these institutions face, but actual business environments are often ignored. This is why Chapter 2 starts with a discussion of banks' crucial financial metrics, divided into industry-specific profit indicators and regulatory-mandated variables. Comprehending what executives aim to maximize (or minimize, in the case of regulatory capital) is crucial to building feasible sustainability-related solutions.

It is still common to hear excuses for why institutions are not moving faster. "We need better models," "We need more studies," and "The data is not good enough for us to do anything, so we shouldn't rock the boat." The present work details all the steps necessary for banks to accelerate their green transition. Here, these excuses are not salient. Banks are no different than other profit-maximizing organizations. Pushed by the competitive or regulatory environments, they will change faster. Some institutions may take proactive actions, but we can't count on that as the only mechanism for climate change mitigation.

Another challenge distinguishing green banking from other companies' environmental actions is the potential for systemic risks. In most markets, when a competitor goes under, surviving firms benefit. As the great financial crisis has shown us, that is not the case for financial institutions, especially those that pose systemic risk. Bears Sterns and Lehman Brothers go under, and the stock of other institutions crash, with several needing to be rescued by taxpayers. On the one hand, central banks and banks can always shout "Systemic risk!" as a jail-free card to any stakeholder, aiming to hold them accountable for climate change and their social impact. On the other hand, these are increasingly significant risks that could potentially topple whole financial systems.

Greening banks is a long, arduous process. Sometimes, we see two steps forward and one step backward. Other times, it feels like five steps backward for every step forward. Still, regulators and financial institutions have developed numerous initiatives. I hope this book helps advance this agenda even more pragmatically.

CHAPTER 2

Financial Statements, Banks' Operations, and Systemic Risk

"Profits are our blood and the stock price our currency," noted the president of a multinational bank in our meeting about designing a course for the bank's senior managers. His goal was to ensure that the managers' understanding of the profit indicators was aligned, given that the institution's goal was to enter a growth phase planned to last five years. Managers should understand how a rising stock price was crucial for the institution's expansion by acquiring local and international competitors.

Climate change can impact a bank's bottom line, and banks are likely the most aggressive companies in squeezing all drops of profit from their operations. The business case for sustainability requires that directors, shareholders, and other stakeholders understand all dimensions of how environmental and other nonfinancial measures drive or limit profits. Organizational inertia is a formidable obstacle, but it is even harder to shake banks out of their business-as-usual path if we can't register the changes in how nonfinancial factors affect banks' balance sheets.

As with any substantial changes, improving banks' environmental outcomes requires either gradual processes in which institutions slowly adapt to changing market conditions or traumatic transformations from significant risk events. We can't count on the latter, but we can certainly provide a roadmap for the former.

This book embeds sustainability-related actions in good old-fashioned bank profit maximization behavior. While climate change is an immediate

R. Zeidan, *The Green Banking Transition Manual*,
https://doi.org/10.1007/978-981-96-2852-0_2

danger, it is unlikely that global governments will upend their financial systems to prioritize mitigation. Thus, this book is about robust banking management as much as about "greening" financial institutions. Details about capital adequacy ratios are the priority instead of long discussions about the shortcomings of financial capitalism.

We start by analyzing banks' financial statements and profit ratios, which differ from those of nonfinancial companies. Significant differences exist between accounting and economic definitions of financial gains on profit indicators. "Revenue is ego; profit is fleeting; the only thing that matters is cold, hard cash (flow)" is a famous saying regarding nonfinancial companies in some corners of the world. This is no different for financial institutions; banks must have enough resources to meet their immediate obligations, even if they rise unexpectedly.

Some economic-based profit indicators specific to financial institutions are RAROC (risk-adjusted return on capital) and RANPV (risk-adjusted net present value). Even if they are primarily specific to financial institutions, these profit indicators follow a similar logic to that of all companies. There are several measures of "profit" in income statements, from gross profits to net income. Before establishing these indicators, we analyze financial institutions' regular income and cash flow statements to understand the drivers of earnings in financial institutions.

2.1 Income Statements

The standard simplified income statement for a financial institution is described in Table 2.1. To wit, income statements for nonfinancial companies start with revenue, deduct variable costs (determining the gross margin), and then fixed costs, resulting in operating income (EBIT).

EBITDA is to a company what gross wage is to a family. Households are comfortable if their labor income is sufficient to pay off taxes, mortgages (or rent), interest from previous loans, and family expenses. Similarly, EBITDA is the cash a company generates to maintain productive capacity and pay the government, banks, and shareholders (and, in addition, to support a firm's growth if required, as in Fig. 2.1).

Depreciation and amortization are used to expense the cost of the property, equipment, and intellectual property, among other tangible and intangible investments. A straightforward way to interpret depreciation and amortization is the required resources for a company to maintain its

Table 2.1 Bank of America's consolidated statement of income

(In millions, except per share information)	*2021*	*2020*	*2019*
Net interest income			
Interest income	$47,672	$51,585	$71,236
Interest expense	4738	8225	22,345
Net interest income	42,934	43,360	48,891
Noninterest income			
Fees and commissions	39,299	34,551	33,015
Market making and similar activities	8691	8355	9034
Other income	(1811)	(738)	304
Total noninterest income	46,179	42,168	42,353
Total revenue, net of interest expense	89,113	85,528	91,244
Provision for credit losses	(4594)	11,320	3590
Noninterest expense			
Compensation and benefits	36,140	32,725	31,977
Occupancy and equipment	7138	7141	6588
Information processing and communications	5769	5222	4646
Product delivery and transaction-related	3881	3433	2762
Marketing	1939	1701	1934
Professional fees	1775	1694	1597
Other general operating	3089	3297	5396
Total noninterest expense	59,731	55,213	54,900
Income before income taxes	33,976	18,995	32,754
Income tax expense	1998	1101	5324
Net income	$31,978	$17,894	$27,430
Preferred stock dividends	1421	1421	1432
Net income applicable to common shareholders	$30,557	$16,473	$25,998
Per common share information			
Earnings	$3.60	$1.88	$2.77
Diluted earnings	3.57	1.87	2.75
Average common shares issued and outstanding	8493.3	8753.2	9390.5
Average diluted common shares issued and outstanding	8558.4	8796.9	9442.9

Source Bank of America, 2022. https://investor.bankofamerica.com/annual-reports-and-proxy-statements

productive capacity. Machines break, and properties must be renovated now and then.

Companies must report operating income (EBIT), usually the difference between EBITDA, depreciation, and amortization. Of course, some companies voluntarily report some type of "Adjusted EBITDA" that is tailored to their realities. Here, we will not detail all the accounting rules for EBITDA, EBIT, and the following cash flow items. We are not

Fig. 2.1 EBITDA's flow

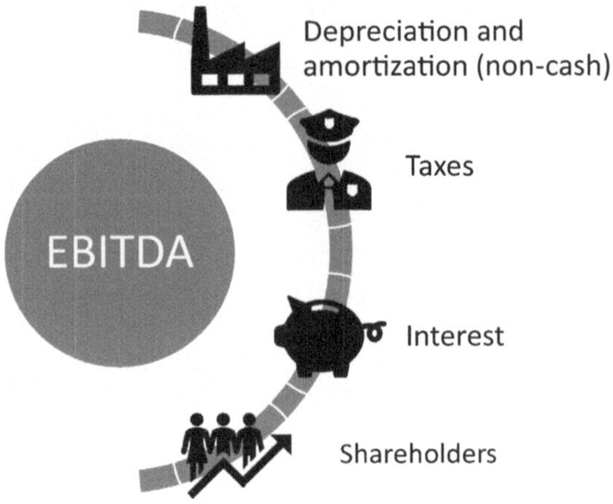

interested in how nonfinancial companies build their financial reports but consider the peculiarities of financial institutions' reports.

For financial institutions, the main distinction is in separating interest and noninterest income. Furthermore, all expenses are divided according to interest and noninterest income. The equivalent of operating income is the net income before taxes, and after adjustments for income taxes, minority interest expenses, and extraordinary items, we arrive at the resulting net income. As in the case of nonfinancial companies, income before taxes is the most relevant account for a financial institution. From it, income flows to the government via taxes, risk management (and other dimensions related to changes in the value of banks' financial positions), and shareholders (Table 2.1).

The main distinction between the income statements of financial and nonfinancial companies is expressed in Table 2.2, which describes charges against net income due to risk management and changes in the value of banks' financial positions. Regarding 2021, we can see positive changes to Bank of America's positions in debit valuation, employee benefit plan adjustments, and negative charges on debt securities, derivatives, and foreign currency adjustments.

By analyzing banks' financial statements, we can see why stress tests' initial focus (Chapter 5) is on the effects of economic shocks on net income. Banks can create credit, but that does not mean they can't lack

Table 2.2 Bank of America's consolidated statement of comprehensive income

(Dollars in millions)	*2021*	*2020*	*2019*
Net income	$31,978	$17,894	$27,430
Other comprehensive income (loss), net of tax:			
Net change in debt securities	(2077)	4799	5875
Net change in debit valuation adjustments	356	(498)	(963)
Net change in derivatives	(2306)	826	616
Employee benefit plan adjustments	624	(98)	136
Net change in foreign currency translation adjustments	(45)	(52)	(86)
Other comprehensive income (loss)	(3448)	4977	5578
Comprehensive income	$28,530	$22,871	$33,008

Source Bank of America, 2022. https://investor.bankofamerica.com/annual-reports-and-proxy-statements

funds. Banks can suffer a liquidity crisis, but it does not take the same form as an industrial firm's bank account lacking funds.

Unlike nonfinancial companies, where cash is king, and net income and cash flow can deviate for years, that is not the case for banks. That is due to several (non-exhaustive) reasons.

First, banks' core businesses result in a mismatch between short-term assets and liabilities. As depositors can withdraw their funds at will, a significant share of liabilities is "instantaneous" because they can be immediately redeemed. Second, net income is tied to banks' regulatory capital, and financial institutions can go under swiftly if their capital is not considered adequate by regulators. The third reason is that interbank markets are incredibly liquid, and banks have access to special credit lines with their central banks as a last line of defense. Hence, reserves, not cash, matter the most for banks. For financial institutions, "capital adequacy is king," which does not seem to have the same ring as "cash is king," right?

Distinctions between income statements for financial and nonfinancial companies also hold for cash flow statements. While for nonfinancial companies, cash flow statements are particularly relevant because they track variations in actual expenditures instead of accounting measures, such statements serve a different purpose for banks. Cash flow statements mostly show how much money was actually paid or received by the financial instruments transacted by banks. While net changes in derivatives in the income statement were −U$2.3 billion in 2021, net changes in trading and derivative assets/liabilities in the cash flow statement were −22.1 billion for the same year. Remember that derivatives are commonly used for hedging purposes, and accounting or cash flow losses don't necessarily mean shareholders are taking a hit. Gains in other accounts can offset these losses in fair value or trading of derivates (Table 2.3).

Interestingly, we should reiterate that net income matters more than the net cash provided by financing activities from a regulatory perspective. Moreover, answering central banks' requirements makes financial statements even more critical for banks than for the average nonfinancial firm.

Another consequential distinction between nonfinancial companies' cash flow statements for banks is the (non)treatment of capital expenditures (CAPEX) and operational expenditures (OPEX)—neither feature in Bank of America's cash flow statement in Table 2.2. The cash flow statement includes adjustments to reconcile net income to net cash provided by operating activities, such as provision for credit losses, gains on sales of debt securities, depreciation, and amortization, but not the typical lines encountered in such statements for industrial or other service companies. Similarly, investing activities, instead of fixed assets, comprise net changes in deposits, federal funds, debt securities carried at fair value, proceeds from sales, paydowns, maturities, etc.

In addition, several rules make the accounting and the market value of investments, intangible assets, and capital expenditures differ in the financial statements of industrial companies. However, banks must mark-to-market most of their holdings, with updated fair value calculations that can be quite complex.

Also of interest are banks' sources of income. After all, greening banks is easier if economic incentives are aligned. The more banks must invest or forfeit income, the harder it will be to overcome organizational inertia. Bank of America and many banks report net interest and noninterest income sources, as shown in Table 2.4.

We can summarize these categories for 2021 in Table 2.5.

The choice of Bank of America as an example is due to its peculiar revenue structure for 2021, which is split almost equally between interest (U$47.5 billion) and noninterest (U$46.2 billion) income. The pattern was similar in 2020 (U$43 vs. 42 billion) and not much different in 2019, with interest income representing a larger share than in the following years (U$49 vs. 42 billion).

Table 2.3 Bank of America's consolidated statement of cash flows

(Dollars in millions)	*2021*	*2020*	*2019*
Operating activities			
Net income	$31,978	$17,894	$27,430
Adjustments to reconcile net income to net cash provided by operating activities:			
Provision for credit losses	(4594)	11,320	3590
Gains on sales of debt securities	(22)	(411)	(217)
Depreciation and amortization	1898	1843	1729
Net amortization of premium/discount on debt securities	5837	4101	2066
Deferred income taxes	(838)	(1737)	2435
Stock-based compensation	2768	2031	1974
Impairment of equity method investment	–	–	2072
Loans held for sale:			
Originations and purchases	(43,635)	(19,657)	(28,874)
Proceeds from sales and paydowns of loans initially classified as held for sale and instruments from related securitization activities	34,684	19,049	30,191
Net change in:			
Trading and derivative assets/liabilities	(22,104)	16,942	7920
Other assets	(34,455)	(12,883)	(11,113)
Accrued expenses and other liabilities	16,639	(4385)	16,363
Other operating activities, net	4651	3886	6211
Net cash provided by (used in) operating activities	(7193)	37,993	61,777
Investing activities			
Net change in:			
Time deposits placed and other short-term investments	(598)	561	387
Federal funds sold and securities borrowed or purchased under agreements to resell	53,338	(29,461)	(13,466)
Debt securities carried at fair value:			
Proceeds from sales	6893	77,524	52,006
Proceeds from paydowns and maturities	159,616	91,084	79,114
Purchases	(238,398)	(194,877)	(152,782)
Held-to-maturity debt securities:			
Proceeds from paydowns and maturities	124,880	93,835	34,770
Purchases	(362,736)	(257,535)	(37,115)
Loans and leases:			
Proceeds from sales of loans initially classified as held for investment and instruments from securitization activities	10,396	13,351	12,201
Purchases	(5164)	(5229)	(5963)
Other changes in loans and leases, net	(58,039)	36,571	(46,808)

(continued)

Table 2.3 (continued)

(Dollars in millions)	*2021*	*2020*	*2019*
Other investing activities, net	(3479)	(3489)	(2974)
Net cash used in investing activities	(313,291)	(177,665)	(80,630)
Financing activities			
Net change in:			
Deposits	268,966	360,677	53,327
Federal funds purchased and securities loaned or sold under agreements to repurchase	22,006	5214	(21,879)
Short-term borrowings	4432	(4893)	4004
Long-term debt:			
Proceeds from issuance	76,675	57,013	52,420
Retirement	(46,826)	(47,948)	(50,794)
Preferred stock:			
Proceeds from issuance	2169	2181	3643
Redemption	(1971)	(1072)	(2568)
Common stock repurchased	(25,126)	(7025)	(28,144)
Cash dividends paid	(8055)	(7727)	(5934)
Other financing activities, net	(620)	(601)	(698)
Net cash provided by financing activities	291,650	355,819	3377
Effect of exchange rate changes on cash and cash equivalents	(3408)	2756	(368)
Net increase (decrease) in cash and cash equivalents	(32,242)	218,903	(15,844)
Cash and cash equivalents on January 1	380,463	161,560	177,404
Cash and cash equivalents on December 31	$348,221	$380,463	$161,560
Supplemental cash flow disclosures			
Interest paid	$4,506	$8,662	$22,196
Income taxes paid, net	2760	2894	4359

Source Bank of America, 2022. https://investor.bankofamerica.com/annual-reports-and-proxy-statements

More importantly, it clearly shows which areas generate significant revenue for large financial institutions (some small banks specialize in niche segments). Net income mostly comes from loans and debt securities, as expected. Noninterest income is more spread out, with investment and brokerage services comprising over one-third of that category and the rest evenly divided into card income, service charges, investment banking fees, and market making. All these categories can be tied to better environmental outcomes, as we will see in later sections.

Table 2.4 Net interest and noninterest income, Bank of America, 2021

(Dollars in millions)	*2021*	*2020*	*2019*
Net interest income			
Interest income			
Loans and leases	$29,282	$34,029	$43,086
Debt securities	12,376	9790	11,806
Federal funds sold and securities borrowed or purchased under agreements to resell	−90	903	4843
Trading account assets	3770	4128	5196
Other interest income	2334	2735	6305
Total interest income	47,672	51,585	71,236
Interest expense			
Deposits	537	1943	7188
Short-term borrowings	−358	987	7208
Trading account liabilities	1128	974	1249
Long-term debt	3431	4321	6700
Total interest expense	4738	8225	22,345
Net interest income	$42,934	$43,360	$48,891
Noninterest income			
Fees and commissions			
Card income			
Interchange fees	$4560	$3954	$3834
Other card income	1658	1702	1963
Total card income	6218	5656	5797
Service charges			
Deposit-related fees	6271	5991	6588
Lending-related fees	1233	1150	1086
Total service charges	7504	7141	7674
Investment and brokerage services			
Asset management fees	12,729	10,708	10,241
Brokerage fees	3961	3866	3661
Total investment and brokerage services	16,690	14,574	13,902
Investment banking fees			
Underwriting income	5077	4698	2998
Syndication fees	1499	861	1184
Financial advisory services	2311	1621	1460
Total investment banking fees	8887	7180	5642
Total fees and commissions	39,299	34,551	33,015
Market making and similar activities	8691	8355	9034
Other income (loss)	−1811	−738	304
Total noninterest income	$46,179	$42,168	$42,353

Source Bank of America, 2022. https://investor.bankofamerica.com/annual-reports-and-proxy-statements

Table 2.5 Categories for typical banks' balance sheets

Net income	*2021*	*% Total*
Loans and leases	29,282	61.4
Debt securities	12,376	26.0
Trading account assets	3770	7.9
Other interest income	2334	4.9
Total interest income	$47,672	100.0
Total card income	6218	13.5
Total service charges	7504	16.2
Total investment and brokerage services	16,690	36.1
Total investment banking fees	8887	19.2
Market making and similar activities	8691	18.8
Other income (loss)	−1811	−3.9
Total noninterest income	$46,179	100.0

Source Bank of America, 2022. https://investor.bankofamerica.com/annual-reports-and-proxy-statements

How can climate change impact banks' financial statements? Fig. 2.2 illustrates the evolution of banks' net income components as in the stress test exercise (see Chapter 5) by Hosseini et al. (2022).

Figure 2.2 shows rising costs, decreased revenue, and required capital investments that should make institutions less profitable in the long run. Chapter 5 describes how stress test exercises bring materiality to the effects of climate change on banks. What matters most is that profitability indicators can be expected to suffer if institutions work diligently to maintain the status quo; business-as-usual is not a riskless proposition.

2.2 Profit and Efficiency Ratios

Return on assets (ROA), on equity (ROE), on invested capital (ROIC), on capital employed (ROCE), operating, gross, pretax, and profit margins, and economic value added (EVA) are some of the most used profit margins in financial accounting. Liquidity ratios include current, acid test, absolute liquidity, and net working capital ratios.

These profit and liquidity ratios underpin investment strategies and corporate finance. However, bank management and employees do not use all of them to track the financial performance of their institutions. Many of these indicators are of little importance to financial institutions' performance.

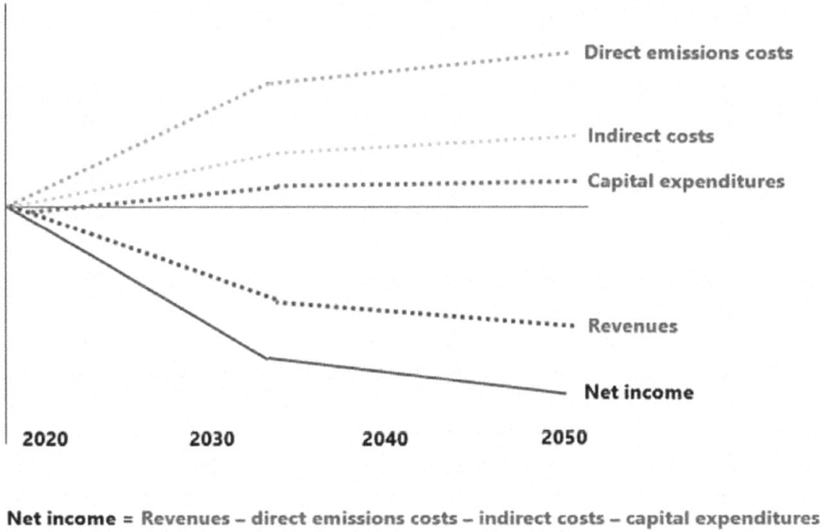

Fig. 2.2 Illustrative evolution of the components of net income (% change relative to baseline) (*Source* Hosseini et al. [2022])

Some economic-based profit indicators specific to financial institutions are RAROC (risk-adjusted return on capital), Net economic profit growth, and RANPV (risk-adjusted net present value). In contrast, efficiency indicators include expenses to income, credit-to-deposits, and cash productivity ratios. Banks also routinely use standard indicators, such as revenue and EPS growth, ROE, and total shareholder return. Here, we detail a few relevant indicators used primarily for financial institutions, large or small, commercial or investment.

RAROC, or risk-adjusted return on capital (RAROC), is a profit indicator of return on investment that accounts for different risk profiles. Lower-risk investments should generate lower returns, and riskier assets should pay higher premia. For most nonfinancial corporations, the weighted average cost of capital is similar across business units, and managers don't commonly adjust their performance indicators by the risk profile of their projects. Similarly, the estimation of RANPV is done by modifying a standard net present value (NPV) to different risk profiles.

Net economic profit (NEP) represents cash available to common shareholders after deducting a capital charge. NEP growth is similar to economic value added (EVA) for nonfinancial companies, an adequate measure of short-term economic profit.

The expense-to-income ratio or cost-to-income ratio is a simple relation between operating expenses and operating income, including net interest and noninterest income. The credit-to-deposit ratio is also a simple relationship, this time between time deposits and loans. Commercial banks create credit as financial intermediaries based on their expected funding, much of which is client deposits. An 80 to 90% ratio is considered standard in the industry.

Net interest margin is a bank's net interest revenue as a share of its average interest-bearing assets. This indicator informs managers about the profitability of a bank's loans. It describes how much a bank earns compared to the amount it pays in interest on deposits. Notably, only interest-bearing assets are included in the calculation.

Take the expense-to-income ratio, for instance. The map (Fig. 2.3) below shows the share of the cost-to-income ratio for countries with data for 2021. For most of Europe, expense-to-income is higher than 50%, topping 70% in the case of Germany. The ratio is below 30% for only ten countries and regions, including the United Kingdom, Uruguay, Vietnam, Zambia, and Macau. In the case of the UK, this can be explained by London being a robust offshore financial center that allows for significant economies of scale (which would likely explain the data for Uruguay and Macau as well).

On the other side of the spectrum, German banks, sometimes considered inefficient, post the fourth-highest expense-to-income ratio (88%) among the 134 countries with available data, behind Cyprus (89%), Syria (91%), and Iraq (92%). German bank profitability is low by international standards (IMF, 2022), not due just to this ratio (which, before the pandemic, stood at 77%, 13% higher than the EU average). Damyanova and Taqi (2020) note that "German banks have struggled with inefficiency for a long time as fierce competition and limited opportunities for consolidation in their highly fragmented and overpopulated home market restrained profitability and kept costs high. Years of extremely low interest rates have exacerbated their profitability problems, triggering large-scale restructurings across the sector, including Germany's top two players—Deutsche Bank AG and Commerzbank AG." German banks rank more favorably in risk-adjusted terms, as low profitability is partially compensated by lower volatility of returns. However, German banks rank among the least profitable in Europe in terms of many measures, such as

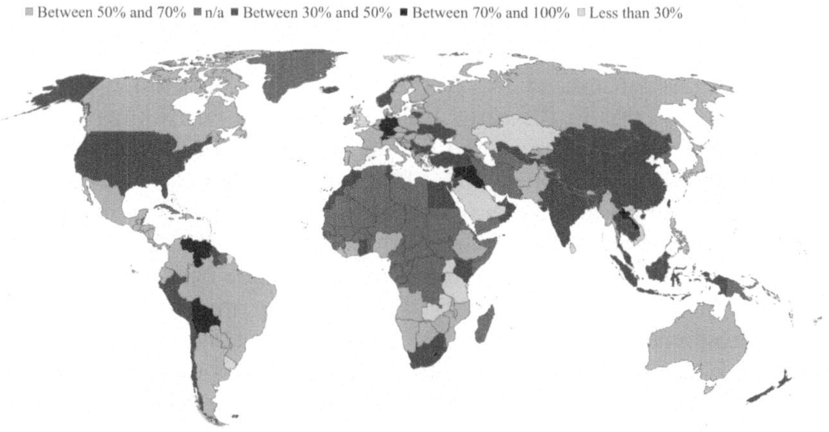

Fig. 2.3 Expense-to-income ratio globally (%) in 2021 (*Source* World Bank [2023])

returns on assets, equity, and risk-weighted assets (IMF, 2022). Among the factors that affect bank profitability are a complex tiered industry structure with barriers to entry and an explicit mandate of a large part of the banking system—cooperative and savings banks—to maximize the welfare of stakeholders rather than profits (IMF, 2022).

Finally, low bank profitability could undermine bank resilience if banks use more capital than earnings to absorb losses in case of shocks (IMF, 2022). McKinsey & Company (2021) even argues that if trends continue and German banks take no action, ROEs could fall to 0% by 2030.

Interestingly, the interests of regulators and shareholders are usually aligned regarding banks' profits. A financial crisis is less likely to happen if banks make more money. For instance, the European Bank Authority has noted that low profits and high costs remain critical challenges for the EU banking sector (European Bank Authority, 2019). Figure 2.4 describes the pattern of net interest margins worldwide in the early 2020s. Unlike the pattern for expense-to-income ratio, there seems to be a clear pattern regarding net interest margins globally. In developed countries, such margins are low, typically less than 2% per year. There are some exceptions, such as in the United States, where the average bank's margin was 2.77% in 2021, and in Afghanistan, a developing country where banks averaged a paltry 1.77% net interest margin in the same year. For middle-income countries, such as Eastern Europe, margins rise to 2–4%, increasing even further for poor countries, such as Sub-Saharan Africa, where margins can exceed 7%. Another anomaly is Argentina, mired in an inflationary crisis in the early 2020s. In such an environment, credit became scarce and expensive, and the net interest margin for the average bank in the country topped 10% (10.44%) in 2021. Not coincidently, the highest margin among the countries with available data in 2021 is Zimbabwe, another country facing high inflation, which reached 12.83%. One may think that high net interest margins mean banks are raking in money, but that is not necessarily true. For Argentina and Zimbabwe, net interest margins above 10% are a symptom of dysfunctional credit markets; banks lend much below their potential, and defaults are much more common than in other countries. Margins may be high, but volumes are low.

Looking at the pattern for banks' return on equity globally, we can see that even with extremely high net interest margins, the profit ratio of banks in Argentina (8.05%) doesn't stand out. Banks in Europe have similar returns on equity, ranging from 6 to 10%. In contrast, the highest rates of return are found in Sub-Saharan Africa and some Central Asia countries (Syria, 31.55%; Kazakhstan, 30.35%; and Georgia, 23.52%).

For return on equity, there is an overall pattern of higher rates of return for banks in poorer and riskier countries. In other words, with higher risk,

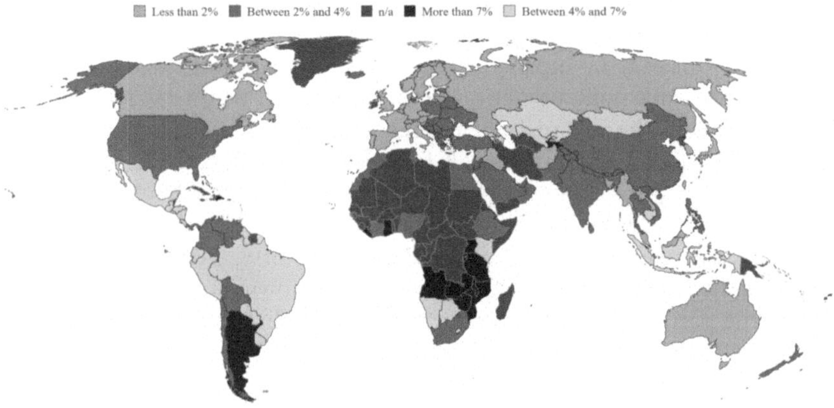

Fig. 2.4 Net interest margin (%) in 2021 (*Source* World Bank [2023])

banks can expect higher returns. But also, a riskier environment can lead to substantial losses, and the three countries with negative ROE in 2021 (Fig. 2.5) are evidence of that: Greece (−16.32%), Lebanon (−1.88%), and Iraq (−0.11%).

We explore the disconnect between the broader societal goals and the specific targets of regulators in Chapter 5. Here, the main message is that we can't build a better world without a deep understanding of the incentives embedded in the profit indicators of financial institutions. Should greening banks be done in a manner that protects banks' profits? If so, this poses a moral dilemma, as most would disagree with governments implicitly subsidizing banks. Thus, what should we make of claims like those in McKinsey & Company (2021): "Even if they achieve the 3 to 4% ROE mark, Germany's banks will still face a shortfall of €30 billion to €40 billion in operating profit, rendering them incapable of making required investments in digitization and addressing environmental, social, and governance (ESG) concerns?"

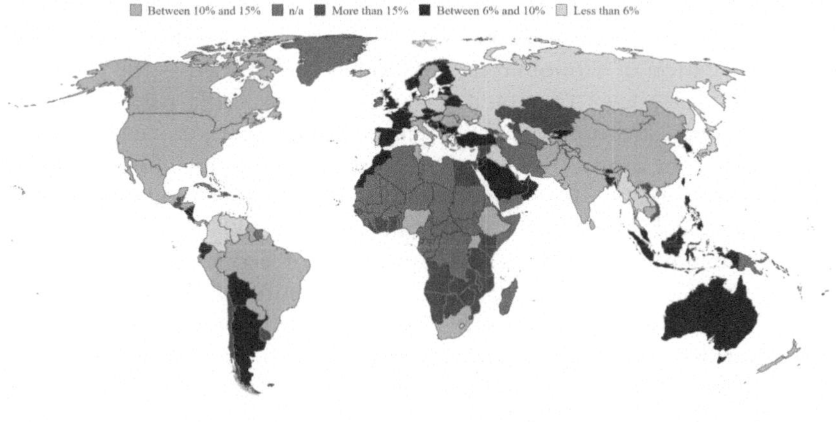

Fig. 2.5 Return on equity (%) in 2021 (*Source* World Bank [2023])

2.3 RAROC

RAROC is a measure of risk-adjusted return on capital. There is no single way to calculate it, but some straightforward formulas are:

$$\text{RAROC} = \frac{\text{Expected profit}}{K} = \frac{\text{Net Income}}{\text{risk} - \text{adj. } K}$$
$$= \frac{\text{OperInc} - \text{ExpLosses} + K\text{Charges} * r}{K}$$

OperInc is operating income, KCharges is capital charges, r is the risk-free interest rate, and K is the economic capital.

We should note that economic capital is a measure of risk, not capital held as in the case of nonfinancial companies. Banks assess capital differently, as what matters for them is not the ability to produce goods and services based on fixed assets or intangible investments but credit. Thus, banks can lend more based on the financial capital at their disposal, which is at risk from counterparties, changes in the economic environment, and more. Thus, economic capital for financial institutions is distinct from the familiar accounting and regulatory capital measures. The computation of economic capital models is expressed as the currency (say, US dollars) level of capital to support the specific risks the institution assumes. Economic capital relates capital to risks, regardless of the existence of assets. Because it is based on potential future losses, it is forward-looking. Banks typically develop internal models to tailor economic capital estimates to their reality (FDIC, 2004).

In some ways, RAROC is the equivalent of economic value added to nonfinancial companies. RAROC is a measure of short-term profitability. It is not designed to track a financial institution over the business cycle, as it does not track capital intensity, growth, and other long-term value drivers. Similar measures, such as RORWA, track the potential to maximize return at a branch level vis-à-vis appetite for risk (Girotra, 2020).

RORAC is not adjusted for return measures, as it uses basic accounting measures from financial statements. However, it is adjusted for both return and allocated capital for the banks' aggregate capital risks (Girotra, 2020). By adjusting capital charges by the risk-free interest rate, RAROC reduces profits by the opportunity cost of the bank's expected losses. This process makes the measure robust and internally consistent (estimates are comparable over time without resorting to other benchmarks).

More importantly, RORAC can be computed at various organizational levels (bank-wide, business units, branch, product, relationship manager, customer segment, customer, portfolio, or account level) to evaluate performance. In addition, they can be aggregated from the account level to any desired level within an organization (Girotra, 2020).

Why does understanding RAROC matter? Banks will resist any changes to the status quo that significantly affect RAROC and other profit measures negatively. Any regulation that requires more use of capital or reduces operating income will be opposed. This dilemma is particularly acute when proposals such as the exclusion of sin stocks (Chapter 4.3.1) from portfolios or credit limits on polluting companies (Chapter 4.3.2) are brought forward.

One challenge in computing RAROC is estimating a bank's economic capital. For nonfinancial companies, economic capital is the number of resources employed to operate, usually equating to specific measures of long-term assets and the total operating working capital required to sustain firms' production and sales.

Still, we can establish some benchmarks for that and other profit indicators. Given that banks' cost of capital usually hovers around 10–15%, that is typically the target for RAROC. In other words, much like EVA and other short-term profit measures, RAROC aims to measure profits generated by the institutions' operations against the opportunity cost of shareholders' equity.

Both EVA and RAROC incorporate opportunity costs and, in the latter case, risk adjustments to improve decision-making. Take a comparison with return on equity, for instance. We have seen regions where ROE was below 6% in the early 2020s. However, because the denominator of ROE is a pure accounting measure and there is no adjustment for opportunity costs, there is no way to tell if a bank with a 6% ROE is doing well. However, RAROC can be directly compared to the risk-free interest rate or other costs of capital indicators. In addition, as we mentioned before, its estimates are comparable over time, so analysts and managers can track the evolution of the institutions' performance.

2.4 Marking-to-Market or Fair Value Accounting

Another essential distinction between accounting for nonfinancial companies and financial institutions is that marking-to-market is usually required in the latter. Mark-to-market is generally an alternative to historical cost accounting, in which the value of an asset is tied to its purchase value. Mark-to-market is a method for valuing assets at the current market conditions. It is also known as fair value accounting; a value is fair if it is the amount the company would receive for selling an asset today without significant obstacles. Nonfinancial companies rarely have to mark-to-market their assets; book and market values tend to differ substantially for these companies.

Marking-to-market is more challenging for illiquid assets. Fair value assessment for such assets is done through the default or interest rate risk method. Default risk is based on incorporating the probability that the investment isn't worth its original value. The interest rate risk method is based on comparing the asset's value to similar assets.

Here is an illustrative example of the difference between historical and fair value accounting. Take a zero-coupon government bond purchased for 909.1 with a year to maturity. The bank expects to hold this bond to maturity, receiving 1000 at maturity. The implicit effective interest rate of this bond is 10% per year. After six months, the yield-to-maturity drops to 5% per year. Hence, the market price of the bond would be:

$$\mathrm{PV} = \frac{\mathrm{FV}}{(1+r)^n} = \frac{1000}{(1+5\%)^{180/360}} = 975.9$$

However, the bank is locked into a 10% return, as it purchased the bond for 909.1, and if it takes the bond to maturity, that will be the bank's return. Historically, banks could account for their assets by the expected value given the effective yield-to-maturity from their original purchase. In this instance, that would be U\$953.46. Figure 2.6 illustrates the distinct paths of the bond's price if the yield-to-maturity (YTM) is constant at 10% or if it slowly drops to 5% and continues at that value till the end of the bond's life.

Which value is correct, U\$953.46 or U\$975.9? If the bank takes the bond to maturity, it doesn't matter, as regardless of the intervening YTM, the institution will receive U\$1,000 at maturity. However, the bank may want or be forced to sell this security before maturity. And therein lies

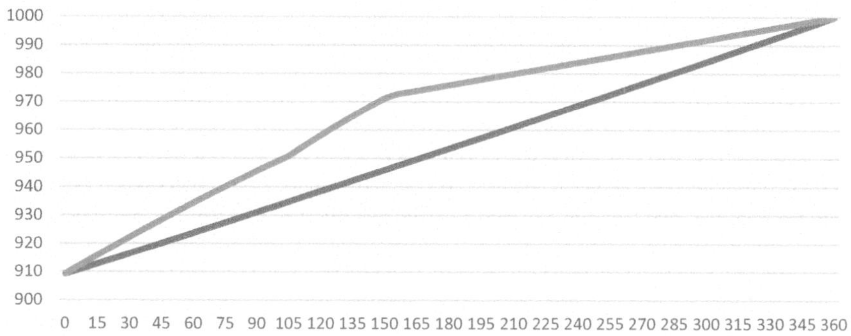

Fig. 2.6 Simulated path of a bond's price at different yield-to-maturities

the requirements for fair value accounting. Its goal is for banks to report updated values for their assets and liabilities.

Basel II capital requirements were pro-cyclical (more about it in Chapter 2.6), although the rules for Basel III have tried to mitigate this characteristic (Argimon et al., 2015). Such requirements don't come without costs, however. Marking-to-market may have contributed to the great financial crisis. If banks require liquidity, they will be forced to sell assets. As institutions look to sell similar assets simultaneously, prices plummet, likely resulting in even larger sales and plummeting asset prices.

Accounting standards have evolved to incorporate regulatory requirements. For instance, Novotny-Farkas (2016) shows that the IFRS 9 ECL accounting standard incorporates earlier and larger impairment allowances. So, earlier recognition of credit losses should reduce the build-up of loss overhangs and the overstatement of regulatory capital. In addition, loan loss provisioning under the IFRS 9 and the prudential filter for unrealized fair value losses form the central link between accounting and regulatory capital, aligning loss recognition and measurement methods (Rugilo, 2021).

Below is a summary of the rules for marking-to-market and to-model from the Bank of International Settlements (BIS, 2019). "Banks must mark-to-market as much as possible. The more prudent side of bid/offer should be used unless the institution is a significant market-maker in a particular position and can close-out at mid-market. Banks should maximize the use of relevant observable inputs and minimize the use of unobservable inputs when estimating fair value using a valuation technique. However, observable inputs or transactions may not be relevant, such as in a forced liquidation or distressed sale, or transactions may not be observable, such as when markets are inactive. In such cases, the observable data should be considered but may not be determinative. Marking-to-market is at least the daily valuation of positions at readily available close-out prices sourced independently. Examples of available close-out prices include exchange prices, screen prices, or quotes from reputable independent brokers."

If marking-to-market is unavailable, banks can mark-to-model, extricating value from a structural financial model, with marking-to-model defined as any valuation benchmarked, extrapolated, or otherwise calculated from a market input (BIS, 2019). This approach must be demonstrated to be prudent, and banks must use extra degrees of conservatism. For instance, if a bank values an art collection, it cannot mark-to-market in the traditional sense. It will have to create a model for valuing such products, ensuring that the outcome is conservative: assets shouldn't be valued at a price higher than what the bank could get if it disposed of them quickly.

Using a practical example of standard approaches, Bank of America describes its fair value approach in its financial statements (Bank of America, 2022). Its strategy is based on estimating fair value regarding an investment's exit price. The institution must maximize the use of observable inputs and minimize the use of unobservable inputs. Measurements fall into one of the three categories:

> Level 1, always used if available, is based on unadjusted quoted prices for identical assets or liabilities in active markets. Level 1 securities include debt and equity, derivative contracts traded in an active exchange market, and specific highly liquid US Treasury securities.
> Level 2 includes the valuation of assets and liabilities with observable inputs other than Level 1 prices, such as quoted prices for similar assets or liabilities, quoted prices in markets that are not active, or other inputs that are observable or can be corroborated by observable market data for substantially the entire term of the assets or liabilities. At this level, securities are traded less frequently than exchange-traded instruments. In addition, derivative contracts are priced using models with observable inputs in the market. For

Bank of America, this category generally includes US government-backed, mortgage-backed (MBS) and asset-backed securities (ABS), and corporate debt securities, among others.
Level 3 securities see little or no market activity, primarily financial instruments for which determining fair value requires significant judgment. This category incorporates consumer MSRs, specific ABS, highly structured, complex, or long-dated derivative contracts, IRLCs, and CDOs where independent pricing information cannot be obtained for a significant portion of the underlying assets. Fair value in such cases is generally determined using pricing models, discounted cash flow, or similar methodologies.

As we can see, Bank of America's fair value accounting practices align with BIS guidelines. Marking-to-market is an essential regulatory tool. Because of this, banks change their behavior to account for it. For instance, some banks may sell some securities and buy others to keep capital thresholds above definite amounts or avoid certain assets or liabilities because of difficulties marking them to market. This type of behavior is uncommon. Most companies won't change their decisions to buy particular machines because of fair value assessment considerations (although depreciation schemes might affect decision-making).

Regardless, we will later see how fair value assessment plays a role in credit rating and other commercial banking-related climate change initiatives. More importantly, how can central banks change fair value practices to encourage banks to become greener? And, more importantly, would there be unintended consequences for environmentally-minded regulations that change marking-to-market guidelines? Before we shift toward specific policy proposals, we must wrap up the understanding of risk management reports.

2.5 Systemic Risk in Financial Systems: Robust Yet Fragile

Banks are regulated differently from most other companies. The main reason is systemic risk, the interconnection between financial institutions that can bring the whole market down if one bank goes under.

Capital adequacy ratios, including liquidity coverage ratios, aim to build resiliency in financial systems, which are famously "robust yet fragile" (Gai & Kapadia, 2010). If a competitor goes bankrupt, a firm will likely benefit by getting some of its customers. Not so with commercial banks. Banks are interdependent due to the form of lending or liquidity provisions,

Banks' interdependence has momentous implications. Jackson and Pernoud (2021) present a two-layer taxonomy of systemic risks that distinguish between (a) contagion through direct externalities and (b) various feedback effects that allow for multiple equilibria and self-fulfilling prophecies. The former is about contagion from a bank's default to distress for another or assets fire sale that depresses the value of another bank. The latter is when beliefs about the poor condition of a bank become self-fulfilling as they lead investors to call in their loans. The intuition behind contagion comes from banks' interconnectedness, as shown in Fig. 2.7.

Their primary model can be summarized as follows (p. 174): Let $N = \{1, \ldots, n\}$ be a set of financial institutions. They call them banks, but they should be understood more broadly as any institution in the financial system whose actions affect others. The network is characterized by a matrix $\boldsymbol{G} = (g_{ij})_{ij}$ such that g_{ij} captures the connection between

Fig. 2.7 A weighted, directed network with five nodes (*Source* Gai and Kapadia [2010])

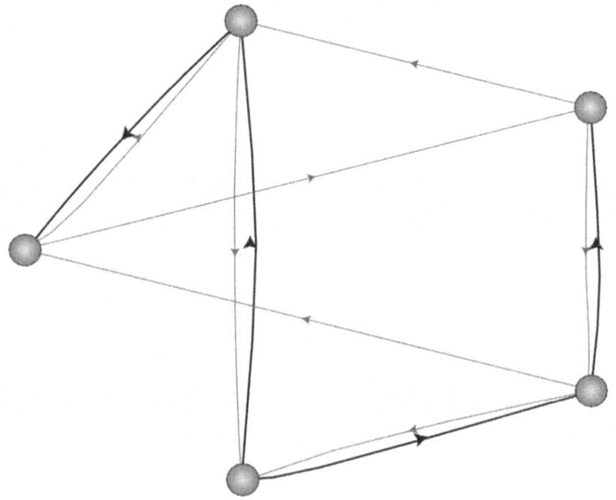

bank i and j. A connection g_{ij} can have multiple components, each corresponding, for instance, to a different type of financial contract. The authors' key object of interest is the vector of values associated with each institution, $\boldsymbol{V} = (V_i)_i$, accounting for all assets and liabilities, including any defaults and associated bankruptcy costs. Because banks are interconnected, their values depend on each other. The value of bank i is a function of other banks' values, denoted by $V_i = F_i\ (\boldsymbol{V} \mid \boldsymbol{G})$. Banks' values are then the solution to a system of n equations in n unknowns, written as:

$$\boldsymbol{V} = F(\boldsymbol{V}|\boldsymbol{G})$$

The two sources of systemic risk come from a change in the value of bank i affecting bank j and the multiplicity of equilibria, with possible shifts from one equilibrium to another. Network interdependencies can lead to self-fulfilling "prophecies" whereby belief changes become realized. As Jackson and Pernoud (2021) point out (p. 174): "The first type of systemic risk captures how a change in fundamentals can move through the network—formally, how much equilibrium values $\boldsymbol{V}$ change in response to some initial change in fundamentals, while keeping the equilibrium constant—whereas the second type of systemic risk captures shifts between equilibria." Allen and Gale (2009) define the two sources of systemic risks similarly: financial crises can start with fundamental changes or self-fulfilling prophecies solely from beliefs and behaviors.

As our goal is to illustrate systemic risk, we focus only on the example of cascading insolvencies. For some reason, a bank cannot pay its debts. Given the banks' default, other institutions see their balance sheets weaken. Some may become insolvent. The remaining institutions' balance sheets deteriorate further, and losses percolate through the network. Formally, consider a two-bank relationship. Let g_{ij} be a debt claim in which bank j owes a debt D_{ij} to bank i. Then, V_i is:

$$V_i = F_i(V|G) = \pi_i + \sum_i \left(d_{ij}(\boldsymbol{V}) - D_{ij}\right)$$

In addition, given that π_i is the value of bank i's portfolio of outside investments, $d_{ij}\ (\boldsymbol{V})$ is the amount bank j can manage to pay bank i and is defined by:

$$d_{ij}(V) = \min\left\{D_{ij}, \frac{D_{ij}}{\sum_k D_{kj}}\left[\pi_j + \sum_k d_{jk}(V)\right]\right\}$$

Implicit assumptions are that banks have limited liability and all debts have equal priority. Then, $\pi_j + \sum_k d_{jk}(V)$ is how much bank j has available to meet its obligations. The bank's debts are divided across creditors in proportion to their claims on j. More generally, the function would be a nested function reflecting priorities.

As Jackson and Pernoud (2021) note (p. 175), "to see how interdependencies generate systemic risk, let $D_{ij} = 1$ and $\pi_i = 0.5$, and suppose that j's outside portfolio value drops from $\pi_j = 1.5$ to $\pi_{j'} = 0.5$. Bank values start at $V_i = 1.5$ and $V_j = 0.5$ under π, but under $\pi_{j'} = 0.5$, they fall to $V_i = 1$ and $V_j = -0.5$ (or effectively to 0, given limited liability). Though the shock affects the portfolio of bank j, it also depresses the value of the other bank. The decrease in the bank i's value could lead to its default if i has debts to others."

In this version of the model, there are no bankruptcy costs. Introducing one would make cascading more likely, with values for V_i and V_j under any regime. More importantly, additional insolvencies lead to deadweight losses in the entire system, as the overall cost can significantly exceed the initial shock; lost are some of the investment and lending services of the insolvent banks. In other versions of the model, contagion comes from externalities in asset prices as insolvent banks prematurely sell significant amounts of assets at steep discounts. As banks hold similar assets, price drops simultaneously shift their correlated exposure downwards (Jackson & Pernoud, 2021).

Investors with imperfect knowledge of the value of a bank's portfolio make inferences about that and other banks' values. The financial network structure may also be imperfectly known, and interbank cross-exposures can lead risk-averse banks to pull back funding from one another when a negative shock hits. Finally, the authors model self-fulfilling prophecies, which require information asymmetries between investors and financial institutions. For the entire model, see Jackson and Pernoud (2021).

Counterintuitively, Allen and Gale (2000) show that when banks' networks are complete, in the sense that all banks are exposed to each other, such that interbank deposits are evenly spread, a shock doesn't spread through the network. When banks are exposed to just a few counterparties, the network is said to be "incomplete" and is more fragile. Here, what matters is that environmental risks and other sources of financial uncertainty may add to factors destabilizing financial systems.

As Jackson and Pernoud (2021) describe, commonalities in exposures across banks can worsen the cascades of insolvencies. Take, for instance, a three-level interaction between two counterparties that have similar exposures in their investments. First, they both tend to be vulnerable and near insolvency simultaneously. Second, if one is forced to sell off some of its assets, the price effect can hurt the other's balance sheet. Third, if one defaults on the other, the latter can become insolvent, especially in light of the first two interactions, which means that this bank is already distressed. Combined, these three outcomes can lead to cascades when the direct default impact, the common exposure, or the indirect price impact would not have led to further insolvencies.

Systemic risk does not emerge from just one source of economic shocks. The premise of this book and much of climate finance is that climate change makes financial systems more fragile. However, we can't disregard regulatory constraints in the greening of banks. Any measure that would make banks more sustainable but more systemic fragile would likely face resistance from regulators. Details matter. One example is capital requirements, as we discuss in Chapter 2.6. A straightforward proposal to make banks direct credit to more sustainable companies is reducing capital requirements for loans to "sustainable" companies. While that may be possible and desirable, at first glance, it violates the assumption that climate finance reduces systemic risks, at least in the short run. Liberating credit to greener companies comes at the cost of reduced capital in the case of a sizable shock (that may have nothing to do with climate change).

Constraints to greener banking don't come just from regulators. Public authorities may balk at limits to credit to "strategic" companies or industries supported by the State, directly or indirectly. And that does not even include the investors' dilemma, for whom a preference for more responsible banking may cost short-term profits. We discuss these tradeoffs in more detail in the following sections.

2.5.1 *A Primer on the Basel Committee on Banking Supervision and risk management*

Most central banks worldwide use standards developed via the Bank for International Settlements (BIS), a bank for central banks. The Bank for International Settlements was established in 1930. Today, it is owned by 63 central banks that represent countries that account for approximately 95% of the world's GDP (BIS, 2022a, 2022b, 2022c).

Still, financial regulation is both global and local. The BIS develops broad global standards. Primary standards are similar worldwide, but financial regulators maintain their autonomy, designing and enforcing rules that may find no counterpart elsewhere, customizing rules to their realities.

The rest of this chapter focuses on the constraints for banks to become more sustainable. Here, we present a primer on Basel III, tying it to systemic risk and its impacts on financial statements. Banks are severely restricted in their actions by local regulators, who tend to implement Basel III regulations. There is no systemic change possible in financial institutions without understanding their behavioral drivers.

Institutions that aim to ensure compliance with commercial banks' risk management systems must meet the Basel Committee on Banking Supervision requirements. The most recent version of these reforms is commonly known as Basel III. The guidelines for the Basel III reforms were initially published in December 2017. The minimum capital requirements for market risk were finalized in January 2019. Central banks worldwide implemented these reforms on January 1, 2023.

The Basel III guidelines are based on three pillars, as indicated in Table 2.6. The first includes the capital adequacy ratios, risk coverage, and leverage. This pillar concerns fundamental consolidated financial indicators indicating whether a bank has enough capital to meet its current obligations and whether leverage levels magnify potential risks from market shocks.

The second pillar establishes the criteria for banks to address firm-wide governance and risk management systems. These include risks not present in standard financial reports. It also sets up how banks must perform stress tests. For instance, in previous versions of the Basel guidelines, banks had significant discretion in running proprietary self-designed stress tests. The

Table 2.6 Basel committee on banking supervision reforms—Basel III

Capital					
	Pillar 1			*Pillar 2*	*Pillar 3*
	Capital	*Risk coverage*	*Containing leverage*	*Risk management and supervision*	*Market discipline*
All Banks	**Quality and level of capital** • **Raising minimum common equity** to 4.5% of risk- weighted assets, after deductions • **A capital conservation buffer** comprising common equity of 2.5% of risk-weighted assets brings the total common equity standard to 7%. Constraints on a bank's discretionary distributions will be imposed when it falls into the buffer range • **A countercyclical buffer** within a range of 0–2.5% comprising common equity will apply when credit growth is judged to result in an unacceptable build-up of systematic risk	**Revisions to the standardised approaches** for calculating • **credit risk;** • **market risk;** • **credit valuation adjustment risk;** and • **operational risk** mean greater risk-sensitivity and comparability **Constraints on using internal models** aim to reduce unwarranted variability in banks' calculations of risk-weighted assets **Counterparty credit risk** More stringent requirements for measuring exposure; capital incentives to use central counterparties for derivatives; a new standardised approach; and higher capital for inter-financial sector exposures	A non-risk- based **leverage ratio** including off-balance sheet exposures is meant to serve as a backstop to the risk-based capital requirement. It also helps contain system- wide build-up of leverage	**Supplemental Pillar 2 requirements** address firm-wide governance and risk management, including the risk of off-balance sheet exposures and securitization activities, sound compensation practices, valuation practices, stress testing, corporate governance and supervisory colleges **Interest rate risk in the banking book (IRRBB)** Extensive guidance on expectations for a bank's IRRBB management process: enhanced disclosure requirements; stricter threshold for identifying outlier banks; updated standardized approach	**Revised Pillar 3 disclosure requirements** Consolidated and enhanced framework, covering all the reforms to the Basel framework Introduces a dashboard of banks' key prudential metrics

(continued)

Table 2.6 (continued)

Capital					
	Pillar 1			*Pillar 2*	*Pillar 3*
	Capital	*Risk coverage*	*Containing leverage*	*Risk management and supervision*	*Market discipline*
		Securitizations Reducing reliance on external ratings, simplifying and limiting the number of approaches for calculating capital charges and increasing requirements for riskier exposures **Capital requirements for exposures to central counterparties (CCPs) and equity investments in funds** to ensure adequate capitalization and support a resilient financial system A **revised output floor**, based on Basel III standardized approaches, limits the regulatory capital benefits that a bank using internal models can derive relative to the standardized approaches			

Capital					
	Pillar 1			*Pillar 2*	*Pillar 3*
	Capital	*Risk coverage*	*Containing leverage*	*Risk management and supervision*	*Market discipline*
	Capital loss absorption at the point of non-viability Allowing capital instruments to be written off or converted to common shares if the bank is judged to be non-viable. This will reduce moral hazard by increasing the private sector's contribution to resolving future banking crises				

(continued)

Table 2.6 (continued)

Capital					
	Pillar 1			*Pillar 2*	*Pillar 3*
	Capital	*Risk coverage*	*Containing leverage*	*Risk management and supervision*	*Market discipline*
SIBs	The Committee identifies global systemically important banks (G-SIBs) using a methodology that includes both quantitative indicators and qualitative elements. In addition to meeting the Basel III risk-based capital and leverage ratio requirements, G-SIBs must have higher loss absorbency capacity to reflect the greater risks that they pose to the financial system. The Committee also developed principles on the assessment methodology and the higher loss absorbency requirement for domestic systemically important banks (D-SIBs)				
Liquidity					
Global liquidity standards and supervisory monitoring The **Liquidity Coverage Ratio** (LCR) requires banks to have sufficient high-quality liquid assets to withstand a 30-day stressed funding scenario that is specified by supervisors The longer-term, structural **Net Stable Funding Ratio** (NSFR) is designed to address liquidity mismatches. It covers the entire balance sheet and provides incentives for banks to use stable sources of funding The Committee's 2008 guidance ***Principles for Sound Liquidity Risk Management and Supervision*** takes account of lessons learned during the crisis. It is based on a fundamental review of sound practices for managing liquidity risk in banking organizations **Supervisory monitoring** The liquidity framework includes a common set of intraday and longer- term monitoring metrics to assist supervisors in identifying and analyzing liquidity risk trends at both the bank and system-wide level **Large exposures** Large exposures regime established to mitigate systemic risks arising from interlinkages across financial institutions and concentrated exposures					

Source BIS. https://www.bis.org/bcbs/basel3/b3_bank_sup_reforms.pdf

regulatory pendulum has swung from self-regulation to stringent guidelines for estimating the likelihood of banks going under from unexpected market shake-ups.

The third pillar describes which information banks must disclose to regulators and the rest of society. It also introduces a dashboard of banks' key prudential metrics.

Financial regulation is primarily based on systemic risk, the connection between banks in which the failure of one institution may lead to a cascading effect that brings the entire financial system to its knees. Banks respond to these regulations by establishing explicit risk management policies and reporting indicators to regulators. Of course, banks must define their internal risk management culture organizationally, which is a challenge to every institution as such regulations sometimes get in the way of conducting business. The primary risks that financial institutions face are credit, market, interest rate, liquidity, operational, reputation, legal, and strategic.

The Hong Kong Monetary Authority offers detailed loss event type classification for operational risks to illustrate how detailed risk management reports can be (Table 2.7) (Hong Kong Monetary Authority, 2022).

Thus, banks have more incentives to develop robust risk management systems than the average nonfinancial company. Usually, banks setup sophisticated governance structures to manage and report on such risks. For instance, Itau reports having different lines of defense, as in Fig. 2.8.

Unlike nonfinancial companies, banks must report detailed risk management outcomes. Accounting standards vary; in the United States, companies report financial data using Generally Accepted Accounting Principles (GAAP), while European firms publish data created via International Financial Reporting Standards (IFRS). Banks' reports are also not uniform due to differences in accounting standards and local regulations. Still, they are similar enough for our purposes.

Figure 2.9 illustrates the paths banks take in their risk management journey. It breaks down this journey into five steps: vulnerable, reactive, compliant, proactive, and resilient.

Vulnerable institutions lack systematic approaches to risk management, don't train their employees well, and are negligent regarding best practices. The resulting culture is that risk events happen, and there is nothing much to be done. Some researchers have argued that banks are inherently

Table 2.7 Detailed loss event type classification

Event-type category (Level 1)	*Categories (Level 2)*	*Activity examples (Level 3)*
Internal fraud	Unauthorized activity	Transactions not reported (intentional); Transaction type unauthorized (with monetary loss); Mismarking of position (intentional)
	Theft and fraud	Fraud/credit fraud/ worthless deposits; Theft/ extortion/embezzlement/ robbery; Misappropriation of assets; Malicious destruction of assets; Forgery; Check kiting; Smuggling; Account takeover/impersonation etc.; Tax noncompliance/ evasion (willful); Bribes/ kickbacks; Insider trading (not on firm's account)
External fraud	Theft and fraud	Theft/robbery; Forgery; Check kiting
	Systems security	Hacking damage; Theft of information (with monetary loss)
Employment practices and workplace safety	Employee relations	Compensation, benefit, termination issues; Organized labor activity
	Safe environment	General liability (slip and fall, etc.); Employee health and safety rules events; Workers' compensation
	Diversity and discrimination	All discrimination types

(continued)

Table 2.7 (continued)

Event-type category (Level 1)	*Categories (Level 2)*	*Activity examples (Level 3)*
Clients, products, and business practices	Suitability, disclosure, and fiduciary	Fiduciary breaches/ guideline violations; Suitability/disclosure issues (know-your-customer etc.); Retail customer disclosure violations; Breach of privacy; Aggressive sales; Account churning; Misuse of confidential information; Lender liability
	Improper business or market practices	Antitrust; Improper trade/market practices; Market manipulation; Insider trading (on firm's account); Unlicensed activity; Money laundering
	Product flaws	Product defects (unauthorized, etc.); Model errors
	Selection, sponsorship, and exposure	Failure to investigate client per guidelines; Exceeding client exposure limits
	Advisory activities	Disputes over the performance of advisory activities
Damage to physical assets	Disasters and other events	Natural disaster losses; Human losses from external sources (terrorism, vandalism)
Business disruption and system failures	Systems	Hardware; Software; Telecommunications; Utility outage/disruptions

(continued)

Table 2.7 (continued)

Event-type category (Level 1)	*Categories (Level 2)*	*Activity examples (Level 3)*
Execution, delivery, and process management	Transaction capture, execution, and maintenance	Miscommunication; Data entry, maintenance, or loading error; Missed deadline or responsibility; Model/system misoperation; Accounting error/entity attribution error; Other task misperformance; Delivery failure; Collateral management failure; Reference data maintenance
	Monitoring and reporting	Failed mandatory reporting obligation; Inaccurate external report (loss incurred)
	Customer intake and documentation	Client permissions/ disclaimers missing; Legal documents missing/ incomplete
	Customer/client account management	Unapproved access given to accounts; Incorrect client records (loss incurred); Negligent loss or damage of client assets
	Trade counterparties	Non-client counterparty misperformance; Miscellaneous non-client counterparty disputes
	Vendors and suppliers	Outsourcing; Vendor disputes

Source Hong Kong Monetary Authority (2022)

reactive regarding sustainability practices, with traumatic risk events triggering the incorporation of new management practices (Weber, 2005). Reactive firms are one step above, plugging holes that show up constantly due to weak risk management systems. In this stage, firms focus on finding culprits and assigning blame without systematic investigations, which would lead to better training.

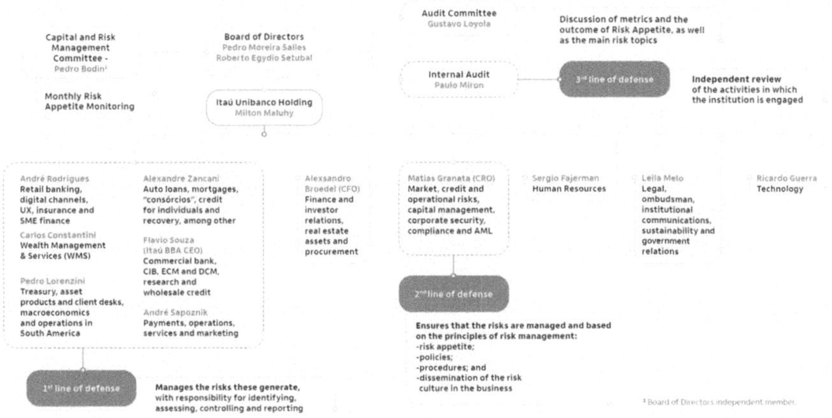

Fig. 2.8 Itau's Governance Structure

The compliant institution is the poster child for business as usual. It has well-established systems that are updated according to regulatory mandates. Compliant banks address regulatory changes as quickly as possible. They follow market benchmarks and train their employees well. However, they don't innovate or aim to anticipate market movements. Compliant firms are not merely reactive but are also not proactive in establishing a risk management ownership culture.

Proactive banks have formal risk assessment processes that are pervasive throughout the institutions. Incidents are not covered up, and the focus is improving systems beyond regulatory mandates. Resilient banks take that approach one step further, turning robust risk management into a way of life.

This general classification may seem fluffy, but there is merit in explicitly delineating the steps banks must take to become more resilient. Accountability is valuable in business, especially regarding commercial and investment banking risk management. In many aspects of life, risk management consists of little more than reactive systems that look to assign blame instead of learning from it.

Can we say that any bank has been proactive in managing risks related to climate change? Most banks now publish sustainability reports. Are these reports meaningful? Throughout this book, one main message is that banks know how to manage risks. Claiming that climate change is

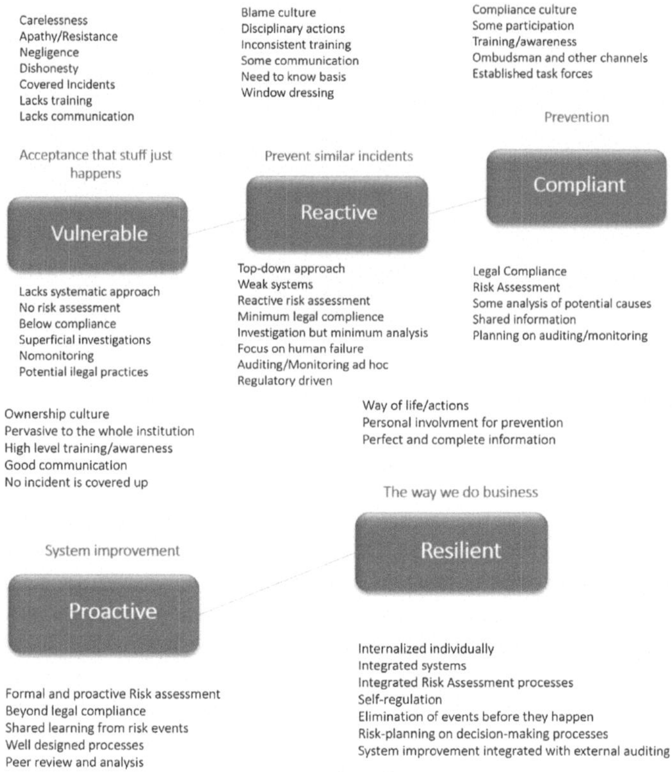

Fig. 2.9 Risk management paths

too diffuse a risk does not fly; institutions can choose to be reactive but can't claim they are proactive when they aren't.

We now move to capital adequacy ratios, which will play a prominent role in determining the main avenues for regulatory climate policies. The following subsection describes how to interpret the primary financial indicators related to capital adequacy ratios, risk coverage, and leverage.

2.5.2 Capital Adequacy Ratios

The main reason for establishing the basics of risk management in the financial statements chapter is the relevance of capital adequacy ratios for strategic decision-making in financial institutions. Even more so than profit indicators, banks are managed to keep capital adequacy ratios above certain levels due to regulatory pressure.

Banks are fundamentally leveraged institutions. The central measure for ensuring that banks have enough money to meet their short-term obligations is the capital adequacy ratio (CAR). CAR is defined as:

$$\text{CAR} = \frac{\text{Tier 1 capital} + \text{Tier 2 capital}}{\text{Risk} - \text{Weighted assets}}$$

Banks' tier 1 capital represents the most liquid resources at the institution's disposal, which can absorb losses immediately as they occur. It is formally divided into common equity tier 1 and additional tier 1 capital, equivalent to a bank's equity (including retained earnings). According to the BIS, tier 1 capital is neither secured nor covered by the issuer's or related entity's guarantee (BIS, 2019).

In contrast, tier 2 capital is related chiefly to provisions for losses (gone concern capital), which must absorb losses before depositors and general creditors do. Banks can make several adjustments to tier 1 and 2 capital if they follow the list of regulatory adjustments and deductions from regulatory capital from Basel III. Deductions typically address the high uncertainty regarding the fair value of assets under regular and stress conditions. Significant deductions are goodwill and other intangible assets, deferred tax assets, and investments in other financial entities (BIS, 2019).

Conceptually, determining risk-weighted assets for credit risk is straightforward, as a weighted sum of balance sheet and off-balance sheet assets held by a financial system. Each dollar exposure on a bank's balance sheet is assigned a risk weight ranging from 0 to 100%. Off-balance sheet exposures can be included by being converted into credit equivalents using a conversion factor and, second, being risk-weighted (Caruana & Narain, 2008).

Of course, determining the weights and what constitutes off-balance sheet items is challenging. Under Basel I, banks had to hold capital equivalent to at least 8% of risk-weighted assets (RWA), with local central banks able to require large shares depending on their circumstances (Caruana & Narain, 2008). Basel II didn't change the basic threshold of 8% of RWA but retooled the system of assigning weights to estimate capital adequacy ratios. Risk weights were assigned by qualified external agencies or by more transparent banks' models and internal rating systems. For internal systems, the bar was raised significantly regarding data and processes. In addition, Basel I did not cover operational risk (the risk of loss resulting from inadequate internal processes, people, systems, or external events).

After the great financial crisis, regulations for the calculation of CAR have been tightened further, culminating in Basel III. In the current framework, banks must carry more and better quality capital. BIS (2019) noted that regulatory capital under Basel III focuses on high-quality capital, predominantly in the form of shares and retained earnings that can absorb losses. It also introduces an explicit going- and gone-concern framework by clarifying the roles of Tier 1 capital (going concern) and Tier 2 capital (gone concern). The central requirement is that all capital instruments must be able to fully absorb losses at the so-called point of non-viability (PoNV) before taxpayers are exposed.

Banks must maintain specified levels of CET1, tier 1, and total capital, each set as a percentage of risk-weighted assets. Total available regulatory capital is the sum of these two elements—tier 1 capital, CET1 and AT1, and tier 2 capital (BIS, 2019). Table 2.8 specifies the minimum levels of tier 1 and 2 capital on Basel III.

How does the conversion or write-off happen? The PoNV condition requires all AT1 and tier 2 instruments to be converted into common

Table 2.8 Minimum levels of capital, Basel III

Tier 1 (going concern)	Common Equity Tier 1	Sum of common shares (equivalent for non-joint stock companies) and stock surplus, retained earnings, other comprehensive income, qualifying minority interest, and regulatory adjustments	CET1 > 4.5%
	Additional Tier 1	Sum of capital instruments meeting the criteria for AT1 and related surplus, additional qualifying minority interest, and regulatory adjustments	CET1 + AT1 > 6%
Tier 2 (going concern)		Sum of capital instruments meeting the criteria for Tier 2 and related surplus, additional qualifying minority interest, qualifying loan loss provisions, and regulatory adjustments	CET1 + AT1 + Tier 2 > 8%

*The standard requires instruments issued by non-joint stock companies to meet criteria deemed equivalent to common shares and included in CET1

Source BIS (2019). https://www.bis.org/fsi/fsisummaries/defcap_b3.htm

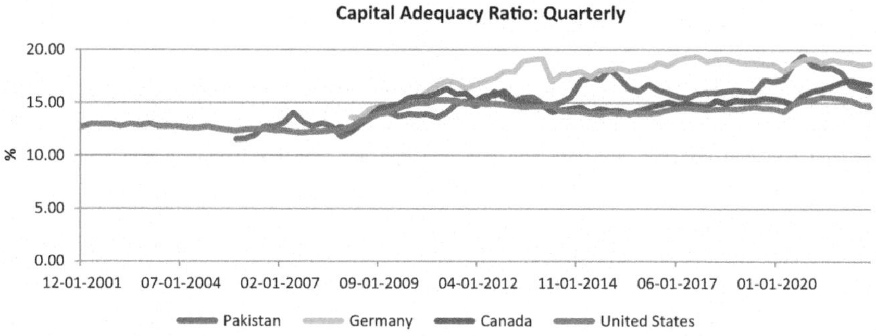

Fig. 2.10 Capital Adequacy Ratio: Quarterly (selected countries)

equity or written off. The earlier of these two conditions must be met: (i) a decision of the relevant authority that the conversion/write-off is necessary, given that the bank is assessed as non-viable and (ii) a decision to inject public funds to prevent the bank's failure. In other words, regulators must consider that the bank is under significant stress and may go bankrupt. Such write-offs induce banks to search for new sources of capital if they want to continue operating.

Banks today carry much higher capital adequacy ratios in response to more stringent regulations than before the crisis. Given how stringent Basel III rules are compared to earlier versions, banks reacted by becoming more conservative, holding more capital than they used to before the great financial crisis. Figure 2.10 illustrates the evolution of CAR in a few selected markets (chosen due to data availability).

For the United States, the average CAR was around 13% before 2008, averaging more than 14% since then. Changes in Pakistan were even more remarkable, with CAR reaching almost 20% in early 2020.

How do banks present capital adequacy indicators to regulators and the public? We answer that with the examples of Bank of America and Itau.

2.5.3 *Capital Adequacy Ratios: Some Illustrations*

This subsection aims to understand how banks usually present their capital adequacy ratios to the public. Greening banks require changing how banks report the possible impact of climate and social events on their balance sheets.

Figure 2.11 illustrates the critical capital metrics reported by Bank of America in 2019 and 2022. In the figure, the bank reports the values for common equity tier 1 capital, tier 1 capital, total capital, risk-weighted assets (advanced and standardized), and supplementary leverage exposure. The bank also reports the common equity tier 1 capital ratio and the supplementary leverage ratio.

As we can see, many indicators have barely budged in these three years. Tier 1 capital was U$191 billion in 2019 and U$205 billion in 2022, growing almost in line with the bank's revenue. Similarly, the bank's risk-weighted assets have changed by less than 10% over the same period (the standardized metric increased, while the advanced metric decreased slightly). This lack of change in key capital metrics is all the more surprising because of the intervening global pandemic. The bank's common equity tier 1 capital ratio is around 11% in both periods. Why this value and not, say, 8 or 15%? Because the Federal Reserve estimates and publicizes individual capital requirements for all large banks. In 2022, the value for Bank of America was 10.5%. It is not a coincidence that Bank of America targets a value a bit higher than the minimum required by the regulator. Any capital tied in such a manner brings opportunity costs; borrowers could pay the institution for its use.

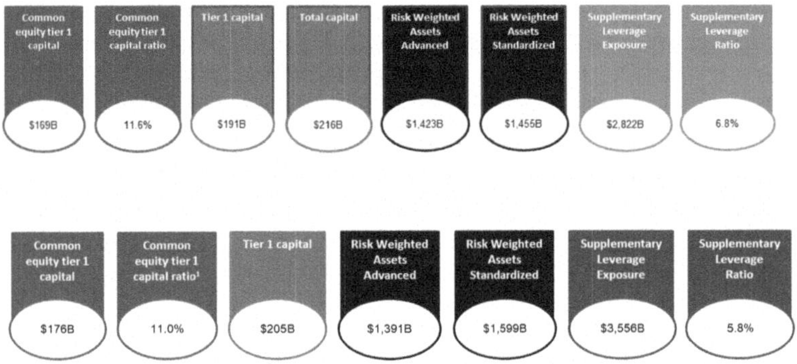

Fig. 2.11 March 31, 2019, and September 30, 2022, key capital metrics—Bank of America Corporation (*Source* Bank of America, 2022. https://investor.bankofamerica.com/regulatory-and-other-filings/basel-pillar-3-disclosures/pillar-3-regulatory-capital-disclosures)

Table 2.9 Regulatory Capital—Bank of America Corporation

Regulatory Capital—Bank of America Corporation		*September 30, 2022*
(Dollars in millions, except ratios)	**Bank of America Corporation Basel III Standardized CECL Fully Phased-In**	**Basel III Advanced CECL Fully Phased-In**
Regulatory Capital		
Common equity tier 1 capital	$ 173,673	$173,673
Tier 1 capital	202,794	202,794
Total capital[2]	235,952	227,490
Assets		
Risk-weighted assets	$1,599,898	$1,389,671
Adjusted quarterly average assets[3]	3,026,294	3,026,294
Supplementary Leverage Exposure		3,553,697
Capital Ratios		
Common equity tier 1 capital (%)	10.9	12.5
Tier 1 capital	12.7	14.6
Total capital	14.7	16.4
Tier 1 leverage	6.7	6.7
Supplementary Leverage Ratio		5.7
Regulatory Capital—Bank of America, NA		September 30, 2022
(Dollars in millions, except ratios)	**Bank of America, NA Basel III Standardized CECL Fully Phased-In**	**Basel III Advanced CECL Fully Phased-In**
Regulatory Capital		
Common equity tier 1 capital	$183,382	$183,382
Tier 1 capital	183,382	183,382
Total capital[2]	198,672	189,478
Assets		
Risk-weighted assets	$1,375,626	$1,053,083

(continued)

Table 2.9 (continued)

Regulatory Capital—Bank of America Corporation		*September 30, 2022*
Adjusted quarterly average assets[3]	2,380,788	2,380,788
Supplementary Leverage Exposure		2,812,431
Capital Ratios		
Common equity tier 1 capital (%)	13.3	17.4
Tier 1 capital	13.3	17.4
Total capital	14.4	18.0
Tier 1 leverage	7.7	7.7
Supplementary Leverage Ratio		6.5

Bank Holding Company		*Insured Depository Institutions*
Regulatory Minimum[4]		*Regulatory Minimum*[5]
Capital Ratios		
Common equity tier 1 capital (%)	9.5	7.0
Tier 1 capital	11.0	8.5
Total capital	13.0	10.5
Tier 1 leverage	4.0	5.0
Supplementary leverage ratio	5.0	6.0

Source Bank of America, 2022. https://investor.bankofamerica.com/annual-reports-and-proxy-statements

1. As of September 30, 2022, capital ratios are calculated using the regulatory capital rule, allowing a five-year transition period related to adopting CECL.
2. Total capital under the advanced approach differs from the Standardized approach due to differences in the amount permitted in Tier 2 capital related to the qualifying allowance for credit losses.
3. Reflects total average assets adjusted for certain Tier 1 capital deductions.
4. The capital conservation buffer and G-SIB surcharge were 2.5% on September 30, 2022. On September 30, 2022, the Corporation's SCB of 2.5% was applied in place of the capital conservation buffer under the Standardized approach. The countercyclical capital buffer was zero. The CET1 capital regulatory minimum is the sum of the CET1 capital ratio minimum of 4.5%, our G-SIB surcharge of 2.5%, and our SCB, or the capital conservation buffer, as applicable, of 2.5%. The SLR minimum includes a leverage buffer of 2.0%.
5. Risk-based capital regulatory minimums at September 30, 2022, are the minimum ratios under Basel III, including a capital conservation buffer of 2.5%. As of September 30, 2022, the regulatory minimums for leverage ratios are the percent required to be well-capitalized under the PCA framework.

There is an old joke that banking should be boring. Table 2.9 describes Bank of America's regulatory capital situation in more detail. In that sense, BoA's data reflect remarkably stable capital adequacy indicators. Common tier capital is less than 5% higher in 2022 than in 2019 (U$176 billion versus U$169 billion) in absolute terms and almost similar in relative terms (11% in 2022 versus 11.6% in 2019). As we can see, the institution describes its common equity tier 1 capital, tier 1 capital, and total capital according to two methodologies for the corporation and Bank of America, SA (there are additional reporting for other subsidiaries). Such reporting is the backbone of risk management reporting.

In addition, Table 2.9 details BoA's risk-weighted assets based on the fully phased-in Basel III regime (the transition was supposed to be completed by the end of 2022, so we omit the other data in the original report with the transitional values). Another significant distinction is between standardized and advanced Basel III regulations. Here, we are not interested in the dissimilarities between these two regimes. Still, one may ask which set of values represents a financial institution's actual robustness to shocks. The answer is none. No unambiguous set of values exists, and Basel III indicators are guidelines, no matter how sophisticated their calculation is. More than the percentages, it is more important that the indicators are solid estimates and that the assets in a bank's balance sheet are well-priced.

BoA's capital adequacy ratios align with those expected of a multinational bank under Basel III. A note in the financial statement from the bank reads: "As of September 30, 2022, Bank of America and its insured depository institution subsidiaries are well-capitalized and meet all capital requirements to which each is subject. Bank of America's capital conservation buffer of 6.48% and leverage buffer of 2.76% are above the capital conservation buffer requirement of 5.0% and the leverage buffer requirement of 2.0%, respectively."

The Federal Reserve introduced a new capital buffer recommended by the BIS when implementing Basel III in the United States, the supplementary leverage ratio. Banks must estimate and hold at least 3% of common equity capital relative to their total leverage exposure. The reasoning for that is explicit in a BIS document detailing the new guidelines: "An underlying cause of the Great Financial Crisis was the build-up of excessive on- and off-balance sheet leverage in the banking system. Banks often build-up excessive leverage while maintaining seemingly strong risk-based capital ratios. The ensuing deleveraging process at the height of the crisis created a vicious circle of losses and reduced credit availability in the real economy (BIS, 2017).

Later, we will discuss whether authorities must review their prudential frameworks to account for the implications of climate-related financial risks for financial stability (Coelho & Restoy, 2022). Here, the capital adequacy ratios allow us to understand how financial regulators require banks to mobilize capital against possible shocks and how to report them to society.

We can see that banks in other countries report capital adequacy ratios similar to BoA. Itau, a Brazilian bank, illustrates its leading indicators for the second quarter of 2022 in Fig. 2.12.

In the second part of the figure, Itau describes how the common equity tier 1 ratio and tier 1 ratio changed from the first to the second quarter. Alongside the detail of Table 2.10, we can see how Itau, much like BoA, shows remarkably consistent capital adequacy ratios.

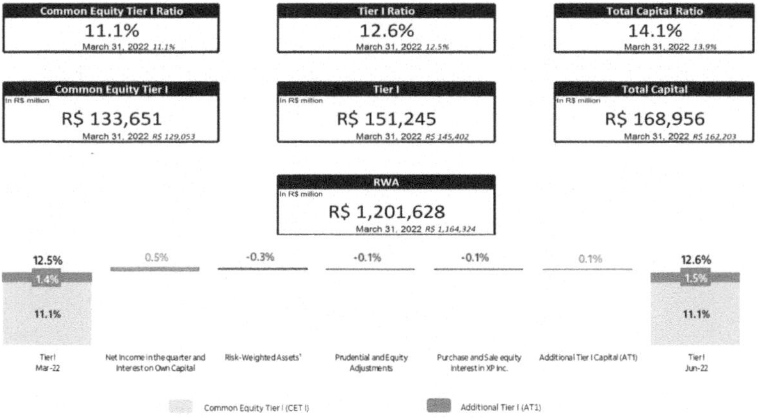

Fig. 2.12 Key indicators, Itau, 2Q 2022 (*Source* Itau (2022) Risk and Capital Management—Pillar 3—2Q22—Banco Itaú, available at: https://www.itau.com.br/download-file/v2/d/42787847-4cf6-4461-94a5-40ed237dca33/7e7cb53e-ef18-1000-fa28-9591f5675fe7?origin=2)

The report notes that the bank's primary goal is to illustrate how "safe" it is. Itau described its results as such: "The Basel Ratio reached 14.1% as of June 30, 2022, an increase of 20 basis points compared to 13.9% as of March 31, 2022, due to the result for the period, partially offset by the increase of the credit Risk-weighted Assets (RWAcpad), prudential adjustments and acquisition of XP Inc. shares. Besides, Itaú Unibanco has a R$ 72,826 million capital excess concerning its minimum required Total Capital. It corresponds to 6,1 pp above the minimum requirement (8%) and higher than the Capital Buffer requirement of 3.5% (R$ 42,057 million). Considering the Capital Buffers, the capital excess would be 2,6 pp. The fixed assets ratio shows the commitment percentage of adjusted Referential Equity with the adjusted permanent assets. Itaú Unibanco falls within the maximum limit of 50% of adjusted PR established by BACEN. On June 30, 2022, the fixed assets ratio reached 19.0%, showing a surplus of R$ 52,441 million."

As we can see, in almost every sentence, Itau relates its excess capital to the minimum regulatory requirements. Amounts are significant: R$42 billion to capital buffers, R$73 billion to total capital, and R$52 billion to fixed assets. There are substantial opportunity costs to this amount of

Table 2.10 Itau's regulatory capital

R$ million	*06/30/2022*	*03/31/2022*	*12/31/2021*	*09/30/2021*	*06/30/2021*
Available capital (amounts)					
Common Equity Tier 1 (CET1)	133,651	129,053	130,716	123,547	124,964
Tier 1	151,245	145,402	149,912	141,409	141,674
Total capital	168,956	162,203	169,797	161,099	156,561
Risk-weighted assets (amounts)					
Total risk-weighted assets (RWA)	1,201,628	1,164,324	1,153,841	1,095,194	1,048,628
Risk-based capital ratios as a percentage of RWA					
Common Equity Tier 1 ratio (%)	11.1	11.1	11.3	11.3	11.9
Tier 1 ratio (%)	12.6	12.5	13.0	12.9	13.5
Total capital ratio (%)	14.1	13.9	14.7	14.7	14.9
Additional CET1 buffer requirements as % of RWA					
Capital conservation buffer requirement (%) (1)	2.5	2.0	2.0	0.625	0.625
Countercyclical buffer requirement (%) (2)					
Bank G-S1B and/or D-S1B additional requirements (%)	1.0	1.0	1.0	1.0	1.0
Total of bank CET1 specific buffer requirements (%) (3)	3.5	3.0	3.0	2.625	2.625
CET1 available after meeting the bank's minimum capital requirements (%)	2.6	2.9	3.5	4.0	4.2
Basel Ill leverage ratio					
Total Basel Ill leverage ratio exposure measure	2,102,773	2,015,946	2,018,692	1,969,517	1,883,388
Basel Ill leverage ratio (%)	7.2	7.2	7.4	7.2	7.5
Liquidity Coverage Ratio					
Total high-quality liquid assets (HQLA)	279,847	293,573	307,280	315,791	324,440
Total net cash outflow	192,124	196,328	193,093	184,568	179,322
LCR (%)	145.7	149.5	159.1	171.1	180.9

R$ million	*06/30/2022*	*03/31/2022*	*12/31/2021*	*09/30/2021*	*06/30/2021*
Net Stable Funding Ratio					
Total available stable funding	1,070,719	1,021,581	1,016,989	978,802	949,811
Total required stable funding	894,427	852,481	839,830	811,430	774,165
NSFR (%)	119.7	119.8	121.1	120.6	122.7

Source Itau (2022) Risk and Capital Management—Pillar 3—2Q22—Banco Itaú, available at: https://www.itau.com.br/download-file/v2/d/42787847-4cf6-4461-94a5-40ed237dca33/7e7cb53e-ef18-1000-fa28-9591f5675fe7?origin=2

excess capital. Each dollar kept as excess capital means the bank is losing the opportunity to lend it at the high interest rates in the country (or any of its subsidiaries worldwide). Brazil has one, if not the highest, lending rates to individual and corporate customers globally (Zeidan, 2020).

Itau's case illustrates the importance of regulation in driving banks' behavior. The Brazilian Central Bank is considered particularly stringent, heavily favoring prudence (Zeidan, 2020). Thus, it makes sense that multinational banks headquartered in the country report capital adequacy ratios highlighting excess capital.

The primary lesson is that regulators hold significant sway over banks' behavior; any measure requiring that banks report on environmental risks, to name a single factor, would likely change banks' operations.

Finally, the significant difference between BoA and Itau's capital adequacy reports is that the latter also reports liquidity indicators in the main capital adequacy ratio tables. BIS's goal with the LCR is to promote the short-term resilience of banks. Institutions should have an adequate stock of unencumbered high-quality liquid assets (HQLA) that can be converted easily and immediately in private markets into cash to meet their needs for a 30 calendar-day liquidity stress scenario (BIS, 2018). LCR is the percentage of HQLA a bank holds in proportion to the possible net cash outflows in stress periods. Banks should keep an LCR above 100% on an ongoing basis. As we can see in the case of Itau, the bank holds an LCR that averages 165% over the data period, much above the minimum required according to Basel III indicators.

The European Central Bank has been publishing data for regional banks since 2016. Figure 2.13 shows the LCR for European banks from 2016 to 2022. Alongside data for Europe, there is data for Australian banks. Interestingly, as the pandemic hits, banks' LCRs rise significantly at first, mainly because banks' net cash outflow goes down. As the economies recover, the banks' liquidity ratios go down.

Still, they are never below 100%, indicating that banks in Europe and Australia comply with the Basel III requirements even after the complete transition period.

Finally, banks usually report their total loss-absorbing capacity. As the name implies, the concept estimates how much losses the institution can take without resorting to the lender of last resort or, ultimately, becoming insolvent.

Table 2.11 presents Bank of America Corporation's TLAC and long-term debt ratios and related information. As we can see, BoA targets

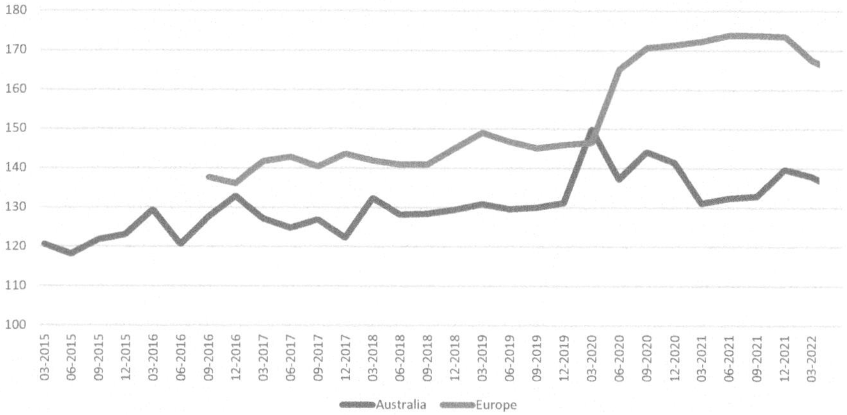

Fig. 2.13 Liquidity Coverage Ratio (minimum required = 100%), Euro-countries, and Australia (*Source* European Central Bank, 2022. https://sdw.ecb.europa.eu/home.do;jsessionid=C1EE79740BDECEDBA1C24E35220171D2)

capacity much higher than the regulatory minimum. In this case, funding interval matters. For commercial banks, systemic risk is mainly (but not solely) tied to short-term debt, primarily demand deposits. Thus, banks that can fund their operations with long-term debt are, *ceteris paribus*, less risky than their competitors. Unlike capital adequacy ratios, no opportunity costs are lost if the actual TLAC is significantly above the regulatory minimum. Thus, a TLAC of 29% against a minimum target of 22% is not a particularly risk-averse strategy, as long as TLAC is financed by long-term debt and not by putting aside potentially value-creating capital.

1. As of September 30, 2022, TLAC ratios are calculated using the regulatory capital rule that allows a five-year transition period related to the adoption of CECL.
2. The TLAC RWA regulatory minimum consists of 18.0% plus a TLAC RWA buffer of 2.5% plus the Method 1 G-SIB surcharge of 1.5%. The countercyclical buffer is zero for this period. The TLAC supplementary leverage exposure regulatory minimum comprises 7.5% plus a 2.0% TLAC leverage buffer. The TLAC RWA and leverage buffers must be comprised solely of CET1 capital and Tier 1 capital, respectively.

Table 2.11 Total loss-absorbing capacity and long-term debt, September 30, 2022

(Dollars in millions)	*TLAC*[1]	*Regulatory Minimum*[2]	*Long-term Debt (%)*	*Regulatory Minimum*[3] *(%)*
Regulatory Capital				
Total eligible balance	$ 461,928	$ 242,473	15.2	8.5
Percentage of risk-weighted assets[4] (%)	28.9	22.0%	15.2	8.5
Percentage of total supplementary leverage exposure (%)	13.0	9.5	6.8	4.5

Source Bank of America, 2022. https://investor.bankofamerica.com/annual-reports-and-proxy-statements

3. The long-term debt RWA regulatory minimum is 6.0% plus an additional 2.5% requirement based on the Corporation's Method 2 G-SIB surcharge. The regulatory minimum for long-term debt leverage exposure is 4.5%.
4. The approach that yields the higher RWA is used to calculate TLAC and long-term debt ratios, which was the Standardized approach as of September 30, 2022.

What is the main lesson? Greening banks must consider the constraints that financial institutions face. "Green" capital requirements, sustainable lending, ESG investing, and other ways to incorporate nonfinancial performance into banks' activities cannot be understood in a vacuum. Incentives matter, and these are crystal clear for commercial banks: first and foremost, compliance with regulators constrains what institutions can do.

2.6 Green Capital Requirements

Should central banks require green capital requirements? Central banks usually require that banks adopt a countercyclical capital buffer, released in case of severe financial shocks, to avoid credit crunches (Masciandaro & Russo, 2023). However, in the case of green capital requirements, we don't have a holistic understanding of its possible costs and benefits.

Recent works have started modeling the implications of mandatory green capital requirements. This section summarizes Oehmke and Opp (2022), one of the first works to analyze the issue and then explore other models, such as those by Dafermos and Nikolaidi (2021), Dunz et al. (2021), and Lamperti et al. (2021). Each model advances solid arguments for our understanding of green capital requirements.

One fundamental criterion for green capital requirements is the tradeoff between financial stability and the possibilities for climate change mitigation. We must add internal incentives for regulators to those tradeoffs. Central banks will move more slowly regarding climate finance if they feel it will make their jobs harder. Before, we have seen how capital requirements shape banks' decisions. Unlike lightly regulated nonfinancial companies, banks must answer to regulators in ways that may be counterintuitive to most businesspeople. And that is why proper modeling of expected responses to green capital requirements is so important: are we sure this is the best way to funnel credit to less unsustainable companies?

In the model by Oehmke and Opp (2022), banks extend loans to two types of borrowers: dirty and clean. The authors explicitly make the tradeoff between profitability and social value; in other words, if banks abandon lending to dirty borrowers, they lose money. Dirty borrowers are more profitable due to production technologies that generate significant carbon emissions. Clean borrowers use other technologies that are less profitable but produce lower carbon emissions.

Instead of looking at all possible forms to establish green capital requirements, Oehmke and Opp (2022) focus on two of the most commonly proposed interventions: the green supporting factor (lower capital requirements for clean loans) and the brown penalizing factor (higher capital requirements for dirty loans). These two interventions are not identical. The former loosens banks' balance sheet constraints, especially relevant when banks have plenty of profitable opportunities but are constrained on how much credit they can create. In contrast, the latter tightens balance sheet constraints.

The first aim of the model is to distinguish between the income and substitution effects of policy interventions. The income effect is about overall profitability and the likelihood that banks may reduce overall credit supply given changes in capital requirements. The substitution effect is about the relative profitability of clean versus dirty loans. Policies ideally should not generate adverse income effects, focusing on incentives to more clean loans and fewer dirty loans. Is this possible to achieve? Let's look at the model.

It is a two-period model ($t = 0, 1$) in which agents are risk-neutral and have no time discounting. Besides the regulator, numerous firms with investment opportunities and competitive banks exist.

Firms are one of two observable types: clean and dirty, $q \in \{C, D\}$. The population fraction of type q is fixed and given by π_q. Production requires a fixed investment I at $t = 0$ for each type. At date $t = 1$, cash flows are realized. We assume that cash flows for each type q follow a lognormal distribution with parameters μ_q and σ_q so that the firm's expected cash flow is given by:

$$\overline{X_q} = \exp\left[\mu_q + \sigma_q^2 / 2\right]$$

A lognormal distribution implies that cash flows cannot be negative; see Fig. 2.14 for an illustration of a lognormal distribution for variable X. Lognormal distributions are commonly used to price derivatives and other financial instruments in which assets, such as stock prices, cannot take negative values. Formally, for a standard normal variable Z with a mean of its' logarithm μ and standard deviation σ, the lognormal distribution of the random variable X is given by:

$$X = e^{\mu + \sigma Z}$$

In addition, for lognormal distributions, the probability density function (PDF), cumulative density function CDF), mean, median, mode, and variance are, respectively:

$$\text{PDF} = \frac{1}{x\sigma\sqrt{2\pi}} \exp\left(-\frac{(\ln(x) - \mu)^2}{2\sigma^2}\right)$$

$\text{CDF} = \frac{1}{2}\left[1 + \text{cef}\left(\frac{\ln x - \mu}{\sigma\sqrt{2}}\right)\right]$, where cef is the complementary error function.

$\text{Mean} = \exp\left(\mu + \frac{\sigma^2}{2}\right)$

$\text{Median} = \exp(\mu)$

$\text{Mode} = \exp(\mu - \sigma^2)$

$\text{Variance} = \left[\exp(\sigma^2) - 1\right]\exp(2\mu + \sigma^2)$

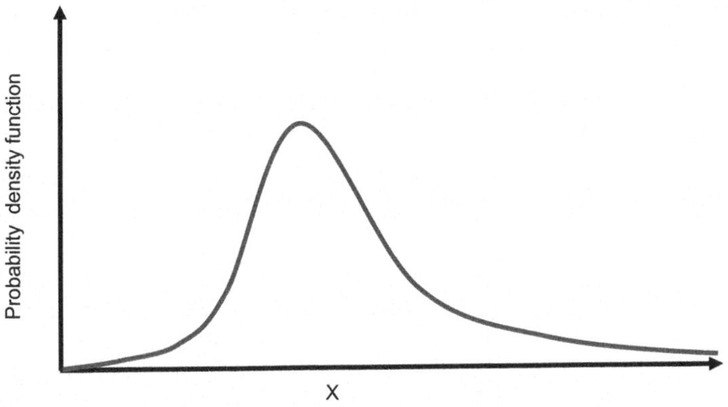

Fig. 2.14 Probability density function

Oehmke and Opp (2022) assume that the variance of the clean and dirty types is identical. Dirty firms are more profitable than clean firms, which is represented by the net present value of each firm, such as:

$NPV_D > NPV_C$,

One notable characteristic of the model is that banks' capital structure matters. They are endowed with equity E. They can raise additional deposit funding D from competitive depositors to finance asset A. Thus, $A = E + D$.

Equity is fixed, and deposit insurance is an effective subsidy for deposit financing. Banks' goals are to maximize their equity:

$$V = \max_{e,w} E[1 + r_E(w, e)]$$

where e is a bank's equity ratio, $r_E\ (\boldsymbol{w}, e)$ is the expected return on equity (ROE), and $\boldsymbol{w} = (\boldsymbol{w}_C, \boldsymbol{w}_D)$ is the vector of bank loan portfolio weights. Given capital requirements e_q as a function of q, the bank then faces the equity ratio constraint:

$$e \geq e_{\min}(w) := \sum_q w_q e_q$$

Harris et al. (2020) first analyzed the equilibrium given e_q. Banks end up specializing in funding clean or dirty firms. In addition, given the maximum interest rate a borrower is willing to pay (r_q^{max}), the expected

ROE is:

$$r_q^{\max}(e_q) = \frac{\mathrm{NPV}_q + \mathrm{PUT}_q(e_q)}{Ie_q}$$

where NPV_q is the (always positive) net present value of the firm of type q, and $\mathrm{PUT}_q(e_q)$ is the contribution of the loan to the bank's deposit insurance.

The expected surplus that accrues to the banks' equity holders is the sum of the NPV of the firm's project and the deposit insurance put. Figure 2.15 illustrates the equilibrium for $e = 16\%$ capital requirements for both firm types. Dirty firms are depicted in red, and clean firms in green—the equilibrium ROE is denoted by r^*. The figure is a typical supply and demand graph in which equity supply is given and completely inelastic (banks cannot issue debt in the model). Bank demand is stepwise: dirty firms have a higher demand than clean firms, as they are more profitable. Banks cannot take all producer surplus because they face perfect competition from other banks. Still, clean firms do not have a (consumer) surplus, as the equilibrium ROE is at their reservation price.

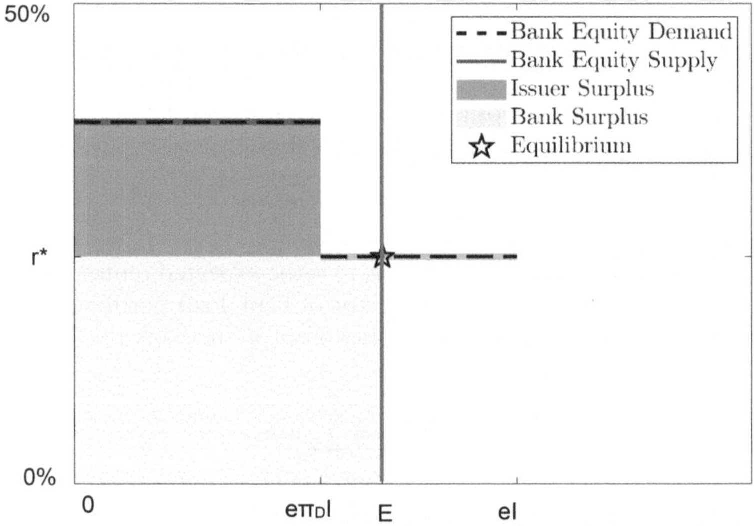

Fig. 2.15 Banking sector equilibrium (*Source* Oehmke, and Opp, (2022))

If banks were allowed to price discriminate, they could collect the (consumer) surplus from the dirty firms. Also of note is that dirty firms are fully funded (inframarginal), but not all clean firms can access credit (marginal), as there is a limited credit supply. Formally, all borrowers with $r_q^{max} > r_E^*$ are fully funded. Marginal borrowers satisfying $r_q^{max} = r_E^*$ are partially funded. The banking sector's equilibrium ROE is:

$$r_E\left(w^*, e_{\min}\left(w^*\right)\right) = r_E^*$$

The authors then turn to the most relevant part for our purposes. They analyze the green supporting and the brown penalizing factors. Above, capital requirements are the same for both firm types: $e_C = e_D = e < 1$. Figure 2.16 shows the effects of the two brown penalizing factors. The first leaves the relative ranking of firm types unchanged. The second has a significant impact as it reverses the relative ranking of firm types.

There is a counterintuitive result—a small brown penalty crowds out lending to clean firms. The reservation price of brown firms goes down, but that does not change the market equilibrium. The penalty reduces overall credit. Banks reduce their credit to clean firms while brown firms are still fully funded. The minor brown penalty only successfully reduces the surplus of brown firms but limits the credit to clean firms.

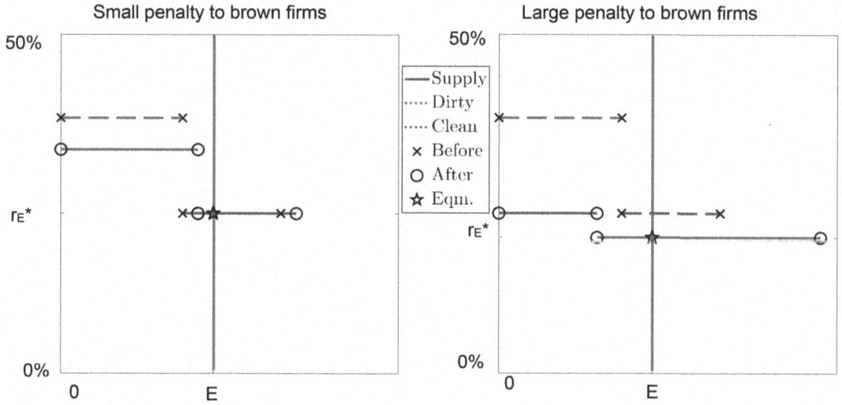

Fig. 2.16 Effects of small and large brown factor penalization (*Source* Oehmke, and Opp, (2022))

The right part of Fig. 2.17 illustrates how the brown penalizing factor can be significant enough to make loans to clean firms relatively cheaper. In that instance, banks fund (fully funded) clean firms first, and brown firms cease to be fully funded. Overall, credit supply is also lower than the benchmark instance of no extra capital requirements as equity becomes scarcer.

What is the difference between a brown penalizing and a green supporting factor? Fig. 2.17, like before, illustrates the equilibrium impact of small and large green supporting factors. The small factor leaves the relative ranking of firm types unchanged. The large green supporting factor induces banks to consider clean firms more profitable.

As before, banks fully fund clean firms after introducing the significant supporting factor, but only brown firms remain entirely financed under a small factor regime. The crucial difference is due to overall credit. Green support enhances banks' total equity, meaning that overall credit supply increases for small and large factors. The authors show that the effect of a marginal decrease in capital requirements for clean loans depends on the capitalization of the banking sector. If $E \in (\pi_D eI,\ eI)$, this change in capital requirements would increase lending to clean firms, having no effect otherwise.

What are the main conclusions? For small interventions, brown penalizing and green supporting factors have quite different effects, driven by

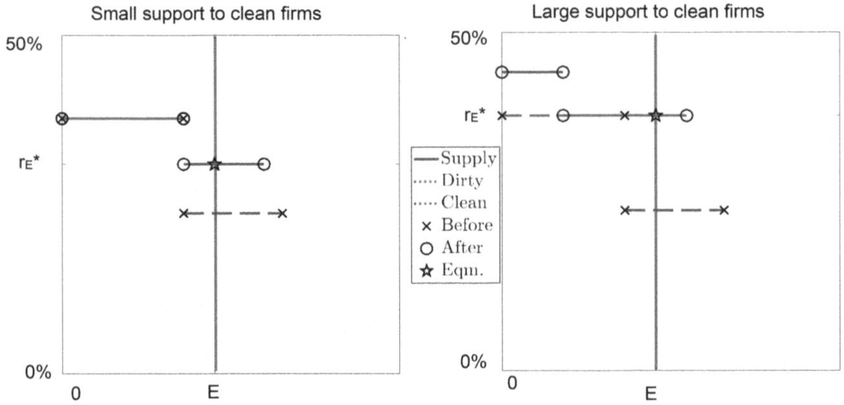

Fig. 2.17 Different levels of support to clean firms (*Source* Oehmke, and Opp, (2022))

opposite income effects. The substitution effect becomes dominant for prominent factors, so their effects are qualitatively similar.

Counterintuitively, a larger fraction of dirty firms are funded due to the significant green supporting factor. That results from higher aggregate credit due to a supporting versus a penalizing factor.

Does this counterintuitive result hold if there are many types of firms and not only two? The authors explore a many-type set-up where banks would continue to rank firm types according to their reservation price. As the authors note, the critical difference is that both income and substitution effects will now be present. Still, the central result remains: changes to capital requirements of inframarginal borrower types will crowd out lending to the marginal borrower type. For example, suppose clean and dirty firms populate the economy, each with a distribution of productivity levels. In that case, a small change to capital requirements will affect both a fraction of clean and dirty borrowers.

Given the model's details, the authors analyze the possibility of optimal capital requirement policies. They establish three principles of optimal prudential regulation: banks use all their equity to fund loans; for low levels of bank equity, the regulator induces banks to lend to their preferred type; if both firm types are funded, marginal deposit insurance puts are equalized across types.

Figure 2.18 illustrates the equilibrium funding decisions (upper panel) and capital requirements (lower panel) under optimal prudential bank capital regulation. The dotted green line indicates the lower bound on the capital requirement for (unfunded) clean firms in the region where only dirty loans are funded, and the capital requirement for dirty loans is set to e^*.

There are four intervals of optimal capital requirements in Fig. 2.18: $0 < E < E_1$, $E_1 < E < E_2$, $E_2 < E < E_3$, and $E > E_3$. The first represents scarce equity: only the regulator's preferred (dirty) type is funded in this instance. Capital requirements for the (unfunded) clean type are set high, which imposes a lower bound on the capital requirement for clean loans (the dotted green line). As aggregate equity in the banking sector increases, the proportion of dirty firms funded increases until they are fully funded (in the second interval). The authors write: "Intuitively, once all dirty lending opportunities in the economy have been exhausted, the marginal benefit of funding the next best investment opportunity, the clean type, is lower by a discrete amount. Therefore, it is initially optimal

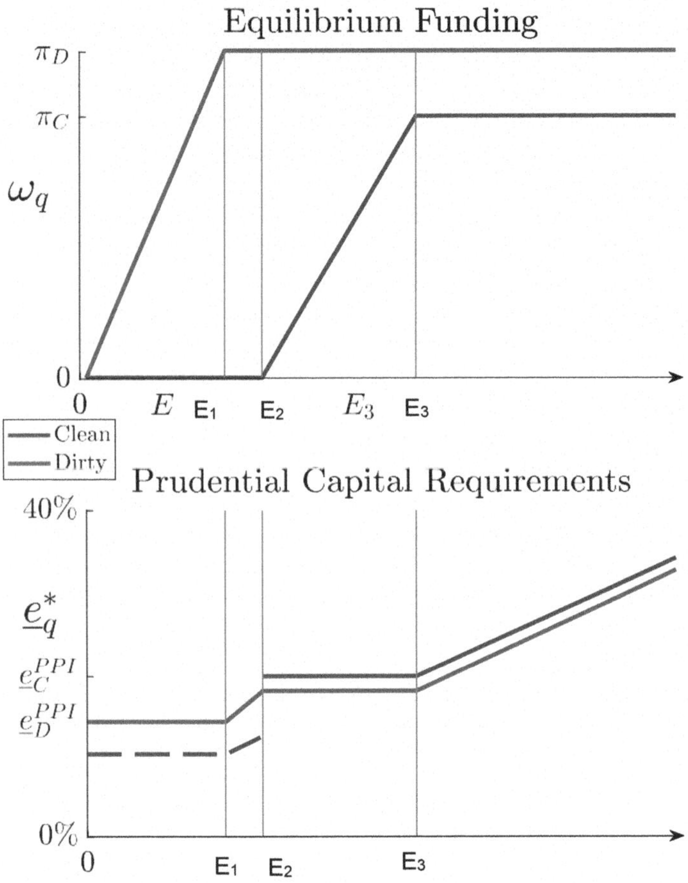

Fig. 2.18 Optimal prudential capital regulation (*Source* Oehmke, and Opp, (2022))

to use additional equity in the banking sector to reduce the deposit insurance put associated with funding dirty firms rather than inducing banks to fund clean firms." Only in region three does the regulator find it optimal to induce banks to fund clean firms; in region four, both types are fully funded. Any additional equity is used to phaseout the deadweight costs arising from deposit insurance.

Table 2.12 Climate risk categorization

		Effect on	
		Firms funded by financial sector	*Other*
Caused by	Firms funded by financial sector	Financial- Financial (TBD)	Financial-Other (✓)
	–Other	Other-Financial (✓)	Other–Other (✗)

Finally, the authors analyze the dynamic effects of climate change on the optimal prudential policy. Table 2.12 summarizes the categorization of climate risk regarding direct and indirect impacts from banks and firms.

The authors analyze the scenario in which the regulator is only concerned about climate-related financial risks to the extent that they affect banks (FF-risks and OF-risks). Interestingly, in their framework, the regulator cannot address other–other risks, such as risks caused by firms or consumers outside the banking sector.

The model captures transition risks as decreasing in dirty firms' expected cash flow and volatility. The optimal regulatory response to moderate risks combines brown penalizing and green supporting factors; the exact calibration depends on aggregate equity. The result, counterintuitively, is that there is crowding out of lending to dirty firms if bank equity is low but crowding out of lending to clean firms if equity is moderate. However, clean types are funded first for significant risks, switching the funding order in Fig. 2.18, similar to the effect of a large brown penalizing factor.

For the climate-related effects of the financial system on economic activity, i.e., the externalities of lending to dirty and clean firms, the optimal prudential policy is unaffected, regardless of their size. The final result that the authors advance is that even with a broader (climate) mandate, capital requirements are not the most natural tool to address externalities. For instance, banks may find dirty loans still financially profitable even at maximal requirements.

Of course, if the regulator can impose Pigouvian taxes, tradeoffs between financial stability and negative consumption externalities would not arise.

What are the conclusions the authors make? First, the brown penalizing and green supporting factors are not equivalent and have potentially subtle counterintuitive outcomes. Second, optimal capital requirements depend on the regulatory objective (a prudential or a broader green mandate) and the nature of climate-related risks. Finally, climate-related risks that affect bank stability can be optimally addressed by combining green supporting and brown penalizing factors. Still, capital regulation is less effective in addressing carbon externalities outside the banking sector.

These results are broadly supported by Dunz et al. (2021). They analyze a combination of green supporting factors and a global carbon tax. Their results crucially depend on central banks' and agents' reactions to such policies. One of the main transmission mechanisms of monetary policy and financial regulation is related to the moderating effecting of central banks' actions on agents' expectations. Regarding their model, Dunz et al. (2021) find that investors' climate sentiments can play a prominent role in avoiding a disorderly low-carbon transition.

Other recent models provide support for more aggressive green capital requirements. Dafermos and Nikolaidi (2021) also analyze penalizing and supporting green-related factors, finding they can reduce physical financial risks. Such a reduction is slight but is enhanced when both factors are implemented simultaneously or combined with green fiscal policies. Lamperti et al. (2021) employ an agent-based macro-financial model to assess green financial policies. They find that green capital requirements spur productivity without hampering financial stability. However, carbon risk adjustment and green public guarantees mitigate emissions but increase instability. They conclude that a policy mix comprising all three policies is sufficient for a virtuous cycle.

We know that green fiscal policies can immensely help climate change mitigation. While combining such policies with a change in financial regulation could be ideal, it is unlikely to become a reality. Central banks have some measure of autonomy in most countries precisely because fiscal and monetary policies are uncoordinated. We will likely see increasing use of both brown penalizing factors and green supporting factors, but not on a large scale.

2.7 Estimation of Expected and Unexpected Losses

The idea behind the estimation of possible bank losses is straightforward. For a portfolio of assets during a specific period, the aggregate losses are nothing more than the probability of default times the losses from default events. Banks must calculate EL as the probability of default (PD) x loss given default (LGD) for corporate, sovereign, bank, and retail exposures not in default (BIS, 2022a, 2022b, 2022c). The devil, as they say, is in the details. Take, for instance, the probability of default (PD). A bank can use data on the past performance of its loan portfolio and complement it with estimations about possible adverse scenarios that have not happened before. Financial crises are rare, so modeling PD with historical data that includes a few data points related to a crisis may be insufficient to estimate the correct amount of capital to safeguard a bank against extreme risk events.

Given regulatory scrutiny, even loss must be defined precisely (BIS, 2022a, 2022b, 2022c). In the Basel III framework, "The definition of loss used in estimating LGD is economic loss. When measuring economic loss, all relevant factors should be taken into account. This must include material discount effects and material direct and indirect costs associated with collecting on the exposure. Banks must not simply measure the loss recorded in accounting records, although they must be able to compare accounting and economic losses. The bank's own workout and collection expertise significantly influences recovery rates. It must be reflected in their LGD estimates, but adjustments to estimates for such expertise must be conservative until the bank has sufficient internal empirical evidence of the impact of its expertise."

Expected losses (EL), applicable for most asset classes, are the losses a bank expects by holding a specific asset. It can incorporate PD, loss-given default (LGD), and exposure at default (EAD). Loss given default is the fraction of the credit exposure lost if the borrower defaults (Bastos, 2010).

Exposure is not a static concept. Current, expected, and peak exposure might all differ and require distinct approaches to relate them to expected losses. Here, we assume that current and expected exposure don't vary significantly, simplifying the estimation of expected and unexpected losses.

We have seen in the previous section that, generally, in the foundation approach, banks estimate the probability of default and rely on supervisory estimates for other risk components. In contrast, in the advanced approach, they use their own estimates. However, that is not strictly the case for all risk exposures. Banks use their best estimate of expected loss for corporate, sovereign, bank, and retail exposures in default, relying on the supervisory LGD in the foundation approach. There are many rules that banks must follow to determine their own LGD. For instance, the minimum data observation period for building LGD estimates is five years for retail and seven years for other exposures. Still, data should cover at least one complete economic cycle. The fewer data points, the more conservative estimates must be (European Central Bank, 2019).

For a simple example, assume that a bank has three loans, as shown in Table 2.13.

The three loans' loss-given defaults are 50, 75, and 80%, respectively. As for the exposure at default, the values are U$10 million, U$20 million, and U$30 million, respectively. Assuming a recovery rate of 100% on the collateral, the expected loss is:

$$\mathrm{EL} = \sum_{i=1}^{N} \mathrm{PD}_i \times \mathrm{EAD}_i \times \mathrm{LGD}_i$$

$$\begin{aligned} EL &= 10 \times 50\% \times 1.5\% + 20 \times 75\% \times 2\% + 30 \times 80\% \times 2.5\% \\ &= U\$975,000 \end{aligned}$$

For this simple example, the bank has expected losses of U$975,000. Of course, the bank's total exposure is U$44 million, even assuming a 100% recovery rate on the collateral.

Unexpected loss (UL) refers to the credit loss above the expected loss. There is no single way to estimate UL. Forjan (2019) describes UL when PD is a Bernoulli variable with a binomial distribution. In that case, the UL_i for an asset value V_i is calculated as the standard deviation from the mean at a certain confidence level.

$$\mathrm{UL}_i = \sqrt{\mathrm{var}} \times V_i$$

Table 2.13 Simple example of the calculation of the probability of default

Loan	*Rating counterparty*	*Mark-to-market value*	*Collateral*	*Exposure*	*PD (%)*
A	A	10,000,000	5	5	1.5
B	A-	20,000,000	5	15	2.0
C	BB	30,000,000	6	24	2.5

As the variance of PD is defined as PD*(1 − PD), the unexpected loss from holding the asset is:

$$\mathrm{UL}_i = \mathrm{EAD} \times \sqrt{\mathrm{PD} \times \sigma^2_{\mathrm{LGD}} + \mathrm{LGD}^2 \times \sigma^2_{\mathrm{PD}}}$$

Thus, for the first loan on Table 36 (for which the EL is U$75,000), the unexpected loss is determined as:

$$UL_i = 10 \times \sqrt{1.5\% \times 25\% + 25\% \times 1.478\%}$$

$$= 10 \times \sqrt{0.7444\%}$$

$$= U\$862,772$$

We can see that the unexpected loss is much higher than expected, which is an intuitive result. The same is true for the other loans, as shown in Table 2.14.

Unexpected losses cannot be aggregated similarly to expected losses by summing the value of each loan. The reason is that it is unlikely that crisis events would make all counterparties default simultaneously.

Table 2.14 Unexpected losses

Loan	*A*	*B*	*C*
Rating counterparty	A	A-	BB
Mark-to-market value	10,000,000	20,000,000	30,000,000
Collateral	5,000,000	5,000,000	6,000,000
Exposure	5,000,000	15,000,000	24,000,000
PD (%)	1.50	2.00	2.50
LGD (%)	50	75	80
σ^2_{PD} (%)	1.478	1.960	2.438
σ^2_{LGD} (%)	25	18.75	16.00
LGD^2 (%)	25.00	56.25	64.00
$\mathrm{PD} \times \sigma^2_{\mathrm{LGD}}$ (%)	0.375	0.375	0.400
$\mathrm{LGD}^2 \times \sigma^2_{\mathrm{PD}}$ (%)	0.369	1.103	1.560
$\mathrm{PD} \times \sigma^2_{\mathrm{LGD}} + \mathrm{LGD}^2 \times \sigma^2_{\mathrm{PD}}$ (%)	0.744	1.478	1.960
$\sqrt{\mathrm{PD} \times \sigma^2_{\mathrm{LGD}} + \mathrm{LGD}^2 \times \sigma^2_{\mathrm{PD}}}$	0.0863	0.1216	0.1400
UL_i	862,772	2,431,049	4,200,000

Source Forjan (2019)

Usually, we also need effective maturity (M) and correlation factor (CF) for unexpected loss calculation.

From estimations of expected and unexpected losses, regulators derive capital requirements that must be available to absorb losses in the case of severe adverse scenarios.

For our purposes, greening banks require estimating expected and unexpected losses. In Chapter 5, we see that climate stress testing does that by tying the economic and financial effects of climate change to banks' balance sheets. ESG investing and other sustainability-related initiatives must also consider marking-to-market and the potential impact on expected and unexpected losses. Finally, they must take into account risk management approaches, as in the following section.

2.8 AIRB; CVA, BA-CVA, and SA-CVA

Banks had more leeway in developing internal risk management models in the past. Since the great financial crisis, regulations have become stricter, even if the practice of allowing internal models has not gone away completely.

Supervisors globally establish distinct rules for the use of internal models. One example is the estimation of LGD using the AIRB approach in the UK. The Prudential Regulation Authority (PRA) has proposed an alternative method for LGD modeling in cases where firms lack sufficient data to model collateral recoveries (Bank of England, 2022). The LGD under the alternative methodology would be calculated as (Bank of England, 2022):

$$\text{LGD} = \text{LGD}_U \frac{E_U}{E * (1 + H_E)} + \text{LGD}_S \frac{E_S}{E * (1 + H_E)}$$

where:

LGD* is the LGD applicable to a collateralized transaction;

LGD_U is the estimated LGD of the exposure disregarding collateral (i.e., treating the exposure as unsecured);

LGD_S is the foundation collateral method secured LGD applicable to the collateral type;

E is the current value of the exposure after the effect of on-balance sheet netting;

E_S is the current value of the collateral after the application of the applicable volatility adjustment (H_c)

E_U is the value of the unsecured exposure calculated as follows:

$$E_U = E * (1 + H_E) - E_S$$

H_c is the volatility adjustment applied to the collateral (as defined according to the financial collateral comprehensive method for financial collateral and according to the foundation collateral method for nonfinancial collateral), and

H_E is the volatility adjustment applicable to the exposure.

Of course, the regulations for AIRB models have numerous details that can't be covered here. What matters in our case is how to explicitly incorporate climate factors into such models to account for climate change and other environmental factors.

Banks face the risk of mark-to-market losses if the creditworthiness of the counterparties deteriorates. The estimation of Credit Valuation Adjustment (CVA) aims to aggregate a bank's exposure to counterparty and other market risk factors. CVA calculations depend on a counterparty's default risk, known as counterparty credit risk (CCR); CVA can be interpreted as the price of CCR (Corna & Zorzi, 2020). The estimation of the CVA is carried through an adjustment to the fair value (or price) of derivative instruments to account for counterparty credit risk.

Banks have two general approaches for calculating capital requirements from CVA: the standardized approach (SA-CVA) and the basic approach (BA-CVA), or a customized approach. Banks above the materiality threshold (i.e., those deemed "too big to fail") must use the BA-CVA unless they receive approval from their relevant supervisory authority to use the SA-CVA. Other banks, such as those whose aggregate notional amount of non-centrally cleared derivatives is less than or equal to 100 billion euros, may skip the calculation of CVA. In this case, financial institutions must set their CVA capital requirement equal to 100% of the capital requirement for counterparty credit risk (CCR). In addition, CVA hedges are not recognized under this treatment, and they must be applied to the bank's entire portfolio. Also, a bank's relevant supervisory authority can remove this option if it determines that the CVA risk resulting from its derivative positions materially contributes to overall risk. Finally, the regulatory CVA must be reported monthly, thus likely differing from the CVA used for accounting purposes (BIS, 2020a, 2020b, 2020c).

Central banks can restrict the use of CVA types. The Deutsche Bundesbank, the German central bank, is discontinuing the internal CVA model approach is being discontinued, which means that only the Standardized Approach for CVA will be available (Deutsche Bundesbank, 2022).

There are two steps: estimating risks and calculating capital requirements based on the assessed risks. In the two approaches described in the Basel III framework, the goal of the CVA capital charge is to capitalize on possible future changes in CCR. The CVA of a single counterparty is determined by (Forjan, 2019):

$$\text{CVA}_n = \text{LGD}_n^* \times \sum_{j=i}^{T} \text{EE}_n^*(t_j) \times q_n^*(t_{j-1}, t_j)$$

where

LGD_n^* is the risk-neutral loss-given default for counterparty *n*. This term is usually set from market spreads.

$\text{EE}_n^*(t_j)$ is the discounted expected exposure during the j_{th} period computed under a risk-neutral measure for counterparty n. This term depends on the derivative contract's values with the counterparty.

$q_n^*(t_{j-1}, t_j)$ is the risk-neutral marginal default probability for counterparty n between periods t_{j-1} and t_j, with T being the final maturity. This term is derived from the counterparty's credit spread.

The BA-CVA formula that aggregates N counterparties in a portfolio is:

$$\text{CVA} = \sum_{n=1}^{N} \text{LGD}_n^* \times \sum_{j=i}^{T} \text{EE}_n^*(t_j) \times q_n^*(t_{j-1}, t_j)$$

However, this is the first approximation for a complete CVA estimation, as the formula does not incorporate correlated risks.

Banks can choose one of two options regarding BA-CVA: a reduced version or a full version. The main difference between the two versions is that the full version recognizes counterparty credit spread hedges and is intended for banks that hedge CVA risk. Since the reduced version is part of the full version, banks must calculate the reduced version even if they don't calculate capital requirements from it (BIS, 2020a, 2020b, 2020c).

Banks should incorporate methods for dealing with material counterparties whose credit spread is significantly and adversely correlated with the risk factors that drive the CVA. For that purpose, they must judge whether a more conservative application of their standard methodology would be appropriate (The European Bank Authority, 2022).

From the estimated risks, banks must then calculate capital requirements. The capital requirements for CVA risk under the reduced version of the BA-CVA, when hedges are not recognized, are (BIS, 2020a, 2020b, 2020c):

$$K_{\text{reduced}} = \sqrt{\left((\rho \sum_{c} \text{SCVA}_c) + (1 - \rho^2) \sum_{c} \text{SCVA}_c^2\right)}$$

where ρ is the supervisory correlation parameter, usually set to 50%, and SCVA_c is stand-alone CVA, the CVA capital requirement counterparty c would receive if considered on a stand-alone basis (as seen above).

We should note that ρ (and its square, $\rho^2 = 25\%$) represents the correlation between the credit spreads of any two counterparties. As credit spreads of counterparties are typically not perfectly correlated, ρ^2 is not close to 1 (BIS, 2020a, 2020b, 2020c).

SCVA_c is calculated as:

$$\text{SCVA}_c = \frac{1}{\alpha} \times \text{RW}_c \times \sum_{\text{NS}} M_{\text{NS}} \times \text{EAD}_{\text{NS}} \times \text{DF}_{\text{NS}}$$

where α is the multiplier used to convert Effective expected positive exposure (EEPE) to EAD and is set at 1.4; RW_{C} is the risk weight for counterparty c that reflects the volatility of its credit spread; M_{NS} is the effective maturity for the netting set NS; EAD_{NS} is the exposure at default (EAD) of the netting set NS; DF_{NS} is a supervisory discount factor (BIS, 2020a, 2020b, 2020c). Table 2.15 presents the supervisory risk weights, which depend on credit quality: investment grade (IG), high yield (HY), or not rated (NR).

As we can see, the risk weights are the same for industrial and consumer goods companies. We can see no differentiation regarding criteria other than essential recovery rate-related or systemic risk criteria.

Finally, the capital requirements for CVA risk in the reduced version of the BA-CVA are:

Capital requirements $= \text{DS}_{\text{BA-CVA}} \times K_{\text{reduced}}$, where the discount scalar $\text{DS}_{\text{BA-CVA}} = 0.65$ (as set by the Bank for International Settlements).

Table 2.15 Supervisory risk weights, RW_C

Sector of counterparty	*Credit quality of the counterparty*	
	IG (%)	*HY and NR (%)*
Sovereign risks, including central banks and multilateral development banks	0.5	2.0
Local government, government-backed nonfinancials, education, and public administration	1.0	4.0
Financial companies, including government-backed financials	5.0	12.0
Basic materials, energy, industrials, agriculture, manufacturing, mining, and quarrying	3.0	7.0
Consumer goods and services, transportation and storage, administrative and support services	3.0	8.5
Technology and telecommunications	2.0	5.5
Health care, utilities, professional and technical activities	1.5	5.0
Other sectors	5.0	12.0

Source BIS (2020a, 2020b, 2020c)

Moving to the full version of the BA-CVA, it recognizes the effect of counterparty credit spread hedges. Still, only single-name credit default swaps (CDS), single-name contingent CDS, and index CDS can be eligible hedges (BIS, 2020a, 2020b, 2020c). The capital requirements' calculation also assumes $DS_{\text{BA-CVA}} = 0.65$, and it adds a β term set as 0.25:

$$K_{\text{full}} = \beta \cdot K_{\text{reduced}} + (1 - \beta) \cdot K_{\text{hedged}}$$

In turn, the part of capital requirements that recognizes eligible hedges (K_{hedged}) is calculated as:

$$K_{\text{hedged}} = \sqrt{\left(\rho \cdot \sum_c (\text{SCVA}_c - \text{SNH}_c) - \text{IH}\right)^2}$$
$$\sqrt{+(1-\rho^2) \cdot \sum_c (\text{SCVA}_c - \text{SNH}_c)^2 + \sum_c \text{HMA}_c}$$

Which (BIS, 2020a, 2020b, 2020c):

$$\left(\rho \cdot \sum_c (\text{SCVA}_c - \text{SNH}_c) - \text{IH}\right)^2$$

aggregates the systematic components of CVA risk arising from the bank's counterparties, the single-name hedges, and the index hedges.

$$\left(1 - \rho^2\right) \cdot \sum_c (\text{SCVA}_c - \text{SNH}_c)^2$$

aggregates the idiosyncratic components of CVA risk arising from the bank's counterparties and the single-name hedges.

$$\sum_c \text{HMA}_c$$

aggregates the components of indirect hedges that are not aligned with counterparties' credit spreads.

For that estimation, SNH_c is defined as:

$$\text{SNH}_c = \sum_{h \in c} r_{hc} \cdot RW_h \cdot M_h^{SN} \cdot B_h^{SN} \cdot DF_h^{SN}$$

The risk weights for the full version of the BA-CVA are identical to those of the reduced version (Table 2.15).

The main differences between the BA-CVA and the standardized approach for credit valuation adjustment risk (SA-CVA) are (BIS, 2020a, 2020b, 2020c):

(1) the SA-CVA features a reduced granularity of market risk factors; and
(2) the SA-CVA does not include default risk and curvature risk.

We skip more details about the calculation of regulatory values. It should be noted that drifts of risk factors must be consistent with a risk-neutral probability measure; the volatilities and correlations of market risk factors must be calibrated to market data whenever sufficient data exist in a given market (otherwise, historical calibration is permissible); the distribution of risk factors must account for the possible non-normality of the distribution of exposures, including the existence of leptokurtosis ("fat tails"), where appropriate (BIS, 2020a, 2020b, 2020c).

The SA-CVA capital requirements are also calculated as the sum of the delta and vega risks calculated for the entire CVA portfolio (including eligible hedges) for the following six risk classes for delta and five, excluding counterparty credit spread risk, for vega (BIS, 2020a, 2020b, 2020c):

(1) interest rate risk;
(2) foreign exchange (FX) risk;
(3) counterparty credit spread risk;
(4) reference credit spread risk (i.e., credit spreads that drive the CVA exposure component);
(5) equity risk; and
(6) commodity risk.

Finally, the net weighted sensitivity of the CVA portfolio to risk factor k (which means that hedging can reduce risks) is:

$$\mathrm{WS}_k = \mathrm{WS}_K^{\mathrm{CVA}} - \mathrm{WS}_K^{\mathrm{Hdg}}$$

The weighted sensitivities must be aggregated into a capital requirement K_b within each bucket b given by (BIS, 2020a, 2020b, 2020c):

$$K_b = \sqrt{\left(\sum_{k\in b} \mathrm{WS}_k^2 + \sum_{k\in b}\sum_{t\in b, t\neq k} \rho_{kt}\mathrm{WS}_k\mathrm{WS}_t\right) + R\cdot\sum_{k\in b}\left(\left(\mathrm{WS}_k^{\mathrm{Hdg}}\right)^2\right)}$$

Much of the rest of the document, "Credit valuation adjustment framework (BIS, 2020a, 2020b, 2020c)," describes the operational details for these buckets for determining risk exposures. The instructions for banks to assign risk exposures to a sector are of particular interest (Table 2.16).

That can be contrasted with the buckets for commodity risk in Table 2.17.

As we can see in these tables, the risk weights are purely commercial risks, without concern for any other dimension. In fact, carbon trading has a much higher risk weight (60%) than coal (30%). The effect is that banks need to put aside less capital in loans to coal companies than those engaging in carbon trading.

Regulation concerning significant exposures is intuitive; it limits the maximum loss of a bank in the event of a sudden counterparty failure

Table 2.16 Buckets for equity risk

Bucket number	*Risk-Weight (%)*	*Size*	*Region*	*Sector*
1	55	Large	Emerging market economies	Consumer goods and services, transportation and storage, administrative and support service activities, healthcare, utilities
2	60			Telecommunications, industrials
3	45			Basic materials, energy, agriculture, manufacturing, mining, and quarrying
4	55			Financials including government-backed financials, real estate activities, technology
5	30		Advanced economies	Consumer goods and services, transportation and storage, administrative and support service activities, healthcare, utilities
6	35			Telecommunications, industrials
7	40			Basic materials, energy, agriculture, manufacturing, mining, and quarrying
8	50			Financials including government-backed financials, real estate activities, technology
9	70	Small	Emerging market economies	All sectors described under bucket numbers 1, 2, 3, and 4

(continued)

Table 2.16 (continued)

Bucket number	*Risk-Weight (%)*	*Size*	*Region*	*Sector*
10	50		Advanced economies	All sectors described under bucket numbers 5, 6, 7, and 8
11	70	(Not applicable)		Other sectors
12	15	Large-cap, advanced economies		Qualified Indices
13	30	Other		Qualified Indices

Source BIS (2020b)

(BIS, 2020a, 2020b, 2020c). Regulations about large exposures depart from the assumptions regarding VaR, CVA, and other methods. Usually, estimating tier 1 and other forms of capital implicitly assumes that a bank has a portfolio of loans that may or may not be correlated but is not concerned with individual positions.

In the case of considerable exposure risks, the goal is to determine the level of exposure to a single counterparty that would require special attention. More importantly, limits differ for regular banks and those deemed "too big to fail" worldwide (global systemically important banks; G-SIBs). The Bank for International Settlements also encourages central banks to differentiate between regular local banks and domestic systemically important banks, D-SIBs. Central banks should consider applying stricter limits to exposures between D-SIBs and smaller banks' exposures to G-SIBs. For most banks, the sum of all the exposure values of a bank to a single counterparty must not be higher than 25% of the bank's Tier 1 capital at all times, but for G-SIBs, that figure is set at 15%. Also, banks must report to the supervisor all exposures equal to or above 10% of the bank's Tier 1 capital (BIS, 2020a, 2020b, 2020c).

Table 2.18 indicates how banks must report data on counterparty risks.

2.9 Value-at-Risk (VaR)

Value-at-risk (VaR) models date back to the 1950s, and the idea behind them is straightforward: it is a statistic that quantifies how often financial losses are higher than a certain threshold during a period. It is common for analysts to misinterpret VaR models. Some define VaR as measuring

Table 2.17 Buckets for commodity risk

Bucket number	*Risk-Weight (%)*	*Commodity group*	*Examples*
1	30	Energy—Solid combustibles	coal, charcoal, wood pellets, nuclear fuel (such as uranium)
2	35	Energy—Liquid combustibles	crude oil (such as Light-sweet, heavy, West Texas Intermediate and Brent); biofuels (such as bioethanol and biodiesel); petrochemicals (such as propane, ethane, gasoline, methanol, and butane); refined fuels (such as jet fuel, kerosene, fuel oil, naphtha, heating oil, and diesel)
3	60	Energy—Electricity and carbon trading	electricity (such as spot, day-ahead, peak, and off-peak); carbon emissions trading (such as certified emissions reductions, in-delivery month EU allowance, Regional Greenhouse Gas Initiative CO2 allowance, and renewable energy certificates)
4	80	Freight	dry-bulk route (such as Capesize, Panamax, Handysize, and Supramax); liquid-bulk/gas shipping route (such as Suezmax, Aframax, and massive crude carriers)
5	40	Metals—non-precious	base metal (such as aluminum, copper, lead, nickel, tin, and zinc); steel raw materials (such as steel billet, steel wire, steel coil, steel scrap and steel rebar, iron ore, tungsten, vanadium, titanium, and tantalum); minor metals (such as cobalt, manganese, molybdenum)
6	45	Gaseous combustibles	natural gas; liquefied natural gas
7	20	Precious metals (including gold)	gold; silver; platinum; palladium

(continued)

Table 2.17 (continued)

Bucket number	*Risk-Weight (%)*	*Commodity group*	*Examples*
8	35	Grains & oilseed	corn; wheat; soybean (such as soybean seed, soybean oil, and soybean meal); oats; palm oil; canola; barley; rapeseed (such as rapeseed seed, rapeseed oil, and rapeseed meal); red bean, sorghum; coconut oil; olive oil; peanut oil; sunflower oil; rice
9	25	Livestock and dairy	cattle (such as live and feeder); hog; poultry; lamb; fish; shrimp; dairy (such as milk, whey, eggs, butter, and cheese)
10	35	Softs and other agricultural	cocoa; coffee (such as arabica and robusta); tea; citrus and orange juice; potatoes; sugar; cotton; wool; lumber and pulp; and rubber
11	50	Other commodities	industrial minerals (such as potash, fertilizer, and phosphate rocks), rare earths; terephthalic acid; glass

Source BIS (2020b)

the extent of potential losses, but that is incorrect. We can illustrate that difference by analyzing Fig. 2.19. This figure assumes that a portfolio's value at the end of a trading day is normally distributed, with a mean of U$500 million and a standard deviation of U$50 million.

If a portfolio is normally distributed, it means that at the end of a trading day, there is a 68.27% probability that its value will be between U$450 million and U$550 million, which refers to the mean plus or minus one-standard-deviation. In addition, there is a 95.45% probability that the portfolio's value will be between U$400 million and U$600 million (two standard deviations) and 99.73% that it will be in the interval of U$350–650 million (three standard deviations). The number of standard deviations for a 99% confidence interval is approximately 2.32. Thus, in 1% of trading days (or something like 2 or 3 days in a year if we consider 252 trading days), the portfolio's value will not be contained in the interval between U$384 million and U$616 million.

Table 2.18 Questions on CCR

Q-1	Please provide the number of transactions subject to counterparty credit risk capital requirements as reported in panel A of this worksheet
Q-2	Please provide the number of transactions subject to central clearing (house and client trades) as reported in panel A of this worksheet
Q-3	For IMM banks only: Please provide your current level of alpha as used to determine exposures and RWA in panel A of this worksheet
Q-4	For IRB banks only: Do you plan to apply the discretion of MAR50.12 (2023 version) to cap the maturity adjustment factor at 1 year in the IRB formula for netting sets subject to the revised CVA capital requirements? Yes, for all eligible netting sets Yes, for some eligible netting sets No, the bank does not yet intend to use this discretion **Note:** If your answer is "2: Yes, for some eligible netting sets," please provide further explanations regarding the reasons in either the "Remarks" column D or a supplementary document
Q-5	If yes to Q-4 (answer 1 or 2), to which extent is the use of the 1-year cap of the maturity adjustment factor already reflected in the numbers reported in lines 21 to 51 of panel A under the revised framework (columns P, R, and S)? Estimate the share of RWA from netting sets for which the maturity adjustment factor is capped at 1 year relative to the total CCR RWA, 0% (use of discretion intended, but not yet implemented) less than 10% between 10 and 20% between 20 and 30% between 30 and 40% between 40 and 50% share of RWA for netting sets where the maturity adjustment factor is capped at 1 year equals to or is larger than 50% **Note:** If your answer is " $\geq$ 50%," please report the share in the "Remarks," column D

Source European Bank Authority (2022). https://www.eba.europa.eu/sites/default/documents/files/document_library/Risk%20Analysis%20and%20Data/Quantitative%20impact%20study-Basel%20III%20monitoring/1026539/EU%20specific%20BM%20instructions%20v.4.4.pdf

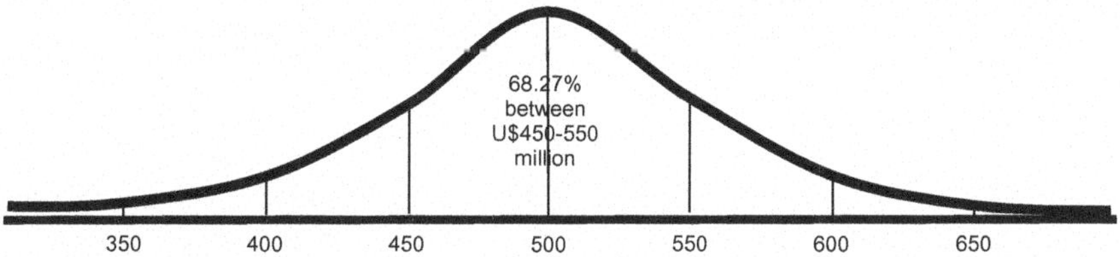

Fig. 2.19 Potential outcomes of a portfolio are normally distributed with a mean of U$500 million and a standard deviation of U$50 million (*Source* Created by the author)

For only one tail, as we are interested in potential losses, the number of standard deviations for a 99% confidence interval is approximately 2.58. Hence, for this example, we expect that in 99% of the trading days, the portfolio's value will be higher than U$371 million. Some may interpret the value-at-risk as U$129 million, the loss related to 2.58 standard deviations. Yet again, that is incorrect. The portfolio's value is expected to be below U$371 million on two or three trading days a year. It can be U$200 million. Or U$50 million. Or −U$500 million, as normal distributions are unbounded.

VaR models are a cornerstone of financial supervision, but banks cannot over-rely on them, as the financial crisis has shown us. VaR models work best when periods of turbulence are similar to past periods. In that sense, one could interpret expected losses as the portfolio's value-at-risk. However, if financial markets have "fat tails" (extreme events more likely than those captured by a normal distribution), VaR models underestimate the probability of meaningful losses. Before the great financial crisis, self-reported value-at-risk models were the cornerstone of financial supervision. Precisely because the crisis unearthed systemic risks that couldn't be captured by analyzing past data, financial regulation has evolved to introduce more robust stress tests. Still, VaR models remain helpful, as the standard deviation of potential losses, under normal conditions, is highly informative for banks and regulators. After all, even if VaR models are unbounded under normal conditions, it does not mean that all possible losses are equally probable.

VaR models are also advantageous because they have a long history as supervisory tools in almost real-time. Unlike most regulatory reports, banks must meet daily capital requirements. Many other capital buffers are reported monthly or quarterly, but requirements related to values-at-risk are calculated and reported daily.

Reporting on VaR is given by (BIS, 2020a, 2020b, 2020c):

$$c = \max\left(\mathrm{VaR}_{t-1}, m_c \times \mathrm{VaR}_{\mathrm{avg}}\right) + \max\left(s\mathrm{VaR}_{t-1}, m_s \times s\mathrm{VaR}_{\mathrm{avg}}\right)$$

where VaR_{t-1} is the previous day's value-at-risk number; $\mathrm{VAR}_{\mathrm{avg}}$ is the average of the daily value-at-risk measures on each of the preceding sixty business days, m_c is a multiplication factor; sVaR_{t-1} is the latest available stressed-value-at-risk number; $\mathrm{sVaR}_{\mathrm{avg}}$ is an average of the stressed value-at-risk numbers, and m_s is another multiplication factor.

The stressed value-at-risk (*s*VaR) measure results from regulatory changes responding to the global financial crisis. Regulators did not aim for *s*VaR to be a measure of tail risk, but its addition was supposed to reduce the procyclicality of the minimum capital requirements for market risk (BIS, 2011). Stressed value-at-risk calculations were introduced at the tail end of Basel II and are fully incorporated into Basel III, even if VaR modeling is not as relevant to determining capital requirements as before the crisis.

Banks still have the flexibility in determining the precise nature of their VaR models, but Basel III establishes several minimum standards; national supervisory authorities have the discretion to apply stricter standards (BIS, 2022a, 2022b, 2022c). Value-at-risk must be computed daily, based on a 99th percentile, one-tailed confidence interval. In addition, banks must estimate the effects of an instantaneous price shock equivalent to a 10-day price movement (the minimum "holding period"). Also, the minimum historical observation period (sample period) is one year. For banks that use a weighting scheme, the average time lag of individual observations cannot be less than six months (BIS, 2022a, 2022b, 2022c). Finally, banks must update their data sets more frequently if there is a significant upsurge in market volatility, aiming to minimize tail risk somewhat.

As banks have a long history of developing VaR models, they enjoy the flexibility to establish their procedures, such as variance–covariance matrices, historical simulations, or Monte Carlo simulations, as long as they capture the nonlinear price characteristics of options positions. They also can recognize empirical correlations within broad risk categories (e.g., interest rates, exchange rates, equity prices, and commodity prices, including related options volatilities in each risk factor category) (BIS, 2022a, 2022b, 2022c).

The stressed value-at-risk (*s*VaR) calculation is based on the 10-day, 99th percentile, one-tailed confidence interval value-at-risk measure of the current portfolio, with model inputs calibrated to historical data from a continuous 12-month period of significant financial stress relevant to the bank's portfolio (BIS, 2022a, 2022b, 2022c). The regulatory material from BIS even includes the note that: "As an example, for many portfolios, a 12-month period relating to significant losses in 2007/2008 would adequately reflect a period of such stress; although other periods relevant to the current portfolio must be considered by the bank." (BIS, 2022a, 2022b, 2022c). Unlike regular daily VaR outcomes, the stressed value-at-risk should be calculated at least weekly (BIS, 2022a, 2022b, 2022c).

If we divide financial system supervision into regular and crisis modes, VaR models feature prominently in the former but not the latter. VaR models, while still highly relevant for daily monitoring of banks' positions, have diminished in importance since the great financial crisis. Even stressed VaR models are more useful in regular periods. Once central banks realized that the statistical distributions of banks' results have fat tails and extreme risk events are less rare than expected, they introduced new micro and macroprudential measures.

VaR methods fall into four broad categories (Badrinarayanan & Akhter, 2023):

- Historical VaR: This is based on the historical performance of an investment and uses past data to estimate the potential loss on an investment over a given period.
- Parametric VaR: This type of VaR uses statistical models to estimate the potential loss on investment based on assumptions about the distribution of returns.
- Monte Carlo simulations: Here, simulations are used to estimate the potential loss on an investment by generating a large number of possible future scenarios and calculating the potential loss for each scenario.
- Variance–covariance VaR: a simplified method of calculating VaR that assumes that the returns on an investment are normally distributed, often used for portfolio risk management.

Table 2.19 describes how banks must report value-at-risk data to regulators.

2.10 Greening Value-at-Risk

As we have seen, commercial banks commonly use VaR models to estimate their portfolios' potential loss in value due to market movements. Incorporating ESG factors or other nonfinancial indicators can provide a more comprehensive assessment of the bank's risk exposure:

Table 2.19 Excerpt of reporting data of internal models approach

47	F, G	Internal models approach (VaR and SVaR-based measures), **actual capital requirement**	Capital requirement for general market risk based on internal models and inclusive of all products that receive IMA treatment. This measure must include modeled specific product risk requirements with model approval from the bank's national supervisor. The value reported should reflect the firm's VaR and SVaR-based measures calculated per requirements outlined in the Revisions to the market risk framework and should reflect the current effective multiplier
48	F, G	Current 10-day 99% value-at-risk (**without** applying the multiplier)	The reported value-at-risk estimate should represent the bank's estimate of the 10-day, 99% value-at-risk of the bank's trading book portfolio as of the reporting date, **excluding the regulatory multiplier**
50	F, G	10-day 99% stressed value-at-risk (**without** applying the multiplier)	The reported **stressed** value-at-risk estimate should represent the bank's estimate of the 10-day, 99% **stressed** value-at-risk of the bank's trading book portfolio as of the reporting date, **excluding the regulatory multiplier**

1. Identifying the relevant ESG factors: banks must first identify the most material ESG factors in their portfolio.
2. Determine the risk impact of ESG factors: After identifying the relevant ESG factors, banks must determine how these factors will impact their portfolio risk. For example, climate change risks, such as physical risks (e.g., extreme weather events) and transition risks (e.g., policy changes), can significantly impact specific sectors, such as energy and agriculture, and affect a bank's exposure to credit and market risks.
3. Integrate ESG factors into VaR models: This step involves adjusting the inputs and assumptions used in the VaR models to reflect the impact of ESG factors on the portfolio risk.

4. Conduct scenario analysis: To test the portfolio's sensitivity to ESG risks, banks can conduct scenario analysis using the VaR models incorporating ESG factors. Scenario analysis involves simulating different scenarios that reflect different levels of exposure to ESG risks and estimating the potential losses to the portfolio.
5. Monitor and report: organizations must monitor and report their ESG risk exposure and performance. This process involves tracking progress toward its sustainability goals, disclosing ESG performance metrics to stakeholders, and regularly reviewing and updating the VaR models to ensure they remain relevant and practical.

Formally, one approach is to adjust the portfolio's expected returns to reflect the impact of ESG factors. This involves incorporating ESG ratings or other sustainability indicators for each security in the portfolio, which measures the security's ESG performance. The expected return is then adjusted based on the security's ESG rating or score, where higher ESG ratings or scores indicate lower risk and vice versa. The formula for the adjusted expected return is:

$$\begin{aligned}\text{Adj.Expected Return} = {} & \text{Expected Return} \times (1 - \text{ESG Weight}) \\ & + \text{ESG Rating/Score} \times \text{ESG Weight}\end{aligned}$$

where:

ESG Weight = the weight of the ESG factor in the overall VaR model

ESG Rating/Score = the ESG rating or score of the security

Another approach is to adjust the portfolio's covariance matrix to reflect the impact of ESG factors. This involves incorporating ESG-related correlations between securities in the portfolio. For example, securities in the same sector may be more likely to be impacted by the same ESG risks, such as climate change or social issues. The formula for the adjusted covariance matrix is:

$$\begin{aligned}\text{Adj.Covariance Matrix} = {} & \text{Covariance Matrix} \times (1 - \text{ESG Weight}) \\ & + \text{ESG Covariance Matrix} \times \text{ESG Weight}\end{aligned}$$

where:

ESG Correlation Matrix = the matrix of ESG-related correlations between securities in the portfolio

Finally, we can use a stressed VaR model that simulates different scenarios reflecting different levels of exposure to ESG risks. The process involves incorporating ESG-related shocks or stresses into the VaR model, such as sudden changes in regulatory policies or extreme weather events. The formula for the stressed VaR is the standard:

$$\text{Stressed VaR} = \text{Portfolio Value} \times (\text{Expected Loss} + \text{Unexpected Loss} \times Z)$$

where:

Expected loss = the expected loss due to ESG-related shocks or stresses

Unexpected loss = the unexpected loss due to ESG-related shocks or stresses, which is calculated using the VaR formula

Z = the standard deviation of the shocks or stresses

Expected Loss:

The expected loss due to ESG-related shocks or stresses can be estimated using historical data and statistical methods. Commercial banks can analyze past ESG events, such as extreme weather events or regulatory changes, and assess the potential impact of similar events on their portfolio. The expected loss can be calculated using the standard expected loss formula:

$$\text{Expected loss} = \text{exposure} \times \text{Probability of Default} \times \text{Loss Given Default}$$

where:

Exposure = the bank's exposure to the security or asset affected by the ESG event

Probability of Default = the probability that the security or asset will default due to the ESG event

Loss Given Default = the expected loss if the security or asset defaults due to the ESG event

Unexpected Loss:

The VaR formula calculates the potential loss of the portfolio at a given confidence level based on the portfolio's historical performance. However, the VaR model must be adjusted to reflect the impact of ESG factors. The formula for the VaR with ESG factors is:

$$\text{VaR} = \text{Portfolio Value} \times Z \times (\text{Standard Deviation} + \text{ESG Factor})$$

where:

Portfolio Value = the market value of the portfolio

Z = the number of standard deviations from the mean, which corresponds to the confidence level

Standard deviation = the standard deviation of the portfolio's returns, adjusted to reflect the impact of ESG factors

ESG Factor = the adjustment factor that reflects the impact of ESG factors on the portfolio's risk

All these formulas help, but greening value-at-risk seems, at first, an impossible task. After all, the goal of the value-at-risk procedure is to estimate, for instance, the 10-day, 99% value-at-risk of the bank's trading book portfolio as of the reporting date. Is it possible to reconcile the long-run risks of climate change to the short intervals embedded into estimates of the value-at-risk of current portfolios?

Dietz et al. (2016) tackle this issue in their article for Nature Climate Change. Their estimates of VaR from climate change can be seen as a measure of the potential for asset price corrections due to climate change. However, they present estimates for the long-run impact of climate change on the value of global financial assets. Table 2.20 presents different estimations of changes in the present value of assets due to expected warming of 2.5% and below 2% until 2100.

They use an extended version of Nobel Prize winner Nordhaus's DICE model to estimate the impact of climate change on GDP growth. They fall into the category of parametric VaR (Badrinarayanan & Akhter, 2023). Figure 2.20 illustrates the discounted cash flows lost to climate change for an initial stock of assets of US$143 trillion in the two scenarios. Dashes are mean/expected values; the column corresponds with the 5–95% range.

In 2013 prices, the authors find that the expected climate VaR under BAU is US$2.5 trillion, rising to US$24.2 trillion at the 99th percentile.

Table 2.20 The present value-at-risk of global financial assets from climate change between 2015 and 2100—the climate VaR

Emissions scenario	*1st pctl*	*5th*	*Mean*	*95th*	*99th*
BAU (expected warming of 2.5 °C in 2100) (%)	0.46	0.54	1.77	4.76	16.86
Mitigation to limit warming to 2 °C with a 2/3 probability (%)	0.35	0.41	1.18	2.92	9.17

Source Dietz et al. (2016)

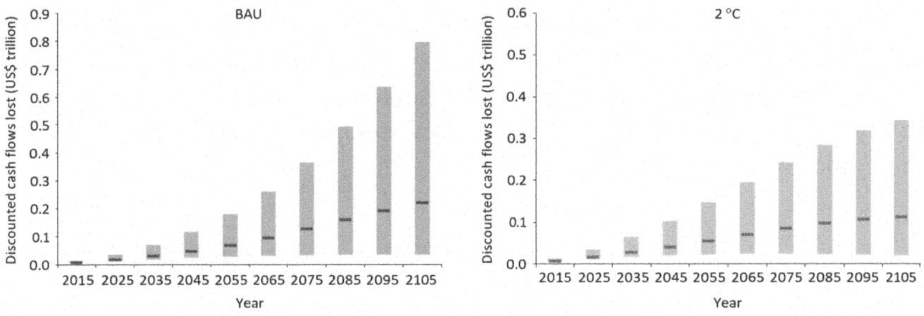

Fig. 2.20 Discounted cash flows lost to climate change in the BAU and 2% mitigation scenarios (*Source* Dietz et al. [2016])

And under the 2 °C mitigation scenario, it is US$1.7 trillion, rising to US$13.2 trillion at the 99th percentile.

Climate Value-at-Risk models do not work adequately as supervisory tools presently. Historically, central banks used VaR models to modulate banks' capital requirements. The development of parametric VaR and Monte Carlo simulations has refined the connection between VaR models and capital requirements, even though these types of models ceased to be the primary determinant of capital buffers.

The accuracy and credibility of VaR models depend on the quality of data, particularly high-frequency, granular, materially relevant data. While it is possible to relate historical climate observations for a range of physical risks to assets and collaterals, they are better suited for estimating long-term impact, as in Dietz et al. (2016). As such, climate value-at-risk can be part of a suite of stress tests but is not amenable as a regulatory tool as traditional VaR models are to financial supervision.

MSCI ESG Research (MSCI, 2020, 2023) describes its version of a climate VaR that aims to offer insights into how climate change can affect company valuations. Regarding its importance for banks, MSCI writes that calculations should help institutions identify optimal low-carbon investment projects within a loan book or credit portfolio, allowing them to establish a process to protect credit portfolios and establish a disclosure framework. These areas fall into ESG Investing (Chapter 5).

There does not seem to be a procedure that would be amenable to incorporating ESG indicators into regulatory-mandated VaR models. Climate Value-at-Risk models, such as those by Dietz et al. (2016) or MSCI, have a longer horizon. These models require the estimation of potential losses higher than a certain threshold in short periods. Of course, long-term measures of the impact of climate change on financial assets may be crucial for portfolio building and policymaking. Still, we should prefer distinct methodologies, such as climate stress testing, for regulatory reporting.

2.10.1 Case Study: Lessons from SVB to Sustainable Banking

Federal regulators shut down the Silicon Valley Bank (SVB) on March 10, 2023, the largest bank failure in the United States since the great financial crisis of 2008. At the time, the bank held over U$200 billion in assets and was the country's 16th largest bank. Bank failures cannot usually be explained by one single factor, and SVB is no exception.

SVB's downfall resulted from a bank run that the institution couldn't stave off. As clients started to redeem their deposits, Silicon Valley Bank sold a $21 billion bond portfolio of US Treasuries. The portfolio yielded an average of 1.79%, far below the then 10-year Treasury yield of around 3.9%. This forced SVB to recognize a $1.8 billion loss, which it needed to fill through a capital raise (Reuters, 2023). That made clients lose confidence in the bank's ability to meet future withdrawals, accelerating clients' exit. Figure 2.21 presents the timeline of events.

The timeline describes the market events that resulted in the deposit flight and the supervisory and regulatory developments. SVB's failure was a combination of lax regulation, inadequate risk management practices, and the speed at which information can travel on social media, a cautionary tale for financial institutions. Notably, the Board of Governors of the Federal Reserve System released a post-mortem review of the Federal Reserve's supervision and regulation of Silicon Valley Bank six weeks after the main events took place (Board of Governors, 2023).

To illustrate the slow response of regulators, Fig. 2.22 describes the evolution of the estimated unrealized losses of SVB's investment portfolio. By the end of the first quarter of 2022, unrealized losses topped U$5 billion, reaching almost U$20 billion six months later.

By the end of 2022, SVB held a peculiar balance sheet compared to its peers, as shown in Table 2.21.

In their review, the Board of Governors argues that four main factors contributed to SVB's collapse:

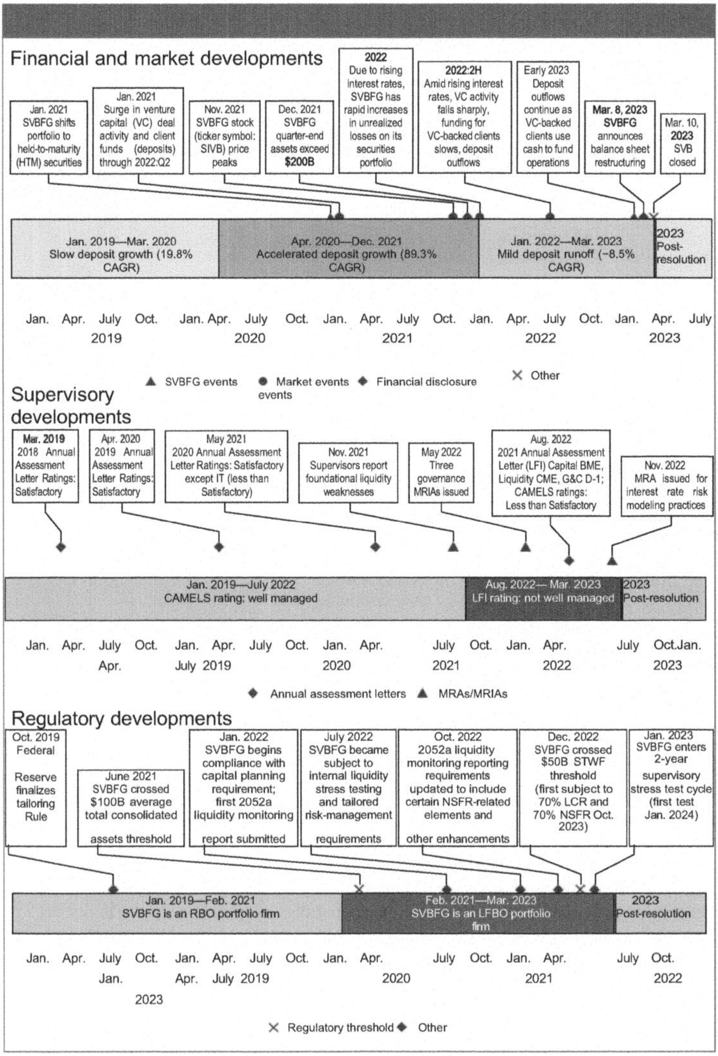

Fig. 2.21 Timeline of key developments (*Note* CAGR = compound annual growth rate. Mild deposit runoff (−8.5% CAGR) period calculated as January 2022 through December 2022. *Source* Board of Governors [2023])

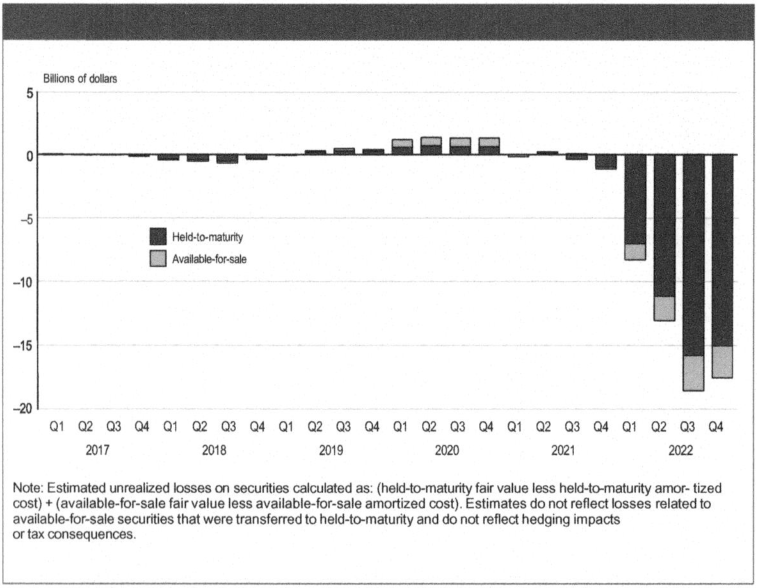

Fig. 2.22 Estimated unrealized gains (losses) on SVBFG's investment portfolio securities (*Source* Board of Governors [2023])

Table 2.21 Comparison between SBV and other regional banks

Peer comparison, 2022:Q4 Percent		
Metric	*SVBFG*	*LBOs*
Loans as a percentage of total assets	35	58
Securities as a percentage of total assets	55	25
Held-to-maturity securities as a percentage of total securities	78	42
Total deposits as a percentage of total liabilities	89	82
Uninsured deposits as a percentage of total deposits	94	41
Common equity tier 1 capital as % of total risk-weighted assets	12	10

Note Values for large banking organizations (LBOs) represent weighted averages of all US bank-holding companies and savings and loan-holding companies with total assets greater than $100 billion, except for banking organizations in the Large Institution Supervision Coordinating Committee (LISCC) supervisory portfolio
Source Board of Governors (2023)

1. Silicon Valley Bank's board of directors and management failed to manage their risks.
2. Supervisors did not fully appreciate the extent of the vulnerabilities as Silicon Valley Bank grew in size and complexity.
3. When supervisors did identify vulnerabilities, they did not take sufficient steps to ensure that Silicon Valley Bank fixed those problems quickly enough.
4. The Board's tailoring approach in response to the Economic Growth, Regulatory Relief, and Consumer Protection Act (EGRRCPA) and a shift in the stance of supervisory policy impeded adequate supervision by reducing standards, increasing complexity, and promoting a less assertive supervisory approach.

There are two structural and two managerial issues among these four options. SVB was lax in its risk management (especially the hedging of interest rate risks), while supervisors did not ask for immediate action on the vulnerabilities they identified at SVB.

More important for this book's scope is identifying vulnerabilities and the changes in the regulatory framework that happened in 2017–2018.

From the regulator's point of view, the supervisory framework must be updated anytime such a crisis happens to limit the possibility that the same mistakes will happen again. Of course, financial regulation is sometimes like shutting the barn door after the horse has bolted: too little, too late. Still, the SVB's case illustrates the dangers of deregulation or lack of proper regulation, which can affect climate finance supervision.

Getting regulation right is almost impossible. Either regulation will constrain banks' behavior significantly or be too lax, allowing for a higher probability of a financial crisis. As one of the lessons of the SVB debacle, the Fed has indicated it wants to raise the baseline for resilience to a broader set of firms, revisiting the tailoring framework for banks with $100 billion or more in assets (Board of Governors, 2023). In the same report, we have the details of the Federal Reserve supervisory activities from 2017 to 2023 and the issues related to SVB from 2019 to 2023.

Figure 2.23 shows the number of open Matters Requiring Attention (MRA) and Immediate Attention (MRIA) each year from 2019 to 2023 regarding SVB. Figure 2.24 shows the timeline for each MRA and MRIA and each corresponding category. Most were closed quickly. Central banks use MRAs as one of the building blocks of financial supervision; MRAs are supposed to formalize the supervisory process, granting institutions clear directions on what is needed to change.

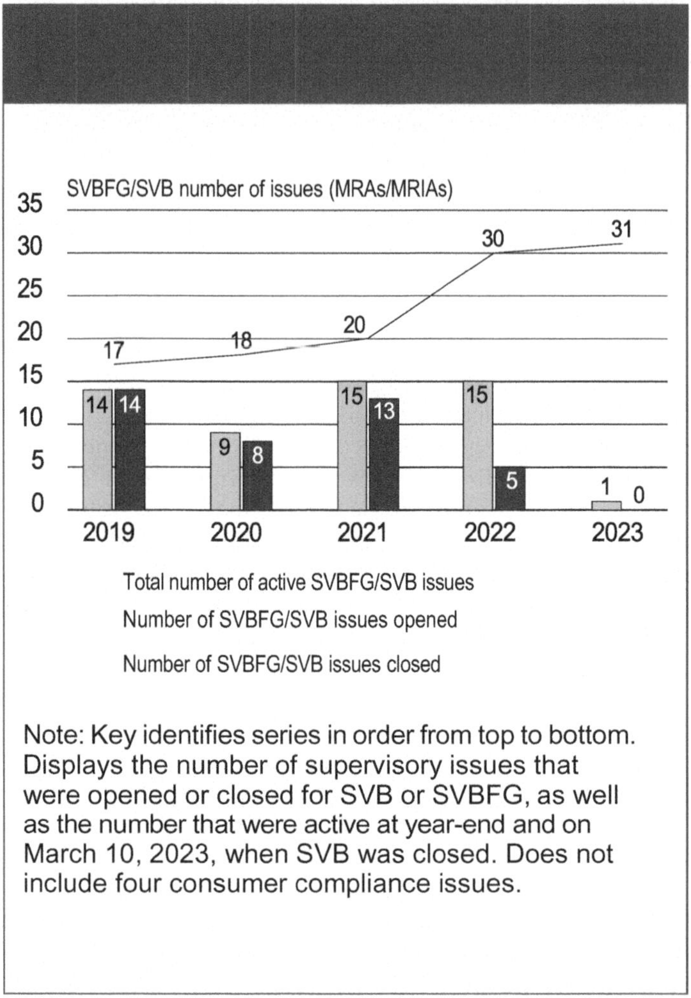

Fig. 2.23 SVBFG/SVB number of supervisory issues (MRAs/MRIAs) (*Source* Board of Governors [2023])

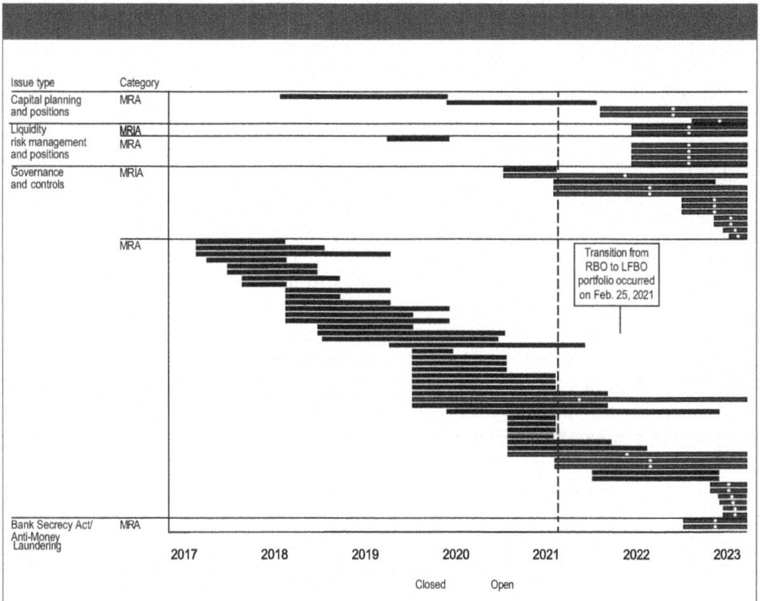

Note: Includes MRAs and MRIAs opened from 2017 to 2023 on SVB and SVBFG. Does not include issues opened prior to 2017 or consumer compliance issues. Issue status reflects the status of each supervisory issue when the firm was closed on March 10, 2023.

Fig. 2.24 Timeline of SVBFG/SVB supervisory issues (MRAs/MRIAs) (*Source* Board of Governors [2023])

Table 2.22 details the issues and their respective categories that remained open when SVB collapsed. Most are related to governance issues, but some central ones concern risk management.

The institution received many more MRAs and MRIAs than the average bank, as the Fed usually has around 2000 issues open to the thousands of banks in the United States. The Fed categorizes institutions into four types (Federal Reserve, 2019):

- The Broadly Meets Expectations rating indicates that the firm is safe and sound.
- The Conditionally Meets Expectations rating indicates that specific material, financial, or operational weaknesses in a firm's practices or

Table 2.22 Open supervisory issues (MRAs/MRIAs) at SVBFG/SVB by category and date opened

Date opened	*Category*	*Issue*
Capital planning and positions		
8/17/2021	MRA	Governance process for lending procedures
8/17/2021	MRA	Loan risk rating granularity
8/19/2022	MRA	Allowance for credit loss (ACL) stress methodology
Liquidity risk management and positions		
11/2/2021	MRIA	Enhanced liquidity risk management project plan
11/2/2021	MRIA	Weak risk management and audit oversight of liquidity
11/2/2021	MRA	Contingency funding plan
11/2/2021	MRA	Deposit segmentation
11/2/2021	MRA	Internal liquidity stress testing design
11/2/2021	MRA	Liquidity limits framework
Governance and controls		
6/5/2019	MRA	Systems/technology second line of defense
6/3/2020	MRIA	Vulnerability remediation
6/3/2020	MRA	Identity access management
2/11/2021	MRIA	IT asset management
2/11/2021	MRIA	Vendor management
2/11/2021	MRA	Data governance
2/11/2021	MRA	Data protection
5/31/2022	MRIA	Board effectiveness
5/31/2022	MRIA	Internal audit effectiveness
5/31/2022	MRIA	Risk management program
10/7/2022	MRIA	Identity and access management governance and oversight
10/7/2022	MRIA	Privileged access management (PAM)
10/7/2022	MRA	Identity access management life-cycle
10/7/2022	MRA	Identity access management logging, monitoring, and detection
11/15/2022	MRA	Interest rate risk (IRR) simulation and modeling
11/21/2022	MRA	Trust and fiduciary services (T&FS) oversight and risk management
12/21/2022	MRIA	Gramm–Leach–Bliley Act 501(b) information security program
12/21/2022	MRA	Cybersecurity risk assessment

(continued)

Table 2.22 (continued)

Date opened	*Category*	*Issue*
12/21/2022	MRA	Systems development/deployment methodology and practices
1/31/2023	MRIA	Third-party risk management governance and risk identification
Bank Secrecy Act/Anti-Money Laundering		
6/24/2022	MRA	Oversight of compliance monitoring and testing
6/24/2022	MRA	Sanctions country of interest risk management

Note Supervisory issues include MRAs and MRIAs (highlighted). The list comprises supervisory issues open as of March 10, 2023, for both SVB and SVBFG. "Date opened" indicates the date the issue was communicated to the firm. Does not include four open consumer compliance issues at the time of the report

Source Internal Federal Reserve supervisory databases

capabilities may place the firm's prospects for remaining safe and sound through a range of conditions at risk if not resolved promptly during the ordinary course of business.

- The Deficient-1 rating indicates that financial or operational deficiencies in a firm's practices or capabilities put the firm's prospects for remaining safe and sound through a range of conditions at significant risk.
- The Deficient-2 rating indicates that financial or operational deficiencies in a firm's practices or capabilities threaten the firm's safety and soundness or have already put the firm in an unsafe and unsound condition.

Notably, throughout the 2010s, many banks were deficient in risk management procedures (Federal Reserve, 2019). Even though the American banking system is much more fragmented than most countries, the lessons from the SVB case can be applied to other financial systems.

In many ways, the Fed is one of the least potent central banks in the world. In America's legalist system, laws and regulations constrain the institution's possible supervisory and regulatory activities. The cases of SVB and, in April 2023, of First Bank show how quickly regulators can act when incentivized to do so. In the case of climate change, central banks could speed up decarbonization if they were to act, even if most have refrained from explicitly incorporating climate change goals in their regulatory framework. What are the lessons we can learn from SVB's case?

Lesson 1: Central banks hold inordinate sway in banks' behavior.
Lesson 2: There will always be tension between regulators and regulated.
Lesson 3: Banks will answer supervisors' calls but will not necessarily be proactive.

Lesson 1 is underappreciated because both banks and supervisors have little reason to overplay that hand. Banks, especially publicly listed institutions, have a duty to shareholders. Still, their profit-seeking behavior is severely constrained by rules such as those emanating from the Basel Accord. Central banks don't stress their supervisory duties because financial systems rely on credibility. Reports pointing out the financial system's fragilities could undermine confidence in the solvency of institutions. Thus, supervisory authorities have to tread a fine line, documenting and proposing changes to institutions' behavior while doing so quietly.

After the great financial crisis, when central banks tightened regulations, commercial banks had little choice but to comply. The additional regulations restricted some profitable operations and required expensive compliance investments. However, failing to comply was not an option, as financial regulators can cut off commercial banks' licenses to operate in extreme cases or give them access to central bank money and services they depend on in mild instances of noncompliance.

The swinging pendulum of financial deregulation during good times and strict rules after crises comes from the inherent tension between regulators and regulated. There is an intrinsic tension between regulators and the institutions they regulate. Regulators aim to ensure the safety and soundness of the financial system, protect consumers, and maintain financial stability. Regulated institutions, on the other hand, seek to maximize profits and shareholder returns. These competing priorities set the stage for conflicts of interest and pushback against regulations. The tension plays out in recurring cycles of regulatory action and industry reaction. Regulators tighten rules in response to risk-taking excesses, market developments, or new risks; institutions then push back, seeking relief on the grounds of overreach or unintended consequences. However, severe regulatory lapses can also prompt reactive crackdowns.

Compliance with new rules requires investments in people, processes, and technology that cut into profits. Regulators frequently impose restrictions that raise costs or limit revenue opportunities for regulated firms. Regulations also often prohibit certain business practices or product features that generate substantial profits. It is in the self-interest of regulated firms to lobby regulators for less stringent rules and more flexibility.

At the same time, regulators depend on the compliance and cooperation of regulated institutions to achieve their policy objectives. They work to balance controlling risk-taking with allowing profitable banking activities that support economic growth. However, regulators have limited resources to monitor institutions and enforce rules. They rely on regulated firms to willingly embrace the intent and spirit of regulations.

An example of this ebb and flow in regulatory pressure, pertaining to SVB and similar cases, comes from Gandel and Smith (2023). They report that in 2019, "three of the largest US regional banks successfully lobbied regulators to ease their capital requirements by excluding paper losses on their investment portfolios. Doing so, they claimed, would allow them to increase lending—thus supporting the American economy—and better manage interest rate risk." Of course, it seems patently clear that relaxing these rules contributed to the market turmoil in early 2023. Still, the regional banks in the United States remained steadfast in their opposition to any rollback that would tighten capital requirements.

We should expect climate-green central banking to play out alongside similar lines, with regulatory authorities pressured by financial institutions that would likely claim they could be greener with fewer (and not more) rules. Financial models posit two hypotheses regarding the tradeoff between credit supply and regulatory strength, such as stress tests (Acharya et al., 2018): the Risk Management Hypothesis, under which stress-tested banks reduce credit supply—particularly to relatively risky borrowers—to decrease their credit risk; and the Moral Hazard Hypothesis, in which these banks expand credit supply—particularly to relatively risky borrowers that pay high spreads—increasing their risk.

2.11 Principles for Responsible Investment

The United Nations Environment Programme Finance Initiative (UNEP FI) was founded in 1992, aiming to engage the finance sector on sustainability. This organization later formalized the Principles for Responsible Investment (UNEP, 2023a). Formally, over 450 banks and insurers with assets exceeding US$100 trillion work to facilitate the implementation of UNEP FI's Principles for Responsible Banking and Principles for Sustainable Insurance, as well as three UN-convened net zero alliances (UNEP,

2023a, 2023b). Maybe we are overthinking the idea of greening banks, as the UNEP Finance Initiative seems well poised to climate-proof the financial system without much outside help. After all, (lack of) coordination is one of the major obstacles for companies to overcome organizational inertia. Later, we formalize a model in which the lack of coordination in a supply chain leads to low-value market equilibria. Simultaneously, many analysts are skeptical about sustainable finance as currently organized.

There are six principles for responsible banking, as shown in Fig. 2.25. These principles, by themselves, make it very easy for banks to sign on. They don't provide hard targets or operational details that genuinely constrain banks' activities. They are abstract to the point of maybe being useless. Of course, these principles may be a solid first step in a long process of incorporating sustainability into a bank's operations. Still, by themselves, they don't mean much. However, signatories should implement these principles, and the guidelines by the UNEP FI are much better in steering institutions toward best practices.

UNEP Fi recommends three implementation steps: impact analysis, target-setting and implementation, and public reporting. Regarding the first, UNEP FI defines impact analysis as identifying the most relevant and

Fig. 2.25 Principles for Responsible Banking (*Source* UN Environment Programme [2023a]. https://www.unepfi.org/banking/more-about-the-principles/)

significant positive and negative impacts of a bank's operations on its societies, economies, and environments. UNEP FI also provides examples of what impact analysis in this context is not: a review of internal operational impacts, financial materiality assessment, stakeholder analysis, or whether it is supposed to be final or permanent (UNEP, 2022a). Impact analysis includes reviewing the bank's portfolio composition and considering the proportional composition of portfolios globally and per geographical scope (% sectors and % type of customers). It also requires that the institution understand context, i.e., the most relevant challenges and priorities related to sustainable development in the countries/regions where the bank operates. The organization should analyze its products and services' most significant positive and negative impacts (not internal operational impacts). Finally, the bank should prioritize the two most considerable impact areas by engaging with internal and external stakeholders.

As for target-setting and implementation, signatories must implement a governance framework to oversee and ensure progress. Progress is defined as following milestones and actions to meet targets. Ideally, signatories must determine targets for the two challenges identified in the impact analysis step. Finally, the targets must be ambitious enough to align the bank's business and portfolio objectively with the Sustainable Development Goals and the Paris Climate Agreement. Finally, signatories must regularly report in English how they are implementing the Principles for Responsible Banking, the targets they have set, and the progress made using the reporting and self-assessment template (UNEP, 2023b).

UNEP FI also publishes interesting methodologies, such as the impact radar, that allow lagging organizations to start planning sustainability actions. The impact radar is detailed in Fig. 2.26.

In some ways, the impact radar could foster meaningful changes if taken seriously, but it can also be used merely for greenwashing. Some categories, such as modern slavery and child labor, seem like checklist items already on the radar from most, if not all, regulators. Also, as many initiatives are based on ESG and SDGs, nonfinancial performance is measured as the prospective risks to banks' operations and the global society.

Should banks go through all the trouble of signing UNEP Fi's Principles for Responsible Banking if they require significant bureaucracy for seemingly little benefit? The answer is likely yes, not because these principles are the be-all and end-all but because they provide a roadmap for the first stage in the evolution process of genuine green banking. Such

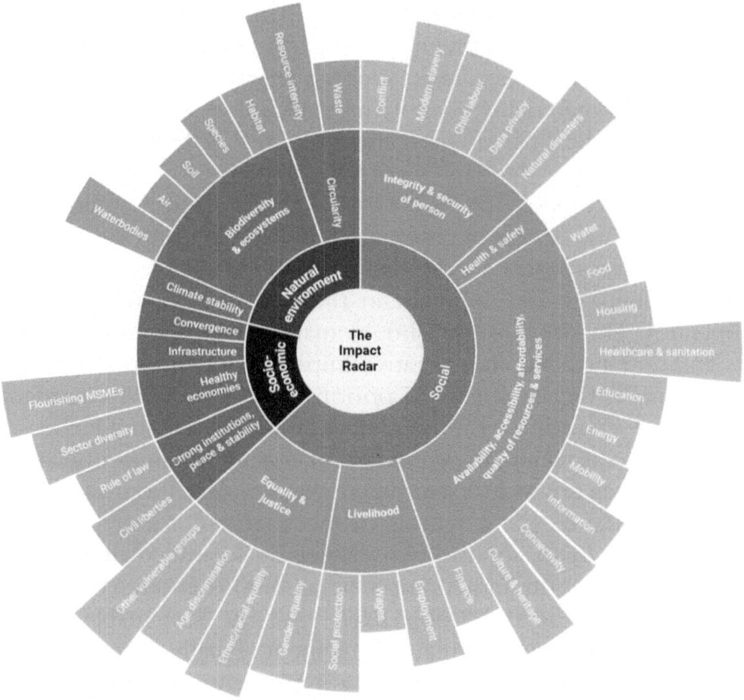

Fig. 2.26 Impact radar at a glance (*Source* UN Environment Programme [2023a]. https://www.unepfi.org/banking/more-about-the-principles/)

commitments are more relevant for large institutions, which are more visible but have more resources to deal with the bureaucracy surrounding the PRI.

For instance, UNEP FI publishes useful tools for impact assessments that are particularly useful for banks without robust methods. Among these tools, signatories have access to the following (UNEP, 2022b):

- The Portfolio Impact Analysis Tool: it enables banks to perform a holistic impact analysis of their portfolios, helping organizations set targets to drive their contribution to society's goals, as required by the Principles for Responsible Banking.

- The Investment Portfolio Impact Analysis Tool: first, banks input data about their portfolios' nature, content, and context. The data is combined with in-built impact mappings to help users identify the most significant impact areas.
- The Corporate Impact Analysis Tool: it helps banks summarize information about the impact status and possibilities of their clients and investee companies. It uses information on the reality of those companies' business activities and the needs of the countries where they operate, whether for sourcing, production, or sales.
- The Real Estate Impact Analysis Tool: it brings decision-making and due diligence in asset acquisition, fund/portfolio review and management, impact target-setting, and impact and SDG reporting regarding the real estate industry.

What are the main drawbacks of the PRIs? It has nothing to do with the principles per se but how organizations approach their implementation. Suppose a bank signs the principles but silos them to the sustainability department without integration with the rest of the institution's operations. In that case, nothing will come out of it. Still, the principles don't offer groundbreaking methods for integrating nonfinancial indicators into regular lending or investing operations. Mature institutions should have no significant issues meeting all the criteria for achieving adequate performance. Nevertheless, genuinely greening its operations requires that banks go beyond PRIs. For that, we move on to green central banking and its implications for financial institutions.

2.12 Governance Structure

A solid corporate governance structure is such that the incentives of companies' managers and owners are well-aligned. The basic tenets of agency theory, which motivates much of contemporary stock market regulations, is that companies should behave as agents of shareholders. When managers and owners are the same, we shouldn't expect any conflict of interest.

Banks' well-designed governance structure is paramount to their survival. Most financial scandals can be traced to failures in the checks and balances that should be correctly embedded in risk management systems. For instance, in 1995, Barings Bank collapsed due to over U$1 billion in losses incurred by a single trader in derivatives. The primary governance flaw was allowing Nick Leeson to simultaneously hold the derivatives trading desk and the clearing, settling, and accounting operations. We also saw how the SVB collapse can be traced to an inadequate structure.

Nonfinancial companies have much more leeway in designing their governance structure than commercial banks. Privately owned companies are not as regulated as listed companies. However, in the case of banks, the difference between those with concentrated and dispersed ownership is not acute. Regulators treat banks similarly, with size and ability to bring down the entire financial system, a more relevant feature for a central bank than the nature of ownership. In that case, Baring Bank's downfall did not trigger a systemic financial crisis. Still, it is due to this possibility that regulators aim to enforce strict governance rules for financial institutions.

Financial institutions' governance is constantly evolving. Gone are the days of short-term bonuses linked to immediate profits. Today, clawback clauses are standard; even artificial intelligence systems help compliance officers instantly identify noncompliance events.

Of course, no governance structure can eliminate all risks, especially from ill-intended executives. Still, sound governance can limit potential damages and speed up the flow of information so that internal checks and balances can react accordingly. Take the example of a company that lost over U$1.5 billion on bad derivatives contracts, Sadia. For our purposes, the details of Sadia's case don't matter. Still, these details and those of 40 companies that lost billions in these types of contracts during the great financial crisis can be found in Zeidan and Mullner (2015).

The company's pre-crisis governance structure had the CFO controlling the entire flow of financial information, including instances of noncompliance. Other financial executives didn't have opportunities to discuss the firm's operations and potential problems with other high-level executives (other than whistleblowing). For all they knew, the CFO informed the Board and the Finance Committee of the noncompliance issues and the mounting losses with the derivatives contracts.

The board retooled its governance structure after the firm reported its catastrophic losses (Fig. 2.27). The risk management department stopped reporting to the CFO; its oversight became the responsibility of the CEO and the Audit Committee. More importantly, the CFO did not centralize the flow of financial information. Conversely, the new structure saddled the CEO with more responsibilities.

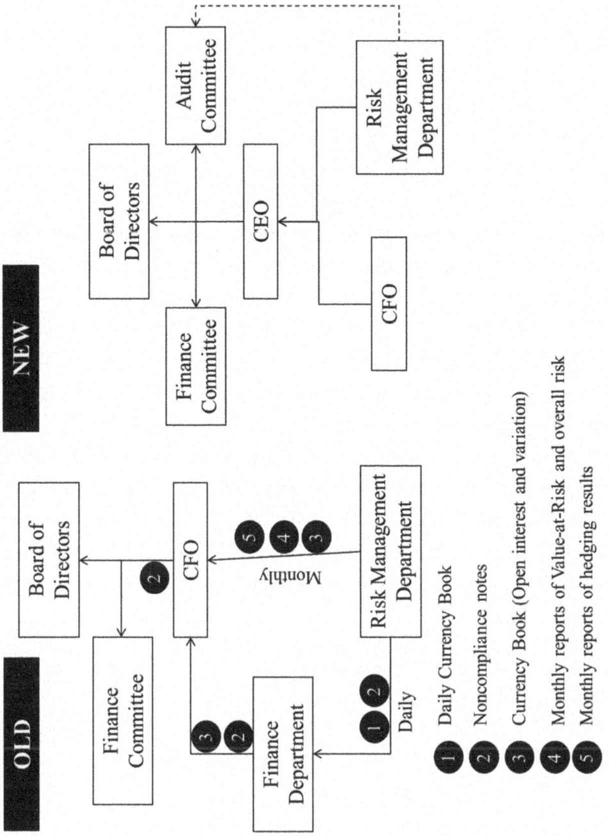

Fig. 2.27 Old and new corporate governance structure of Sadia, 2008

Below are two examples of the governance structure of multinational banks: Bank of America's overall structure and the specific risk management structure of Itau.

Bank of America's governance (Fig. 2.28) is notable for the direct link between the disclosure committee, which reports to the CEO and CFO, and the audit committee. That serves as a check against potential risk management issues. Interestingly, there is no link between the ESG management and board committees and the rest of BoA's governance structure; in contrast, the Management Risk committee is connected to the Audit and Enterprise Risk committees.

Banks detail the specific risk management structure more than the average corporation. Itau (Fig. 2.29) explicitly states that risk management is akin to a line of defense. The bank divides its lines of defense into three levels. The first is the responsibility of each department (auto loans, mortgages, retail banking, etc.), the second is the risk management department, and the third is the audit and internal committees.

Interestingly, the risk management structure delineates that the banks' goals derive from risk appetite guidelines. In addition, Itau aims for a coordinated risk culture in which metrics and outcomes are detailed.

As in the case of BoA, Itau does not integrate sustainability risks into its specific risk management structure. In its 2021 annual report, ESG warrants a separate section, but these indicators are, by and large, not referenced in the other parts of the document.

More importantly, while sustainability committees constitute a significant step forward, the praxis of environmental practices in the companies

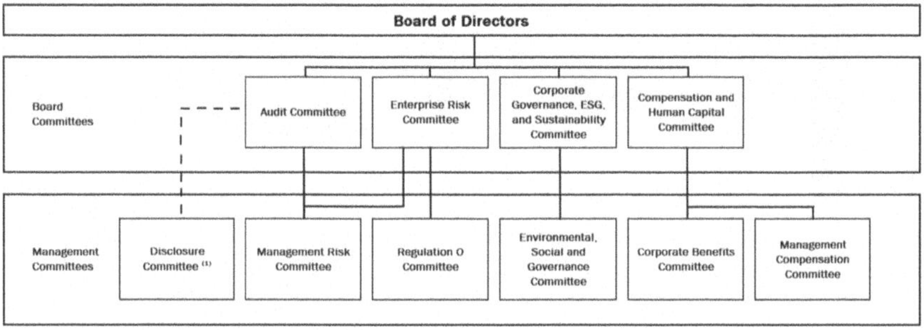

Fig. 2.28 Bank of America's governance structure (*Source* Bank of America, 2022. https://investor.bankofamerica.com/annual-reports-and-proxy-statements

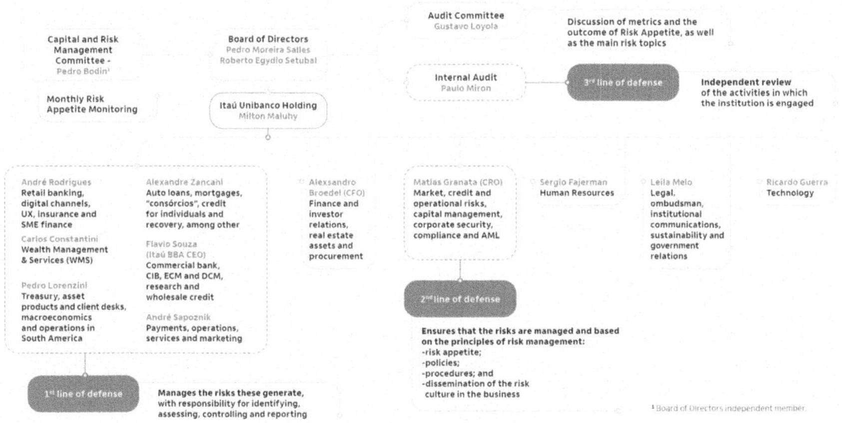

Fig. 2.29 Itau's governance structure (*Source* Itau (2022) Risk and Capital Management—Pillar 3—2Q22—Banco Itaú, available at: https://www.itau.com.br/download-file/v2/d/42787847-4cf6-4461-94a5-40ed237dca33/7e7cb53e-ef18-1000-fa28-9591f5675fe7?origin=2)

matters the most. How do institutions incorporate ecological factors into regular decision-making? Environmental reports are a good first step for banks to understand where they are in the dynamic greening process, but most look toward selling existing initiatives to institutions' stakeholders.

Structure, conduct, and performance is an industrial organization theory that posits that market structures (competition, oligopoly, or monopoly, to name a few) determine firms' behavior, which translates into individual firms' performance. A solid corporate governance structure is a necessary but not sufficient condition for banks to improve their environmental performance.

Greenwashing can happen even amidst a robust corporate governance structure. It is easier for a proactive firm to act greener than for a carefully structured institution to do so if the governance pillars are primarily for show. The most important criterion for banks to improve their nonfinancial performance is incorporating sustainability into the business processes. There is a limit to the value of reports and marketing initiatives, including corporate social responsibility. Even when companies sign climate pledges, change won't be forthcoming if the goals are not internalized. Take the Renewable Energy 100% (RE100) global initiative by the Carbon Disclosure Project (CDP). Companies that sign it commit to using 100% renewable energy by a specific date. By 2021, RE100 member companies report consuming 49% renewable electricity, up from 45% in 2020 and 41% in 2019, and the average member is committed to 100% renewable energy by 2029 (CDP, 2023). More than 200 corporations have signed on to RE100 (Grove & Clouse, 2021), but there are many ways to transition to renewable energies. Companies may use creative accounting for that purpose, shift operations without changing business practices, or work with regulators to transform the grid at scale.

Below, we present a formal model for optimal corporate governance for green banks. Unfortunately, there is no standardized solution. In many ways, every institution must find its way to empower internal climate policies.

2.12.1 An Optimal Corporate Governance Model for Green Banks

Corporate governance is constantly evolving. In an uncertain world, the interests of shareholders, board members, and managers may be aligned for some time. Still, shocks can shake up things, allowing managers to divert resources or board members to become complacent in their monitoring roles. Such shocks may include climate and social changes but are broader in the model below.

This subsection summarizes the model by Noe and Rebello (2012). If you want to skip the model's technical details, jump to the following subsection, which details the model's implications for the optimal corporate governance for a "green" bank.

Noe and Rebello (2012) aim to find optimal corporate governance and compensation in a dynamic world. The idea behind their model is straightforward. There are three types of agents: shareholders, directors that make up the board, and managers. The board sets up the compensation and monitoring policies. Shareholders decide, every period, on funding for the company. Managers either invest productively or divert shareholder funds for personal consumption.

In the present instance, the insights come from two main drivers: information asymmetry and recurring shareholder investments. The crux of the issue is that shareholders and the board must make their decisions without first observing managers' actions. The shareholders' capital contribution, the manager's compensation, and the monitoring policy are common knowledge and verifiable.

Formally, shareholders provide managers with investment capital, k, at the start of each period before observing the firm's current position, which is not verifiable *ex-ante*. The shareholders and board are the last to observe the firm's current position and do so only after the manager has chosen whether to invest or divert. Figures 2.30 and 2.31 summarize the timeline of events.

This figure presents the sequence of actions within each period when the firm is in a strong position, S, and the shareholders have funded operations.

This figure presents the sequence of actions within each period when the firm is weak, W, and the shareholders have funded operations.

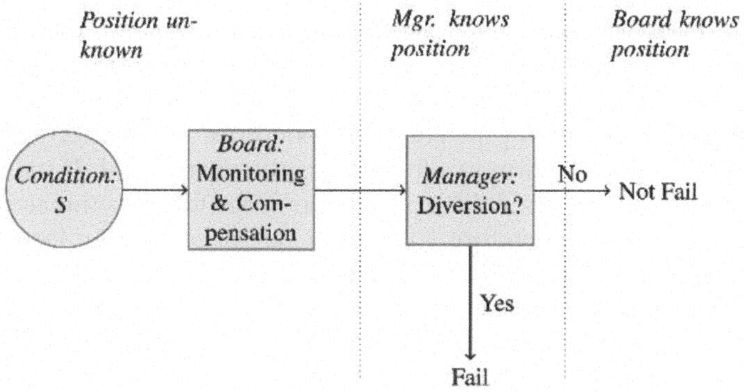

Fig. 2.30 Timeline in position S (*Source* Noe and Rebello [2012])

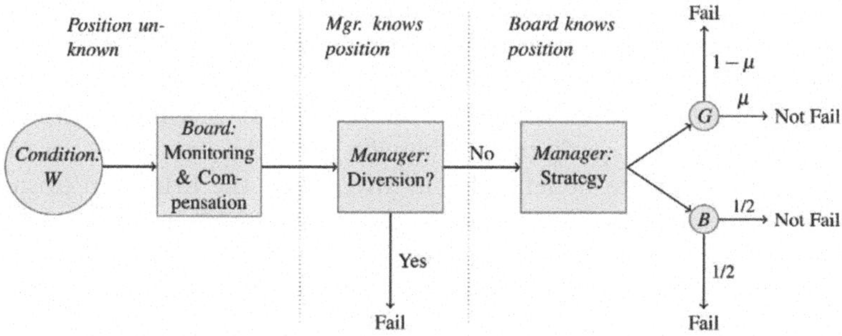

Fig. 2.31 Timeline in position W (*Source* Noe and Rebello [2012])

A firm's "position" (p) in any given period that it produces a positive output can be either strong, S, or weak, W. The firm is owned by risk-neutral shareholders and managed by risk-neutral managers; in turn, executives are supervised by a board that aims to maximize the shareholders' payoff. The firm may survive indefinitely; periods are indexed $1, \ldots, \infty$.

After managers observe the firm's position, compensation, and monitoring policy, they invest the shareholders' funds in the firm or divert them to personal consumption. Diversion by the manager is observable but not verifiable.

If shareholders provide k (condition 1), and managers invest in operations (2), the firm generates one dollar of revenue at the end of the period. The revenue is common knowledge, verifiable, and insensitive to the firm's current position. If shareholders don't provide k or managers divert funds, the firm "fails," which means it cannot function in any future period.

If the firm is in a strong position, S, conditions (1) and (2) are sufficient to ensure that the firm can function in the next period. If the firm is in a weak position, W, its ability to function in the future is threatened by an exogenous shock. Therefore, (1) and (2) are necessary but insufficient to ensure the firm can function in the next period.

The managers must make an unobservable and unverifiable strategic decision, which can be "good" (G) or "bad" (B). The strategic decision determines the firm's probability of functioning in the next period. It also determines the nonpecuniary private benefit managers receive in the current period. The board learns the firm's current position before the managers decide.

For strategy G, the firm functions in the next period with probability $\mu > 1/2$, and the managers' private benefits are $\beta/2$. The variable μ captures the managers' strategic competencies and is common knowledge. Under strategy B, the firm functions in the following period with a probability of $1/2$, and the manager's private benefit is β. The manager also earns a nonpecuniary private benefit of β in any period the firm is in position S and operates. Here, the "good" strategy is defined as the managers maximizing the firm's survival chances. The "bad" strategy indicates that managers prefer to keep their private benefits instead of sacrificing them to maximize the firm's survival.

Managers don't receive private benefits, which are not verifiable if the firm fails to operate. The board sets the managers' compensation and monitoring incentives for each period. The managers' reservation wage in each period is zero. They receive a fixed salary of $w \in [0, 1]$ if the firm operates but receive nothing if the firm does not operate.

Monitoring limits the manager's ability to divert the shareholders' capital contribution. Managers may divert funds from the company for personal consumption. The cost for such actions is $1 - \varphi$ per dollar diverted, which is common knowledge and represents the quality of the legal system and the intensity of scrutiny by the media and financial analysts. The best monitoring systems would make $\varphi = 0$, making the cost for diversion equal to the firm's entire potential revenue; managers would not be incentivized to divert any funds in that case.

If shareholders believe that managers may divert funds, they can spend $\left(\frac{1}{2}\right)\gamma\alpha^2$ to make a fraction of the investment capital, represented by $\alpha \in [0, 1]$, "nondivertable." The monitoring cost and the constant γ are common knowledge. The constant γ captures the effect of the firm's operations' complexity and internal controls' quality. The managers' single-period payoff from diversion, reflecting both the board's monitoring policy and their personal costs, is thus $\varphi(1 - \alpha)k$.

Finally, firms can be invulnerable, INV or vulnerable, VN, latent state variables never observed directly by shareholders or the manager. The firm's current position is always S if it is invulnerable. In contrast, if the firm is vulnerable, its position is S with probability $1 - \delta$ or W with probability δ. Thus, $\delta \in [0, 1]$ represents the degree of the firm's vulnerability to shocks.

At the start of period 1, all agents believe that the firm is vulnerable with a probability of π_1. In subsequent periods, their assessment of the firm's vulnerability, π, evolves as they acquire more information about the firms' actions.

In the model, shareholders usually have no incentive to shut down operations, as the cash flow from investment and the transition probabilities are constant over time. The only source of dynamics is the evolution of the latent state variable x. Shareholders' and managers' strategies depend only on x.

The model is designed to be a series of one-off decisions. Decisions don't depend on past performance or past actions. Once a company goes bankrupt, it ceases production.

The managers' expected payoffs depend on their salary and private benefits in the current period, the probability that the firm will continue operating, and their continuation value. Take the case that the firm's current position is S. Managers can be sure the company will survive, and thus, their expected payoff from operating the firm is

$$w + \beta + \rho V(x\prime)$$

where $V(x')$ represents the continuation value from the state variable x. Furthermore, let $V_0 = V(1 - \delta)$ represent the continuation value when the firm is vulnerable.

Following a shock, the expected payoff from operating the firm and choosing strategy G is

$$w + \frac{1}{2}\beta + \mu\rho V_0$$

while the gain from choosing strategy B is:

$$w + \beta + \frac{1}{2}\rho V_0$$

Comparing these two possibilities, it is clear that managers prefer strategy G when their private benefits are low or either the discount factor and their strategic competence are high:

$$\frac{\beta}{\rho(2\mu - 1)} \leq V_0$$

The diversion decision is represented by $D \in \{0, 1\}$, where zero represents no diversion and one represents diversion that provides the manager with a payoff of $\varphi(1 - \alpha)k$. The managers' decisions depend on their current salary, w, the level of monitoring, α, the firm's current position, p, and their belief about the firm's type, x. Therefore, their best response to the board's choices is defined by

$$\mathrm{BR}_M(w, a, p, x) = \underset{D\in\{0,1\}}{\arg\max}\ D\phi(1 - \alpha)k +$$

$$(1 - D)\begin{cases} w + \beta + \rho V(x') & \text{if } p = S \\ \max\begin{bmatrix} w + \frac{1}{2}\beta + \mu\rho V_0, \\ w + \beta + \frac{1}{2}\rho V_0 \end{bmatrix} & \text{if } p = W \end{cases}$$

Meanwhile, the board's decision is given by:

$$u(w, a, D) = \begin{cases} 1 - w - (1/2)\alpha^2 - k \text{ if } D = 0 \\ \alpha k - (1/2)\alpha^2 - k \quad \text{if } D = 1 \end{cases}$$

Finally, the probability that the firm will operate in the following period, m, is given by:

$$m(p, D) = \begin{cases} 1 \quad \text{if } D = 0 \text{ and } p = S \\ \mu \quad \text{if } D = 0,\ p = W, \text{ and } \frac{\beta}{\rho(2\mu-1)} \leq V_0 \\ 1/2 \text{ if } D = 0,\ p = W, \text{ and } \frac{\beta}{\rho(2\mu-1)} \leq V_0 \\ 0 \quad \text{if } D = 1 \end{cases}$$

In the model, the board has a clear information disadvantage that prevents it from conditioning the manager's salary and monitoring policy on the firm's position.

What is the central outcome of the model regarding the options for how the board monitors managers? The board is restricted to choosing between two governance regimes: a partial deterrence regime, under which the manager's best response is to divert if the current position is W but not if the position is S, and a complete deterrence regime, where the manager's best response is not to divert in either position. Since the board chooses only current-period compensation and monitoring, it cannot influence the manager's choice between strategies G and B, even if it implements a deterrent regime. In other words, if the board maximizes the probability of the firm's survival, it cannot stomp down entirely on the possibility that managers divert funds. Formally, that means that the board cannot pick policies that induce the manager to divert when the firm's condition is S but not when it is W.

The board's choice depends on the state variable, x. The solution to the board's problem is nonstationary when the firm's type has not been revealed and $x \in (1 - \delta, 1)$. The solution is stationary once the firm is revealed vulnerable, as the state variable remains $x = 1 - \delta$ for all subsequent periods. If the company survives and produces uninterruptedly, the state variable approaches one.

In the partial deterrence governance regime, the board ensures the managers operate the firm in position S and divert in position W. Therefore, it sets the managers' payoff from operating the firm in position S to exceed her payoff from diverting shareholders' funds and also leaves the managers better off diverting than operating the firm in position W:

$$w + \rho V(x') + \beta \geq \varphi k(1 - \alpha)$$

and

$$\max\left[w + \frac{1}{2}\beta + \mu\rho V_0, w + \beta + \frac{1}{2}\rho V_0\right] < \phi(1 - \alpha)k$$

The tradeoffs determining the relation between x, the likelihood of the strong position, and the manager's salary under a partial deterrence regime are relatively straightforward. Under such a regime, in position W, each dollar of cash flow monitored reduces the shareholders' loss from actual diversion by one dollar. In position S, the manager does not divert. Therefore, the only benefit from monitoring in position S is that each dollar of monitored cash flow reduces the amount shareholders pay the manager by $\varphi \leq 1$. Therefore, provided that $\varphi < 1$, the monitoring intensity chosen by the board will never be high enough to protect shareholder funds completely.

Moreover, the higher the probability of position S, i.e., the higher x, the smaller the marginal gain from monitoring. Consequently, except for the limiting worst-case governance environment in which diversion is costless (i.e., $\varphi = 1$), the marginal benefit of monitoring falls as x increases. For this reason, the optimal monitoring intensity falls as x rises. Furthermore, the better the governance environment, the smaller the benefits from increases in x.

Since the board never finds it optimal to protect shareholders' funds via monitoring, it must also use compensation to incentivize the managers. The managers' salaries are set to ensure that they are indifferent between operating the firm and diverting in position S. *Ceteris paribus*, reducing monitoring increases the manager's incentive to divert. This incentive to divert is partially countered by the increase in the manager's continuation value caused by the increase in x.

Under a complete deterrence regime, the managers operate the firm in both positions S and W. Therefore, the board has to choose the manager's compensation and monitoring policy to ensure that the manager's payoff from operating the firm in position W is no lower than her payoff from diversion, i.e.

$$\max\left[w + \frac{1}{2}\beta + \mu\rho V_0, w + \beta + \frac{1}{2}\rho V_0\right] \geq \phi(1 - \alpha)k$$

Under a complete deterrence regime, monitoring has only an indirect benefit; it lowers the manager's gain from diversion and hence lowers the salary necessary to induce the managers to operate the firm by $\varphi \leq 1$ for each dollar of cash flow. That contrasts with the partial deterrence regime, where each dollar of cash flow that is monitored reduces the shareholders' loss from actual diversion by one dollar in position W. Since the benefit from monitoring is smaller under a complete deterrence regime, so is the optimal level of monitoring.

What happens when the firm is known to be vulnerable? Beliefs cease to evolve. The managers' continuation value becomes higher under a complete deterrence regime than a partial one. Therefore, switching from a complete deterrence regime to a partial one results in lower compensation.

Given all these details, the authors establish the details of the optimal governance policy. The board trades off the higher likelihood of long-run survival generated by the complete deterrence regime against the possible lower cost of implementing the partial deterrence regime. Before experiencing a shock, a firm's optimal governance structure changes as performance-generated information regarding the firm's type accumulates. A shock prompts a change in governance structure and perhaps a regime shift. The firm's characteristics dictate these dynamics, the manager's competence, and the external governance environment. As we have seen, managers must be paid a premium under a complete deterrence regime. The benefits of this premium are increasing in the likelihood that the premium will affect the firm's survival. This likelihood drops as the probability that the firm is in a strong position (x or $1 - \delta$) rises. Therefore, shareholders strictly prefer a partial deterrence regime when x and $1 - \delta$ are sufficiently large.

Also, firms will adopt a complete deterrence regime if they do not have a long history of good performance. More importantly, a firm initially judged to have a high likelihood of experiencing a shock will only switch to a partial deterrence regime after a sufficiently long history of good performance.

If a firm experiences a shock early in its history, before transitioning to a partial deterrence regime, its governance regime ensures a positive probability of surviving the shock. However, given that a partial deterrence regime does not deter managers from diverting resources, a shock results in the firm's collapse (Fig. 2.32).

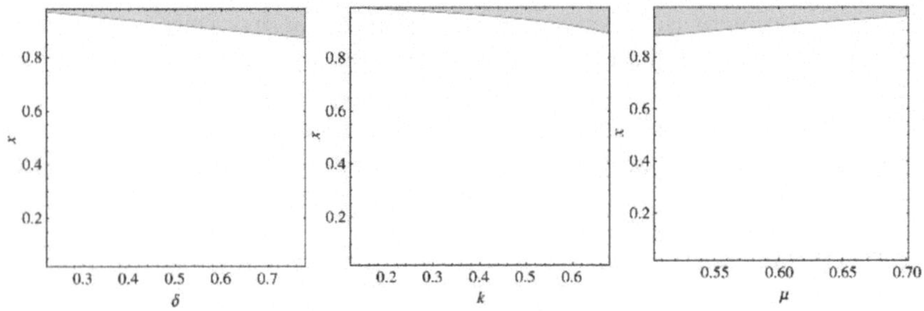

Fig. 2.32 The effect of parameter shifts on the choice between complete and partial deterrence (*Source* Noe and Rebello (2012). The shaded region in each panel represents the parameter set in which the partial deterrence regime is optimal. In contrast, the unshaded region represents the parameter set where the complete deterrence regime is optimal. In the figure, $\delta = 0.50$, $\mu = 0.60$, $\beta = 0.02$, $\rho = 0.95$, $k = 0.40$, $\gamma = 3.0$, and $\varphi = 0.90$)

2.12.2 Barriers to Sustainability Evolution: A Case Study

This case study describes the sustainability trajectory of a large multinational bank (hereby, the bank) that offers many lessons regarding the (lack) of governance institutionalization in commercial banks and illustrates some of the dilemmas formalized in the previous subsections.

The bank has its headquarters in Europe, but most of the events described below happened in the subsidiaries in the Americas.

In the mid-2000s, the bank acquired a rival's European operations in the Americas. At the time, no part of the bank's organizational structure dealt with sustainability, even remotely. The institution had a reputation for being extremely aggressive, having grown significantly in the previous two decades through mergers and acquisitions in various global regions. The acquired company in the Americas had a reputation as the leading sustainability bank in the area. The bank had a decision to make: get rid of the sustainability initiatives or find a way to incorporate them into an organization with no history of dealing with the subject.

The CEO of the local subsidiary met with the group's board in Europe. They reached an agreement. The bank would not only incorporate all the employees of the sustainability department of the acquired institution but would empower them to develop initiatives for the firm. The rationale was straightforward: they would treat the subsidiary as an environmental

R&D department for the entire group. The sustainability department would develop initiatives and fight to implement them locally. The board would work with the other subsidiaries to turn these initiatives into worldwide policies if successful. After a while, if the sustainability department failed to develop initiatives picked up locally or deemed inconsequential, the bank could even eliminate the department.

Initially, the sustainability department was moderately successful in steering the subsidiary toward less unsustainable operations. The first significant policy proposal dealt with the subsidiary's operation in a sparsely populated region with significant deforestation risks. The sustainability department generated a report about the subsidiary operations with a straightforward recommendation: the bank should stop credit operations for small and medium-sized enterprises, keeping only individuals and some of their largest corporate clients. The report showed that the institution could not discern if its corporate loans directly or indirectly supported deforestation. Much of the bank's activities were likely tied to companies profiting from higher regional deforestation rates. The sustainability department estimated that the costs for properly adjudicating risks and designing credit policies limiting the reputational and operational risks associated with tying its actions to deforestation would be much higher than the bank's regional profits. Of course, the commercial department firmly opposed that proposal, arguing, among other things, that leaving the market to its competitors wouldn't achieve anything for society and would put the bank in a more precarious position.

The bank's CEO thought this was such a momentous decision that it was up to headquarters to decide. Since the goal of keeping the sustainability department was to be the R&D department for the entire group, the determination had commercial implications for subsidiaries with similar issues. Surprisingly, the board decided that the bank should follow the sustainability department's recommendation and withdraw from the region.

Notably, the sustainability department functioned like every other department till the mid-2010s. The executives had productivity metrics and were integrated into the aggressive commercial culture of the institution. Still, they played a dual role. They helped design green funds for the Asset Management department, created nonfinancial rating methodologies, and supported new ESG-related investment products. However, many policies to improve the institution's financial performance put the managers of the sustainability departments in conflict with executives of other sectors, as in the example discussed above. The department was viewed internally as a cost center, even if they supported numerous revenue generation initiatives.

As ESG-related issues became more pressing, the bank established other sustainability departments but still relied on this subsidiary to develop its most sophisticated strategies. However, an example of the nonlinearity of sustainability initiatives' evolution is that the department was almost dissolved in the mid-2010s. Due to an economic crisis that pressured the company's profits and other issues, the CEO was replaced. The incoming executive focused on short-term gains, looking closer to the aggressive nature of other subsidiaries. He didn't believe his subsidiary should focus on environmental and nonfinancial issues. The new CEO found that the sustainability department was an easy cost-cutting source. While the Board could have prevented the new CEO from almost dismantling the sustainability department, it allowed him carte blanche to redesign the bank's operations to lift profits in the short run.

And therein lies the short vs. long-run dilemma of genuine sustainability policies in commercial and investment banks. Executives find it easy to commit to sustainability goals during periods of significant economic growth. Still, these initiatives are readily abandoned when the business cycle turns. Robust corporate governance structures don't sacrifice long-term profitability for short-term gains. That should be even more so when an institution has mature departments with a long history of providing services to the organization.

Formally, the new CEO didn't dismantle the sustainability department, but he dismembered it. The director, who had headed the department for 17 years, was let go with the argument that she "didn't fit the mold of a bank executive." The department's focus shifted toward providing environmental reports without substantial organizational change proposals. The local subsidiary lost its bite regarding environmental management policies. The CEO argued that the best ideas had already been disseminated; if the board wanted more changes in that area, they should empower headquarters to do so.

Of course, sustainability departments evolve, and maybe it was time for the era of that particular department as the generator of the leading R&D proposals for the group to be over. Still, this case shows how systemic changes depend on many dimensions, from robust governance structures to executives' fickle opinions on how banks should develop environmental managerial policies.

References

Acharya, V. V., Berger, A. N., & Roman, R. A. (2018). Lending Implications of US Bank Stress Tests: Costs or Benefits? *Journal of Financial Intermediation, 34*, 58–90.

Allen, F., & Gale, D. (2000). Financial Contagion. *Journal of Political Economy, 108*(1), 1–33.

Allen, F., & Gale, D. (2009). *Understanding Financial Crises*. OUP Oxford.

Argimon, I., Düllmann, K., Foos, D., Francis, B., Gaul, L., Georgescu, O., Nordal, K., & Pramor, M. (2015). The Interplay of Accounting and Regulation and its Impact on Bank Behaviour: Literature Review. Working Paper 28, Bank for International Settlements. https://www.bis.org/bcbs/publ/wp28.pdf

Badrinarayanan, C., & Akhter, Z. (2023). *Understanding Climate Value-at-Risk (VaR) for Financial Risk Management, Blue Sky Analytics*. https://blueskyhq.io/blog/understanding-climate-var-for-financial-risk-management

Bank of America. (2022). *Annual Report*, avaible at: https://investor.bankofamerica.com/regulatory-and-other-filings/annual-reports/content/0000070858-23-000121/0000070858-23-000121.pdf

Bank of England. (2022). *CP16/22 – Implementation of the Basel 3.1 standards*, available at: https://www.bankofengland.co.uk/prudentialregulation/publication/2022/november/implementation-of-the-basel-3-1-standards

Bastos, J. A. (2010). Forecasting Bank Loans Loss-Given-Default. *Journal of Banking & Finance, 34*(10), 2510–2517.

BIS. (2011). *Revisions to the Basel II Market Risk Framework*. https://www.bis.org/publ/bcbs193.pdf

BIS. (2017). *Basel III Leverage Ratio Framework—Executive Summary*. https://www.bis.org/fsi/fsisummaries/b3_lrf.htm

BIS. (2018). *Liquidity Coverage Ratio (LCR)—Executive Summary*. https://www.bis.org/fsi/fsisummaries/lcr.htm

BIS. (2019). CAP50—Prudation Valuation Guide. Bank for International Settlements. https://www.bis.org/basel_framework/chapter/CAP/50.htm?&inforce=20191215

BIS. (2020a). *LEX—Large Exposures*. https://www.bis.org/basel_framework/standard/LEX.htm

BIS. (2020b). MAR50 Credit Valuation Adjustment Framework, Version Effective as of 1 January 2023. https://www.bis.org/basel_framework/chapter/MAR/50.htm?inforce=20230101&published=20200708&export=pdf

BIS. (2020c). *Targeted Revisions to the Credit Valuation Adjustment Risk Framework*. https://www.bis.org/bcbs/publ/d507.htm

BIS. (2022a). *CRE35—IRB Approach: Treatment of Expected Losses and Provisions, Bank for International Settlements*. https://www.bis.org/basel_framework/chapter/CRE/35.htm?inforce=20220101&published=20191215

BIS. (2022b). *Instructions for Basel III Monitoring*. https://www.bis.org/bcbs/qis/biiiimplmoninstr_jan22.pdf

BIS. (2022c). *About BIS—Overview, Bank for International Settlements*. https://www.bis.org/about/index.htm

Board of Governors. (2023). *Review of the Federal Reserve's Supervision and Regulation of Silicon Valley Bank*. https://www.federalreserve.gov/publications/files/svb-review-20230428.pdf

Board of Governors of the Federal Reserve System. (2022). *Large Bank Capital Requirements*. https://www.federalreserve.gov/publications/files/large-bank-capital-requirements-20220804.pdf

Caruana, J., & Narain, A. (2008). Banking on More Capital. *Finance and Development, 45*(2), 24–28.

CDP. (2023). *Driving Renewables in a Time of Change*. https://www.there100.org/driving-renewables-time-change

Coelho, R., & Restoy, F. (2022). The Regulatory Response to Climate Risks: Some Challenges. Bank for International Settlements [BIS]. https://www.bis.org/fsi/fsibriefs16.htm.

Corna, L., & Zorzi, F. (2020). *New Challenge on SA-CCR: An Overview on Implementation Process*. https://www.iasonltd.com/research/research-paper-series/new-challenge-on-sa-ccr-an-overview-on-implementation-process

Dafermos, Y., & Nikolaidi, M. (2021). How Can Green Differentiated Capital Requirements Affect Climate Risks? A Dynamic Macrofinancial Analysis. *Journal of Financial Stability, 54*, 100871.

Damyanova, V., & Taqi, M. (2020). German Banks Remain Among Europe's Least Efficient in Q1 Ranking, S&P Global Market Intelligence. https://www.spglobal.com/marketintelligence/en/news-insights/latest-news-headlines/german-banks-remain-among-europe-s-least-efficient-in-q1-ranking-59438102

Deutsche Bundesbank. (2022). *Risk of a Credit Valuation Adjustment (CVA)*. https://www.bundesbank.de/en/tasks/banking-supervision/individual-aspects/own-funds-requirements/cva-risk

Dietz, S., Bowen, A., Dixon, C., & Gradwell, P. (2016). 'Climate Value at Risk' of Global Financial Assets. *Nature Climate Change, 6*(7), 676–679.

Dunz, N., Naqvi, A., & Monasterolo, I. (2021). Climate Sentiments, Transition Risk, and Financial Stability in a Stock-flow Consistent Model. *Journal of Financial Stability, 54*, 100872.

European Bank Authority. (2019). Low Profits and High Costs Remain a Key Challenge for the EU Banking Sector, News & Presses. https://www.eba.europa.eu/low-profits-and-high-costs-remain-a-key-challenge-for-the-eu-banking-sector

European Banking Authority. (2022). *2023 EU-wide Stress Test—Methodological Note*. https://www.eba.europa.eu/risk-analysis-and-data/eu-wide-stress-testing

European Central Bank. (2019). ECB Guide to Internal Models, European Central Bank. https://www.bankingsupervision.europa.eu/ecb/pub/pdf/ssm.guidetointernalmodels_consolidated_201910~97fd49fb08.en.pdf

FDIC. (2004). Economic Capital and the Assessment of Capital Adequacy, Supervisory Insights, Winter. https://www.fdic.gov/regulations/examinations/supervisory/insights/siwin04/siwinter04-article1.pdf

Federal Reserve. (2019). Supervisory Developments, Federal Reserve Supervision and Regulation Report—November 2019. https://www.federalreserve.gov/publications/2019-november-supervision-and-regulation-report-supervisory-developments.htm

Forjan, J. (2019) The Evolution of Stress Testing Counterparty Exposure, Analyst Prep. https://analystprep.com/study-notes/frm/part-2/credit-risk-measurement-and-management/the-evolution-of-stress-testing-counterparty-exposure/

Gai, P., & Kapadia, S. (2010). Contagion in Financial Networks. *Proceedings of the Royal Society a: Mathematical, Physical and Engineering Sciences, 466*(2120), 2401–2423.

Gandel, S., & Smith, C. (2023). Regional US Banks Claimed Easier Capital Rules Would Turbocharge Loans, Financial Times. https://www.ft.com/content/c409f7d0-c1ec-4553-8d49-7eb1b54a106d

Girotra, A. (2020). *Risk-adjusted Profitability Management at Banks*. https://assets.kpmg.com/content/dam/kpmg/in/pdf/2020/06/risk-adjusted-profitability-management-at-banks.pdf

Grove, H., & Clouse, M. (2021). Renewable Energy Commitments versus Greenwashing: Board Responsibilities. *Corporate Ownership & Control, 18*(3), 423–437.

Hong Kong Monetary Authority. (2022). Supervisory Policy Manual, OR-1 Operational Risk Management, V.2–25.07.2022. https://www.hkma.gov.hk/media/eng/doc/key-functions/banking-stability/supervisory-policy-manual/OR-1.pdf

Hosseini Jebeli, H., Johnston, C., Logan, C., Molico, M., Shen, X., & Tremblay, M. C. (2022). Assessing Climate-Related Financial Risk: Guide to Implementation of Methods (No. 120). Bank of Canada.

IMF. (2022). Germany Financial Sector Assessment Program Technical Note—the Determinants of Bank Profitability, IMF Country Report No. 22/273. https://www.imf.org/-/media/Files/Publications/CR/2022/English/1DEUEA2022010.ashx

Jackson, M. O., & Pernoud, A. (2021). Systemic Risk in Financial Networks: A Survey. *Annual Review of Economics, 13*, 171–202.

Lamperti, F., Bosetti, V., Roventini, A., Tavoni, M., & Treibich, T. (2021). Three Green Financial Policies to Address Climate Risks. *Journal of Financial Stability, 54*, 100875.

Masciandaro, D., & Russo, R. (2023). Central Banks and Climate Policy: Unpleasant Trade–Offs? A Principal–Agent Approach. BAFFI CAREFIN Centre Research Paper.

McKinsey & Company. (2021). German Banking Returns to the Playing Field, Perspective. https://www.mckinsey.com/~/media/mckinsey/industries/financial%20services/our%20insights/german%20banking%20returns%20to%20the%20playing%20field/german-banking-returns-to-the-playing-field.pdf

MSCI. (2020). Climate Value-at-Risk: Powering Better Investment Decisions for a Better World, MSCI. https://www.msci.com/documents/1296102/16985724/MSCI-ClimateVaR-Introduction-Feb2020.pdf

MSCI. (2023). Climate Value-at-Risk: Scenario Analysis, MSCI. https://www.msci.com/documents/1296102/17413431/ClimateVaR_Brochure.pdf

Noe, T. H., & Rebello, M. J. (2012). Optimal Corporate Governance and Compensation in a Dynamic World. *The Review of Financial Studies, 25*(2), 480–521.

Novotny-Farkas, Z. (2016). The Interaction of the IFRS 9 Expected Loss Approach with Supervisory Rules and Implications for Financial Stability. *Accounting in Europe, 13*(2), 197–227.

Oehmke, M., & Opp, M. M. (2022). Green Capital Requirements. Available at SSRN.

Reuters. (2023). Explainer: What Caused Silicon Valley Bank's Failure? Reuters. https://www.reuters.com/business/finance/what-caused-silicon-valley-banks-failure-2023-03-10/

Rugilo, D. (2021). Analysing the Growing Interplay of Accounting and Regulatory Capital: A State-of-the-art Review. Available at SSRN 3918335.

Smith, C.; Masters, B., Gandel, S., & Vandevelde, M. (2023). Federal Reserve Review Pins Blame for SVB Failure on Donald Trump-era Rule Changes, Financial Times. https://www.ft.com/content/cd7d2d8b-32b9-4f89-8bd0-b23efeb33be2

UNEP. (2022a). Impact Analysis and Target Setting Process, Interactive Guidance v 1.4, UNEP FI. https://www.unepfi.org/wordpress/wp-content/uploads/2022/09/Impact-and-Target-Process-V-1.4-14.09.2022.pdf

UNEP. (2022b). Impact Radar, UNEP FI. https://www.unepfi.org/impact/impact-radar-mappings/

UNEP. (2023a). UNEP Finance Initiative—About US, UNEP FI. https://www.unepfi.org/about/

UNEP. (2023b). How to Implement, UNEP FI. https://www.unepfi.org/banking/resources-for-implementation/

Weber, O. (2005). Sustainability Benchmarking of European Banks and Financial Service Organizations. *Corporate Social Responsibility and Environmental Management, 12*, 73–87.

World Bank. (2023). *Bank cost to income ratio (%)*, available at: https://databank.worldbank.org/source/global-financial-development/Series/GFDD.EI.07

World Bank. (2023). *Bank net interest margin (%)*, available at: https://databank.worldbank.org/source/global-financial-development/Series/GFDD.EI.01

Zeidan, R. (2020). Why is Bank Credit in Brazil the Most Expensive in the World? *Brazilian Review of Finance, 18*(4), 1–22.

Zeidan, R., & Müllner, J. (2015). Firm, Market and Top Management Antecedents of Speculation: Lessons for Corporate Governance. *Journal of Multinational Financial Management, 32*, 42–58.

CHAPTER 3

Sustainable Lending

Banks already incorporate nonfinancial performance into their lending decisions. It is naïve to believe that commercial banks ignore nonfinancial information in their lending decisions. At the same time, there are no standard sustainability credit rating systems.

This section is not about begging financial institutions to change their business models; it is about providing the tools so that banks can improve their overall performance without sacrificing short and long-term profits if possible. For this purpose, this section presents a simplified lending model and extends it to incorporate sustainability-related information beyond ESG indicators. We describe how banks lend and then provide the required steps for greening the lending process.

Notably, we focus not only on downside risks, as exemplified by ESG indicators, but also on opportunities. BlackRock, one of the largest investment management companies, explicitly states, "We believe an underappreciated opportunity for investors seeking to drive the transition lies in identifying carbon-intensive companies that are positioning themselves to lead decarbonization within their industries (BlackRock, 2023)." We take a similar approach. Any genuine sustainability-related rating system must include opportunities and downside risks, even if the latter may be more relevant in the short run.

R. Zeidan, *The Green Banking Transition Manual*,
https://doi.org/10.1007/978-981-96-2852-0_3

3.1 Why a General Sustainability-Related Rating System?

Credit rating is at the heart of bank lending. Banks rate firms (or specific financial instruments, such as a particular corporate bond) on their overall capacity to meet their financial obligation and, in most cases, on the possibility of recovery in the case of partial or total default.

Securing a commercial loan is standard across the industry, with some differences depending on the jurisdiction, the clients' size, etc. The general process for securing such a loan includes pre-approval, loan application, review of the loan application package, loan underwriter/committee, term sheet, and closing documents (CFI Team, 2022).

Several of these steps are self-explanatory. During pre-approval, a lender will evaluate the firm's history, investigate existing debt and current credit lines, and analyze the loan's purpose. Some lenders require that the formal credit application is submitted to a credit adjudicator or loan committee, and then the processor will present the borrower with a term sheet (CFI Team, 2022).

The standard credit rating process follows a "CAMEL" analysis, which is divided into (Egan-Jones, 2020):

- Capital—an equity cushion not diluted by unreserved, non-performing assets.
- Asset Quality—measured by the share of non-performing assets, nonaccrual assets, and corresponding reserve coverage.
- Management—business practices, quality of public disclosures, and corporate governance.
- Earnings—the level and quality of earnings.
- Liquidity—the ability to quickly liquidate assets to meet obligations.

Figure 3.1 describes the leading financial indicators and how they relate to the standard CAMEL approach.

As we can see, many indicators are quantitative, but not all are. In addition, qualitative information complements indicators such as debt-related ratios; for instance, companies growing fast are likely to be less profitable, and banks consider that in generating credit ratings.

Figure 3.2 presents a general process available in any introductory finance text. Complexity increases for more sophisticated methods, such as rating structured finance instruments, as shown in Fig. 3.2. Structured

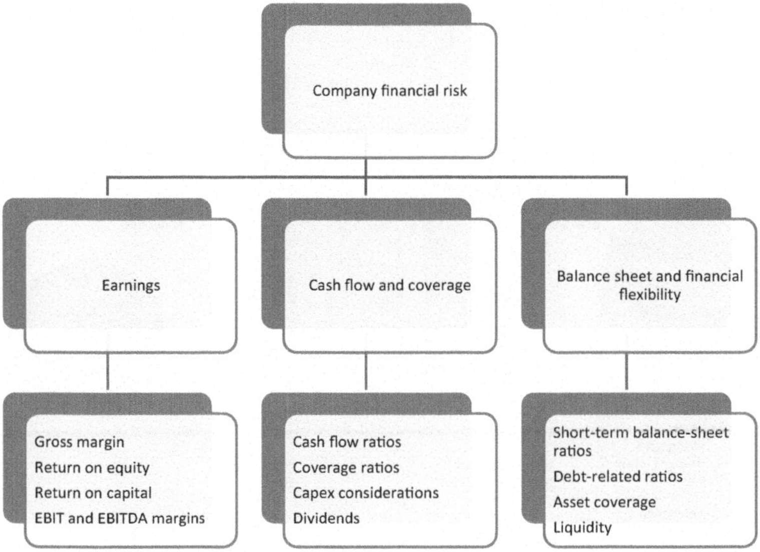

Fig. 3.1 Key financial risks (*Source* Egan-Jones [2020])

finance instruments typically involve pooling individual financial assets and selling separated debt securities to investors, usually having three parties: an originator, an arranger, and a special purpose entity, or SPE, that issue the securities.

Our interest is in improving banks' (usually commercial banks') lending decisions. In particular, the focus is on the process that involves evaluating prospective customers' likelihood of repaying loans in full (other stages include finding customers, assessing collaterals, designing loan agreements, and monitoring compliance). Figure 3.3 describes straight-through commercial banking lending processes.

Integrating climate and social risks in credit decision-making involves minor changes in the steps of the lending process: origination, servicing, and asset management. We are primarily concerned with credit risk assessment for lending origination. Specifically, by incorporating environmental and social factors into the gathering data step, banks could improve their credit decisions, making them fairer (especially for external stakeholders), more robust, and consistent.

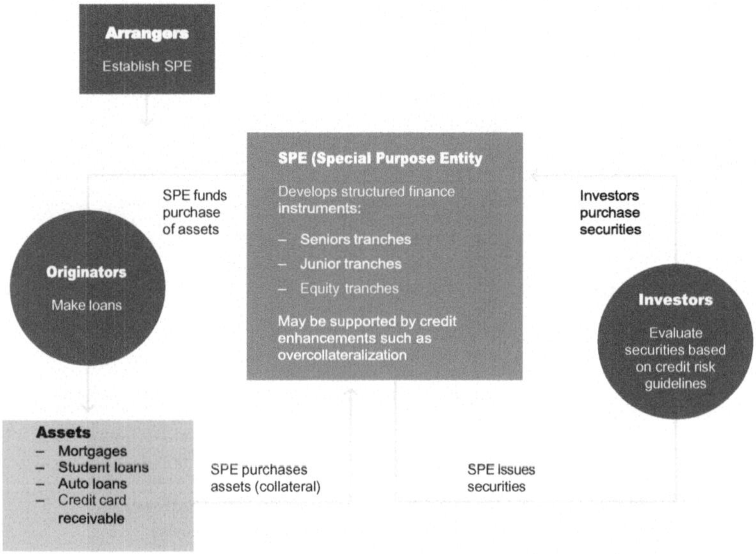

Fig. 3.2 Structured Finance Instruments (*Source* S&P Global [2022])

The literature has called for and analyzed the possibility of incorporating environmental and social factors into lending decisions for over twenty years [e.g., Case (1999), Cowton and Thompson (2000), and Acharya and Abuyuan (2002)]. However, we still don't have a standard method for it. There are a few reasons for this: there is no consensus on which environmental factors should be included in credit rating systems, no single method has outcompeted others, and no global regulatory mandates have emerged, among others.

A few robust initiatives come close to standardizing social and environmental factors in risk management models.

For instance, the Equator Principles (EP) aim to serve as a common baseline for financial institutions to identify, assess, and manage environmental and social risks when financing projects. However, the Equator Principles (now in its fourth version) apply to a narrow subset of commercial operations. It only applies to large infrastructure and industrial projects with capital costs of U$10 million and total aggregate loans of at least U$50 million (The Equator Principles, 2020). In addition, the goal

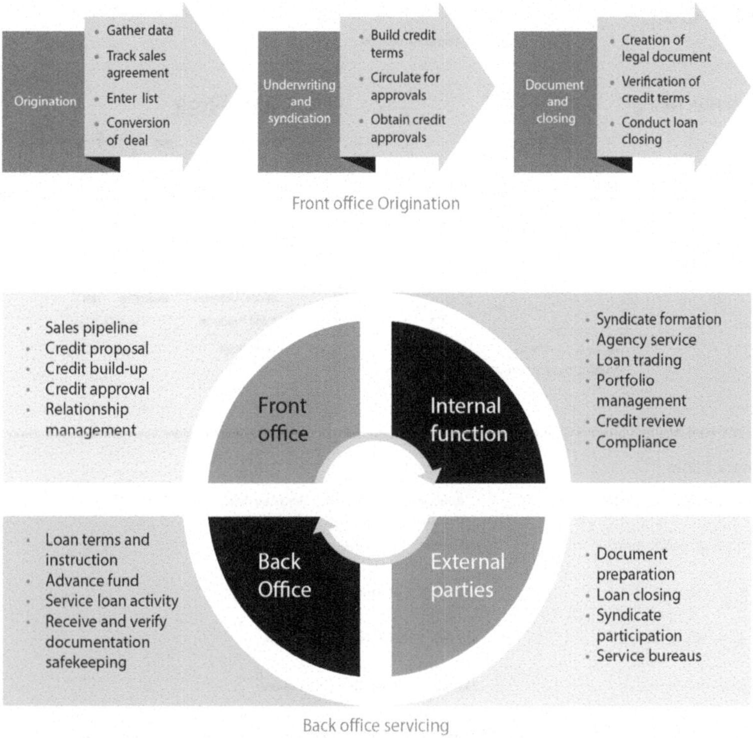

Fig. 3.3 Front office and back office straight-through lending processes (*Sources* Kidder [2004] and Alexandar [2018])

is for the companies applying for loans to create environmental assessment reports and change their behavior.

ESG and reputation risk ratings encompass relative rankings of companies regarding environmental, social, and governance risks. Services like Sustainalytics and Sustainable Fitch generate ESG ratings similar but more limited in scope to reports from credit rating agencies. Figure 3.4 displays a mock report from Sustainalytics, including the scale used in the report. As we can see, there are fewer categories than pure credit reports. More importantly, however, such ratings do not impact lending decisions. They aim to inform investors how exposed portfolios are to material ESG issues (Sustainalytics, 2020).

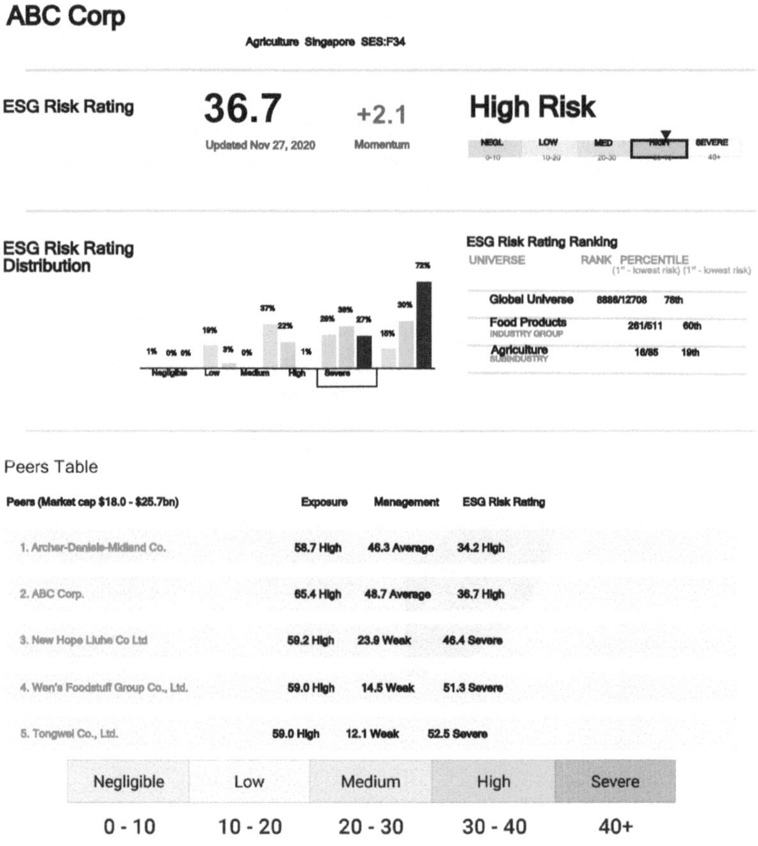

Fig. 3.4 Mock report from Sustainalytics

Recent initiatives have tried to enhance the scope of sustainability risk management. For instance, Ascui and Cojoianu (2019) advance a natural capital (in the sense of ecosystem) credit risk assessment framework. Still, one crucial condition for banks to develop and implement robust sustainability credit rating systems is high-quality, actionable information as inputs. This has been recognized as a challenge for a long time but is still a substantial barrier to disseminating sustainable lending practices. Thompson and Cowton (2004) show that bankers attach importance to firms' annual reports, notwithstanding their traditional limitations as a source of information on corporate environmental impact. They also observe that some desire extensions to environmental disclosure, even if those desired developments are relatively narrow, mirroring banks' principal interest in protecting their loans.

Since the mid-2000s, ESG indicators have emerged as the primary standard for disseminating financial and nonfinancial companies' social and environmental impact. However, there are two main barriers to ESG indicators as the central criteria for informing lending decisions: such indicators are mostly related to downside risk [Zeidan (2022a), Zeidan (2022b)], and there are currently over 360 ESG accounting standards globally (and ESG-related guidelines, such as regulations and standards, have grown from around 700 in 2009 to more than 1,700 today, according to The Economist, 2020). Some authors [e.g., Rezaee and Tuo (2019); Busco et al. (2020)] claim that society faces the ESG trap, the low information content of environmental reports that limits the ability of investors and financial institutions to improve decision-making related to nonfinancial indicators.

Some initiatives aim to improve this landscape. The Corporate Sustainability Reporting Directive (CSRD) is the new European Union (EU) legislation requiring all large companies to publish regular reports on their environmental and social impact activities. Nearly 50,000 companies (15,000 in Germany alone) in the EU must submit their report aligning with the CSRD on January 1, 2025, for the 2024 financial year. The CSRD is one of the measures within the Sustainable Finance Package adopted by the European Commission in April 2021 to help improve money flow toward sustainable activities across the EU.

However, although information content is undoubtedly a significant challenge, it is not the only barrier to robust, sustainable lending processes. In the remaining section, we describe the primary methods for building credit rating systems and detail previous attempts at developing such methods.

3.2 Methods for Sustainable Lending

The steps for building a standard credit rating model are the identification of the segment of interest (perimeter of applicability), the definition of the event to be forecast (the default), analysis of the internal and external regulatory framework, analysis of processes, information technology procedures and data to support the credit unit and data availability, analysis of the portfolio, definition of the modality for dealing with outliers and exceptions, comparison and discussion with the business and credit experts (Izzi et al., 2011). Figure 3.5 describes the typical approach for building a credit rating model.

Credit ratings use quantitative and qualitative information based on different methods. These include multi-criteria decision-making (MCDM), as in the case of Zeidan et al. (2015), based on an analytical hierarchic process (AHP), Roy and Shaw (2022), designed from a fuzzy TOPSIS, and Nabeeh et al. (2021), developed through a Neutrosophic Multiple-Criteria Decision-Making Framework (N-MCDMF).

Bonsall et al. (2017) show that differences in the credit rating agencies' methodologies result in differences in rating properties. In particular, they focus on differences in information processing constraints between a rating agency that utilizes qualitative analysis and direct access to borrowers' management in its rating process compared to one that does not. They also find that as information uncertainty about borrowers increases, the agency's rating accuracy, informativeness, and timeliness without direct access decrease relative to the agency with that access.

This direct access to borrowers' management motivates the Sustainability Credit Score System (SCSS, Zeidan et al., 2015). It is based on the analytic hierarchy process methodology. Its goal is to inform lending decisions by integrating sustainability into regular credit reports. With a bank

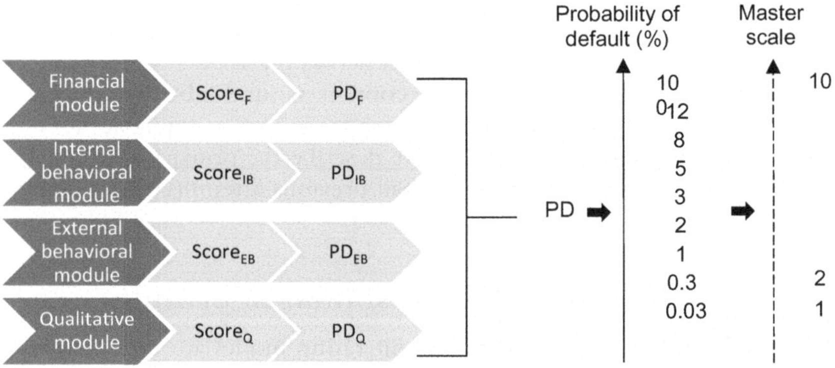

Fig. 3.5 Main steps in the development of statistical models (*Source* Izzi et al. [2011])

as its end user, the SCSS would work by inducing changes in lending decisions regarding credit availability and interest rates. For instance, banks that complement their regular credit score with sustainability data would have better information to decide on the price and quantity of lines of credit. Also noteworthy is that the central condition for generalizing the SCSS is using private information. We argue that this is one of the characteristics that makes the system stand out as an improvement over ESG ratings.

3.3 Private Versus Public Information, Private Versus Public Companies

There is a common misconception that credit ratings rely almost exclusively on quantitative information, with their outputs robustly derived from unambiguous statistical models. However, as Ganguin and Bilardello (2005) and many others have noted, "a diligent credit evaluation of a company's financial performance and profile cannot and should not be done without an understanding of the level of qualitative risk inherent in the entity." ESG ratings are mainly designed for investors and fund managers to use. Naturally, they are based on public information. It is also why several sustainability-related ratings are only available for public companies; they are mostly (but not exclusively) built from self-reported ESG indicators. However, credit ratings that extend to companies of all sizes would be precious for banks and institutional investors.

The SCSS has been designed to encompass ratings for all companies, public and private, large and small. Its methodology is initially designed for account managers of commercial banks to input the required information to generate the final scores. Thus, it uses account managers' private information on their clients. Account managers are responsible for completing the questionnaires, which tap into their private information and generate standard scores. In that sense, it is similar to how regular credit ratings are implemented.

Generalizing the SCSS requires resolving the tension between public and private information. Limiting it to the former would likely make it easier to redesign it but would limit its adoption by commercial banks and other financial institutions. After all, only a fraction of banks' clients are listed companies. Institutions must create credit reports for all their lending operations. Banks mainly acquire credit bureaus' reports when available for small and medium-sized companies and complement them with proprietary information or build their reports.

There are significant limits to public information about companies' environmental and social impacts. Robust credit reports require consistent data for backtesting, but firms' ESG disclosure practices are not uniform (Zeidan, 2022b). For instance, firm-level variables explain most variation in ESG disclosure (Yu & Luu, 2021), disclosure scores are sensitive to outliers (Baldini et al., 2018), and profitable and mature firms disseminate more climate-related information (Drempetic et al., 2019).

Standardized private information allows for the evolution of robust credit ratings. Part of the appeal of the SCSS is that it is supposed to be used by commercial banks that can train their account managers and improve the ratings from each round of ratings they generate. Thus, the main challenge with generalizing the SCSS for different end users is dealing with disparate expectations, abilities, and access to private information. In Sect. 3.3, we describe how we resolve these issues, although only higher adoption would allow researchers to check for the robustness of the final rating system.

3.4 How Do Banks Incorporate Information into "Green" Lending Today?

There is no significant need to motivate green credit rating systems as many firms face climate and other nonfinancial risks. However, the recent scientific literature brings many suggestive insights. This subsection summarizes much of recent works about sustainable lending and is thus reasonably citation-heavy. You should skip it if your goal is the technical description of sustainability-related credit rating systems.

Climate and credit risk may be highly correlated (Capasso et al., 2020), which could drive banks to accelerate incorporating climate factors in regular credit risk models. In fact, it is somewhat of a puzzle why that has not already happened, with some authors arguing that organizational inertia is a more substantial barrier than previously thought. More importantly, Capasso et al. (2020) find that the positive relationship between corporate default risk and carbon footprint is more robust following the Paris Agreement, which may support the argument that banks must adapt or die.

Some of that risk is already priced in the bonds issued by the largest companies. Apergis et al. (2022) find that firms within the S&P 500 with solid ESG scores benefit from lower bond spreads and better bond ratings than firms with weaker ESG scores. Of course, most companies worldwide do not issue bonds, even though the market for green bonds is maturing [e.g., Ehlers and Packer (2016, 2017), Hachenberg and Schiereck (2018) and Chang et al. (2021)] and expanding (Barua & Chiesa, 2019).

There is one counterargument to the need for commercial banks to incorporate nonfinancial performance into standard credit rating systems: banks already charge higher interest rates to firms with higher environmental risks.

Weber et al., (2010, 2015) indicate that sustainability criteria can be used to predict the financial performance of a debtor and improve the predictive validity of the credit rating process. Weber (2012) notes that Canadian banks systematically examine environmental risks for credits, loans, and mortgages. Still, there are no clear benchmarks (at the time).

For instance, Fard et al. (2020) show, using a sample of 27 countries between 1990 and 2014, that banks charge higher interest rates and adjust other contractual features when lending to firms facing more stringent environmental regulations. In addition, they show that firms facing such regulations have fewer participants in their loan syndicates, higher bankruptcy risk, and lower credit ratings despite reducing their leverage. Thus, they conclude that banks' lending practices are already environmentally sensitive. In addition, Guiral et al. (2021) suggest that lenders use CSR performance as a proxy for borrowers' integrity. However, although Semet et al. (2021) confirm that extra-financial criteria are integrated into bond pricing, they find that credit rating agencies undermine the impact of climate change and environmental topics on a country's creditworthiness.

Another relevant empirical evidence for the present context comes from Wellalage and Kumar (2021). On a sample of 3915 unlisted firms, they found that companies with better environmental performance received approximately 6.4% higher loans (as a ratio of total sales) but that ecological performance does not affect loan duration and collateral requirement, indicating no spillover economic effect of corporate environmental performance on loan conditions.

Although there is evidence that ESG indicators are already incorporated into credit risk models, banks don't necessarily do that systematically. For instance, Zhou et al. (2022) show that information and expertise asymmetries limit commercial banks' abilities to evaluate the credit risk of green lending. Moreover, almost all the discussions on "green" lending and bonds focus on downside risks from incorporating ESG "risks" (for a discussion on why ESG indicators are not risk factors, see Zeidan, 2022b) into regular credit risk models.

Ultimately, we have indirect evidence that commercial banks already use nonfinancial information for lending decisions, which isn't surprising. Still, the most substantial evidence is that banks use that information indirectly. Take Fard et al. (2020), for instance. They find that financial institutions use environmental regulation as a proxy for climate-related risks. Banks control some of the ESG indicators in corporate lending. We argue that generalizing credit score systems to incorporate socio-environmental information comprehensively for banks can make financial markets more relevant in mitigating climate change. In addition, rating systems should incorporate upside possibilities and not solely downside risks. Banks don't have robust incentives to use ESG indicators in lending decisions because that would only make credit scarcer and more expensive. Ideally, banks would reduce interest rates for more sustainable and innovative companies through better credit ratings and not only look at increased default probabilities. Thus, we discuss how to generalize sustainability credit systems based on the SCSS (Zeidan et al., 2015), which uses internal information and upside possibilities to generate companies' nonfinancial ratings.

3.5 The Original SCSS

"We already incorporate ESG indicators into our lending procedures," claimed a senior executive for a large development bank in Latin America. "How so?" he was asked. "We make borrowers sign a form stating that they don't use forced labor, comply with environmental regulations, and more." "Do you really think this changes firms' behavior?" I asked the classroom, not the executive, directly. Of course, the consensus was that such a form was not enough.

Commercial banks' lending relies on credit rating systems developed to estimate risk against borrowers' defaults. As seen before, Basel III standards require that banks calculate the loss parameters: the probability of default (PD), loss given default (LGD), and exposure at default (EAD). Usually, banks rely on creditworthiness as the main criteria, and all information for the decision-making is related to financial information or qualitative data on how likely borrowers can repay their loans.

The Sustainability Credit Score System (SCSS) was initially commissioned by a multinational bank that validated its methodology. The project was then published as a scientific article in the Journal of Business Ethics and was later generalized into an open platform. This section describes the original method applied to the sugar industry and the steps toward generalizing the SCSS. Of course, such a method is not the only way to incorporate sustainability into the lending process; other methods differ primarily in the details, not their essence. The SCSS was later transformed into an open platform. The system allows us to generate sustainability-related stand-alone credit scores for companies of all sizes and all industries. The final scores are normalized to the interval between 0 and 1. The outcomes can then be mapped into standard credit ratings (usually triple-A to D).

The original system was developed for a multinational bank. The methodology was supposed to extract the information already possessed by the bank. How? By tapping into the knowledge of each firm through its account manager. The idea behind the model was straightforward: account managers already carry detailed knowledge about each client. They visit firms, know the owners, and likely deal with suppliers and customers. Account managers would have approved loans for types of equipment, innovation processes, and more. For the original SCSS, we interviewed account managers who dealt with companies in the sugar industry and the companies' owners.

For instance, take two examples: company A had much lower environmental standards than the average company in the sector. The interview with the account manager revealed all its details, and the company was rated well below average on an initial mock questionnaire. For instance, the firm was involved in legal embroglios regarding its land, and it still used an old technique for dealing with the sugarcane leaves: burning. The account manager was aware of these and other company business practices. Company B was above average in terms of its environmental management practices. For example, it has installed a system for reusing vinasse, a highly acidic by-product of sugar manufacturing (some other companies just threw it in rivers or used it to settle dirty roads). The account manager rated the company much higher than average, with explicit knowledge of this and other business practices by the company.

The initial design of the SCSS was then to have account managers answer a comprehensive but relatively short and straightforward customized questionnaire about the nonfinancial performance of the companies they managed. Account managers already fill out the forms for regular credit scores, which include more than just accounting information. Because their time was valuable, the SCSS was engineered to be as streamlined as possible without losing effectiveness. Such characteristics were maintained in the transformation to an open platform.

Generalizing the SCSS for companies in all sectors and all types of analysts required the introduction of new weights and categories. We describe the generalization process later.

The bank aimed to complement regular credit rating models by yielding qualitative and quantitative information to improve decision-making. Ideally, for each potential borrower, the credit department would generate two ratings, a regular one and a sustainability one. The sustainability rating could allow banks to distinguish between more and less sustainable companies, with the institutions modulating credit supply and price to this extra piece of information.

For example, let's assume that companies would be rated similarly to regular credit models, with sustainability worthiness ranging from triple-A (prime borrowers) to D (default). Assume a company with a low sustainability rating and below investment grade (usually in the BB range or lower). For this company, this could mean increased interest rates or denial of credit even if the company is otherwise creditworthy. Conversely, companies with high sustainability ratings could get preferred treatment regarding costs or access to capital.

The SCSS may reduce information asymmetry by engaging stakeholders, but its primary purpose is to minimize banks' risks by lowering default rates. Rating scales are commonly used in the financial industry. We follow the standard approach for developing a credit score based on the analytic hierarchy process methodology. There are always important issues related to the development of scale measures [e.g., Churchill and Peter (1984) and Sanjeev (2003)]. As this or similar systems are adopted, available data should allow us to measure reliability and validity.

The final result is a credit score system that rates companies and is composed of six matrices for the six sustainability dimensions; each matrix $A_i = \left(a_{ij}\right)_{1 \leq i.j \leq n}$, in which $a_{ij} = \begin{cases} 1 \text{ if } i = j \\ {}^{1}/_{a_{ji}} \text{if } i \neq j \end{cases}$, and a weighting matrix for the six dimensions.

For each dimension, A_i is composed of 5 questions. A final questionnaire of 30 questions is developed from the analytical model, giving us a final sustainability credit score ranging from 0 to 1. It is used to assess a company's sustainability in the selected industry.

While institutions may adopt the Equator Principles or other ESG commitments as a signal to shareholders and stakeholders, the SCSS is a regular score system to determine the credit score of potential clients. This approach differs from the Equator Principles, which establish that projects over US$10 million should be analyzed through short-term sustainability impacts. The SCSS measures most companies in the industry, even small companies, and focuses on risks and opportunities for future sustainability. Given the industry's sustainability factors, the SCSS aims to measure each firm's potential contribution to sustainable economic production. Because sustainability is multidimensional and dynamic, there is no unique way to measure the impact of a single firm. For the present work, Fig. 3.6 below summarizes the analytical process that generates questions for the scoring system.

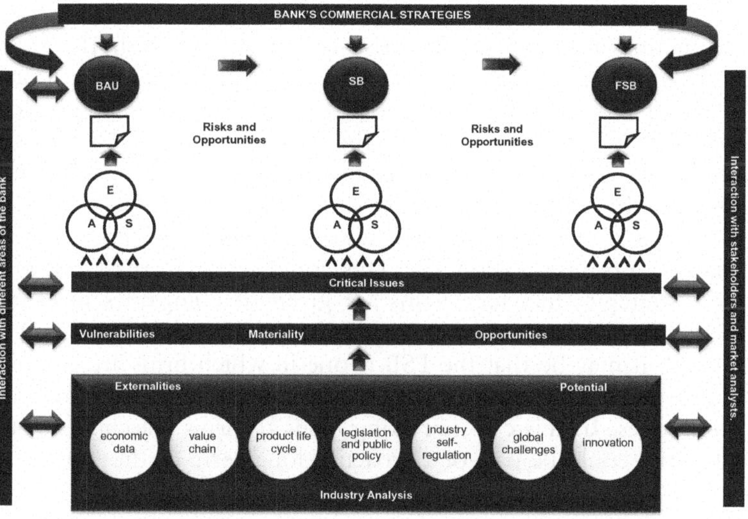

Fig. 3.6 Analytical Methodology for the Sustainability Credit Score System (*Source* Zeidan et al. [2015])

The methodology is based on a bottom-up approach. First is the industry analysis, followed by defining critical issues regarding the industry and its long-term sustainable path. We then distill these issues into their environmental, economic, and social aspects and relate them to the three main paths for sustainable development: business as usual (BAU), sustainable business (SB), and future sustainable business (FSB). Due to the inherent uncertainty of forecasting, we adopta generic conception of these development stages.

BAU refers to the present stage in which the industry practices are directly related to past practices, which may or may not be sustainable. SB is a future stage (mid-term, around 2030) resulting from firms adopting new sustainable practices. These are mainly derived from emerging technologies, new commercial practices, and evolving legislation. FSB is a future stage (long-term, around 2050) marked by the foreseen role of the industry in a sustainable path that would allow continuing economic, social, and environmental development (WBCSD, 2010).

From this relationship, we deduce risks and opportunities, which are the source of the credit score system. The main contribution of this methodology is that the resulting credit score system can help develop proactive short- and long-term commercial practices. We turn to this later, but a simple example of long-term commercial practices follows. By conducting a long-term analysis, we try to establish the possible future sustainability of the industry itself. For instance, let us assume that our study of the sugar industry shows that its long-term yield productivity will be low. The only way for the industry to survive is to expand geographically into protected environments and displace other cultures. In this case, the FSB analysis would show that firms could only achieve FSB practices if they change their core business by focusing on more sustainability-promising products. This could result in the development of credit strategies in which loans are given to companies investing in changing their business model toward a more sustainable one. On the other hand, it may be that the FSB is one in which firms are technological leaders and could obtain much better yields by focusing on new crops and techniques. In this case, directing loans to firms searching for those opportunities could be part of a proactive long-term credit policy.

3.5.1 Methodology of the SCSS

The Sustainability Credit Score System (SCSS) is developed through the following stages:

- Selecting the industry;
- Analyzing the industry: economic outlook, product life-cycle analysis, value chain, legislation, public policy, industry self-regulation, and innovation.
- Developing paths for the average firm: business as usual (BAU), sustainable business (SB), and future sustainable business (FSB).
- Defining variables related to individual firms in each of six sustainability dimensions: economic growth (EG), environmental protection (EP), social progress (SP), socioeconomic development (SD), eco-efficiency (EE), and socio-environmental development (SD).
- Unveiling the materiality issues of the average firm, plus vulnerabilities and opportunities regarding the industry's sustainability.
- Combining the information in the steps above to obtain questions for the composition of the scoring system.
- Defining the weights for the analytical hierarchy process.

The main output is the credit score, which ranges from 0 to 1. Scores are supposed to rank firms in terms of their sustainability. The central advantage of the SCSS is that financial institutions are free to incorporate it into their more established credit models by distilling all the information into a questionnaire that results in a comparable number for each firm. This process allows banks to change lending practices at a granular level, including short-term strategies based on local branches—for instance, the funding of new projects related to R&D or the transportation of vinasse in the case of the sugar industry, detailed later. It can also lead to developments in long-term policies, such as funding research centers and lending to companies in frontier regions.

Building a model based on the analytic hierarchy process (AHP) method requires structuring and evaluation. The AHP demands pair comparisons among criteria/alternatives that belong to the same hierarchical level. Regarding the former, we decompose the critical issues and risks into a hierarchical structure. As for the latter, we define the relationship between the hierarchies. The following steps are:

We compare the relative importance of eco-efficiency (EE), socio-environmental (SA), socio-economics (SE), environmental protection (PA), economic growth (CE), and social progress (PS). At the end of this phase, we obtain a 6 × 6 comparison matrix.

Next, we compare the critical issues for the six previous dimensions. For instance, for social progress, three questions are compared—which, in turn, results in a 3 × 3 comparison matrix.

Finally, the firm's development level, relative to the sustainability criteria relevant to the sugar industry, is established for each question. In this case, for each question, the possible answers are classified as "below business as usual (nBAU)," "business as usual (BAU)," "sustainable business (SB)," and "potential future sustainable business (FSB)."

We establish six dimensions as ideal because they suit the AHP methodology and allow for the seamless establishment of two hierarchies based on ESG indicators. The first level is the intersection between environmental, social, and governance dimensions, and the second incorporates factors related to only one dimension. For instance, socioeconomic and socio-environmental factors are hierarchically superior to social or environmental factors by convention.

Then, we must assign weights to the different development paths and sustainability dimensions for the final measurements. We use subjective criteria. The subjective criteria can be validated by testing the questionnaire in the field through successive iterations of the process. Model validation is paramount to risk modeling using subjective criteria (Jones & Mingo, 1999). In the present case, the absence of extensive quantitative data makes the validation process even more critical. The bank's research department conducted the original validation process. However, as we will describe later, the SCSS is an evolving tool, with changes being incorporated to reflect the feedback from the application of the questionnaires.

The analytical methodology has one main goal: to support the development of a questionnaire that, when applied to the sugar industry firms, reveals their creditworthiness based on sustainability issues.

The comparison matrix has the following generic format:

$$A = \left(a_{ij}\right)_{1 \le i.j \le n}$$

Table 3.1 Saaty's relative importance table

Intensity	*Relative importance*
1	Equal relative importance
3	Slightly superior relative importance
5	Strong relative importance
7	Very strong relative importance
9	Absolute relative importance

where

$$a_{ij} = \begin{cases} 1 \text{ if } i = j \\ {}^{1}/_{a_{ji}} \text{ if } i \neq j \end{cases}$$

The numerical values in the comparison matrix can be obtained in Table 3.1:

We build a six-dimension comparison matrix. Two premises are assumed before the comparisons are carried out: the first defines that the intersections between two dimensions of sustainability are preferable to singular dimensions because practices in the first fields tend to balance distinct objectives better. The second premise prescribes that, when compared, the areas of intersection of dimensions and singular dimensions have similar relative importance. The approach allows us to avoid focusing on a specific aspect (for instance, prioritization of economic growth).

We obtain the following six-dimension comparison matrix (Table 3.2).

For the comparison matrix above, in line with the AHP, the normalized relative-weight vector may be obtained (Table 3.3).

The inconsistency level is 0% (below the usual 10% level, the maximum accepted level in the AHP methodology).

Table 3.2 Six-dimension comparison matrix

	EE	*SA*	*SE*	*PA*	*CE*	*PS*
EE	1	1	1	3	3	3
SA	1	1	1	3	3	3
SE	1	1	1	3	3	3
PA	1/3	1/3	1/3	1	1	1
CE	1/3	1/3	1/3	1	1	1
PS	1/3	1/3	1/3	1	1	1

Table 3.3 The normalized relative-weight vector

PS	*0.25*
SE	0.25
CE	0.25
EE	0.08
OS	0.08
AS	0.08

The next phase requires the preparation of comparison matrices for the indicators associated with each dimension considered. For each indicator, four relative degrees—relative to nBAU, BAU, SB, and FSB—are assigned, as well as the relationship to GRI.

The Global Reporting Initiative is an international organization that publishes standards about business nonfinancial impacts on society. We establish that the most relevant factors for a particular industry are picked from the GRI indicators related to that dimension. Once all factors are selected and the weights determined, we must write the questionnaires that account managers will use to generate firm-specific sustainability ratings. This last step is not presented here, as the questions are too particular to the reality of SMEs in the sugar industry in Brazil. The questions used in generalizing the SCSS are given in Sect. 3.6.

Concerning the comparison matrices and the weights for the sugar industry, we arrive at the following:

3.5.1.1 Eco-efficiency

Use of water (EN9)

Improvements to cultivation and production equipment (EN18)

Productivity and sugar cane variety (EN14)

The comparison matrix is in Tables 3.4 and 3.1

The normalized relative-weight vector is in Table 3.5.

The level of inconsistency for this last comparison matrix is 0.00%.

Table 3.4 Eco-efficiency comparison matrix

	(a)	*(b)*	*(c)*
a)	1	3	1
b)	1/3	1	1/3
c)	1	3	1

Table 3.5 Eco-efficiency normalized relative-weight

a)	42.86%
b)	14.29%
c)	42.86%

Table 3.6 Socio-environmental comparison matrix

	a)	*b)*	*c)*
a)	1	3	1
b)	1/3	1	1/3
c)	1	3	1

Table 3.7 Socio-environmental normalized relative-weight vector

a)	42.86%
b)	14.29%
c)	42.86%

3.5.1.2 Socio-environmental

Environmental impacts on the community (SO1)

Reduction in fossil fuel use (EN17 and EN29)

Elimination of burning practices (EN16)

The comparison matrix is in Table 3.6.

The normalized relative-weight vector is in Table 3.7.

The level of inconsistency for this last comparison matrix is 0.00%.

3.5.1.3 Socio-economics

Compliance (PR9)

Requalification of workers (LA11)

Influence over public policies (SO5)

The comparison matrix is in Table 3.8.

Table 3.8 Socio-economics comparison matrix

	a)	*b)*	*c)*
a)	1	1	3
b)	1	1	3
c)	1/3	1/3	1

Table 3.9 Socio-economics normalized relative-weight vector

a)	42.86%
b)	42.86%
c)	14.29%

Table 3.10 Environmental protection comparison matrix

	a)	*b)*	*c)*
a)	1	1	3
b)	1	1	3
c)	1/3	1/3	1

Table 3.11 Environmental protection normalized relative-weight vector

a)	42.86%
b)	42.86%
c)	14.29%

The normalized relative-weight vector is in Table 3.9.

The level of inconsistency for this last comparison matrix is 0.00%.

3.5.1.4 *Environmental Protection*

Reduction in the use of chemical inputs such as fertilizer and agrochemicals (EN22)

Compliance with natural resources and biodiversity protection legislation (EN28)

Production expansion without an increase in environmental impacts (EN11 to EN13)

The comparison matrix is in Table 3.10.

The normalized relative-weight vector is in Table 3.11.

The level of inconsistency for this last comparison matrix is 0.00%.

3.5.1.5 *Economic Growth*

Company governance/information transparency (LA13)

Product development and evolution (EC1)

Economic development of the community (EC7)

Table 3.12 Economic growth comparison matrix

	a)	*b)*	*c)*
a)	1	1	3
b)	1	1	3
c)	1/3	1/3	1

Table 3.13 Economic growth normalized relative-weight vector

a)	42.86%
b)	42.86%
c)	14.29%

The comparison matrix is in Table 3.12.
The normalized relative-weight vector is in Table 3.13.
The level of inconsistency for this last comparison matrix is 12.32%.

3.5.1.6 *Social Progress*

Adherence to the National Good Labor Practices Commitment (HR7)
Human-rights-related policies and procedures (HR8)
Investments in the development of communities (EC8 and EC9)
The comparison matrix is in Table 3.14.
The normalized relative-weight vector is in Table 3.15.
The level of inconsistency for this last comparison matrix is 0.00%.

Table 3.14 Social progress comparison matrix

	a)	*b)*	*c)*
a)	1	1	3
b)	1	1	3
c)	1/3	1/3	1

Table 3.15 Social progress normalized relative-weight vector

a)	42.86%
b)	42.86%
c)	14.29%

Table 3.16 Resulting matrix

	FSB	*SB*	*BAU*	*nBAU*
FSB	1	1/3	1/5	1/9
SB	3	1	1/3	1/5
BAU	5	3	1	1/3
nBAU	9	5	3	1

Table 3.17 Resulting matrix for the normalized relative-weight vector

a)	53.71%
b)	27.85%
c)	13.53%
d)	4.91%

Given these comparison matrices, the resulting matrix for the four possible answers considered—"FSB," "SB," "BAU," and "nBAU"—is in Table 3.16.

The normalized relative-weight vector of the resulting matrix is in Table 3.17.

The level of inconsistency for this last comparison matrix is 3.81%.

3.5.2 *Industry Analysis*

The Sustainability Credit Score System was initially tested using data from the Brazilian sugar and ethanol industry (referred to as the sugar industry from now on). This industry combines two characteristics that make it suitable for a first adopter. First, it presents pressing environmental, social, and economic issues (ethanol is considered a relatively clean energy source). Second, it is large enough to warrant a sustainability analysis by a commercial bank.

Throughout the 2010s, the sugar industry was responsible for approximately 2% of the Brazilian GDP. It employed around 4 million people and processed around 700 million tons of sugar cane to produce 38 million tons of sugar and 27 billion liters of ethanol annually. The industry comprises dozens of small producers and hundreds of industrial mills, making collecting information to develop rating systems costly.

Brazil is the world's largest sugar cane producer. Sugar cane crops occupy an area of 8.1 million hectares, around 1% of Brazil's territory and 2.5% of the country's arable land. Roughly two-thirds of the refined sugar output is exported.

The industry analysis methodology combines an in-depth examination of the industry practices with an analysis of the global challenges. From the countless challenges and issues regarding sustainability [e.g., KPMG (2012); OECD (2012); WBCSD (2010), among many others], thirteen are selected, either because of their global comprehensiveness (water and climate change issues) their relevance to the industry (transportation and mobility). For each one, we identify possible sources of sustainability risks but also opportunities for the dynamic development of the industry. Table 3.18 shows Brazil's originally selected global challenges for the sugar industry.

The next step is to relate these challenges to the sugar industry by establishing materiality criteria. Then, the group of critical issues is divided into a development path represented by three categories: business as usual (BAU), sustainable business (SB), and future sustainable business (FSB). Each one is defined as follows: BAU—the average firm in the industry; SB—the top tier of firms regarding sustainable practices; FSB—the average sustainable future firm, in which innovations shape the industry according to sustainability requirements. There are two main paths for development: the dissemination of sustainable practices, in which the average firm turns to sustainable practices (from BAU to SB), and the innovation path, which leads firms from their present sustainable practices to future sustainable practices (from SB to FSB).

The last informational step is to determine which of the many potential risks and opportunities would be relevant to the strategies of a commercial bank. We filter the information through two development paths—BAU to SB and SB to FSB. The risks and opportunities can be found in Table 3.19. These inform the final questions for the questionnaire aimed at account managers.

3.6 Generalizing the SCSS

Sustainability credit score systems that generate similar ratings to regular credit rating models are ideal for commercial banks to improve their lending processes. Imperatively, such systems must include upside and not only downside possibilities for the interaction between environmental and social drivers and financial performance. In addition, these systems must be able to generate ratings for companies of all sizes, not relying solely on

Table 3.18 Global challenges and the Brazilian sugar industry

	Selected challenges	*Impacts on the sugar industry*
1	Climate change	This global challenge may have negative impacts, for instance, on the biodiversity of agricultural land to produce sugar cane and the amount (reduction) of water available to irrigate crops in the *Cerrado* region. However, it may allow for new frontiers for production Also, changes in the energy matrix may create a demand for ethanol and energy from biomass as cleaner alternatives to oil and gas
2	Wealth, economy, and consumption	This challenge may represent increased labor costs and migration from this to other industries
3	Biodiversity	The decline in biodiversity and ecosystems may compromise sugar cane productivity and lead to the reduction of agricultural land to preserve threatened biomes
4	Energy	For the sugar and ethanol industry, which generates its own energy, regulatory measures issued by the Government may be a concern. Still, the possibility of an increase in demand may point toward increased business and new consumer markets. The industry shows high potential to contribute to changes in the energy matrix, supplying ethanol for transportation and producing electricity from sugar cane bagasse. One promising new product, for instance, is aviation kerosene produced from ethanol
5	Cities	This global challenge may represent, on the one hand, opportunities to increase the demand for urban mobility products and, on the other hand, disputes over scarce resources such as water
6	Water	This global challenge may represent an increase in the demand for food products. However, it may provoke heated disputes over the raw materials necessary for industrial output

(continued)

Table 3.18 (continued)

	Selected challenges	*Impacts on the sugar industry*
7	Food	The demarcation and the allocation of land for agricultural production intended to limit deforestation demand major productivity improvements in the areas destined for sugar cane cultivation. This requires investment in research on new varieties with higher sucrose content
8	Forests and deforestation	Mechanization of the sugar cane harvest is a consequence of the need to avoid burning its residues and improve labor productivity. However, one of its consequences is the elimination of low-skilled workers. Also, increases in ethanol production under new processing conditions may add green jobs to Brazil's and other economies
9	Jobs and green jobs	The impact of this challenge on the sugar and ethanol industry may affect the ethanol production costs and create pressure on the ecosystem used to produce biomass
10	Shortage of inputs	The impact of this challenge on the sugar and ethanol industry may affect ethanol production costs and create pressure on the ecosystem used to produce biomass
11	Transportation and mobility	Using machines and equipment and transporting sugar cane to the mills and from there to the market requires fossil fuels, increasing CO_2 emissions. At the same time, ethanol represents an essential source of clean energy and contributes to reducing the utilization of fossil fuels

(continued)

Table 3.18 (continued)

	Selected challenges	*Impacts on the sugar industry*
12	Population growth	Population growth may affect the industry as the increase in the consumption of renewable forms of energy results in higher demand for ethanol and, hence greater demand for land. However, new technologies may counterbalance this effect
13	Organizational governance	Corporate governance issues may result in more professional companies, especially as family-owned companies evolve. Better governance should bring transparency, ethics, and better self-regulation. The commoditization of ethanol may require compliance with global regulations related to sustainability matters

publicly available data. We provide a detailed methodology for a sustainability credit rating open platform based on analytical hierarchy processes, summarizing Zeidan and Onabolu (2023).

Zeidan and Onabolu (2023) generalize the closed-platform system in Zeidan et al. (2015) by, among other things, adding country and industry variables, two additional possible answers, and an explicit way to generate forward default probabilities. They also detail the final reports that could be used independently or alongside regular credit rating reports.

We aim to describe an implementable generalized sustainability credit score system launched as a financial service open to subscribers in early 2022, the Sona Sustainability Credit Score System. It is based initially on the SCSS (Zeidan et al., 2015). Still, it has one crucial enhancement: it has been expanded for any end user interested in generating a sustainability credit report. That includes commercial banks, insurers, investors, and any financial institution.

The SCSS model is unique because it provides a single sustainability risk assessment framework through which companies and entities of different sizes, geographies, sectors, and industries can all be reliably measured, scored, and ranked. This system enables an analyst to compare, for example, the sustainability performance of a wind farming company in

Table 3.19 Risks and opportunities for sugar firms

Risks	*Opportunities*
·Non-compliance with legislation	1. Provision of consulting advice to clients on:
·Use of sugar cane varieties inappropriate for the region	·Areas more appropriate for sugar cane cultivation
·Operation in an area where the water supply is compromised	·Varieties appropriate for given regions and biomes and new cultivation techniques
·Low productivity	
·Limited capability to manage the product mix	2. Financing and investments to help the industry:
·Sugar cane planted in areas of declivity higher than 12%	·Face productivity challenges related to the use of adequate sugar cane varieties;
·Manual harvesting is not replaced by mechanized harvesting	·Expand industrial facilities (construction of new mills, renovation of existing facilities);
·Labor practices inadequate for retaining the agricultural labor force	·Introduction of equipment embedding more advanced technologies)
·Inadequate use of water	·Produce second- and third-generation ethanol;
·Contamination of soil and groundwater by fertilizers and agrochemicals	·Replace the existing fleet with vehicles powered by renewable energy;
·Inadequate fertilization of plantations	·Mechanize production (purchase of equipment, employees' qualification program);
·Inadequate managerial and governance practices	·Develop more sustainable equipment to manage sugar cane plantations;
·Non-use of technological improvements such as new sugar cane varieties, sorghum, precision agriculture, generation of electrical power, etc.	·Tackle the high costs related to compliance, such as the use and disposal of water;
. Use of obsolete equipment throughout the production process	·Change the fertilization processes (construction of vinasse ducts)
·Failure to obtain environmental licenses	·Introduce international governance standards and data transparency;
·Inappropriate contracts with sugar cane suppliers	·Close the water and natural resources cycles in industrial processes;

(continued)

Table 3.19 (continued)

Risks	*Opportunities*
·Negligence in tracking the impacts of climatic changes	·Research on soil type and adequate amounts of fertilizer
·Co-responsibility in lawsuits filed against companies in the industry	
·Illegal use of transgenic varieties;	3. Tracking information on:
·Contamination of soil and groundwater and failure to preserve water;	·Technologies suitable for trucks, machines, and equipment powered by ethanol;
·Uncontrolled product quality and safety during distribution;	·The development of new markets and products from sugar cane;
·Dismissal of large numbers of employees without adequate requalification;	·Initiatives to qualify workers, intra-industry programs, institutions, and NGOs;
·Burning of sugar cane leaves before harvest;	·Research on new sugar cane varieties and new cultivation techniques;
·Use of machines that damage the soil;	·Climate change
·Production of sugar using toxic elements or contaminants	
Financing of companies that are:	
Operating illegally;	
Adopting illegal labor practices and/or committing human rights abuses;	
Using new technologies illegal according to the current legislation;	
Distributing adulterated ethanol or evading sales taxes	

Ghana and a mining company in Norway, all on the same measurement scale.

The central trade-offs in expanding a credit score system refer to the nature of information and the compatibility between scores generated by different analysts. When used by a commercial bank, training analysts or account managers who will input the data to guarantee compatibility and refine the final product is straightforward. In addition, the SCSS has been tested in a single sector, the sugar industry in Brazil. Expanding the system for any industry in all countries and the information asymmetry across end users provides formidable challenges.

There are several challenges to generalizing the SCSS from closed to open platforms, from single to multi-industries, and from one to any country. The crucial ones are the number and content of the sustainability paths, which must be redefined, questions and weights must be redesigned, and a new set of country-specific weights must be created. The following subsection provides a guide for creating an open platform where end users can generate an organization's sustainability credit score.

3.6.1 The Initial Guide to Inputting Information for the SCSS

The model is based on relative comparisons. Thus, comparisons between indicators must be consistent for meaningful results. The analyst must choose, for each indicator, one of four options: NBAU (which indicates that a company is worse than the industry's average), BAU, SB, or FSB. The simplest way to interpret these options is to rank companies below average, average, above average, and among the best. For each of the 18 indicators, which expands on the initial set in Zeidan et al. (2015), an analyst must choose one of the four alternatives for the company under examination.

However, before answering the specific questions regarding the company for which the sustainability credit rating is being generated, the analyst must answer a few questions that will establish the comparison group for the company under examination.

The antecedent process is due to the credit rating, as is standard, making relative comparisons. Thus, there must be clear benchmarks for each company to be ranked. There are two categories to build the comparison groups (usually for companies in the same industry).

The first category determines if the evaluated company faces the steepest, major, or minor sustainability challenges. For that purpose, three primary variables must be considered: where the company is located, the industry that is the primary source of profits for the company (for instance, by considering the NAICS or SIC identification codes), and the relevant products or services that are the primary sources of environmental and social issues.

It should be noted that the system is qualitative, as is the case with many facets of credit rating systems. In that sense, there are no unique, unambiguous criteria for some classifications below. Still, the system is robust as long as analysts are consistent (as the number of responses increases, consensus calls can be developed to improve the system).

Thus, to make the process of filling out the questionnaire simple and efficient, the analyst must consider the binary choices below:

Region: 0 if the company operates in a region with low-quality institutions; 1 otherwise.

Industry: 0 if the industry is rife with environmental or social challenges (mining, oil & gas, land-intensive agricultural production, etc.); 1 otherwise.

Products: 0 if the production and sales of the firm's primary goods and services bring significant negative externalities; 1 otherwise.

Usually, there will be a strong correlation between industry and products, but not always. For instance, a company that repairs oil platforms may be classified as part of an industry rife with environmental challenges. Still, their services may not pose significant challenges to the ecosystem.

The initial classification will result in the following comparison groups, ordered through the sum of the binary variables (S = Region + Industry + Product; $0 \leq S \leq 3$):

1—The most significant sustainability challenges ($S = 0$)
2—Major sustainability challenges ($S = 1$)
3—Minor sustainability challenges ($S > 1$)

The second goal is related to the information at the analyst's disposal. There are three possible alternatives: no company-specific information ($D = 0$), low-quality information ($D = 1$), and high-quality information ($D = 2$). In many cases, there will not be detailed and trustworthy information about some indicators ($D = 0$), but there will be information about others ($D > 0$). BAU is the standard classification when no actionable information exists for a specific indicator. When there is information available, there are two options:

Low-quality information ($D = 1$): this category incorporates company-generated data that cannot be audited, secondary information, such as reports from industry associations that are not detailed, or other types of information that are better than having no information but cannot be trusted wholesale.

High-quality information ($D = 2$): data tied explicitly to the indicator under consideration from reputable sources that can be trusted at face value. Data generated by the company can be classified as high-quality if the information is transparent, data cannot be easily manipulated, and/or reputable third parties have supervised or audited the data generation process or final reports.

The comparison groups above lead to the following rules for filling out the questionnaire. For a specific indicator:

3.6.1.1 FSB

Analysts should classify companies in this category only if high-quality information is available.

Even so, when S = 0, this category is unavailable unless there are exceptional circumstances.

When S = 1, companies must be in the top 5% among their comparison group to be classified as FSB. Companies should be the main driving force behind decarbonizing their industries for that particular indicator or present an innovative way to deal with the issue at hand.

When S > 1, companies must show actual pursuits to lower their negative environment or social impact to be classified as FSB. Information should describe the companies' actions and how they track the effects of their measures.

3.6.1.2 SB

When S = 0, this category is only available if high-quality information indicates that the company is committed to reducing its harmful environmental or social impact. There should be clear evidence that the company does not incur greenwashing. Information should describe the companies' actions and how they track the effects of their measures.

When S = 1, this category is only available if the information indicates that the company is committed to reducing its deleterious environmental or social impact. Information should describe the companies' actions and how they track the effects of their measures.

When S > 1, the analyst should classify the company as S.B. if it exceeds that indicator's industry standards.

3.6.1.3 BAU

BAU is the standard answer if the analyst has no reason to consider that the company differs from its peers for that indicator.

If high-quality information is available, a company should be classified as BAU if there are no significant risks to its operations or society related to the specific indicator under consideration.

If there is low-quality information, the analyst must consider material risks to society from the company's operations regarding that indicator.

3.6.1.4 NBAU

The analyst should select NBAU with evidence of higher risks than comparable companies for the indicator under consideration, e.g., evidence of repeated fines about the issue, the use of old production methods, the hidden effects of their operations, and active opposition to improved regulatory standards.

Below are some developed questions so analysts can rank companies regarding their nonfinancial performance. Unfortunately, there is no initial way to generate questions that yield unambiguous responses. However, that is not a significant hurdle. As with every credit score system, questions are supposed to be refined as results accumulate. For instance, if there is an indication that the dispersion of the answers from analysts for certain companies is exceptionally high, the questions can be rewritten to limit ambiguity.

The examples below describe the first version of the questions related to the eco-efficiency dimension (Fig. 3.7).

3.6.2 Adding Options and Further Changes After Initial Tests

The five key areas of further development required to generalize the SCSS covered in this paper are the inclusions of country impact, industry and sector impact, additional rating answer options, sustainability forward default probability, and credit rating score comparisons. Within each area are certain limitations and testing requirements in the application to company ratings to normalize relative to the rating of industry peers.

3.6.2.1 Country Impact

When starting a new company rating, the user is asked to select the country where the rated company is based or headquartered. There are 193 countries on the list of country options. According to the U.N. Country Sustainability Report, each country is ranked by its overall score. The overall score measures the progress toward achieving all 17 Sustainable Development Goals (SDGs) as a percentage of SDG achievement, where a score of 100 indicates that all SDGs have been completed. At the top of this list in descending order are Finland, Denmark, Sweden, and Norway, with scores ranging from 86.51(%) to 82.35(%) as of 2022.

The country selected impacts the company's final score, which is rated based on the difference between the relevant country's sustainability development score and the average (mean) score of all 193 countries,

1. Eco-Efficiency			
Water management			
NBAU	BAU	SB	FSB
Does not meet the legal requirements	Compliance with law	Has concrete actions to make consumption and water capacity compatible	Leader in its industry regarding water management
Waste management			
NBAU	BAU	SB	FSB
Does not meet the legal requirements/ poses a grave risk to adjacent ecosystems.	Compliance with law/ Accepts the possibility of disasters	Creates little waste and/or promising practices impede potential disasters.	Leader in its industry regarding waste management. E.g., reuses most waste generated; uses it as biofuel in small electricity generation plants, etc.
Land use, including deforestation			
NBAU	BAU	SB	FSB
Company is set on contested areas; regular conflicts with locals; uncertain if operations are linked to deforestation.	Compliance with the law and/or following standard practices.	Investments in land revitalization, including reforesting in company land, if applicable. Must go beyond regulatory standards. Publishes comprehensive public reports.	Has concrete actions to foster biodiversity; publishes and tracks biodiversity action plans (focus on actions); prioritizes, monitors, and schedules actions related to land-use improvements.
Disaster Resilience			
NBAU	BAU	SB	FSB
The company's operations are particularly prone to natural disasters like floods and hurricanes.	Compliance with the law and/or following standard practices.	Risk management practices include concrete plans for natural disasters and built-in redundancies. Service provision may not suffer from disaster risks. The company is well-insured financially.	Has concrete actions to mitigate natural disaster risks, working alongside the community and regulators to maintain its "social capital" even if natural disasters occur.
Certifications			
NBAU	BAU	SB	FSB
Company does not have standard certifications and thus cannot access specific markets. Company is regularly fined for lack of environmental certifications.	Compliance with the law and/or following standard practices.	Company has advantages over its competitors for holding certifications that are not standard. Company works with NGOs and other stakeholders to improve its operations and the supply chain.	Company is proactive in disseminating best practices. Holds almost all certifications and is the industry leader in the subject.

Fig. 3.7 Initial version of Eco-efficiency questions for the generalized SCSS (*Source* Zeidan and Onabolu [2023])

divided into two parts. For example, if the country of the company being rated is Japan, which has a country score of 79.85(%), this is subtracted from the average (mean) score of 62.09(%) and divided by 2, giving a final country impact score of +8.88(%). Suppose the company's country score is lower than the average (mean) country score. In that case, this will reduce the final sustainability rating of the company in question. For example, suppose the company's country being rated is Liberia, with a 48.65(%) score. In that case, this is subtracted from the average (mean) score of 62.09(%) and divided by 2, giving a final country impact score of -6.72(%).

The current approach is pragmatic. The final country impact score is added to (or subtracted from) the result of the Sustainability Credit Score System, producing a final score and rating. Therefore, two companies are identical in all other sustainability metrics aside from the countries they are based on have different sustainability credit scores. It seems unfair to discriminate against companies geographically, but this is today's market reality. The current approach approximates the difference between sovereign ratings, incorporating these into individual credit ratings, as is standard practice.

3.6.2.2 Industry and Sector Impact

Similarly to the country's impact score, the industry and sector affect the final sustainability credit score.

Economic activities can broadly be classified in several ways. One of the more widely used classification methods puts industries into one of three sectors: primary (extraction and agriculture), secondary (manufacturing), and tertiary (services). Some add quaternary (knowledge) or quinary (culture and research) sectors. Different industry classification methods include the International Standard Industrial Classification of All Economic Activities (ISIC), the North American Industry Classification System (NAICS), the Standard Industrial Classification (SIC), and the Bloomberg Industry Classification Standard (BICS). Users are asked to select the relevant industry from 60 options.

All industry options belong to one of the three sectors. The weightings differ for each sector based on the companies' exposure to the indicators within the six dimensions. For example, industries in the manufacturing sector have the highest exposure to environmental dimension impacts (environmental protection and eco-efficiency). In contrast, service companies have higher exposure to social dimension impacts (socioeconomic and social progress).

3.6.2.3 Additional Rating Answer Options

The four rating options initially available for the SCSS are NBAU, BAU, SB, and FSB. Two additional rating options are introduced: Sustainability

Table 3.20 Weight matrices for the six dimensions and initial four options for analysts

	EE	*SE*	*ES*	*EP*	*EG*	*SP*
EE	1	1	1	3	3	3
SE	1	1	1	3	3	3
ES	1	1	1	3	3	3
EP	1/3	1/3	1/3	1	1	1
EG	1/3	1/3	1/3	1	1	1
SP	1/3	1/3	1/3	1	1	1

	FSB	*SB*	*BAU*	*nBAU*
FSB	1	1/3	1/5	1/9
SB	3	1	1/3	1/5
BAU	5	3	1	1/3
nBAU	9	5	3	1

Default (SD), indicating an adverse sustainability event in the past 12 months, and a Not Applicable (N/A) option, where the specific indicator in question is irrelevant to the rating entity.

The inclusion of the Sustainability Default rating options in the analytical methodology increases the lower end of the range of possible results (of the sustainability credit score) from 1/100 (1%) up to 100/100 (100%). An SD rating represents a score of 1%, NBAU is 25%, a BAU of 50%, S.B. 75%, and FSB 100%. This scale allows for a standardized measurement framework that can be reliably and intuitively tested across companies and sectors.

Moreover, the N/A option is available for all indicators across the six dimensions. Thus, non-relevant indicators have no impact on the final score. Finally, for consistency, the weight matrices for the AHP are standardized, as shown below (Table 3.20), following Zeidan et al. (2015).

3.6.2.4 *Forward Default Probability*

Another feature of the generalized SCSS is the creation of credit reports that include a Sustainability Forward Default Probability, the probability of a sustainability default occurring over five years for the rated company.

A sustainability default explicitly indicates the company's exposure to adverse ESG or sustainability events. Infamous such events include the

Deepwater Horizon oil spill in 2010 and Volkswagen falsifying emission tests due to poor governance, resulting in a loss of $33.3 billion in fines, penalties, financial settlements, and buyback costs. It can be extended to incorporate climate risks, such as the severe flooding in Thailand in 2011, which disrupted automotive and technology supply chain networks, causing an estimated $46.5 billion in economic damages.

The methodology used to assess a company's sustainability forward default probability works by looking at the sustainability ratings of a database of public companies for each year over the past ten years and calculating their average percentage of sustainability default events over the period.

This methodology's primary limitation is the assumption that past averages are informative. As the landscape of ESG and sustainability is evolving rapidly, we will likely see less correlation between market responses to past climate and social events. To overcome this limitation, the plan is to conduct quarterly regression analyses on the historical sustainability performance of the universe of companies.

3.6.3 Credit Rating Score Comparisons

For a particular company, the sustainability score is the weighted average of the 30 indicators (questions) under the six dimensions (economic growth, environmental protection, social progress, socioeconomic development, eco-efficiency, and socio-environmental). This score is then adjusted for a country's impact and normalized relative to industry peers.

The final sustainability score for the entity (e.g., 77%) is matched to a corresponding final sustainability rating (e.g., A+), a credit grade equivalent (e.g., upper medium grade), and a classification of whether or not this equates to an investment grade rating or not. The final sustainability score of the assessed entity corresponds to a rating between AAA (extremely strong) and D (sustainability default). All ratings between AAA and BBB- are considered "investment grade," and those between BB+ and D are considered non-investment grade. These assessments of company performance are not absolute but explicitly intended to be relative to the standards and performance of a company's industry peers.

The choice for this particular scoring system is straightforward: it is similar to the standard credit rating systems used by global rating agencies.

3.6.4 Initial Adjustments

The primary objective of the generalized SCSS is to assess companies' sustainability and ESG exposure and opportunities, generate consistent, reliable results, and provide valuable insights on the sustainability creditworthiness of a given counterparty.

Even though the goal is for a system that can be used to generate ratings for companies of all sizes, the framework of the generalized SCSS model was initially tested on a database of 100+ public companies, with over 1000+ Monte Carlo simulations conducted in six months following the initial assessments. Although the general framework of the initial model has remained unchanged, there have been several refinements to the weightings applied to both the country and sector/industry inputs to align further the assessments and results of company performance relative to industry peers.

Macro data at the segment and geographic levels are continuously collected from academic and NGO datasets (e.g., World Bank, Transparency International, and US EPA), company disclosures (sustainability reports, proxy reports, AGM results, etc.), government databases, and other stakeholder sources regarding specific companies. For the model, essential data includes weekly monitoring of controversies or sustainability default events by companies or other government entities.

The Sustainability Credit Risk Committee reviews all new industry developments and model changes. In subsequent steps, a formal in-depth quality review occurs, including quality checks of data and rating results, industry and market-lead oversight, and sustainability accounting standards and reports. Furthermore, the plan is to conduct an in-depth annual framework review. This review will examine the critical issues assigned to the various dimensions and indicators and the weights applied to each sector and industry model. This process may also identify emerging issues and those that have become less significant.

The framework helps attenuate information biases by extracting private information from the credit score system's analysts. Many outsiders, such as account managers and analysts, have firm-specific information, but there is no structured way to extract it into a coherent framework. Remaining expertise biases could be limited by using robustness checks on the reports generated by the end users of the generalized SCSS. For instance, if dozens of analysts create reports for the same company, we can improve the model by checking for omissions in the questionnaires or patterns from the inputted answers. Finally, the system could also be used by firms, with workers independently filling out the questionnaires so managers could create reports for internal use.

3.6.5 *Analysis of the Final Generalized SCSS*

Ideally, commercial banks would generate sustainability-related ratings or modify their existing credit rating systems to incorporate nonfinancial performance explicitly. The present section details all the steps required to generalize a sustainability credit rating system (based on Zeidan et al., 2015) from a closed to an open platform.

The first step to generalize the SCSS includes adding three primary variables: where the company is located, the industry that is the primary source of profits for the company (for instance, by considering the NAICS or SIC identification codes), and the relevant products or services that are the primary sources of environmental and social issues. The second step is the inclusion of two rating answer options. Then, we determine the weightings for arriving at a sustainability forward default probability and make credit rating score comparisons.

The main output is the Sustainability Forward Default Probability for the rated company. That reflects the possibility of a sustainability default occurring over five years. It should be noted that the system is qualitative, as is the case with many facets of credit rating systems. In that sense, there are no unique, unambiguous criteria for some classifications below. Still, the system is robust as long as analysts are consistent (as the number of responses increases, consensus calls can be developed to improve the system).

The current model may provide a way for society to overcome the ESG trap, the low information content of environmental reports that limits the ability of investors and financial institutions to improve decision-making related to nonfinancial indicators [e.g., Rezaee and Tuo (2019); Busco et al. (2020), Zeidan (2022b)]. Although there is evidence that ESG indicators are already incorporated into credit risk models, banks don't necessarily do that systematically (Zhou et al., 2022). We argue that the present model can help commercial banks overcome information and expertise asymmetries in evaluating the credit risk of green lending by extracting private information from account managers, analysts, insiders, and other market agents.

Below is a sample of the output of the generalized SCSS (Fig. 3.8).

11-07-2022

SONA Sustainability Credit Score System (SSCSS) Results Report

Calculation results for SONA Sustainability Credit Score System

Summary – Model Information

Company Name	CSB
Country	Denmark
Model	SCSS1
Sector	Services
Industry	Education
Analyst	Rodrigo Zeidan

Rating Date	11-07-2022
Comparison Group Scores	
Country	1 or 0
Sector	1 or 0
Industry	1 or 0

Generalized SCSS Results - Summary

Final Sustainability Score	78%
Final Sustainability Rating	A+
Credit Grade Equivalent	Upper Medium grade
Investment Grade? (BBB- or above)	Yes

Fig. 3.8 Sample output of the generalized SCSS

These results are based on the following inputs (Table 3.21). The sample company is a business school. Thus, for some categories, the choice of input is n/a. There is a choice of NBAU and FSB for only one category each, with the rest divided between BAU and SB.

Table 3.21 Inputs for the generalized SCSS

Generalized SCSS Results—Current	
Environmental protection	
Indicator	*Rating*
Business model	SB
Greening of supply chains	SB
CO2 and other climate-related emissions	BAU
Environmental auditing and certifications	BAU
Energy consumption	SB
Economic growth	
Indicator	*Rating*
Corporate governance	SB
Innovation and long-term viability	BAU
Quality of economic growth opportunities	NBAU
Equipment and machinery	SB
Types of consumers	SB
Social progress	
Indicator	*Rating*
Social License to Operate	BAU
Regulatory changes	BAU
Sourcing	SB
Diversity	BAU
Relationship with stakeholders	SB

(continued)

Table 3.21 (continued)

Eco-efficiency	
Indicator	*Rating*
Water management	SB
Waste management	SB
Land use	N/A
Disaster resilience	N/A
Certifications	SB

Socio-environmental	
Indicator	*Rating*
Reporting on labor and environmental issues	BAU
Labor and environmental model	SB
Corruption	FSB
Funding	BAU
Industry associations	FSB

Socio-economic	
Indicator	*Rating*
Labor costs	BAU
Labor training and conditions	SB
Worker's health and risk of accidents	SB
Outsourcing and supply chain risks	N/A
Data disclosure	SB

Finally, Table 3.22 summarizes the outcomes of the generalized SCSS. In the present example, the equivalent rating to the selected answers is A + , generating a five-year sustainability default probability of 3.7%. The A + resulting score is classified as upper medium, just below the high-grade category. Table 3.22 also shows the descriptions of each possible rating and the corresponding interval range inside the broader 0 to 1 interval.

Are there limitations to this method? Of course. The main advantage of the original SCSS is the possibility of standardization from repeated inputs by the same type of user: account managers. The generalized SCSS has network effects that may never be realized. Its quality depends on the number of reports generated by high-level users, which allows the system to improve over time. "Garbage in, garbage out" is another potential risk, as is the possibility of fraud: users who will purposely generate skewed ratings. However, that risk is slight if lenders use the system to modulate credit decisions; they would have incentives to create trustworthy ratings. Otherwise, lenders would be making lending decisions on insufficient data.

Table 3.22 Generalized SCSS results—Forecast

	1-Year	5-Year
Sustainability Default Probability	2.5%	3.7%
Sustainability Rating	A+	A+
Percentile	25%	25%

	Forward Sustainability Default Probability
1-Year	2.5%
2-Year	2.8%
3-Year	3.0%
4-Year	3.3%
5-Year	3.7%

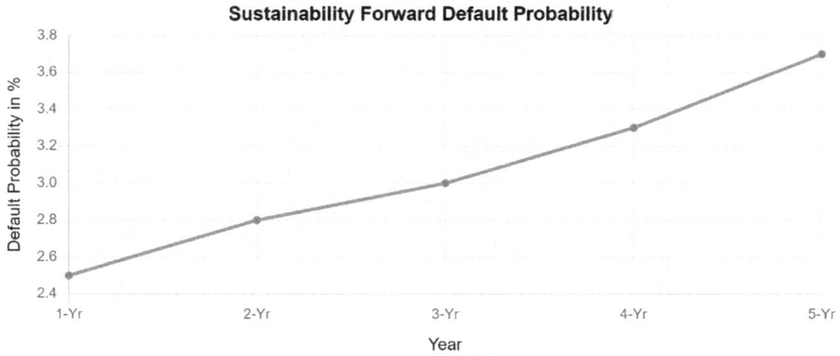

(continued)

Table 3.22 (continued)

Long-Term Rating Comparisons

Description		Value(pts.)	SCSS long-term
AAA	Prime	An obligor has EXTREMELY STRONG capacity to meet its sustainability commitments.	95 to 100
AA+	High grade	An obligor has VERY STRONG capacity to meet its sustainability commitments.	90 to less than 95
AA		It differs from the highest-rated obligors only to small degree.	85 to less than 90
AA-			80 to less than 85
A+	Upper Medium grade	An obligor has STRONG capacity to meet its sustainability commitments but	75 to less than 80
A		is somewhat more susceptible to the adverse effects of changes in	70 to less than 75
A-		circumstances than obligors in higher-rated categories.	65 to less than 70
BBB+	Lower Medium grade	An obligor has ADEQUATE capacity to meet its sustainability commitments.	60 to less than 65
BBB		However, adverse conditions or changing circumstances are more likely to lead	55 to less than 60
BBB-		to a weakened capacity of the obligor to meet its sustainability commitments.	50 to less than 55
BB+	Non-Investment Grade	An obligor is LESS VULNERABLE in the near term than other lower-rated	45 to less than 50
BB		obligors. However, it faces major ongoing uncertainties and exposure to	40 to less than 45
BB-		adverse conditions, which could lead to the obligor "s inadequate capacity to meet its sustainability commitments.	35 to less than 40
B+	Highly Speculative	An obligor is MORE VULNERABLE than the obligor "s rated "BB," but the	45 to less than 50
B		obligor currently can meet its sustainability commitments. Adverse conditions	25 to less than 30
B-		will likely impair the obligor "s capacity or willingness to meet its sustainability commitments.	20 to less than 25
CCC	Extremely Speculative	An obligor is CURRENTLY VULNERABLE and depends upon favorable conditions to meet its sustainability commitments.	15 to less than 20
CC		An obligor is CURRENTLY HIGHLY VULNERABLE.	10 to less than 15
C		An obligor is CURRENTLY HIGHLY VULNERABLE to sustainability breach	5 to less than 10
D	In default	An obligor has failed one or more sustainability obligations (rated or unrated) with negative results.	0 to less than 5
n.r.	Not rated	No rating has been requested, or there is insufficient information on which to base a rating.	Not applicable
r.w.	Rating withdrawn	The sustainability rating was withdrawn.	Not applicable

References

Acharya, A., & Abuyuan, A. M. T. (2002). *A Decade of Environmental Lending*. World Bank.

Alexandar, A. M. (2018). Straight-Through Processing in Commercial Lending: Commercial Banking Lending Perspective, *Infosys White Paper*. https://www.infosys.com/industries/financial-services/documents/straight-through-processing-commercial-banking.pdf

Ascui, F., & Cojoianu, T. F. (2019). Implementing Natural Capital Credit Risk Assessment in Agricultural Lending. *Business Strategy and the Environment, 28*(6), 1234–1249.

Apergis, N., Poufinas, T., & Antonopoulos, A. (2022). ESG Scores and Cost of Debt. *Energy Economics, 112*, 106186.

Baldini, M., Dal Maso, L., Liberatore, G., Mazzi, F., & Terzani, S. (2018). Role of Country-and Firm-Level Determinants in Environmental, Social, and Governance Disclosure. *Journal of Business Ethics, 150*(1), 79–98.

Barua, S., & Chiesa, M. (2019). Sustainable Financing Practices Through Green Bonds: What Affects the Funding Size? *Business Strategy and the Environment, 28*(6), 1131–1147.

BlackRock. (2023). *How to Invest in the Net Zero Transition*. BlackRock.

Capasso, G., Gianfrate, G., & Spinelli, M. (2020). Climate Change and Credit Risk. *Journal of Cleaner Production, 266*, 121634.

Case, P. (1999). *Environmental Risk Management and Corporate Lending: A Global Perspective*. Elsevier.

CFI Team. (2022). *Commercial Loan, Corporate Finance Institute*. https://corporatefinanceinstitute.com/resources/commercial-lending/commercial-loan/

Chang, K., Feng, Y. L., Liu, W., Lu, N., & Li, S. Z. (2021). The Impacts of Liquidity Measures and Credit Rating on Corporate Bond Yield Spreads: Evidence from China's Green Bond Market. *Applied Economics Letters, 28*(17), 1446–1457.

Churchill, G. A., Jr., & Peter, J. P. (1984). Research Design Effects on the Reliability of Rating Scales: A Meta-Analysis. *Journal of Marketing Research, 21*, 360–375.

Cowton, C. J., & Thompson, P. (2000). Do Codes Make a Difference? The Case of Bank Lending and the Environment. *Journal of Business Ethics, 24*(2), 165–178.

Drempetic, S., Klein, C., & Zwergel, B. (2019). The Influence of Firm Size on the ESG Score: Corporate Sustainability Ratings Under Review. *Journal of Business Ethics*, 1–28.

The Economist. (2020, October 3). *The Proliferation of Sustainability Accounting Standards Comes with Costs*. https://www.economist.com/business/2020/10/03/the-proliferation-of-sustainability-accounting-standards-comes-with-costs

Egan-Jones. (2020). *Methodologies for Determining Credit Ratings (Main Methodology)*. Egan-Jones. https://www.sec.gov/Archives/edgar/data/1651331/000165133120000008/EJR_Ex_2_Methodologies.pdf

Ehlers, T., & Packer, F. (2016). Green Bonds–Certification, Shades of Green and Environmental Risks. *Bank for International Settlements*.

Ehlers, T., & Packer, F. (2017). Green Bond Finance and Certification. *BIS Quarterly Review September*.

Fard, A., Javadi, S., & Kim, I. (2020). Environmental Regulation and the Cost of Bank Loans: International Evidence. *Journal of Financial Stability, 51*, 100797.

Ganguin, B., & Bilardello, J. (2005). *Fundamentals of Corporate Credit Analysis*. McGraw-Hill.

Guiral, A., Moon, D., Perez-Garcia, J., & Byun, J. (2021). Do Affective Reactions to Sustainability Performance Unintendedly Influence Lending Decisions? *Corporate Social Responsibility and Environmental Management, 28*(6), 1635–1646.

Hachenberg, B., & Schiereck, D. (2018). Are Green Bonds Priced Differently from Conventional Bonds? *Journal of Asset Management, 19*(6), 371–383.

Izzi, L., Oricchio, G., & Vitale, L. (2011). *Basel III Credit Rating Systems: An Applied Guide to Quantitative and Qualitative Models*. Springer.

Jones, D., & Mingo, J. (1999). Credit Risk Modeling and Internal Capital Allocation Processes: Implications for a Models-Based Regulatory Bank Capital Standard. *Journal of Economics and Business, 51*(2), 79–108.

Kidder, L. A. (2004). Straight-Through Processing in Commercial Lending: A Solution Waiting for Awareness of the Problem. *Com. Lending Rev., 19*, 9.

KPMG. (2012). *Expect the Unexpected: Building Business Value in a Changing World*. KPMG. https://assets.kpmg/content/dam/kpmg/pdf/2012/08/building-business-value-part-1.pdf.

Nabeeh, N. A., Abdel-Basset, M., & Soliman, G. (2021). A Model for Evaluating Green Credit Rating and Its Impact on Sustainability Performance. *Journal of Cleaner Production, 280*, 124299.

OECD. (2012). *OECD Environmental Outlook to 2050. The Consequences of Inaction*. Retrieved February 02, 2013, from http://www.oecd.org/env/indicators-modeling-outlooks/oecdenvironmentaloutlookto2050theconsequencesofinaction.htm

Roy, P. K., & Shaw, K. (2022). Modeling a Sustainable Credit Score System (SCSS) using BWM and fuzzy TOPSIS. *International Journal of Sustainable Development & World Ecology, 29*(3), 195–208.

Sanjeev, A. (2003). The Art of Scale Development. *Marketing Research, 15*(3), 10–12.

Semet, R., Roncalli, T., & Stagnol, L. (2021). ESG and Sovereign Risk: What is Priced in by the Bond Market and Credit Rating Agencies?. *arXiv preprint* arXiv:2110.06617

S&P Global. (2022). *Guide to Credit Rating Essentials*. S&P Global. https://www.spglobal.com/ratings/_division-assets/pdfs/guide_to_credit_rating_essentials_digital.pdf

Sustainalytics. (2020). *The ESG Risk Rating: Frequently Asked Questions—For Companies*. https://connect.sustainalytics.com/hubfs/SFS/Sustainalytics%20ESG%20Risk%20Rating%20-%20FAQs%20for%20Corporations.pdf

Thompson, P., & Cowton, C. J. (2004). Bringing the Environment into Bank Lending: Implications for Environmental Reporting. *The British Accounting Review, 36*(2), 197–218.

WBCSD. (2010). *Vision 2050: A New Agenda for Companies*. WBCSD. https://www.wbcsd.org/contentwbc/download/1746/21728/1.

Weber, O., Scholz, R. W., & Michalik, G. (2010). Incorporating Sustainability Criteria into Credit Risk Management. *Business Strategy and the Environment, 19*(1), 39–50.

Weber, O. (2012). Environmental Credit Risk Management in Banks and Financial Service Institutions. *Business Strategy and the Environment, 21*(4), 248–263.

Weber, O., Hoque, A., & Ayub Islam, M. (2015). Incorporating Environmental Criteria into Credit Risk Management in Bangladeshi Banks. *Journal of Sustainable Finance & Investment, 5*(1–2), 1–15.

Wellalage, N. H., & Kumar, V. (2021). Environmental Performance and Bank Lending: Evidence from Unlisted Firms. *Business Strategy and the Environment, 30*(7), 3309–3329.

Zeidan, R., Boechat, C., & Fleury, A. (2015). Developing a Sustainability Credit Score System. *Journal of Business Ethics, 127*(2), 283–296.

Zeidan, R. (2022a). Obstacles to Sustainable Finance and the Covid19 Crisis. *Journal of Sustainable Finance & Investment, 12*(2), 525–528.

Zeidan, R. (2022b). *Why Don't Asset Managers Accelerate ESG Investing? A Sentiment Analysis Based on 13,000 Messages from Finance Professionals*. Business Strategy and the Environment.

Zeidan, R., & Onabolu, S. (2023). The Generalized Sustainability Credit Rating System. *Brazilian Review of Finance, 21*(1), 21–47.

Zhou, X., Caldecott, B., Hoepner, A. G., & Wang, Y. (2022). Bank green lending and credit risk: an empirical analysis of China's Green Credit Policy. *Business Strategy and the Environment*.

CHAPTER 4

ESG Investing

Bankers cannot avoid ESG investing. In the early wave of job cuts in the industry, bankers devoted to sustainability-related decisions dodged them (Ritchie, 2023) while financial institutions were scrambling to find climate talent (Clark, 2023). However, the critical issue is how to avoid greenwashing. ESG investing is like going to heaven for Christians. Everybody claims they want to be good to go to heaven, but nobody is eager to arrive at their ultimate destination. As asset managers have proprietary methods for asset allocation, firms can easily claim that they are doing good while making money, as they can hide behind black box models. Still, when done right, ESG investing can align investors', managers, and society's interests. In this section, we explore the pitfalls and possible benefits of robust methods for sustainability-related asset allocation and other forms of investing.

Climate-related impacts can change asset prices in many ways, from directly impacting companies' productive capacity to changes in consumer behavior. Campiglio et al. (2022) summarize these mechanisms in Fig. 4.1.

In the section about the sustainability delta, we describe how to relate these steps to the drivers of companies' value. However, ESG investing generally requires (Campiglio et al., 2022):

R. Zeidan, *The Green Banking Transition Manual*,
https://doi.org/10.1007/978-981-96-2852-0_4

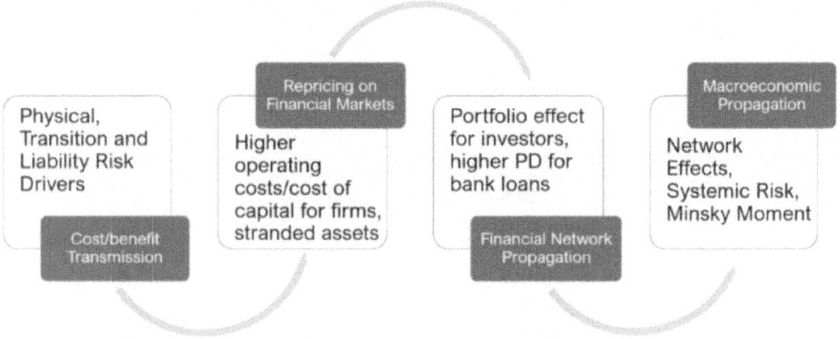

Fig. 4.1 The journey from climate-related impacts to asset price changes (*Source* Campiglio et al. [2022])

1. Determining the exposure of an asset.
2. Determining the financial costs of the economic shock.
3. Including financial and nonfinancial market dynamics.
4. Choosing the measure of impact.

Much of that boils down to materiality, an issue we discuss in Chapter 3 on sustainability credit rating systems. As Campiglio et al. (2022) observe, economic impacts must be translated into financial ones, but methodologies strongly differ across studies.

Typical arguments regarding the relevance of ESG investing include net zero commitments, a tectonic shift of capital, and the growth of ESG-related funds. These arguments don't necessarily hold muster and may even be counterproductive to real systemic change. Of course, they can advance green investing if several stakeholders buy in, which depends on the willingness of market actors to commit to real change.

In this section, we explore theoretical and practical issues regarding ESG investing. In particular, we analyze the main obstacles to this type of investment process and present ESG portfolio construction methods.

ESG investing is embedded into the broader category of sustainable investment, broadly defined as responsible investment and ownership (see Tables 4.1 and 4.2).

Table 4.1 Responsible investment framework (asset selection)

Responsible asset selection				
Screening			*ESG integration*	
Norms-based (static)	*ESG (dynamic)*	*Thematic*	*Valuation*	*Risk*
– e.g.: Coal Tobacco	– Environmental Social Governance	– e.g.: Green Impact	– Environmental Social Governance	– Environmental Social Governance

Table 4.2 Responsible investment framework (ownership)

Responsible ownership			
Voting	*Engagement*	*Activism*	*Direct management*
e.g.: – ESG-focused – ESG-aware	e.g.: – Campaign – Disclose	e.g.: – Board seat – Acquire shares	e.g.: – Private equity – Other illiquids

Source Dunn et al. (2020)

Table 4.3 United Nations principles for responsible investment

Principle 1 We will incorporate ESG issues into investment analysis and decision-making processes	*Principle 2* We will be active owners and incorporate ESG issues into our ownership policies and practices	*Principle 3* We will seek appropriate disclosure on ESG issues by the entities in which we invest
Principle 4 We will promote acceptance and implementation of the Principle within the investment industry	*Principle 5* We will work together to enhance our effectiveness in implementing the Principle	*Principle 6* We will each report on our activities and progress toward implementing the Principle

Source UN PRI, December 2018

The principles for responsible investment encompass ESG investments. Table 4.3 details the United Nations' principles for responsible investment.

As we can see, banks that abide by these principles should create robust ESG investing strategies.

Increasingly, ESG indicators are factoring into bankers' pay. Papadopoullos (2022) indicates that 41 of the top 100 banks considered environmental factors when deciding their chief executive's bonus award. In addition, JP Morgan, Citigroup, Barclays, and HSBC, among other banks, have adopted financed emissions targets.

However, how much of that is real change and how much is lip service is still an open question. We explore the several dimensions of ESG investing in the following sections.

4.1 Codifying ESG and Sustainable Investments

What is the state of the art regarding the regulatory framework for disclosing sustainability-related information? European authorities are widely seen as the most proactive regulators in this dimension. Unfortunately, there isn't precise guidance on the methodologies for reporting sustainability risks, but some organizations should develop guidelines eventually. This subsection describes several of the most up-to-date points regarding ESG investing from a European perspective.

The European Parliament codified sustainability risks as ESG risks in their 2019 regulation about sustainability-related disclosures in the financial services sector (the following sections bring some additional comments on this regulation), which started to be implemented in 2022. The organization also provided a harmonized definition of sustainable investment.

The regulation (EU) 2019/2088 aims to reduce information asymmetries in principal-agent relationships regarding the integration of sustainability risks, the consideration of adverse sustainability impacts, the promotion of environmental or social characteristics, and sustainable investment (European Parliament, 2019). The disclosures were based on two primary principles: members of the financial industry must report the reasons why the sustainability risk assessment leads to the conclusion that there are no sustainability risks deemed to be relevant to the financial product and must provide detailed information on the qualitative and quantitative terms when those risks are considered appropriate (European Parliament, 2019).

As regulations require precise wording, the European Parliament had to present a definition of sustainability-related risks. The choice fell upon ESG indicators. The definition is self-referential and reads (European Parliament, 2019): "A sustainability risk means an environmental, social or governance event or condition that, if it occurs, could cause a negative material impact on the value of the investment, as specified in sectoral legislation, in particular in Directives 2009/65/EC, 2009/138/EC, 2011/61/EU, 2013/36/EU, 2014/65/EU, (EU) 2016/97, (EU) 2016/2341, or delegated acts and regulatory technical standards adopted pursuant to them."

These directives establish the role of financial regulators in Europe, including risk management principles. Directive 2009/65/EC, for instance, specifies the coordination of laws, regulations, and administrative provisions relating to undertakings for collective investment in transferable securities (UCITS) (European Parliament, 2009).

Much of the regulations (EU) 2019/2088 that deal specifically with sustainability risks and investments detail the importance of such concepts. It also establishes that market participants should follow the guidelines for responsible business conduct developed by the Organisation for Economic Co-operation and Development (OECD) and the Principles for Responsible Investment (as seen before).

The most significant part of the regulatory framework is the distinction between sustainability-related funds and impact investing funds. Regarding the former, financial market participants should disclose whether and how the designated index, sustainability index or mainstream index, is aligned with those characteristics. If no benchmark is used, market agents must inform how the sustainability characteristics of the financial products are met. Companies should provide reports to disclose this information annually (European Parliament, 2019). In addition, financial services companies should inform end investors of their methodology to integrate relevant sustainability risks, whether material or likely to be material; they maintain concise information about those policies on their websites (European Parliament, 2019).

Given this context, paragraph 17 of Article 2 of the regulation (EU) 2019/2088 defines sustainable investment as "an investment in an economic activity that contributes to an environmental objective, as measured, for example, by key resource efficiency indicators on the use of energy, renewable energy, raw materials, water and land, on the production of waste, and greenhouse gas emissions, or on its impact on biodiversity and the circular economy, or an investment in an economic activity that contributes to a social objective, in particular an investment that contributes to tackling inequality or that fosters social cohesion, social integration and labor relations, or an investment in human capital or economically or socially disadvantaged communities, provided that such investments do not significantly harm any of those objectives and that the investee companies follow good governance practices, in particular with respect to sound management structures, employee relations, remuneration of staff and tax compliance (European Parliament, 2019)."

As we can see, the definition is relatively vague. The definition of sustainability factors, almost synonymous with sustainability risks throughout the document, is not much better. "Sustainability factors mean environmental, social, and employee matters, respect for human rights, anti-corruption and anti-bribery matters (European Parliament, 2019)."

Article 4 establishes the guidelines for financial market participants' disclosure. Information should include, among others:

(a) policies on the identification and prioritization of principal adverse sustainability impacts and indicators;
(b) the principal adverse sustainability impacts and actions taken or planned;
(c) reference to responsible business conduct codes and internationally recognized standards for due diligence and reporting and, where relevant, the degree of their alignment with the objectives of the Paris Agreement.

In addition, large companies, defined as those with more than 500 employees, must publish and maintain on their websites a statement on their due diligence policies concerning the information provided in their reports.

Information is not detailed throughout the articles that comprise the body of the regulations from the European Parliament. For instance, regarding the methodologies used to assess ESG factors and the performance measures of sustainable investments, market agents must report the "information on the methodologies used to assess, measure and monitor the environmental or social characteristics or the impact of the sustainable investments selected for the financial product, including its data sources, screening criteria for the underlying assets and the relevant sustainability indicators used to measure the environmental or social characteristics or the overall sustainable impact of the financial product. (article 10, European Parliament, 2019)."

European authorities do not provide explicit guidelines on how these methodologies and investment policies should be reported. Interestingly, regulators note that previous disclosure directives are not always clear. For instance, directive 2013/34/EU of the European Parliament and of the Council (18) imposes transparency obligations regarding ESG indicators that may be unsuitable for communications with end investors (European Parliament, 2019). Still, details concerning the most recent regulations haven't improved. Authorities pass the bucket to the next round of regulatory scrutiny. They note that other committees, such as the European Banking Authority (EBA), the European Insurance and Occupational Pensions Authority (EIOPA), and the European Securities and Markets Authority (ESMA), should develop draft regulatory technical standards to specify further the content, methodologies, and presentation of the reports by financial services companies.

As we can see, not even the most proactive regulatory agencies have established comprehensive methodologies to enforce climate-friendly changes in European banks' operations. Further, data disclosure issues may limit regulators' ability to implement systemic changes, as shown in the following section.

4.1.1 SFDR and the Future of Data Disclosure

Sustainability risks entail environmental, social, or governance events or conditions that, if they occur, could cause an adverse material impact on the value of the investment.

In their plan to make Europe a carbon–neutral region by 2050, the European Union has designed a series of measures to help decarbonize the economy. In the realm of sustainable finance, the European Commission developed an action plan with the aims of reorienting capital flows toward sustainable investment to achieve sustainable and inclusive growth, managing financial risks stemming from climate change, resource depletion, environmental degradation, and social issues, and fostering transparency and long-termism in financial and economic activity (European Commission, 2018).

In the sustainable finance space, the EU introduced the first phase of the SFDR on 10 March 2021, the Taxonomy Regulation on 1 January 2022, and the second phase of the SFDR on January 1, 2023 (Maples Group, 2022).

The EU Taxonomy is a list of environmentally sustainable economic activities that provides companies, investors, and policymakers with appropriate definitions to clarify which economic activities qualify as sustainable to help deal with that issue. Introducing transparency to investment products with sustainability-related claims should help investors channel investment capital toward more sustainable companies and activities (Pellegrino, 2022).

The quality of nonfinancial performance data is one of the most considerable obstacles to robust ESG investing. Thus, the EU regulations for sustainable finance are a significant step in bridging asymmetric information between companies and potential investors. Of course, no regulation is perfect, and the SFDR is no exception. Still, we can't deny the potential of mandatory reporting that includes all financial services companies with more than three employees. Even if these small companies are not required to provide written reports, they must consider sustainability risks in their advisory processes (European Commission, 2018).

The regulations also established the International Platform on Sustainable Finance, a group of public and private sector experts that consult on the European Commission's development of further sustainable finance policies and tools (European Commission, 2023). The SFDR classifies funds as gray, light green, or dark green, with stricter reporting requirements for green funds. Investment managers must report on the regulations to ensure companies comply with global standards such as the UN Guiding Principles on Business and Human Rights (Pellegrino, 2022).

For many banks, environmental policy is answering to regulators. Greening banks will be straightforward if climate financial regulation is well-designed and timely. However, the term "well-designed regulation" is almost an oxymoron. Of course, even far-from-perfectly designed regulations are still likely preferable to nothing. There are criticisms regarding SDFR, mainly related to the lack of direction for proper data disclosure. Busch et al. (2022) extensively analyze the EU Taxonomy and the SDFR. They summarize the new classification scheme as based on five distinctive categories: (1) Exclusion-focused investments, (2) Basic ESG investments, (3) Advanced ESG investments, (4) Impact-aligned investments, and (5) Impact-generating investments.

In Table 4.4, Busch et al. (2022) define sustainable investments as investments with at least a low ambition to contribute to a sustainable transition (categories three to five). The authors establish the necessary ("and") and optional ("or") conditions for investments to qualify in each category. They also distinguish between Basic and Advanced ESG investments. The former aims to mitigate risks, while the latter aims to manage ESG risks and opportunities, focusing on financially material ESG issues. Such a distinction is implied in the sustainability credit score system (Chapter 3).

Advanced ESG investments use exclusions and norms-based screenings. Compared to essential ESG investments, they use stronger criteria for approval, such as ESG integration (high commitment). If the requisite information is available, a high degree of commitment to ESG integration will involve an investigation of all issuers in a portfolio that are financially significant ESG factors. Advanced ESG investments, as opposed to essential ESG investments, employ voting or engagement to gather data and assist research, enhance public disclosure, or improve ESG issue practices, all with the goal of better measuring and managing ESG risks and opportunities (Busch et al., 2022).

As for impact-aligned investments, they use positive and negative screens to address environmental and social goals and concerns. The positive screening methods use the SDGs or the EU taxonomy as reference frameworks to identify investees with positive effects on environmental or social variables (positive company impact). Investees having detrimental effects are excluded through exclusions and norms-based screens (Busch et al., 2022).

As with many other initiatives, Busch et al. (2022) and Pellegrino (2022) note that the procedures for reporting nonfinancial data are ambiguous. The breadth and depth of reporting vary with the methodologies used, such as the Impact Management Platform and the EU's Platform on Sustainable Finance (PSF). SFDR provisions do not clarify how to qualify an investment product; ultimately, self-reporting is still the standard practice, with all the problems that this entails.

Given how fragile the ESG criteria are used by funds today, it is unlikely that all these funds consistently track nonfinancial performance similarly to how they track financial performance. Even so, many, if not most, funds will look into being classified as sustainable-related funds. In 2022, before the second phase of SFDR, 31.5% of funds in the EU were already classified as Article 8 (27.9%) or Article 9 (3.6%) (Pellegrino, 2022).

The SFDR falls short in guiding ESG reporting, although it does clarify some issues, as we will see in the following subsection. The

Table 4.4 SFDR classification scheme for sustainable investments

Dimension		*Criteria*	*Exclusions-focused*	*Basic ESG*	*Sustainable investments*		
					Advanced ESG	*Impact aligned*	*Impact generating*
General characteristics		*Ambition level*	No	Marginal	Low	Medium	High
		Main objective	Values-driven	Mitigation of ESG risks	Managing ESG risks & opportunities	Address E/S challenges	Active contribution to solving RWC (i.e., transition of investees)
		Materiality	–	Financial materiality	Financial materiality	Double materiality	Double materiality
Pre-Investment strategies	Negative screening	*Exclusions*	Based on ethical values	Based on ESG risks	Based on ESG risks	Based on negative impacts	
			OR	AND	AND	AND	Based on non-transformable activities
		Norms based screening	✓	✓	✓	Based on negative impacts	
		AND					

Dimension		*Criteria*	*Exclusions-focused*	*Basic ESG*	*Sustainable investments*		
					Advanced ESG	*Impact aligned*	*Impact generating*
	Positive screening	*ESG integration*	–	Low commitment	High commitment		
			OR	OR	OR		
		Best-in-class/ Best-in-universe/ Best-in-progress	–	Low sophistication	High sophistication	Focus on positive company impact through positive screening	Focus on positive investor impact through capital allocation
			OR	OR	OR		
		Sustainability themed	–	–	Financial opportunities		
					AND		OR
Post-investment strategies		*Engagement & voting*	–	–	Transparency ESG risks and opportunities	Transparency company impact	Transition objective investor impact
					AND		
Performance measurement		*Performance measurement*	–	ESG Risks	ESG risks and opportunities	Measurement of company impact	Measurement of expected and generated company & investor impact

(continued)

Table 4.4 (continued)

Dimension	*Criteria*	*Exclusions-focused*	*Basic ESG*	*Sustainable investments*		
				Advanced ESG	*Impact aligned*	*Impact generating*
				AND		
	Objective	√	√	√	√	√
	Pre-investment		Short description	Detailed description	Detailed description	Detailed description
Documentation	*Post-investment*		–	Formal and regular reports	Formal and regular reports (company impact)	Formal and regular reports (investor impact)
	Performance measurement		At least one KPI	> one KPI on ESG matters	> one KPI on company impact + impact monitoring	> one KPI on company & investor impact + impact monitoring
	External verification	–	–	(√)	√	√

Source Busch et al. (2022)

classification system by Busch et al. (2022) helps relate the distinct categories of sustainable funds to the rules of the SFDR. However, as with many ESG-related initiatives, the main issue is standardizing nonfinancial reporting.

4.1.2 *ESG Investing at BlackRock*

There are no firm ESG criteria, and even legislative bodies cannot define such indicators precisely. Still, that does not stop financial institutions from introducing strategies and products related to ESG. In January 2020, BlackRock committed to putting sustainability at the center of its investment process. By 2023, the company has stated that ESG risk analysis was embedded in 100% of regular portfolio risk reviews. Moreover, the institution started to publish strategy-level ESG integration statements for products across the active investment platform (BlackRock, 2023).

Take, for instance, BlackRock's commitment to ESG investing. BlackRock is likely the world's largest hedge fund manager, with over U$10 trillion of assets under management. The company's shift toward ESG investing in 2020 sent shockwaves through the investment community. However, some of the reasons behind the move, expressed in the firm's letter to their clients, are not necessarily sound. BlackRock argued that the share of countries committed to net zero had swelled from 10 to 95% of global emissions, a tectonic capital shift was underway, and ESG investing was growing six times faster than the rate of traditional investments.

Such a surge in country commitments comes from two options: a new consensus in which all participants agree to move swiftly to achieve common goals or lip service, greenwashing at its finest. Regardless, is it something to be celebrated? Maybe even initial greenwashing may become real action as the pressure on countries mounts. Still, even if it signals that countries plan on changing their behavior, it does not support the view that asset managers must immediately follow with meaningful change. The same holds for the growth of "ESG investing." If genuine ESG investing is indeed growing at six times the rate of traditional investments, then it is likely that an asset manager should indeed catch up with the market. However, as for countries' commitments, the true nature of ESG investing matters. Are companies genuinely changing their portfolios to reflect nonfinancial performance, or are they just claiming they are doing so? Therein lies the issue: ESG investing is an area that lends itself to half-serious commitments. Claims of green investing totaling dozens of trillions of dollars can never be verified, as investment strategies are black boxes.

Still, weak claims notwithstanding, BlackRock's public commitment to sustainable investment may fundamentally change the financial industry's makeup. Competitors will have a solid incentive to commit to something similar, even if they don't intend to come through on these promises or justify their decisions not to follow suit.

While the company does not publish its methodologies in detail, mainly because its asset managers have leeway to incorporate ESG indicators into their strategies, BlackRock reports on many dimensions of its strategy.

Figure 4.2 describes BlackRock's description of the emergence of sustainability premia. Mostly, they assume that sustainability premia will come from strategic asset allocations.

Among the initiatives developed since the institution made its big announcement, BlackRock has introduced more than 200 new sustainable funds, built Aladdin® Climate, and formed Decarbonization Partners. Regarding data transparency, the organization has published implied temperature rise metrics for its ETFs and public index funds. BlackRock also planned to deliver the industry's most sophisticated transition tools, analytics, and portfolio advice (BlackRock Institute, 2022a).

So, is BlackRock intent on focusing on transition finance? It is impossible to tell from the outside. At the start of the process, the company stated that its asset managers would be free to incorporate ESG criteria

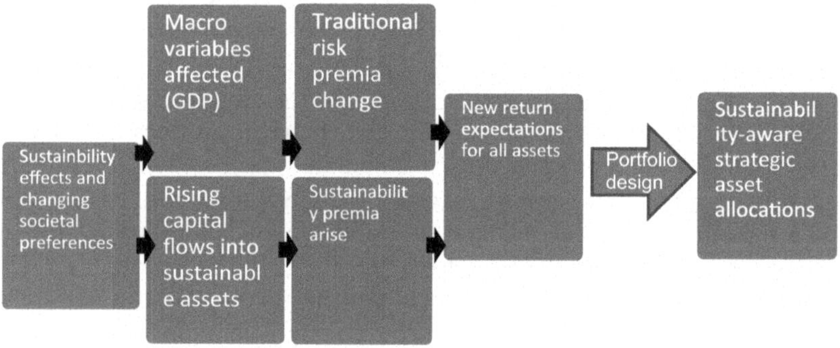

Fig. 4.2 BlackRock's description of how changes in investment patterns imply sustainability premia (*Source* BlackRock [2020])

into their portfolios. Indeed, some managers will make a good-faith effort to do it diligently. However, that may not be true for most fund managers without explicit criteria or incentives.

The institution reports that BlackRock's framework is based on three pillars: navigate, drive, and invent. That includes strategies to enable investors to "green the core" of their portfolio by accessing climate-aware broad-market exposures; new fundamental and systematic active strategies; expansion of iShares® strategies to include climate benchmarks; and growth of the Portfolio Consulting and Outsourced Chief Investment Officer capabilities to incorporate climate transition analytics (BlackRock, 2022).

Still, we know that ESG measures are highly correlated. Table 4.5 describes the correlation between ESG ratings from six ESG rating providers. Regardless of how the firm enacts ESG investing, there is plenty of space for BlackRock to improve its strategies by using robust ESG ratings and for rating providers to enhance their methodologies by having such a large firm using them.

Finally, legal pushback may change the company's strategy. In 2024, class action suits accused BlackRock of violating its fiduciary duty to investors by integrating ESG indicators that would reduce profits, as plaintiffs claimed. Still, while BlackRock's ESG investment strategies are not entirely transparent, there are signs that the firm has incorporated climate transition into its macroeconomic outlooks. For instance, in their full and summarized 2023 Global outlooks, climate transition merits a whole subsection, like many other sources of macroeconomic risk.

Table 4.5 Correlation between ESG ratings from six ESG rating providers

	Asset 4	*Sustainalytics*	*Inrate*	*Bloomberg*	*KLD*
Asset 4					
Sustainalytics	0.77				
Inrate	0.23	0.30			
Bloomberg	0.75	0.72	0.12		
KLD	0.59	0.62	0.29	0.54	
MSCI IVA	0.43	0.47	0.32	0.32	0.47

Source Gibson et al. (2021)

BlackRock even states that it tracks the transition to net zero carbon emissions like any other driver of investment risks and opportunities, such as monetary policy (BlackRock Institute, 2022a, 2022b).

4.2 ESG Portfolio Construction

The ESG investing environment is challenging, as asset managers must decide on a few among hundreds of ESG indicator databases. While there is no precise procedure for portfolio construction, recent research indicates that passive strategies may be dominated by active portfolio management. This section summarizes Branch et al. (2019), Utz et al. (2014), and Pedersen et al. (2021). The former describes a simplified procedure for ESG portfolio construction. The latter presents a more complicated approach for integrating ESG criteria into portfolio management.

Cremers et al. (2023) introduce Active ESG Share as a novel metric of the extent of a fund manager's use of ESG information. This metric compares the entire distribution of portfolios' stock-level ESG ratings to benchmarks. This methodology captures how actively a manager uses ESG information rather than whether the manager favors stocks with high or low-ESG ratings.

As for portfolio implementation, Branch et al. (2019) outline three pairs of ESG portfolio construction. The first two strategies are the simplest, relying on binary (in or out) data to exclude unwanted securities. The second pair relies on ESG scores. The third pair combines the first two, leading to the most complex implementations. The authors note that each pair highlights a trade-off between higher-than-necessary risk and unwanted exposure. Excluding or underweighting unwanted securities in combination with risk minimization leads to overweights in securities correlated with the rejects.

They construct the portfolios using mean–variance optimization with a maximum score objective function. Optimization is on a target ESG score denoted by C (transaction costs are ignored) given by:

$$\min \lambda w_A^T \sum w_A + T(w - w_0)$$

$$s.t.$$

$$w_A^T 1 = 0$$

$$w \geq 0$$

$$w_A^T X = C$$

where w refers to portfolio weights, w_a is active weights, Δw represents changes in portfolio weights, w_0 is the initial portfolio weights, $X(\Delta w)$ is active exposures, $\sum$ is the asset covariance matrix, X is the exposure to ESG factors, 1 is the vector of all 1s, C is the target ESG score, and λ is a measure of risk aversion.

The covariance matrix $\sum$ comes from the Barra US Total Market Equity (USSLOW) model, and optimizations are performed using the software Barra Optimizer 8.7.1.

For the cap-weighted exclusion, which omits unwanted securities from a diversified benchmark and then weights remaining securities in proportion to their market capitalizations, the authors find that the strategy carries excessive tracking error (i.e., higher variability of returns versus the benchmark). That is because the residual risk introduced from the exclusions is not controlled or managed anywhere in the investment process. For the optimized exclusion, which differs from the former by weighting remaining securities to minimize tracking error, the mechanism for lowering tracking error overweights securities correlated with the omitted securities. That can produce unwanted or unintuitive outcomes.

The portfolios with ESG data are constructed with two optimized tilts for a gender diversity strategy based on the MSCI ACWI. Unlike the exclusion portfolios, which the authors note may trouble some investors, both tilts use the number of women on a firm's board.

The final pair of portfolios combines exclusion and tilts. The authors maintain the optimization regarding gender diversity as their priority. As in the previous examples, there is a trade-off between exposure and risk. The tracking error of the customized tilt exclusion was higher than that of the tilt exclusion, and the extra risk of the customized tilt exclusion was rewarded with a lower weight of companies with no female executives.

Table 4.6 summarizes the strategies of the authors.

The benefit of the approach of Branch et al. (2019) is that the procedure is replicable based on a clearly defined objective function. The main drawback is that investors usually do not maximize an ESG factor directly.

Table 4.6 Summary of ESG strategies

Technical goal	*Data granularity*	*Risk aversion*	*Strategy*	*Trade-off*
Exclude Unwanted Securities	Binary	Low	Cap-Weighted Exclusion	Excess Tracking Error
		High	Optimized Exclusion	Risk of Unwanted Exposure
Tilt on a Theme	Scored	Low	Maximum Score	Excess Tracking Error
		High	Minimum Risk	Risk of Unwanted Exposure
Exclude and Tilt	Binary and Scored	Low	Custom Tilt Exclusion	Excess Tracking Error
		High	Tilt Exclusion	Risk of Unwanted Exposure

Source Branch et al. (2019)

The usual approach is for investors to maximize returns given specific ESG considerations (which may refer to excluding unwanted securities). Hence, we describe a more general approach from Pedersen et al. (2021).

Pedersen et al. (2021) establish an ESG-efficient frontier similar to standard efficient frontiers in common financial models. In their theory, portfolios that span the frontier are all combinations of the risk-free asset, the tangency portfolio, the minimum-variance portfolio, and the ESG-tangency portfolio (four-fund separation). Notably, equilibrium asset returns satisfy an ESG-adjusted capital asset pricing model (CAPM), showing when higher ESG assets have lower or higher equilibrium expected returns.

The model divides the types of investors into three categories. Type-U (ESG-unaware) investors maximize their unconditional mean–variance utility and nothing else. Type-A (ESG-aware) investors have mean–variance preferences but use ESG scores to update their views on risk and expected return. Type-M (ESG-motivated) investors prefer high-ESG scores, seeking a portfolio with an optimal trade-off between a high expected return, low risk, and high average ESG score. The authors show that the investor's problem can be reduced to an ESG and Sharpe ratio trade-off. Hence, a stock's environmental, social, and governance (ESG) score plays two roles: (1) it provides information about firm fundamentals, and (2) it affects investor preferences. An ESG-efficient frontier, the highest attainable Sharpe ratio for each ESG level, characterizes the solution to the investor's portfolio problem.

The ESG-efficient frontier and the mean–variance frontiers for all portfolios with specific ESG scores are illustrated in Fig. 4.3.

Panel A shows the ESG-SR frontier, the maximum Sharpe ratio (on the y-axis) achieved for all portfolios with a given ESG score (on the x-axis). The peak of the ESG-SR frontier is the standard tangency portfolio's Sharpe ratio (SR). Investors who care about SR and ESG should choose a frontier portfolio to the right of this portfolio, on the ESG-efficient frontier. Panel B shows the standard mean variance frontier and the corresponding standard tangency portfolio (denoted "all assets"). The slope of the line from the risk-free rate to the tangency portfolio is the maximum SR. Panel B also shows the mean–variance frontier built exclusively for portfolios with a particular ESG score. This frontier is a hyperbola that lies inside (i.e., to the right of) the standard hyperbola and has its tangency portfolio with corresponding Sharpe ratio SR. This Sharpe ratio defines a point on the ESG-SR frontier.

Figure 4.4 describes the preferences of three types of investors.

The model solves an investor's problem of choosing a portfolio of n risky assets and a risk-free security. The risk-free return is r^f, and the other assets have excess returns represented in the vector of random variables $r = (r^1,\dots, r^n)$. The assets have ESG scores given by $s = (s^1,\dots, s^n)$.

Type-U investors take expected excess returns as $E(r)$ with risk given by the variance–covariance matrix, $var(r)$. Type-A investors use assets' expected excess return, $\mu = E(r|s)$, conditional on the ESG information s, and the conditional variance–covariance matrix of excess returns $\sum: = \text{var}(r|s)$. Because the portfolio allocation problem for investors U and A has the standard Markowitz solution, the focus is on type-M investors.

Investor M starts with a wealth of W and chooses a portfolio of risky assets, $x = (x^1,\dots, x^n)$, where x^i is the fraction of capital invested in security i. The investor seeks to maximize utility U over final wealth W and the average ESG score on a mean–variance framework. The ESG score is

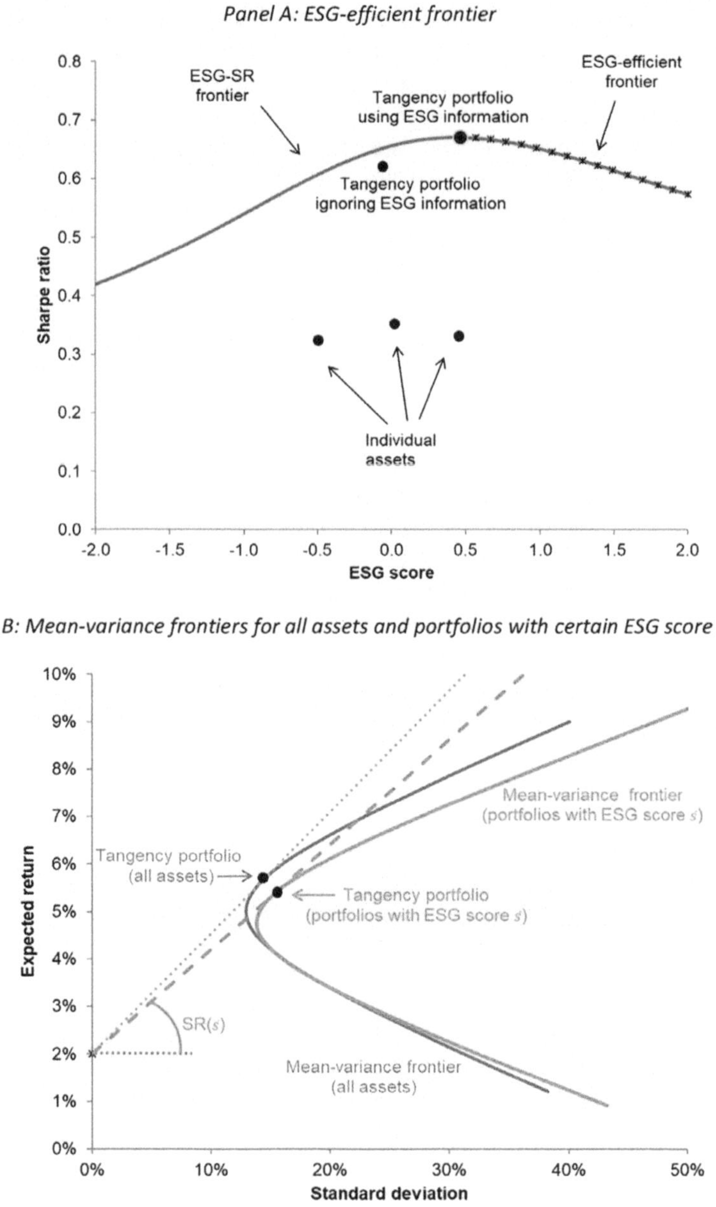

Fig. 4.3 ESG-efficient and mean–variance frontiers (*Source* Pedersen et al. [2021])

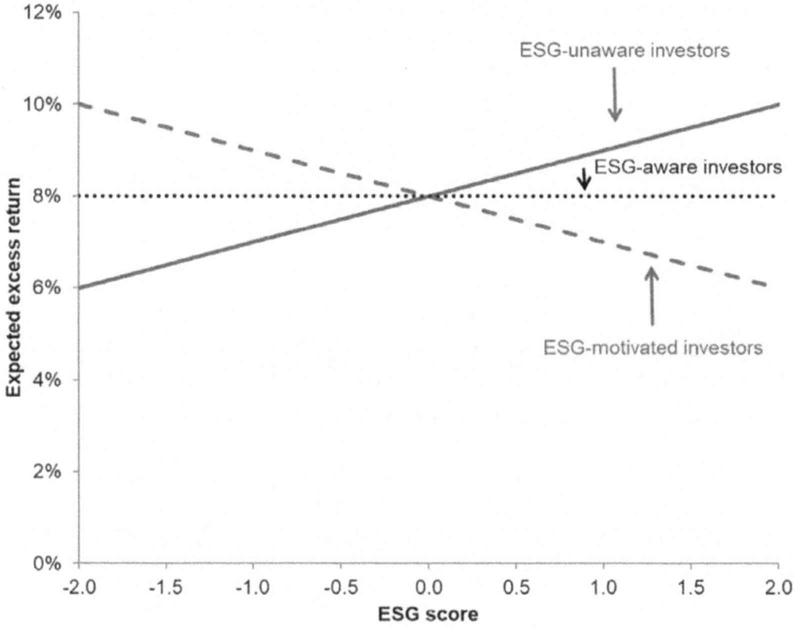

Fig. 4.4 Preferences of ESG-unaware, -motivated, and -aware investors (*Source* Pedersen et al. [2021])

defined as:

$$\bar{s} = \frac{x^{i} s}{x^{i} 1}$$

Future wealth is:

$$\widehat{W} = W(1 + r^{f} + x^{i} r)$$

Utility U is given by:

$$U = E\left(\widehat{W}|s\right) - \frac{\overline{\gamma}}{2} Var\left(\widehat{W}|s\right) + W f(\bar{s})$$

where $\overline{\gamma}$ is the absolute risk aversion parameter, $\bar{s}$ is the average ESG score, and f: $R \rightarrow R \cup \{-\infty\}$ is the ESG preference function. The average ESG score is scaled by the total position in risky assets because the investor gets no ESG utility from investing in the risk-free asset.

Given $\gamma = \overline{\gamma} W$ is the relative risk aversion, and portfolios x are long-biased (the investor does not bet consistently that the market will go down); the utility maximization problem is:

$$\max\left(x^{i}\mu - \frac{\gamma}{2}x^{i}\sum x + f\left(\frac{x^{i}s}{x^{i}1}\right)\right)$$

Solving the utility maximization problem in a standard mean–variance analysis is done via the investor optimally combining the tangency portfolio with the risk-free asset. Remember that an efficient frontier is such that the relation between risk and return is positive; higher risk results in higher expected return. This relationship is represented by the Sharpe ratio, the expected excess return divided by the standard deviation of excess returns. The tangency portfolio is the portfolio that maximizes the Sharpe ratio.

The ESG-SR frontier or the maximum Sharpe Ratio that can be achieved with an ESG score of $\overline{s}$ is:

$$\mathrm{SR}(\overline{s}) = \max\left(\frac{x^{i}\mu}{\sqrt{x^{i}\sum x}}\right), \text{ if } x^{i}1 = 1 \text{ and } x^{i}s = \overline{s}$$

The central proposition of Pedersen et al. (2021) is that: "the investor should choose the average ESG score $\overline{s}$ to maximize the following function of the squared Sharpe ratio and the ESG preference function f":

$$\max_{\overline{s}}\left[(SR(\overline{s}))^{2} + 2\gamma f(\overline{s})\right]$$

The proposition makes the trade-off between ESG factors and Sharpe Ratios explicit. More importantly, the tradeoff can be divided into parts that depend only on securities and others that rely only on preferences. As the authors note, while the mean–variance frontier in the standard Markowitz framework can be computed independent of preference parameters, the ESG-SR frontier can be calculated independent of preferences, with the investor deciding where to place herself in the frontier at the end. The investor's problem is to choose a place in the ESG-SR frontier and then decide on the amount of risk by choosing how much to invest in the portfolio and to hold as cash. Notably, if the investor cares about total instead of average ESG, the theory does not entail an ESG-SR frontier.

Also relevant is that the maximum Sharpe Ratio achieved with an ESG score (SR($\overline{s}$)) is lower than the ratio across all portfolios (SR(s*)):

$$SR(s^*) = \sqrt{c_{\mu\mu}} > SR(\overline{s}) = \sqrt{c_{\mu\mu} - \frac{\left(c_{s\mu} - \overline{s}c_{1\mu}\right)}{c_{ss} - 2\overline{s}c_{1s} + \overline{s}^2 c_{11}}}$$

Finally, the optimal portfolio is a combination of the risk-free asset, the tangency portfolio, $\sum^{-1}\mu$, the minimum-variance portfolio, $\sum^{-1}1$, and the ESG-tangency portfolio, $\sum^{-1}s$:

$$x = \frac{1}{\gamma}\Sigma^{-1}(\mu + \pi(s - 1\overline{s}))$$

where

$$\pi = \frac{\left(\overline{s}c_{1\mu} - c_{s\mu}\right)}{c_{ss} - 2\overline{s}c_{1s} + \overline{s}^2 c_{11}}$$

Parameter π represents the amount of adjustment or the strength of the preference for ESG. Figure 4.5 illustrates the indifference curves for type A and M investors. For the type-M investor, utility increases in the Sharpe ratio and the ESG score, yielding a trade-off illustrated by the downward-sloping indifference curves. For the ESG-aware investor, indifference curves are horizontal because this type of investor does not derive utility from ESG factors.

Pedersen et al. (2021) also incorporate the possibility of stock screening, like Branch et al. (2019). For that purpose, they change the set of allowed portfolios to require that the share of low-ESG stocks is zero or negative:

$$X = \left\{x \epsilon R^n | x^i 1 > 0, \forall i x^i \leq 0 if s^i < s^*\right\}$$

The equation means that below a certain sustainability threshold ($s^i < s^*$), the share of that stock in the portfolio (x^i) should be zero or negative.

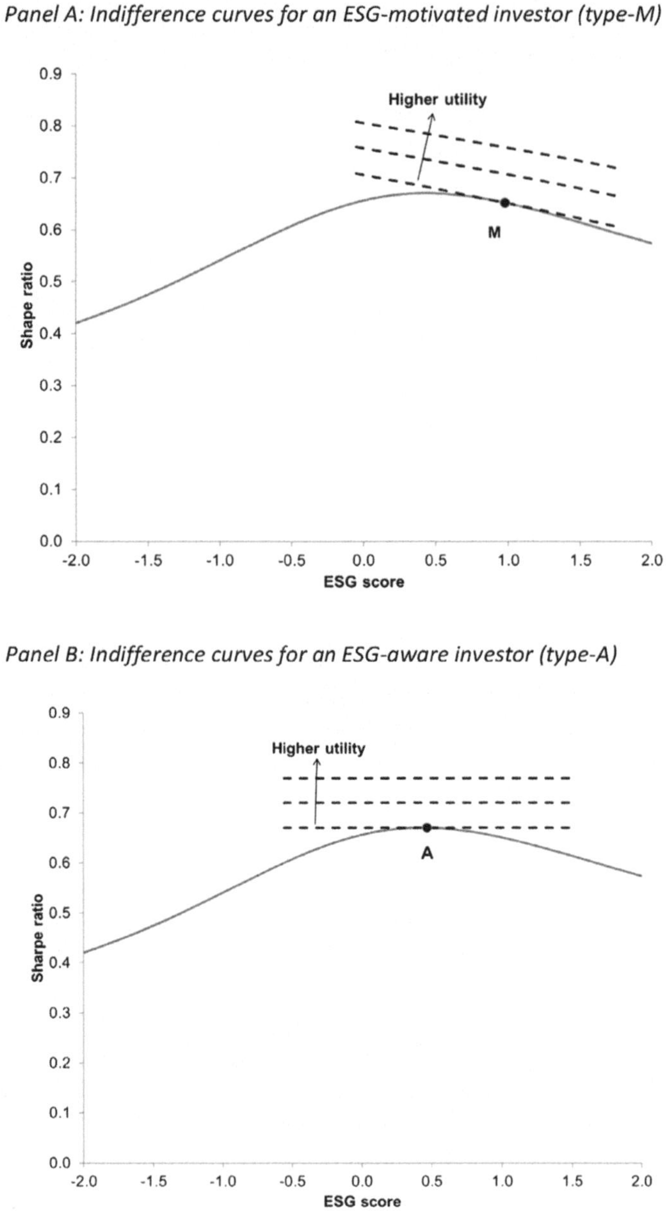

Fig. 4.5 Indifference curves for ESG-aware and -motivated investors (*Source* Pedersen et al. [2021])

Here, ESG-frontier adds to the tools available for portfolio managers. This section describes a general method that allows for specific choices for asset managers. Fund managers develop proprietary models based on mean–variance and other common portfolio management concepts, which are standard in investment processes. Adding explicit ESG-frontier considerations allows for transparent decision-making and communication with clients.

4.3 ESG-Adjusted CAPM

Pedersen et al. (2021) build on their ESG-SR frontier and develop a full-blown ESG-adjusted capital asset pricing model. Their model is based on an overlapping generations (OLG) economy in which, at time t, security prices are $p_t = \left(p_t^1 \ldots p_t^n\right)$ and excess returns are $\left(r_t^1 \ldots r_t^n\right)$. In overlapping generations models, individuals live for two periods, are born in every period, and the population grows at a constant rate. In the standard model, individuals receive an endowment of the only good of the economy at birth. Individuals can consume the product or invest in its production. There are two factors of production: labor and capital; the production function of the economy is $Y = f(K, L)$.

There are only two generations alive at any moment, young and old. The standard model uses the permanent income hypothesis theory. Individuals work in the first period, consuming and saving for retirement in the second period. People smooth their consumption over time, saving for retirement and spending all savings during the second period.

The ESG-adjusted CAPM model takes as exogenous the ESG scores (s), the risk-free rate (r^f), dividend payoffs (v), and the shares outstanding of each stock.

Crucially, ESG scores are informative. Its informational values are defined as:

$$E(v_t|s) = \hat{\mu} + \lambda(s - s^m)$$

where s^m is the weighted-average ESG score of the market portfolio and parameter $\lambda \in R$ determines the relative profitability of ESG-friendly firms. Positive λ indicates that ESG-friendly firms are more profitable than the average firm, and negative λ establishes that low-ESG companies make more money than the average enterprise.

Generally, each security price depends on its current ESG score and the current investors' ESG sentiment. A security's return variance depends on the risk of changes in the overall ESG investor sentiment, the stock's own ESG score, and how ESG predicts dividends and the covariances of all shocks.

Specifically, if all investors are Type-U (ESG-unaware), the model reverts to a standard CAPM. However, this version of the CAPM yields a striking feature. High-ESG firms (those with a positive λ) are priced differently; they have higher conditional expected returns than those with below-average ESG scores. The paradox is that in a world of ESG-unaware investors, they may end up incorporating ESG information due to expected profits from these factors. The result is similar in the world of Type-A (ESG-aware) investors; the informational value of ESG scores is already incorporated into prices.

What happens when all investors are of Type-M, using ESG in their signals and identical ESG preferences? Then, the equilibrium price of any security i and the equilibrium conditional expected excess return are given, respectively, by (for the proof, see the original article):

$$p^i = \frac{\hat{\mu}^i + \lambda(s^i - s^m) - \frac{\gamma}{W} COV(v^I, v^m|s)}{rf - \pi(s^i - s^m)}$$

$$E\left(r_t^i|s\right) = \hat{\beta}^i E\left(r_t^m|s\right) - \pi(s^i - s^m)$$

ESG scores affect asset prices by changing expected cash flows and the discount rate. The standard conditional CAPM expression gives a firm's cost of capital $\hat{\beta}^i E\left(r_t^m|s\right)$ adjusted for the ESG score being above or below the market. Companies with better ESG ratings have lower costs of capital and invest more.

Finally, what happens when all types of investors populate the world? The model does not say much, as there are two countervailing forces. Prices may reflect the content of ESG scores (higher profits or costs), and preferences from type-M investors increase stocks' demand, leading to higher prices and lower required returns.

More direct is the prediction about a possible increase in the adoption of ESG investing. That would result in higher prices for high-ESG stocks. If adoption and ESG informativeness are unexpected, then high-ESG stocks would experience a return boost, but not if these are expected.

As the authors note (pp. 582–583), the testable predictions of the theory are:

1. The ESG-SR frontier can summarize the trade-off between risk, expected returns, and ESG.
2. Using ESG information can increase the investor's SR by improving the ESG-SR frontier.
3. Given the investor's information set, investors with stronger ESG preferences (or higher risk aversion) choose portfolios with higher ESG scores and (marginally) lower SR.
4. Even investors with preferences for the average ESG score optimally choose portfolios with positions (long or short) in almost any security (as opposed to standard models of taste-based discrimination that imply stricter segregation).
5. ESG investors choose a combination of four portfolios (or funds): the risk-free asset, the standard tangency portfolio, the minimum-variance portfolio, and the ESG-tangency portfolio.
6. A security with a higher ESG score has a higher demand from ESG investors, which lowers the expected return, different expected future profits, which can increase the expected return if the market underreacts to this predictability of fundamentals, and more substantial flows from investors, which can increase the price in the short term.

Some testable hypotheses are intuitive because they likely didn't need a formalization. Still, having a proper model that integrates these and other hypotheses into a CAPM-related framework allows us to enhance our understanding of ESG investing. Specifically, their treatment of ESG investing dynamics yields alluring insights.

Higher adoption of ESG investing matters because companies' emissions decrease when the wealth share of green investors and their sensitivity to climate externalities increase, as shown by De Angelis et al. (2022). With the caveat that ESG factors must be informative, a tool for tracking specific changes in high-ESG asset prices from ESG adoption is notable. Finally, one particular hypothesis can change how investors operationalize ESG investing. Since even investors with preferences for the average ESG score ignore stricter segregation, the future of ESG investing may not involve exclusion criteria standard in divestment proposals and several sustainability-related funds. For more on that subject and complementing Branch et al. (2019), we turn to the work of Zerbib (2022).

4.3.1 Divestment, Exclusion Criteria, and Sin Stocks

For an asset manager, the simplest way to implement ESG investing transparently is by excluding entire industries deemed to be problematic in some manner. We have seen in Sect. 4.2 how ESG portfolio constructions can be simplified by allowing for straightforward exclusion criteria (Branch et al., 2019). Here, we summarize an asset pricing model with partial segmentation and heterogeneous preferences that reflect sustainable investors' dual practice of exclusion and integration. This model, by Zerbib (2022), complements the previous models by delineating distinct premia on neglected stocks and tastes that clarify the relationship between ESG and financial performance.

Unlike the model by Pedersen et al. (2021), the present one is a single-period equilibrium model populated by two only investor groups: regular and sustainable investors.

The emergence of sustainable investors generates a taste premium and two exclusion premia. The former comes from three effects: a preference for owning high-ESG investable assets, adjusting the market risk premium by the average taste premium, and commonality on excluded asset returns. The latter exclusion premia result from a reduced investor base and a local segmentation effect (following de Jong & Roon, 2005). The exclusion effect is the sum of the two premia.

Other than basic assumptions about frictionless trading and Gaussian returns, there are two model-specific assumptions:

1. Partial segmentation: regular investors may invest in all assets, but sustainable investors restrict their risky asset allocation to the sub-market of I-investable assets (the regular stocks $I_1,\ldots,I_{nI}$), excluding X-investable assets (the sin stocks $X_1,\ldots.X_{nX}$).
2. Heterogeneous Preferences: investors have mean–variance preferences, and Υ denotes their relative risk aversion. Sustainable investors favor the greenest companies' stocks. They subtract a deterministic private cost of externalities, c_k, from the expected

returns on each investable asset in their mean–variance optimization program. The overall cost of externalities of the value-weighted portfolio of investable assets is c_{mI}.

Figure 4.6 illustrates the market. At a certain threshold, sustainable investors exclude brown assets.

From that set-up, Zerbib (2022) determines the S-CAPM. The expected excess return on any asset $k \in \{I_1,\ldots,I_{nI}, X_1,\ldots X_{nX}\}$ is:

$$\mathbb{E}(r_k) = \beta_{km_I}\left(\mathbb{E}\left(r_{m_I}\right) - pc_{m_I}\right) + \underbrace{pB_{kI}C}_{\text{Taste premium}} \underbrace{+\gamma\frac{p}{1-p}q\mathbb{C}\text{ov}(r_k, r_{m_X}|r_I)}_{\text{Exclusion-asset premium}}$$

$$+ \underbrace{rq\mathbb{C}\text{ov}(r_k, r_{m_X}|r_{mI})}_{\text{Exclusion-market premium}}$$

As we can see, this expression differs significantly from the S-CAPM in the previous section. However, the models' goals also differ. While Pedersen et al. (2021) develop a model based on an overlapping generations economy that extends a general ESG-frontier, Zerbib (2022) is concerned with a particular subset of portfolio strategies based on exclusion criteria. Hence, the current model has exclusion-asset-specific premia and a general Exclusion-market premium. The author also derives the expected excess return for any investable and excludable assets. These are,

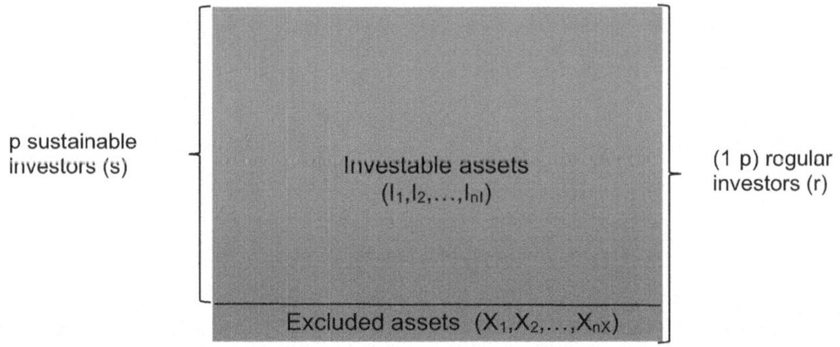

Fig. 4.6 The market set-up (*Source* Zerbib [2022])

respectively:

$$\mathbb{E}(r_{I_k}) = \beta_{I_k m_I}(\mathbb{E}(r_{m_I}) - pc_{m_I}) + \underbrace{pc_{I_k}}_{\text{Taste premium}} + \underbrace{\gamma q \mathbb{C}\text{ov}(r_{I_k}, r_{m_X} | r_{m_I})}_{\text{Exclusion-market premium}};$$

$$\mathbb{E}(r_{X_k}) = \beta_{km_I}(\mathbb{E}(r_{m_I}) - pc_{m_I}) + \underbrace{pB_{X_k I}C}_{\text{Taste Premium}} + \underbrace{\gamma \frac{p}{1-p} q \mathbb{C}\text{ov}(r_{X_k}, r_{m_X} | r_I)}_{\text{Exclusion-asset premium}}$$

$$+ \underbrace{\gamma q \mathbb{C}\text{ov}(r_{X_k}, r_{m_X} | r_{mI})}_{\text{Exclusion-market premium}}.$$

Alongside the two exclusion premia, a taste premium reflects the investors' preferences for green assets. Intuitively, the taste premium for green assets reduces the expected return on the investable market.

Two compelling scenarios and an obvious result follow from this more general specification.

First, what happens if all investors turn "green"? If sustainable investors populate the economy, the result is identical to Acharya and Pedersen's (2005) liquidity-adjusted CAPM with a deterministic illiquidity cost. In that case, there is a unique linear equilibrium in which the conditional expected net return of security *i* is:

$$E_t(r^i_{t+1} - c^i_{t+1}) = r^f + \lambda_t \frac{\text{cov}_t(r^i_{t+1} - c^i_{t+1}, r^M_{t+1} - c^M_{t+1})}{\text{var}_t(r^M_{t+1} - c^M_{t+1})},$$

where $\lambda_t = E_t(r^M_{t+1} - c^M_{t+1} - r^f)$ is the risk premium, and the conditional expected gross return is:

$$E_t(r^i_{t+1}) = r^f + E_t(c^i_{t+1}) + \lambda_t \frac{\text{cov}_t(r^i_{t+1}, r^M_{t+1})}{\text{var}_t(r^M_{t+1} - c^M_{t+1})} + \lambda_t \frac{\text{cov}_t(c^i_{t+1}, c^M_{t+1})}{\text{var}_t(r^M_{t+1} - c^M_{t+1})}$$
$$-\lambda_t \frac{\text{cov}_t(r^i_{t+1}, c^M_{t+1})}{\text{var}_t(r^M_{t+1} - c^M_{t+1})} - \lambda_t \frac{\text{cov}_t(c^i_{t+1}, r^M_{t+1})}{\text{var}_t(r^M_{t+1} - c^M_{t+1})}.$$

The required excess return is the expected relative illiquidity cost $E_t(c^i_{t+1})$ plus four betas (or covariances) times the risk premium. The four betas depend on the asset's payoff and liquidity risks. The required return on an asset increases linearly with the market beta, the covariance between the asset's return and the market return.

The three liquidity risks are:

- $cov_t(c_{t+1}^i, c_{t+1}^M)$ represents the covariance between the asset's and the market's illiquidity. Investors want compensation for holding a security that becomes illiquid when the market turns illiquid.
- $cov_t(r_{t+1}^i, c_{t+1}^M)$ represents the covariance between the security's return and the market liquidity. Investors are willing to accept a lower return on an asset with a high return in times of market illiquidity.
- $cov_t(c_{t+1}^i, r_{t+1}^M)$ represents the covariance between the security's liquidity and the market's expected return. Investors are willing to accept a lower expected return on a more liquid asset during a downturn.

Second, if sustainable investors exclude some assets but have tastes similar to regular investors, the taste premium vanishes, and only the exclusion premium remains. Then, the equilibrium converges to the I-CAPM equilibrium equation for investable assets in de Jong and de Roon (2005):

$$\mathbb{E}(r_{I_k}) = \beta_{I_k m_I}\mathbb{E}(r_{m_I}) + rq\mathbb{C}\text{ov}(r_{I_k}, r_{m_X}|r_{m_I}).$$

Finally, if there are no sustainable investors or they don't act on their preferences, no excluded asset exists, and the equation is the same as the standard CAPM.

Zerbib (2022) then proceeds to bring to data the model by treating sin stocks as excluded assets and proxying sustainable investors' tastes for green assets using green fund holdings. For the empirical estimation, the main question is: what constitutes a sin stock? Divestment movements have a long history. For instance, if there was ever a good reason to pursue such actions, the boycott of South Africa's apartheid government was it. Today, tobacco and alcohol are widely considered sin stocks (gaming stocks are sometimes thrown in alongside tobacco and alcohol but without the same justification).

The author's empirical strategy relies on the tobacco, alcohol, and gaming industries, with robustness checks that include the defense industry. While these industries are not close to being the most important regarding climate change or other social-environmental areas, testing the model's main propositions matters here. Although there could be criticisms about the method for extracting sustainable investors' green tastes, the empirical strategy is straightforward. The revealed preference factor contrasts the weights of stocks in the portfolio of funds' asset allocations with the asset weights in the investment universe. Ultimately, Zerbib (2022) finds that the taste premium significantly impacts excess returns, but only weak evidence supports sin stock exclusion's effect on investable stock returns. However, the main empirical finding related to the sustainability delta later in the chapter is that the impact of sustainable investors on a company's cost of capital can be substantial.

4.3.2 Phasing Out Coal Investments: The Case of HSBC

HSBC does a better-than-average job of communicating its sustainability policies. For instance, instead of creating a narrative in which the bank is the most sustainable globally, the institution is upfront: policies only address risk issues. They are distinct from other actions, such as certifications or memberships to related associations (HSBC, 2022). This matters because the organization does not bundle sustainability policies with different types of reputational risk or corporate social responsibility initiatives. HSBC signed the Equator Principles in 2003. Related to that and its sustainability policies, HSBC relates some of its risks to specific industries. In particular, departments must restrict their actions related to prohibited and restricted businesses. The latter refers to activities the bank may finance but require additional approvals based on information that firms are responsibly managed (HSBC, 2022).

The bank implies it uses a sustainability credit rating system. In the industry dimension, business activities are given sustainability risk ratings categorized as high, medium, or low. Unlike the system in Chapter 3, which is open to companies of all sizes, HSBC gives relevant customers one of the following labels: leader for exceeding standards; compliant for meeting standards; near-compliant for being on a credible path toward standards but without unacceptable impacts; and non-compliant for not materially meeting standards. The bank has closed relationships with non-compliant customers, but complete closure takes longer, where HSBC has committed to loan terms outstanding (HSBC, 2022).

HSBC has not published the details of its sustainability rating sustainability, and from its public documents, it seems they rely on 75 or more sustainability risk experts. However, there is one dimension of its sustainability policy that is well-documented. The 2021 Annual General Meeting (AGM) approved a resolution binding HSBC to phase out thermal coal financing in the EU and OECD by 2030 and globally by 2040 (HSBC, 2021). Analyzing HSBC's public documents is fruitful because some relevant bank policies are public. This resolution implies that the bank must publicize its main strategies and report to shareholders if it's on track to meet the institution's goals. Thus, HSBC's commitment to phasing out coal investments is a rare instance in which the institution demarcates and communicates precisely the path to reducing credit to a specific industry due to sustainability commitments.

Since this is a long-term process, HSBC must publish annual reports updating policies and targets. For that purpose, the bank established a Task Force on Climate-Related Financial Disclosures (TCFD) in 2020 to establish the baselines for the targets. As intermediate goals, the Bank plans to reduce thermal coal financing exposure by at least 25% by 2025 and financing exposure by 50% by 2030.

Significantly, the bank has delineated what it will and won't do. Among the former, HSBC plans to phase out the financing of coal-fired power and thermal coal mining by 2030 in markets in the EU and OECD and by 2040 in other markets, engage with relevant clients on their transition plans, and agree to finance phaseout timelines. Finally, it seeks to withdraw any financing and advisory services with a client that makes a new commitment to or proceeds with thermal coal expansion after 1 January 2021 (unless such expansion was contractually committed or under construction before that date) (HSBC, 2021).

The bank will not finance new coal projects, but what constitutes a coal producer? For the EU and OECD markets, companies for which thermal coal-related revenues are greater than 30% of total revenues. The bank seeks to avoid new relationships with prospective clients with significant thermal coal power capacity, mining production, or revenues, except to reduce greenhouse gas emissions (HSBC, 2021).

How about incorporating such policies in asset management and other bank areas? The bank is committed to spreading these policies to all relevant HSBC entities, products, and businesses to support transitioning from coal-fired power to thermal coal mining within HSBC's 2030/40 timelines (HSBC, 2021). However, there is a caveat. Fiduciary duties or other regulatory obligations constrain this commitment. That is a significant caveat. Asset managers can hide behind the fiduciary duties narrative to avoid incorporating nonfinancial information restricting portfolio composition. Even though groups of asset managers believe that fiduciary duties don't pose a significant obstacle to ESG investing (Zeidan, 2022b), banks can still refrain from incorporating nonfinancial information by claiming that this could lead to lower rates of return.

Another part of the policy that does not detail its operational criteria is the new obligations related to HSBC's Net Zero 2050 plan. HSBC also announced a commitment to stop providing new financing to any client who fails to engage sufficiently in its transition plan or determines that the plan is incompatible with HSBC's Net Zero by 2050 target (HSBC, 2021). However, as always, the devil is in the details. If the bank starts losing customers, will it maintain its net zero commitment? Only time will tell.

4.3.3 ESG Factors and Sustainable Investing in Equilibrium

How do market forces change asset prices when considering investors' preferences for ESG criteria? More importantly, what happens with asset prices if ESG ratings are indeed market factors, unlike the opinion of fund managers reported in Zeidan (2022b) in the following subsection?

Pástor et al. (2021, 2022) answer these questions in two articles. Their 2021 study finds that green assets have low expected returns because investors enjoy holding them and because green assets hedge climate risk. Still, green assets outperform when positive shocks hit the ESG factor. In addition, they find that the ESG investment industry is the largest when investors' ESG preferences differ the most. Finally, they show that sustainable investing produces a positive social impact by making firms greener and shifting real investment toward green firms.

In the 2022 study, they considered a theory with a green factor and showed that this explains much of the underperformance of value stocks in previous years. They also show that green assets delivered high returns in recent years due to more environmental concerns, not high expected returns. Interestingly, they estimate lower expected returns for green stocks than for brown, consistent with the perception of asset managers (Zeidan, 2022b).

The 2021 model has "green" and "brown" firms, with green firms generating positive externalities and brown firms negative. Agents also have different preferences; agents with "ESG preferences" derive utility from holdings of green firms and disutility from brown firms and care about firms' aggregate social impact and climate risk.

The "ESG factor" is a scaled return on the ESG portfolio (generating "ESG betas"); asset prices are derived from a two-factor model. Green assets have positive ESG betas, and brown assets have negative betas. A simple version of the ESG factor is a green-minus-brown portfolio return, where ESG characteristics weigh both green and brown portfolios. Assets' CAPM alphas reflect exposure to the omitted, priced ESG factor. The factor has a negative premium that comes from investors' ESG tastes.

Avramov et al. (2022) incorporate uncertainty about the corporate ESG profile. The authors show that, as expected, the market premium increases and demand for stocks declines under ESG uncertainty. As we have seen before, ESG information is not standardized, so investors have significant costs in determining the signal from noise.

Can ESG noise be corrected? Berg et al. (2022a) tackle this issue. They propose two noise-correction procedures that instrument ESG ratings with ratings of other ESG rating agencies. Interestingly, the effect of ESG performance on stock returns is more robust than previously estimated. After correcting attenuation bias, the coefficients increase by 2.6, implying an average noise-to-signal ratio of 61.7%. Such results are encouraging but do not tackle the central issue: how to make ESG ratings more informative? Maybe the right approach is to ignore them, focusing on firm-specific risks, which should incorporate social, governance, and environmental factors. Or separate them into their components, E, S, and G indicators instead of ESG indicators.

In particular, Pástor et al. (2021) interpret the ESG factor as capturing unexpected changes in ESG concerns, from customers shifting their demand for goods from green providers and investors changing their appreciation for green holdings. Interestingly, a shift in beliefs about green holdings is enough to increase the performance of green investments. This result is noteworthy because firms can be left behind if they don't update their perception of ESG-related holdings.

In their model, sustainable investing leads to positive social impact. The authors define a firm's social impact as the product of the firm's greenness and scale. Greener investors impact firms through two channels: firms choose to invest in becoming greener to capture higher valuation and green firms' costs of capital decrease. Finally, Pástor et al. (2021) extend the model by allowing investors to incorporate climate into their utility functions. Because brown assets have higher climate betas than green assets, this pushes up brown assets' expected returns in our model. Thus, brown stocks also have positive CAPM alphas because of brown stocks' larger exposures to climate risk.

Positive social impact can emerge from other reasons. In the model by Oehmke and Opp (2022), financing constraints and coordination among agents drive positive social impact in higher investment in green versus brown firms.

Given all these channels, why don't asset managers accelerate climate transition? We provide some evidence in the following section.

4.4 Why Don't Asset Managers Already Incorporate ESG Indicators Explicitly? The Praxis of ESG Investing

Should we expect that the absence of a significant relationship between sustainability and returns implies that asset managers are free to implement sustainability mandates? Unfortunately, the answer is not quite. Debates on the praxis of ESG investing include the relation between ESG and financial performance, the quality and breadth of ESG data, the technical aspects of building portfolios that incorporate ESG indicators, and more. This subsection summarizes Zeidan (2022a, 2022b), who uses qualitative information from interviews with asset managers and sentiment analysis on 13,000 messages from finance professionals to understand why asset managers are not accelerating ESG investing.

Portfolio optimization requires consistent data for backtesting. Still, Baldini et al. (2018) show that country-level characteristics such as the political system (legal framework and corruption), labor system (labor protection and unemployment rate), and cultural system (social cohesion and equality opportunities) significantly affect firms' ESG disclosure practices.

Even if disclosures are detailed, ESG indicators do not capture the overall environmental performance. Disclosure scores are generally not distribution-free, have high kurtosis and skewness, and are sensitive to outliers (Baldini et al., 2018). In addition, ESG dissemination appears to be skewed toward larger, more profitable companies. Drempetic et al. (2019) show a relationship between firm size, a company's available resources for providing ESG data, and the availability of a company's ESG data.

Kotsantonis and Serafeim (2019) encapsulate the difficulties in integrating ESG into the investment process in four categories: data inconsistency, benchmarking, ESG data imputation, and issues among ESG data providers. Regarding the first dimension, the authors state plainly that "ESG data inconsistency is worse than you think it is." However, ESG investing cannot be done without backward-compatible ESG data.

Recent initiatives, such as the Sustainable Industry Classification System (SICS) of the Sustainability Accounting Standards Board (SASB), have sought to address this issue; however, even if companies are beginning to adopt ESG, the quality of the reports varies significantly.

Pástor et al. (2022) aim to dissect green returns. They compute stock-level environmental scores based on MSCI ESG rating data. They claim that the advantages of MSCI ESG Ratings are that more than 1700 clients use them, cover more firms than other ESG raters, the research mentioned above by Berg et al. (2022a) find that MSCI's ESG scores are the least noisy and that MSCI's ESG research unit employs more than 200 analysts and incorporates artificial intelligence, machine learning, and natural language processing into its methodology. As with most academic articles, the main obstacle is reliable ESG data.

MSCI ESG Ratings may be the best or one of the best standards in the market, but it still does not accomplish what an ideal system would. It does not have data on private companies, and its ratings, as good as they are, are not unambiguous.

Opposite forces drive the dynamics of sustainability standards. Given that no code is universally accepted, new standards emerge regularly, but reporting costs and the pressure of shareholders induce the consolidation of existing guidelines. The number of ESG-related guidelines and regulations increased from 700 in 2009 to more than 1700 in 2019 (The Economist, 2020). Unfortunately, it seems that society is still years, if not decades, away from standardized (and value-creating) ESG disclosure. Moreover, there are no comprehensive alternatives, although some initiatives are promising. For instance, integrated reporting, created by the International Integrated Reporting Council, provides standards for sustainability-related disclosure. The International Integrated Reporting Council (IIRC) and the Sustainability Accounting Standards Board (SASB) merged to form the Value Reporting Foundation. The Value Reporting Foundation publishes the Integrated Thinking Principles, Integrated Reporting Framework, and SASB Standards. Evidence shows that corporations that voluntarily disclose more SASB-identified sustainability information exhibit greater price informativeness (Grewal et al., 2020).

However, ESG data are open to misrepresentation. When corporations materially misrepresent sustainability information, investors may suffer "hidden value" injuries. Still, there is no technical limit to incorporating ESG data into portfolio building.

Unfortunately, ethical investing seems similar to going to heaven; those who claim they want to end up there are in no rush to reach their destination. The disclosure of environmental, social, and governance (ESG) factors that allow investors to differentiate listed companies in terms of their nonfinancial performance is a necessary but not sufficient condition for reducing global greenhouse emissions. The main lesson of this subsection is that obstacles to disseminating ESG investing remain and that regulators and civil society should continue to search for ways to change fund managers' incentives to guarantee that more ethical investing becomes standard in financial markets.

Zeidan (2022b) analyzed 13,125 messages from 81 finance professionals (most asset managers). No member of the group explicitly includes ESG factors in their portfolio strategies. One fund manager stated in 2019 that its fund included variables related to ESG separately in its models. Still, there are a few out of hundreds of variables that their complex models considered. The lack of use of ESG is an interesting feature as it goes against previous evidence of fund management behavior. For instance, Van Duuren et al. (2016) find that banks use ESG to flag and manage risk. Oliveira et al. (2020) show that sustainability indices are valuable hedging tools for asset managers in some contexts.

The members who are asset managers practice fundamental investing but do not feel that ESG investing is in any way close to it. Of course, the present evidence does not invalidate previous works. Van Duuren et al. (2016) reveal a substantial difference in US and European asset managers' views of ESG. Brazilian professionals may hold more distinct perspectives even if they work in the United States and Europe. Should the absence of a significant relationship between sustainability and returns imply that fund managers are free to implement sustainability mandates? The group has overwhelming support for the idea that the orthogonality between environmental outcomes and financial performance is a necessary but not sufficient condition for ESG investing. The restriction of the strategy space and issues such as data quality are still viewed as overwhelming obstacles. Practical difficulties in backtesting models with accurate data and the learning curve from ESG data complicate the matter. Moreover, members routinely observe significant internal transaction costs, such as manipulating data and developing models, and external, from acquiring expensive access to databases.

Some managers have taken tentative steps toward ESG investing but claim to have found a strong correlation between disclosure quality and firm size. Yet most fund managers have not related ESG scores to portfolio performance. There is a strong consensus, rightly or not, that ESG dissemination is skewed toward larger, more profitable companies. There is also skepticism that ESG indicators reflect financial and nonfinancial companies' actual social and environmental impacts. "ESG is nothing more than marketing" is the view of a member who lives in the United States. One shared view is that asset managers may claim to be doing ESG investing while simply picking large companies with better disclosure practices. "I could easily build an ex-post ESG report to justify my asset allocation that would reveal that mine was one of the greenest portfolios around," wrote another. Another member wrote, "There are dozens of ESG data providers; it would be easy to cherry-pick factors that give me the ESG scores I want." Nevertheless, a few members have expressed views consistent with Xiao et al. (2013), but they have conceded that their institutions have not moved toward the broad implementation of sustainability mandates.

Some of the above arguments may be ex-post justifications for maintaining the status quo. One limitation of the textual analysis is that it cannot answer how organizational inertia shapes ESG indicators' discourse or analyze differences in social norms and the relative morals of ethical investing between the surveyed asset managers and other groups. Another limitation is the lack of internal investments in building models with nonfinancial indicators.

Firm executives' actions are not immutable. Fund managers and shareholders might pressure managers to change investment and operating decisions. Pointedly, shareholders may also pressure fund managers to transform their businesses (Fig. 4.7). Other stakeholders amplify connections between fund managers and ESG factors. In 2008, less than one-third of German banks published CSR reports; by 2013, almost every bank did. More than a decade since the industry started using ESG reports, there has been no universal method of reporting nonfinancial outcomes, and the informational content of ESG reports varies greatly. ESG diffusion provides one substantial obstacle to empirical studies:

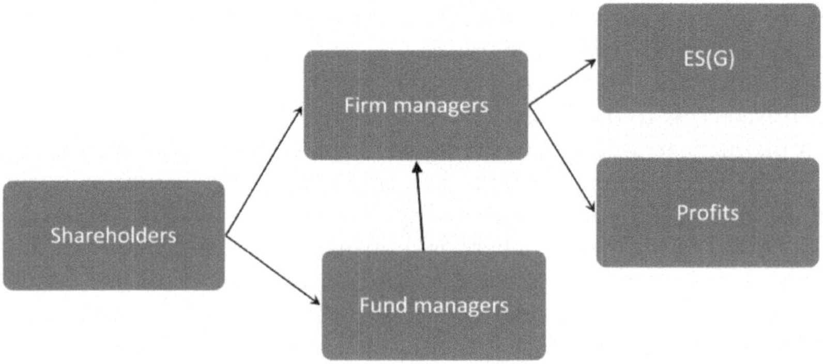

Fig. 4.7 The diffusion of ESG practices (*Source* Zeidan [2022a])

temporal validity. If the content of ESG reports changes significantly over time, studies that find a weak relationship between ESG factors and financial performance may not enlighten future research.

One of the discussions about ESG indicators as risk factors occurred in February 2020. The emerging congruence is that ESG indicators are far from being risk factors today. Factors such as momentum, liquidity, volatility, and others allow asset managers to employ a consistent, systematic, rule-based process that targets a subset of stocks with specific desired characteristics. There is almost unanimity in the lack of sustainability metrics. Data inconsistency, benchmarking, ESG data imputation, and problems with ESG data providers are widespread.

It should be noted that there is a shared view that pressure for ESG adoption must come from investors and shareholders, with asset managers following their lead. Regardless, members do not view ESG as a risk factor. After all, investors expect to be compensated for taking an extra risk, and there is no systematic evidence that high-ESG portfolios outperform more general portfolios.

Some members have expressed that ESG indicators are too loosely related to environmental, social, and governance risks. The models used by asset managers are not readily amenable to restrictions on the strategy space without some counterbalance. In addition, it seems challenging to disentangle ESG indicators from companies that use it for greenwashing and companies that dutifully report threats and actions in these areas. Finally, negative screening can be helpful but has limited practical appeal.

Another salient discussion has been on supply chain ESG. A shared concern is that companies may outsource ESG outcomes. For instance, assume that company A has a verticalized operation that produces intermediary goods and the final good. Furthermore, assume that the production process of one of the intermediary products is particularly polluting. The company might choose to sell its productive capacity in this intermediary good to a nonlisted company that is not expected to publish ESG scores.

It is conceivable that publicly listed companies reduce their environmental damage without having any global effect. Companies that publish ESG indicators will become greener over time, but not much will change for society.

Large companies shepherd many initiatives to turn firms in their supply chains greener. Whelan et al. (2017) describe such efforts in the Brazilian beef industry. Nevertheless, members are skeptical that individual efforts to improve ESG-related outcomes can generate a systemwide transformation. Supply chain sustainability is particularly complex. According to some members, materiality is a crucial feature of ESG data. Conversations include many complaints about the quality of current ESG data. Members have argued that it may be impossible to determine if the intrafirm evolution of ESG indicators generates systemic benefits with the existing data. Finally, members disagree that all companies should report financial risks from climate change. Disclosure is costly, and widespread or mandated reporting may generate low-quality information. Furthermore, significant transaction costs are associated with ever-increasing financial reports. Unless reporting standards disclose meaningful information, there is consonance that companies should not spend resources making such efforts.

The flip side of the view that ESG indicators are not risk factors is that fiduciary duty does not constrain the decision space of fund managers. Fiduciary duty requires that managers put the interests of their clients before their own. Many funds use ESG screening to determine the equities that enter their portfolios or change firms' weights according to their ESG scores without violating this obligation. Usually, the scientific literature states that the relation between ambiguous preferences and asset managers' capital allocation is complicated by fiduciary duty. For instance, fiduciary duty is frequently used by the trustees of pension funds to justify their opposition to ESG investing (Schanzenbach & Sitkoff, 2020).

However, members strongly believe their role is to follow investors' directives but do not view fiduciary duty as a barrier to ESG investing.

The business case for sustainability relies on transparency about ESG-related outcomes generating long-term value. Evidence for the case is inconclusive, and it may be that we will never honestly know if ESG investing is profitable, given that financial markets are increasingly more efficient. Agents adapt to perceived or fundamental changes to their portfolios. Market anomalies tend to disappear after some time (Zaremba et al., 2020), which matters because if the incorporation of ESG information does not generate expected excess financial returns, there must be other forces that speed up ESG diffusion. One such force is investors' preferences.

Nevertheless, ESG investing poses no ethical dilemmas for surveyed fund managers. No member argued that fiduciary duty is a barrier to adopting nonfinancial metrics as investment criteria. A group member wrote: "Fiduciary duty is just a convenient excuse. ESG investing has many problems, but fiduciary conflict is not one of them."

Regardless of fund managers' skepticism about using nonfinancial metrics, investors can get overseers to shift their stance and incorporate ESG factors into financial strategies. According to the textual analysis, pressure from funds' backers should accelerate ESG investing. After all, there are no technical barriers to model building, and ESG can be integrated into regular portfolios.

Of course, group members may be myopic about their reality. The days of non-ESG investing numbered. Organizational inertia and skepticism allow fund managers to behave as business as usual. Asset managers invoke the deus ex machina of investors driving change with their work being an instrument to investors' goals. Regardless of the agreement with this view, without asset managers buying into it, ESG investing will not reach its full potential.

Organization inertia is not the only barrier to ESG investment diffusion. Skepticism by fund managers also plays a role. Some avenues exist for regulators and investors to pressure fund managers into more socially responsible investments.

It seems that the quality of ESG and nonfinancial information is lacking. That must be resolved by a concerted effort of exchanges and supervisory agencies, locally and globally. Today, large companies provide better information, on average. However, capital markets can only allocate resources more efficiently in terms of sustainability if the information for decision-making improves.

In the end, fund managers report to their clients. If investors request that nonfinancial criteria be considered in the investment process, this should force fund managers to comply. Still, as in the case of the quality of information, this is a long process that can speed up ESG investing, but not to the extent that society needs to reduce carbon emissions promptly.

4.4.1 *Difficulties with Measuring Sustainable Performance: The Case of Wright Capital*

Wright Capital's business model focuses on impact investing and sustainable finance. Assets are allocated to investments related to one or more of the ten selected Sustainable Development Goals (SDGs) (Fig. 4.8). For their clients, at least 1% of their portfolio must be allocated to narrowly defined impact investments through a dedicated fund (FIC FIM Wright Social Impact) that charges no management fees. The firm is a consumer of sustainable finance products because it does not invest its clients' wealth directly. It buys shares in specialized funds. As such, if a particular investment is related to quality education, one of the SDGs in the Social Capital fund, Wright Capital's role is to ensure that the invested funds meet impact investing criteria. This case is detailed in Zeidan (2020), and we summarize it here.

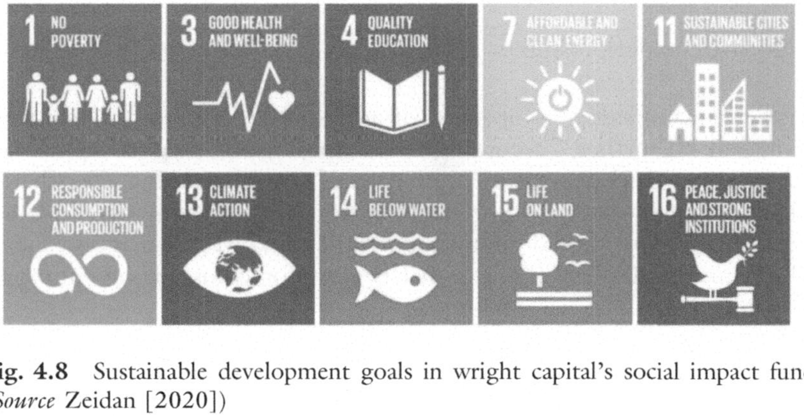

Fig. 4.8 Sustainable development goals in wright capital's social impact fund (*Source* Zeidan [2020])

At first, Wright Capital's social impact strategy mostly involved convincing their clients to increase the share of their wealth devoted to impact investment. Recently, the firm has added lobbying for changes in financial regulations. The company aims to influencing decision-makers by actively participating in associations that drive regulatory change. They aim to accelerate the dynamic processes related to sustainable finance and impact investment.

In an interview with the founders of Wright Capital, they shared three obstacles to ESG investing.

(1) The limits of Environmental Social and Governance (ESG) factors

Most corporations today publish sustainability reports in which ESG factors are dis- closed. However, the quality of the information companies publish varies significantly, and investors cannot easily distinguish between value-creating sustainable initiatives and greenwashing. Funds that screen for ESG factors still rely on "intuition that the laggard's cash flows are riskier and therefore demand a higher cost of capital and thus be valued using a high discount rate" (Davis & Lescott, 2019, 49). ESG factors have one limitation: they present only risks and not opportunities. As such, value-enhancing sustainability initiatives are not captured in regular environmental funds. There are clear practical difficulties about allocating funds to high-performing ESG-screened companies for consumers of financial products. Without dealing with such issues, it will be hard for sustainable finance to thrive.

(2) Shareholder pressure

On the demand side, "companies will go as far as shareholders will take them, and no further," according to the founder of Wright Capital. Of course, some market pressure should lead to greenwashing. Yet shareholder pressure, especially for large corporations without consolidated ownership groups, should limit value-neutral initiatives. Managers cannot hide from shareholders if the signal is clear for companies to improve environmental and social outcomes.

(3) Institutional investors

Scale matters. Institutional investors are vital stakeholders in the sustainable finance domain. Institutional investors are the most influential stakeholders in promoting change. Improving the regulatory framework may speed up the process. Regardless, without institutional investors pressuring companies, small wealth management companies should continue to struggle to find competitive ESG-dedicated funds.

One can't manage what can't be measured. While ESG factors have allowed companies to disclose important information on environmental and social sources of risks, there are limits to its usefulness. There is little standardization in disclosure and no significant evidence that portfolios that screen for ESG factors outperform traditional portfolios.

Nevertheless, business as usual has become less valuable amidst a global pandemic, and resilient companies' market capitalization should rise as the global economy recovers. As the regulatory pendulum swings again to allow more lending for distressed companies, financial regulators can include disclosure rules on environmental and social outcomes as conditions for access to credit.

4.5 Carbon as a Risk Factor

Investors are compensated for holding assets or portfolios with certain risk factors. We have seen that many fund managers don't consider ESG to be a proper risk factor. However, many academic articles have posited that mitigating risks, measured by ESG indicators, should make assets more attractive for investors.

Lioui and Tarelli (2022) chase the ESG factor, comparing two methodologies based on the time series (ratings used to sort stocks) and cross-sectional (ratings used to weight stocks) approaches. They find substantial variations of the factor-alpha in the time series and across vendors. Berg et al. (2022b) tackle the issue of noisy data. They propose two noise-correction procedures, in which they instrument ESG ratings with ratings of other ESG rating agencies. They find that the coefficients of corrected estimates increase on average by a factor of 2.6, implying an average noise-to-signal ratio of 61.7%.

Maybe the correct framework is that the stock price of companies that are intensive in carbon emissions are increasing risk factors. Bolton and Kacperczyk (2021) study whether carbon emissions affect the cross-section of US stock returns. They find that stocks of firms with higher total carbon dioxide emissions (and changes in emissions) earn higher returns, controlling for size, book-to-market, and other return predictors. Partly, this is due to institutional investors implementing exclusionary screening based on direct emission intensity in a few salient industries. They cannot explain this carbon premium through differences in unexpected profitability or other known risk factors (Bolton & Kacperczyk, 2021).

Carbon data in their study comes from the Carbon Disclosure Project (CDP), MSCI ESG Research, and Trucost. The final samples are built on Trucost EDX data, which covers around 1000 listed companies since the fiscal year 2005 and over 2900 listed companies in the United States since 2016. They match these data with the FactSet returns and balance sheet data for all US-listed companies from 2005 to 2017. We should assume that the investors' preoccupation with climate change has strengthened over time. Thus, the authors' results are even more robust, as we would expect that carbon was not a significant risk factor, if at all, in the early years of their sample.

There are three substantial categories of carbon emissions from a company's operations: production emissions (scope 1), indirect emissions from electricity consumption (scope 2), and other indirect emissions from product use, waste disposal, outsourced activities, etc. (scope 3). The latter category is further divided into upstream and downstream indirect emissions.

Notably, the carbon premium is related to the level of (and to changes in) emissions but not to emission intensity, likely because regulations are more likely to target activities where the level of emissions is highest.

The authors find that the carbon premium is economically significant, with a one-standard-deviation increase in the level and change of scope 1 emissions leading to a 15-bps and 26-bps increase in stock returns, or respectively, a 1.8% and 3.1% annualized increase (2.9% and 2.2% for scope 2 emissions and 4.0% and 3.8% for scope 3). They conclude that all other things equal, the carbon premium reflects lower investor demand for stocks of companies associated with high emissions.

Pástor et al. (2022) support these results. They find that US green stocks outperformed brown as climate concerns strengthened. The value-weighted portfolio of stocks in the top third of greenness outperformed the bottom third by a cumulative return difference of 174%. Still, despite that outperformance, they estimate lower expected returns for green stocks than for brown, consistent with a carbon premium. As seen before, the Pástor et al. (2021) model predicts a carbon premium (brown assets with a higher expected return than green assets) for two reasons: investors have green tastes, and greener assets are a better hedge against climate risk. Pástor et al. (2022) estimate expected returns on green and brown assets in the US market on data from 2012 to 2020. They assign greenness measures to individual stocks using MSCI ESG Ratings. How can the authors explain the apparent paradox between green stocks having higher realized returns but less expected returns? They demonstrate that green stocks outperform brown due to surprises over the sample period; shocks related to climate change reduce brown stocks' returns. In addition, industry-level greenness, as opposed to differences within the industry, largely accounts for the superior performance of green stocks and the importance of climate shocks in explaining that performance. Figure 4.9 illustrates the difference in returns between value-weighted green and brown portfolios. The values of the green and brown lines at the end of 2020 are 264.9 and 91.3, implying green stocks outperformed brown by 174 percentage points over this period (Pástor et al., 2022).

Concerning the higher expected returns of brown assets, Bolton and Kacperczyk (2021) convincingly argue that several institutional investors treat high carbon emissions stocks as sin stocks (see Sect. 4.2). They find that insurance companies, pension funds, and mutual funds underweight stocks high in scope 1 emission intensity. The negative ownership effect of moving from high to low scope emission-intensity firms accounts for 15%–20% of the cross-sectional variation in the ownership variable (Bolton & Kacperczyk, 2021). However, divestment is based only on scope 1 emission intensity, both in aggregate and for each institutional investor category (Bolton & Kacperczyk, 2021).

The authors also argue that their results contradict the carbon alpha hypothesis, whereby investors buying shares of companies with low-carbon emissions and shorting companies with high emissions generate positive abnormal returns. Finally, they also document that the carbon premium has materialized recently; there is no indication of such a premium in data from the 1990s (Bolton & Kacperczyk, 2021).

While there are signs that the preference for green investments fundamentally changes market dynamics, we must consider the uncertainty of this evolutionary process. For instance, we may be unable to predict how prices of green and brown assets will evolve during the climate transition.

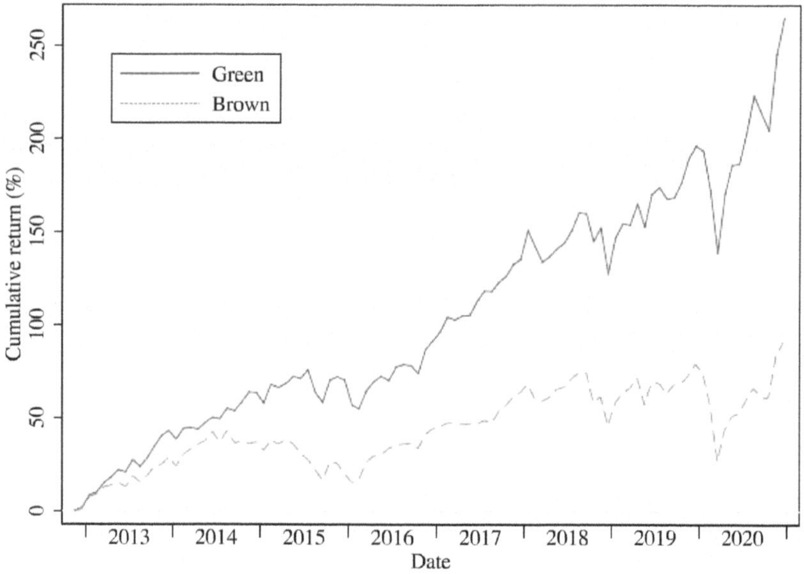

Fig. 4.9 Returns on value-weighted green and brown portfolios (*Source* Pástor et al. [2022])

In a rational expectations model, Goldstein et al. (2022) show that the equilibrium price may not be uniquely determined because traditional and green investors trade in opposite directions based on the same information. As the number of green investors grows and ESG information improves, price informativeness may counterintuitively be reduced.

There is plenty of evidence that climate risk is not well-priced. One of the most convincing studies is Acharya et al. (2022). The authors find that local exposure to damages related to heat stress equaling 1% of GDP is associated with municipal bond yield spreads that are higher by around 15 basis points per annum. This effect is mostly from increased energy expenditures and decreased labor productivity. As for equities, one-standard-deviation increase in exposure to heat stress is associated with yield spreads that are higher by around 40 bps for sub-investment grade corporate bonds, with little effect for investment grade bond spreads, and with conditional expected returns on stocks that are higher by around 45 bps.

Meanwhile, Duan et al. (2021) find that the bonds issued by carbon-intensive firms underperform, which cannot be fully explained by divestment from institutional investors. They argue that investors underreact to the predictability of carbon intensity for firm cash flow news, creditworthiness, and environmental incidents. Regarding the other side, that of the premium related to green bonds, Pietsch and Salakhova (2022) provide evidence that a critical factor explaining the greenium is associated with the issuer's credibility, as measured by bonds under external review (that includes signatories to the UNEP FI). Also, investors' demand grows over time as the greenium becomes more statistically and economically significant.

Does their work indicate that institutional investors are penalizing carbon-intensive companies coherently? Not quite. They note that investors price a carbon emission risk premium in all industries even though divestment is concentrated in the sectors with the highest CO_2 emissions (oil & gas, utilities, and transportation) (Bolton & Kacperczyk, 2021). Even though ESG indicators are almost 20 years old, ESG investing is in its infancy, as these and other studies and the practice of fund managers show. We discuss green bonds in more detail in the following subsection.

4.6 Green Bonds

The widespread use of green bonds could change how financial systems allocate capital to more sustainable projects. Nevertheless, green bonds are not necessarily green and are unlikely to be mandated by regulators. The market should continue to be underutilized in the next decade and should, at most, complement other initiatives for improving the nonfinancial performance of financial institutions. Still, incorporating green bonds in a bank's portfolio is necessary to appease regulators and investors. Hopefully, the market will mature toward disseminating green bonds that will promote real change, but even if that is not the case, asset managers cannot escape it.

On the one hand, shareholders benefit from green bond issuance (Tang & Zhang, 2020). On the other hand, green bonds often make vague commitments, and these promises have weakened over time (Curtis et al., 2023). So, what gives? Should banks treat green bonds as applicable or just play the greenwashing game?

Green bonds are fixed-income financial instruments intended to raise funds earmarked by the issuer for environmentally friendly projects consistent with a climate-resilient economy (Reboredo et al., 2020). Third parties monitor compliance; the funds must be spent on the goals established in the bonds' prospectus.

Although we focus on corporate bonds, most debt instruments lend themselves to green classifications. For instance, in September 2013, the Nordic city of Gothenburg in Sweden issued a municipal green bond totaling SEK500m. Proceeds funded the city's greening of public transport, water management, energy, and waste management projects. Local authorities committed to publicly available post-issuance and independent verification by CICERO. The bond received ratings of AA+ and AAA from S&P and Moody's. The bond was oversubscribed and was followed by a second green bond in May 2014, this time for SEK1.8bn. Both bonds had a 6-year tenor (IISD, 2015).

Any type of bond can be green if the proceeds go to green assets or projects. Companies that regularly issue corporate bonds can, in principle, issue green bonds if they have qualifying green assets or projects (IISD, 2015). For issuers, the only significant transaction cost is the monitoring, which mostly does not happen with regular bonds. Issuing green bonds is a straightforward process. There are five steps (IISD, 2015):

- Identify qualifying green projects and assets. The "greenness" of a company does not matter—it's about the physical assets or projects.
- Arrange independent review. Verifiers include Clean Development Mechanism (CDM) or Emission Trading Schemes (ETS)-qualified organizations and Climate Bonds-approved verifiers.
- Set up tracking and reporting. The issuer needs to track the value of the assets or projects that must stay equal to, or greater than, the bond amount.
- Issue the bond. This step includes seeking required issuance approval from regulators; structuring the bond, usually with an investment bank or advisor; getting a credit rating; and marketing and pricing the bond.
- Monitor the use of proceeds and report annually. Usually, this is done through an audited annual public report.

Table 4.7 presents some more details about distinct types of green bonds.

Table 4.7 A non-exhaustive categorization of green bonds

Type	*Proceeds raised*	*Debt recourse*	*Example*
Green use of proceeds Bond	Earmarked for green projects	Standard/full recourse to the issuer; therefore same credit rating applies as to the issuer's other bonds	European Investment Bank has issued more than EUR7bn (RMB60bn) in "Climate Awareness Bonds" in various currencies since 2007. Proceeds are earmarked for renewable energy and energy efficiency projects
Green use of proceeds Revenue Bond	Earmarked for green projects	Revenue streams from the issuer, such as fees, are the source of repayment for the bond	New York State Environmental Facilities Corp issued a US$213m (RMB1.33bn) green water bond in June 2014. Proceeds are earmarked for drinking water and wastewater infrastructure projects
Green Project Bond	Ring-fenced for the specific underlying green project	Recourse is only to the project's assets and balance sheet	Big60million Ltd issued a Climate Bonds Standard certified GBP4.6m bond (RMB43m) specifically for the Willersey Solar Farm project in September 2014
Green Securitised Bond	Either earmarked for green projects or go directly into the underlying green projects	Recourse refers to loans or assets grouped as collateral (e.g., solar loans)	Hannon Armstrong, a US-listed sustainable infrastructure investor, issued a US$100m (RMB626m) asset-backed securitization of cash flows from wind, solar, and energy efficiency installations in December 2013

Source IISD (2015)

Because green bonds are regular bonds with some extra caveats, we skip some technical aspects in favor of sharing some recent research on the topic that may inform strategic decisions by financial institutions. We discuss the case for issuing these bonds and their limitations, starting with the latter.

One recent study about green bonds examines the legal terms in the market for green bonds (Curtis et al., 2023). They analyze a sample of nearly 1000 bonds over the entire market history, supplementing it with interviews with over 50 market participants and policymakers. They are concerned about the lack of enforceability of green promises. Incidentally, these promises have been getting weaker over time. The authors also conclude that commitments are vague, default events are not adequately reported, and sometimes obligations are omitted. The interviews reveal that market participants know of the shortcomings.

Still, the global green bonds market should not stop growing soon. In 2014, green global bond issuance totaled EUR 14 billion, according to Bos (2023). By 2023, annual global issuance should surpass EUR 600 billion (Fig. 4.10). Still, such figures may be understatements. S&P Global (2022) estimates sustainable bond issuance surpassed U$1.5 trillion in 2022.

The source of the disagreements between data providers is likely due to national definitions of green or sustainable bonds. Regardless, the actual amount matters less than the trend, which is clear.

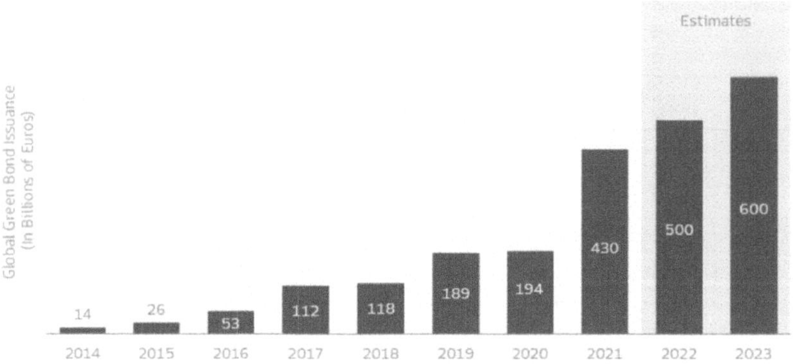

Fig. 4.10 Global green bond issuance (*Source* Bos [2023])

Even though many climate-related commitments may not be worth the paper they are written on, the Paris Agreement induces changes in financial markets. Tolliver et al. (2020) use a database of over $300 billion in green bonds issued in 49 countries between 2007 and 2017 to study the drivers of green bond market growth. The authors build a Paris Agreement Nationally Determined Contribution robustness index and find that Paris pledges exerted the most considerable impact among all variables they tested as green bond drivers.

So, how should banks address green bonds? Should they ignore "brown bonds" in favor of green-only bond portfolios?

The answer is probably no, although following developments in green bonds may spur improved response to regulators. We have seen that exclusion strategies in ESG investing may not be optimal. However, there is a mechanism by which monitoring green bonds may generate value for asset managers in commercial and investment banks.

Green bond issuances signal to investors that companies are more profitable or engender lower risk than similar enterprises. Tang and Zhang (2020) show that stock prices positively respond to green bond issuance, and institutional ownership, primarily from domestic institutions, increases after the firm issues green bonds, resulting in higher stock liquidity.

The first natural way for banks to deal with green bonds is by advising companies in the process of green bond issuance. In that sense, this business practice would be no different from regular corporate bond issuance structuring. However, banks are setting up new departments to deal with sustainability-linked bonds or changing current practices in existing departments to incorporate them.

Barclay's set up a Sustainable Capital Markets team responsible for implementing changes in current business practices. The team is also responsible for helping the specialized areas of the bank to structure bond issuances or other organizational and sustainability goals (Cass et al., 2022).

Juvyns (2023) describes some strategies by J.P. Morgan in dealing with green bonds. Some asset management teams believe that green bonds will continue to benefit from substantial fundamental, quantitative, and technical factors. Regarding fundamentals, green bonds seem more defensive, with lower duration-adjusted volatility, than traditional bonds, but they have similar duration-adjusted returns. Using green bonds in the asset management portfolio of J.P. Morgan requires active management, as the lack of global standards for green bonds makes passive investments trickier. Without the ability to analyze the use of the proceeds from the bonds' issuance, an asset manager could fail to avoid greenwashing and regulatory risks.

In the following subsection, we describe the case of BBVA, the first Spanish bank to issue green bonds.

4.6.1 *How Banks Incorporate Green Bonds: J.P. Morgan, BBVA, and Barclay's Evidence*

In 2018, BBVA was the first Spanish bank to issue a green bond. The total value of the issuance was €1 billion, and it was structured as non-preferred senior debt with a 7-year maturity period. Proceeds from the issuance were directed at financing renewable energy and sustainable transport projects. In 2019, the bank issued another bond with similar characteristics, but this time, it was almost three times oversubscribed (BBVA, 2021).

Reports related to these projects tracked carbon emission avoidance, water treatment, and waste management. The projects reduced carbon emissions that would otherwise exist, totaling 724,000 tons of CO_2 equivalent, treated a volume of water equivalent to the annual consumption of more than 140,000 people, and managed waste equivalent to that produced by 600,000 people (BBVA, 2021).

Even more interesting is BBVA's third sustainable-related bond issuance on July 7, 2020. The bank issued convertible contingent bonds or CoCos. These are hybrid issues that combine debt and equity elements. CoCos can be converted into stock if the CET1 capital ratio drops below a certain level. These bonds are also perpetual instruments. However, the issuer can exercise an option to redeem the bond after a specific period (typically five years after launch) (BBVA, 2021).

How did BBVA square issuing a perpetual bond with the sustainability-related requirements (and their disclosure)? The bank committed to reinvesting and preserving that reinvestment in green projects throughout the bond's life (BBVA, 2021). This commitment allowed the bank to match the bond's maturity without perpetual green assets. For the specific case of BBVA's CoCo, the commitment includes (BBVA, 2021):

- Building a solid portfolio of eligible assets that proves the bond's reinvestment capability. For that purpose, the bank obtains independent opinions from DNV GL. This firm certifies the assets' quality (greenness) and that proceeds are directed toward projects that comply with the bond issuance rules.
- Having a reliable and robust capacity to generate eligible assets. In that case, the projects are part of BBVA's Pledge 2025. In it, the bank pledged to mobilize €100 billion through 2025 in green financing, sustainable infrastructure, social entrepreneurship, and financial inclusion.
- Having a solid governance model. The bank enrolled another certifying agency to ensure independence between the Initial Assessment (DNV GL) and the Reinvestment Certification (PWC). PWC conducts auditing for the annual reports. The consulting firm's role is to verify that the selection of assets meets the eligibility criteria and also certify the environmental impact of the projects. Internally, the institution set up the committees and internal structure required to identify, determine eligibility, and ensure the traceability of the assets.

The BBVA experience illustrates some relevant issues regarding green bonds:

(1) The process is amenable to greenwashing unless the organization is willing to pay hefty transaction costs;
(2) The projects' pipeline is likely not an issue;
(3) The demand for green bonds is also likely not an issue;
(4) The separation between sustainability and operations is not conducive to issuing green bonds.

Points 1 and 2 are intertwined. Because banks routinely fund green (and brown and all other sorts) projects, picking among regularly funded projects classified as green is a matter of internal bureaucracy. Issuing €1 billion for green projects is not a hurdle for a bank with over €300 billion in loans and advances to customers in its balance sheet. HSBC aims to provide USD750bn–USD1trn of sustainable finance and investment to support customer transitions and a sustainable future. Even though HSBC is larger than BBVA, it is not by a significant amount. If such a monumental commitment is more than greenwashing, HSBC (and likely any other commercial bank) would have no problem issuing green bonds as part of this trillionaire supply of sustainable finance.

Still, banks have significant costs to issue green bonds, both organizationally and in monetary disbursements. The governance structure with multiple certification and auditing companies mitigates the possibility of greenwashing. However, setting up such structures increases the bond's cost of capital in relation to regular bonds issued by the bank. That BBVA can issue green bonds at a more favorable interest rate is almost necessary for their viability. After all, regular bonds don't need to remunerate the bank for an extra governance structure.

More importantly, such bond issuance forces a bank's sustainability department to work together with the operational side of the bank. Organizational inertia is one of the main governance challenges for green banking. Changing business practices is a crucial hurdle as asset managers, analysts, loan officers, and other operational personnel aren't usually incentivized to consider sustainability dimensions in their decision-making. Thus, issuing sustainability-related debt instruments can have a considerable internal impact on the bank's business processes.

One notable aspect of BBVA's experience is that the bank eschewed the second mover advantage. In sustainability, institutions often opt to follow instead of braving the way. As banks still view ESG indicators and other sustainability-related factors as risks and not opportunities, the mindset is that leading the way will make an institution incur all the fixed costs of developing a new strategy. Copying the strategy of another bank, however, means reducing the expenses related to the learning curve of the sustainability process. By being the first Spanish bank to issue green bonds and doing so with a large issuance, BBVA took it upon itself to develop the market by paying the set-up costs of this strategy, which may not be recoverable and that competitors might not incur.

Is there a reason for a bank, especially a large bank, not to dip its toes into the green bonds market? Not really. The most important question is: are green banks contributing to climate change mitigation? That is a much more difficult question to answer, and it is beyond the scope of this book. Still, if the other option is doing nothing, an institution might as well try, as these actions have little downside risk.

4.7 Sustainability Delta

Firm valuation is a significant issue for commercial and investment banks. Analysts must have companies to incorporate them into portfolios, and any M&A operation requires various valuation rounds.

Valuation methods include multiples, discount cash flow (DCF), and others, but DCFs are the most common way to measure a company's worth. This section presents two methods for incorporating sustainability components into regular valuation models. The first is described by Zeidan and Spitzeck (2015), and the second by Whelan et al. (2017). In both cases, the goal is to incorporate the opportunities generated by renewable energy, better modes of production, and other sources of "greenium."

Of course, banks already incorporate ESG indicators as downside risks in regular valuation models. Firms are increasingly subject to environmental and social risks, and one does not need to go far for examples of disasters that transformed several of the largest businesses globally. The BP oil spill wiped off US$30 billion of market value in weeks, and the company restructured its business to diminish its dependency on oil. However, it is not clear if institutions do that systematically. Thus, the Sustainability Delta is a straightforward methodology that separates ESG indicators and their materiality in driving firm value Fig. 4.11.

There are three main categories of valuation techniques (Damodaran, 2012): comparable analysis (such as multiples, precedent analysis, and SOTP), liquidation models (asset-based and fair-based values), and discount cash flow methods. The first requires information on company peers, adjusting it for company-specific information. Liquidation models, as the name implies, assume the company will be liquidated. Discounted cash flow methods look at future cash flows, assuming a company is only as valuable as its capacity to generate value for shareholders in the future. It is the most common valuation method, and we argue it is best suited to incorporate sustainability issues.

The main concern in relating sustainability issues to valuation methods is that neither is well defined. The impact of sustainability issues on firms' value is a multidimensional issue. An ideal model that would incorporate sustainability into valuation models should have the following desired characteristics:

- to be able to bring materiality to sustainability issues;

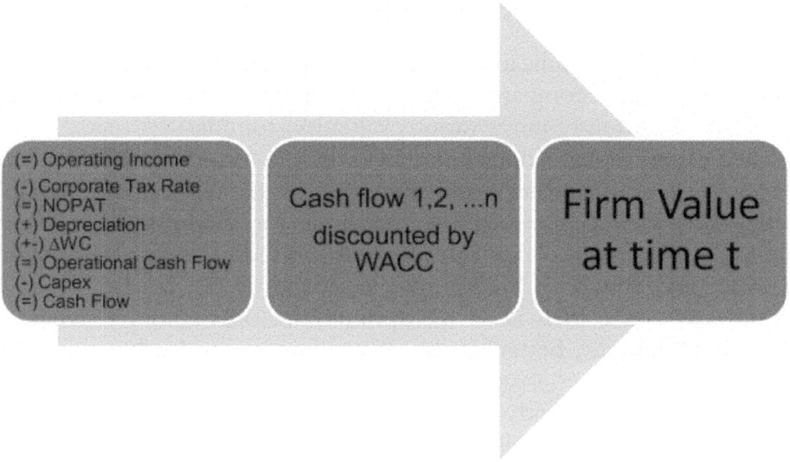

Fig. 4.11 A simple cash flow method for firm valuation

- to be relatable to issues in the chosen valuation method;
- to be amenable to the creation of different simulation scenarios.

The first issue is one of the main hurdles in incorporating sustainability issues into financial modeling. First, sustainability reporting standards need to improve sector-specific materiality because the usual way of reporting does not readily allow the creation of financial information based on self-reported sustainability. Many firms already use AA1000 certification or develop a materiality matrix but have difficulties explaining how relevant materiality issues impact financial performance.

The Sustainability Delta presented in Fig. 4.11 considers a variant of ESG opportunities, which can potentially increase the present firm value at t_1. It also incorporates scenario building, a regular procedure in valuation models.

The ESG methodology tries to solve the materiality issues by ranking the possible impact of ESG factors on firm value. The data requirements are specific to companies and industries and relate to variables in a cash flow statement. For instance, prices can be affected by price premiums based on sustainable goods and services, and the quality of such goods can affect the quantity of goods and services sold. The result is that long-term revenue is affected by investments in more sustainable goods and services. Other variables are affected by sustainability issues in different ways. The cost of capital is based on reputation and the eco-premium perceived by financial institutions. In contrast, capital expenditures may be higher in the short run and lower in the long run for companies that are first entrants in promoting sustainable means of production.

The methodology goes from general principles to firm-level analysis, as in Fig. 4.12. The first stage establishes the variables relevant to a specific firm, going from general variables regarding six sustainability dimensions to the specific ones that impact a firm's future cash flow. The qualitative analysis comprises a life-cycle analysis of the products, identifying the main social and environmental impacts and their financial impact. The six sustainability dimensions evaluated are similar to that of the SCSS: economic growth (EG), environmental protection (EP), social progress (SP), socioeconomic development (SD), eco-efficiency (EE), and socio-environmental development (SD). In the second step, the impacts of the value drivers on future cash flows are evaluated, including revenue and costs. In the final valuation stage, the sustainability delta is calculated regarding ROIC (return on invested capital) and WACC, considering different scenarios with associated probabilities to allow us to simulate different valuation results.

The sustainability delta distances itself from the ESG methodology because it has the same focus on opportunities as it has on risks, being closer to the idea of ESG being nothing special (Edmans, 2023). Hence, it analyzes the probability of increased revenue through new products or

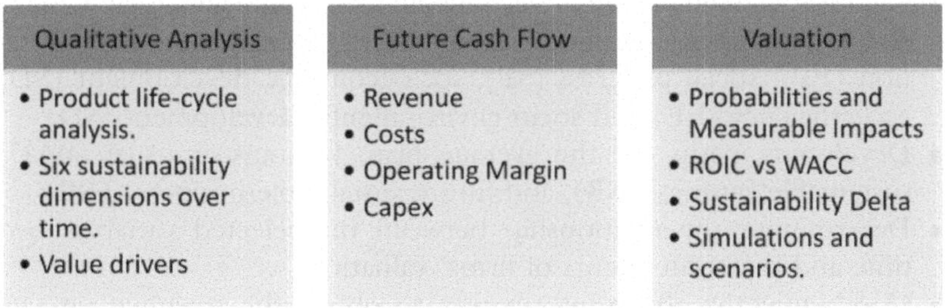

Fig. 4.12 The process of the sustainability delta (*Source* Zeidan and Spitzeck [2015])

services, decreasing costs by targeted, sustainable practices, and increased social capital by renegotiating the social contract between the company and its stakeholders. Another difference is the focus on the time dimension. Impacts on cash flows depend on investments and decisions toward more sustainable production and final goods and services. We analyze such a path through three phases: business as usual (BAU), sustainable business (SB), and future sustainable business (FSB), which are also similar to the SCSS, as in Fig. 4.12.

Since we are dealing with cash flows, it is paramount to understand the path of a company regarding sustainability issues. Take long-term costs, for instance. Assuming a company invests in innovation and sustainable means of production, costs should be lower in the long run, and thus operating income should be higher. If companies already comply with best practices, their costs should not rise shortly, impacting cash flow as in Fig. 4.12. Significant fines for labor practices and environmental issues that could be prevented happen constantly and show how some companies are far from embodying the best practices of many industries.

Discount cash flow methods rely on operating income as the primary variable to be discounted to the present, and a decrease in costs leads to a higher valuation. The main issue is measuring such cost savings on future cash flows. Here, we are explicitly concerned with the sustainability impacts on firms' future cash flows by establishing a probability that the variables related to a firm's valuation are related to sustainability events. Given a selected industry, the process involves the following.

- Value drivers: product life-cycle analysis, value chain, legislation and public policy, industry self-regulation, and innovation.
- Defining variables related to individual firms in each of six sustainability dimensions: economic growth (EG), environmental protection (EP), social progress (SP), socioeconomic development (SD), eco-efficiency (EE) and socio-environmental development (SD).
- Developing paths for the average firm: business as usual (BAU), sustainable business (SB), and future sustainable business (FSB).
- Determining the relationship between the selected variables over time and the components of firms' valuation.
- Combining the above information to obtain the coverage on each variable and measurable impacts on cash flow and WACC.
- Calculating the sustainability delta.
- Establishing scenarios for simulations of the results.

The result is a matrix of coverage and impact that affects the valuation of a company, as represented in Table 4.8, which shows a typical simplified cash flow statement used in valuation methods.

The first question is whether sustainability plays a role in addressable markets. For companies like The Body Shop or Natura, sustainability is related to all its addressable markets. Hence, the coverage of the addressable market affected by sustainability issues would be 100%. In another case, take a construction company in a poor country. For such a company, most of the addressable market is related to local infrastructure projects, which are hardly affected by sustainability opportunities. There is no demand for sustainability-specific projects in government purchases in several emerging countries.

In addition, some markets will bear an eco-premium while others won't. In contrast, if we analyze another industry that has been the target of sustainable finance initiatives, the sugar industry in Brazil, we can establish positive probabilities to the addressable market about the path from BAU to FSB. Sustainably farmed sugar commands an eco-premium, with prices around 20% above regular refined sugar. Companies rated higher in sustainable production could improve their margins and sales, commanding higher valuations. The exact change in valuation is due to the production process and cost management. Take water management, which is one of the most critical challenges in agriculture. It is not an issue for every firm but can become significant in some areas. Depending on the region, its probability of impact on costs ranges from 5 to 20% of variable costs. Companies rated higher in the path from BAU to FSB in water management increase their valuation by lowering future variable costs. However, companies that want to pursue sustainability strategies have, at first, to increase their capital expenditures, which can reduce their value. Addressing a comprehensive sustainability delta involves assumptions about the necessary investments and future cash flows generated by sustainability strategies.

4.7.1 Application of the Sustainability Delta

We describe the SD impact on the valuation of a sugar manufacturer. This case is based on actual data (with some approximations for simplicity) from a small sugar manufacturer. Its valuation is based on the following assumptions:

Table 4.8 Basic cash flow statement for a sustainability path

	BAU		*SB*		*FSB*	
	% Coverage	*Measurable impact*	*% Coverage*	*Measurable impact*	*% Coverage*	*Measurable impact*
Addressable market						
Market-share						
Revenue						
(−) Variable costs						
(−) Fixed costs						
(=) EBITDA						
(−) Depreciation and amortization						
(=) EBIT						
(−) Corporate income tax						
(=) NOPLAT						
(+) Depreciation and amortization						
(±) Working capital						
(=) Operational cash flow						
(−) Capex						
(+) Terminal value						
(=) Enterprise cash flow Discounted by WACC						
(=) Enterprise value						

Source Zeidan and Spitzeck (2015)

The company produces white sugar. It is located in a frontier region where the industry is expanding, with lower productivity than in other areas but growing at 1% yearly. It has seven-year contracts with farmers that supply sugar cane in close vicinity.

The initial valuation period is five years, from 2025 to 2029. We assume that the values of 2029 are going to be constant from then on, arriving at a terminal value equal to the present value of a perpetuity based on NOPAT less working capital and capex discounted by the WACC of the company.

Today, the firm produces 400,000 pounds of sugar annually, expanding toward 700,000 tons in 5 years. Its production is growing by roughly 15% a year. Sugar prices are estimated to be US$15 a pound in 2025 and should be constant at US$16 a ton for the rest of the period.

Variable costs are US$10 per pound in 2025 and grow by 3% a year during 2025–2029 (accounted for the productivity growth). Fixed costs are US$800,000 in 2025 and grow at 10% a year. Capital expenditures are US$500,000 in 2025 and increase by 10% annually. Investments in working capital are US$100,000 in 2025, and given a constant financial cycle of 40 days, its values are US$151,111 in 2026, US$122,667 in 2027, US$141,067 in 2028 and US$162,227 in 2029. All values are inclusive of taxes.

Regarding terminal values, we assume no change in operating profit. The firm does not need to spend on new investments, but its operating margin decreases by the same value as the CAPEX, for simplicity. Results for the base scenario are in Table 4.9.

The capital structure comprises 40% of debt and 60% of equity and is assumed constant for the whole period. The cost of capital is also steady, with 7% a year for debt and 14% for equity. Given all these assumptions, the final cash flow is found in Table 4.9. In the BAU scenario, the enterprise value is around US$9.6 million.

The sustainability delta is estimated from two sustainability-related projected investments: an impact on cost management and an eco-premium on organic sugar.

The former opportunity is related to best practices in energy management. These practices include bioenergy production from sugarcane bagasse, a by-product of the production process. We estimate that the coverage rate is only 2% of total fixed costs, a very conservative estimate. The measurable impact follows the typical cash flow profile of an investment in bioenergy production for a small sugar producer.

Table 4.9 Base scenario (Business as usual) of a frm valuation. US$

	2025	*2026*	*2027*	*2028*	*2029*
(=) Revenue	6,000,000	7,360,000	8,464,000	9,733,600	11,193,640
(−) Variable costs	−4,000,000	−4,738,000	−5,612,161	−6,647,605	−7,874,088
(=) Operating margin	2,000,000	2,622,000	2,851,839	3,085,995	3,319,552
Operating margin (%)	*33*	*36*	*34*	*32*	*30*
(−) Fixed costs	−800,000	−864,000	−933,120	−1,007,770	−1,088,391
(=) EBITDA	1,200,000	1,758,000	1,918,719	2,078,226	2,231,161
(−) Depreciation and amortization	−200,000	−220,000	−242,000	−266,200	−292,820
(=) EBIT	1,000,000	1,538,000	1,676,719	1,812,026	1,938,341
(−) Income taxes (34%)	−340,000	−522,920	−570,084	−616,089	−659,036
(=) NOPLAT	660,000	1,015,080	1,106,635	1,195,937	1,279,305
(+) Depreciation	200,000	220,000	242,000	266,200	292,820
(±) Working capital	−100,000	−151,111	−122,667	−141,067	−162,227
(=) Operational cash flow	760,000	1,083,969	1,225,968	1,321,070	1,409,898
(−) Capex	−500,000	−550,000	−605,000	−665,500	−732,050
(+) Terminal value					12,483,461
(=) Enterprise cash flow	260,000	533,969	620,968	655,570	13,161,310
			Enterprise value	9,662,930	

Source Zeidan and Spitzeck (2015)

- Capex of US$200,000 in the first year and US$100,000 in Years 2 and 3.
- Energy savings (the firm is not large enough to sell excess energy until Year 5, but this would require more investments in connecting the company to the grid, which we disregard at this point) of US$15,000 beginning in Year 2.
- Subsidized credit for the investment, reducing the firm's total cost of capital by 0.2% a year.

As for organic sugar, the firm production would range from 5 to 20% of the total sugar production for the local market or exports. The firm could, with its current infrastructure, quickly produce up to 5000 tons of organic sugar a year with minimal investments, resulting in a coverage rate of less than 1.5%. It could choose to produce more, but that would involve distribution, marketing, and investment risks. We assume the following measurable impacts:

- Prices 20% higher than regular sugar.
- Sales in the local market, diversifying revenue streams (the company is mainly an exporter). The effect is not shown as cash flow.
- Production begins in Year 2 and grows at the same rate as total production (which stays the same over the period).

The results are in Table 4.10. The sustainability delta, the difference between the BAU situation and the exploration of sustainability opportunities, is 1.24%. Companies moving toward more sustainable means of production and looking to sell more sustainable goods and services should become significantly more valuable as markets develop to incorporate it in their cash flows.

Theory on sustainable finance demonstrates that current ESG methodologies lack a consideration of opportunity exploration to enhance future cash flows and a scenario–building exercise. Methods such as the sustainability delta allow analysts to consider nonfinancial risks and opportunities explicitly.

Table 4.10 Sustainable business scenario and Frm valuation. US$

	2025	*2026*	*2027*	*2028*	*2029*
(=) Revenue	6,000,000	7,376,000	8,482,400	9,754,760	11,217,974
(−) Variable costs	−4,000,000	−4,738,000	−5,612,161	−6,647,605	−7,874,088
(=) Operating margin	2,000,000	2,638,000	2,870,239	3,107,155	3,343,886
Operating margin (%)	*33*	*36*	*34*	*32*	*30*
(−) Fixed costs	−800,000	−849,000	−918,120	−992,770	−1,073,391
(=) EBITDA	1,200,000	1,789,000	1,952,119	2,114,386	2,270,495
(−) Depreciation and amortization	−200,000	−220,000	−242,000	−266,200	−292,820
(=) EBIT	1,000,000	1,569,000	1,710,119	1,848,186	1,977,675
(−) Income taxes (34%)	−340,000	−533,460	−581,440	−628,383	−672,410
(=) NOPLAT	660,000	1,035,540	1,128,679	1,219,803	1,305,266
(+) Depreciation	200,000	220,000	242,000	266,200	292,820
(±) Working capital	−100,000	−152,889	−122,933	−141,373	−162,579
(=) Operational cash flow	760,000	1,102,651	1,247,745	1,344,629	1,435,506
(−) Capex	−700,000	−650,000	−705,000	−665,500	−732,050
(+) Terminal value					12,990,302
(=) Enterprise cash flow	60,000	452,651	542,745	679,129	13,693,758
		Enterprise value		9,782,791	

Source Zeidan and Spitzeck (2015)

There are three main limitations to this methodology:

- information requirements;
- the fact that it works better with single-product companies;
- difficulty of assumptions regarding SB and FSB paths and their impacts on future cash flows.

Any valuation method suffers from the first two issues, but they are more relevant when incorporating sustainability into future cash flows. It is particularly difficult to estimate the needs for present-day investments and future savings and improved cash flows from sustainability issues. The third requirement relates to qualitative information on the industry's future and the place of the typical firm as a future sustainable business.

4.7.2 Bringing Materiality to the Fore: A Case Study for the Beef Industry

This case study summarizes Whelan et al. (2017). The article aims to describe a materiality methodology for companies in the beef industry that is freely shared with the community. The work was commissioned by multinational companies that made public commitments to zero deforestation but found it challenging to implement. For the companies, making explicit the benefits of sustainability-related investments could incentivize their supply chain to change their current behavior.

As some stakeholder interviews indicated, many business owners, especially ranchers, were highly resistant to change. Many felt that they didn't have a direction for sustainability-related investments, skeptical that green expenditures would generate enough profits to make them worthwhile. For modernizing the supply chains, the focal companies wanted to distribute better managerial tools to the small companies.

The project also shows the importance of the largest firms, financial and nonfinancial, leading the climate transition. Several multinational companies have signed zero-deforestation agreements but haven't been able to track their supply chains adequately. Creating a methodology to show the benefits of sustainability measures could potentially speed up the improvement of environmental outcomes in their supply chains.

Like the sustainability delta, the monetization methodology is a detailed process for bringing materiality to sustainability-related factors. Unlike the former, the monetization methodology customizes valuation tools, adapting them to the realities of the beef industry.

Table 4.11 details the main categories for which sustainability-related investments could increase firm value. Like the sustainability delta, the goal is to divulge actionable information for managers and investors of all sizes.

4.8 Social Impact Bonds

Social impact bonds (SIBs) are a tiny fraction of financial markets. Unfortunately, such instruments can't be scaled like regular bonds. Still, they can meaningfully improve social outcomes, so we describe their essential characteristics here without extensive details.

SIBs are performance-based financial instruments that align social and financial objectives. They are designed to incentivize private investors to

Table 4.11 NPV of expected benefits for ranchers, slaughterhouses, and retailers, based on the monetization methodology

	Ranch		*Slaughterhouse*		*Retailer*	
	NPV of expected benefit *Conservative*	*Aggressive*	*Conservative*	*Aggressive*	*Conservative*	*Aggressive*
Costs	**$12,320,338**	**$13,286,798**				
Better cost management (inputs)						
Cost reduction: techniques and innovation	$6,642,897	$6,642,897				
Cost avoidance: land productivity	$5,677,441	$6,643,901				
Revenue	**$1,901,615**	**$3,303,163**	**$68,192,911**	**$227,309,703**	**$17,684,092**	**$53,052,276**
Price premiums	$1,332,378	$1,332,378	$7,576,990	$45,461,941	$1,367,892	$4,103,675
'No discount'	$44,860	$269,163				
Volume Increase: Future demand	$340,848	$1,022,543	$60,615,921	$181,847,763	$16,316,201	$48,948,602
Volume increase: Higher land productivity						
New revenue stream—additional land	$183,528	$679,079				
Risk	**$1,580,543**	**$4,599,380**	**$66,805,941**	**$228,084,242**	**$19,904,637**	**$85,082,304**
Operational	$158,054	$632,217	$8,901,351	$35,605,406	$683,946	$2,735,783
Market	$237,081	$987,839	$53,408,109	$178,027,028	$16,414,698	$68,394,576
Regulatory	$1,185,407	$2,963,518	$935,941	$3,770,186	$70,210	$273,030
Reputational		$15,805	$3,560,541	$10,681,622	$2,735,783	$13,678,915
Cost of capital and valuation	**$3,467,162**	**$6,341,076**	**$4,048,810**	**$12,146,431**	**$948,281**	**$3,176,787**

	Ranch		*Slaughterhouse*		*Retailer*	
	NPV of expected benefit *Conservative*	*Aggressive*	*Conservative*	*Aggressive*	*Conservative*	*Aggressive*
Cost of Debt			$3,756,046	$11,268,139	$331,944	$1,327,775
Market Capitalization			$292,764	$878,291	$616,337	$1,849,012
Land value appreciation	$3,467,162	$6,341,076				
Other	**$465,792**	**$2,945,702**	**$10,052,374**	**$36,983,392**	**$3,916,156**	**$21,913,456**
Talent attraction	$62,474	$562,264	$5,372,598	$18,132,517	$2,939,576	$13,228,094
Employee retention	$3,645	$14,581	$263,542	$1,185,939	$546,645	$6,965,627
Brand						
Corporate ecosystem			$4,416,234	$17,664,936	$429,934	$1,719,736
Environment: Emission Avoidance	$380,219	$2,281,312				
Environment: Carbon Sequestration	$19,454	$87,545				
Total	**$19,735,449**	**$30,476,118**	**$149,100,036**	**$504,523,768**	**$42,453,166**	**$163,224,824**

Source Whelan et al. (2017)

fund social programs, with returns tied to achieving predefined social outcomes. SIBs have been used to fund various social programs, such as reducing prison recidivism rates and improving educational outcomes for disadvantaged children.

There are four types of organizations: the government, issuers, monitoring organizations, and NGOs. The idea behind an SIB is straightforward: the government and the issuer work closely together to determine the parameters of a social issue that private investments can ameliorate. Of course, the selected social issue must have clear success metrics. For investors, SIBs are like most other government-backed bonds with one main difference: if the project is successful, investors receive the principal plus interest as agreed, but if the project is not, they usually lose all principal (similarly to unsecured bonds).

As for 2023, the average contract duration for an SIB was 52 months, the upfront capital was U$3.3 million, and the average number of beneficiaries was 19,474 (but the median SIB serviced less than 500 beneficiaries). The total invested capital in the SIB industry in 2023 was almost U$500 million (Gustaffson-Wright & Painter, 2023). It is still a small part of financial markets, but SIBs may continue to grow in the following decades. The main challenges are well-designed instruments in which competent governments work seamlessly with private organizations to outsource some issues that can be funded privately. Of course, SIBs complement governments' social policies; many social challenges are not amenable to this type of financial arrangement.

Below is the usual process for an SIB issuance.

1. Identify a Social Issue: The first step in issuing a social impact bond is to identify a specific social issue that needs to be addressed, such as reducing homelessness or improving education outcomes.
2. Develop a Project Plan: Once a social issue has been identified, the issuer must develop a project plan that outlines the specific goals of the project, the target population, and the metrics that will be used to measure the project's success. The project plan should also include a budget and timeline for the project.
3. Determine the Payment Structure: Social impact bonds are structured to repay investors based on the project's success. The issuer must determine the payment structure for the bond, which may involve payments based on specific outcomes or milestones achieved by the project.

4. Establish a Special Purpose Vehicle: To issue a social impact bond, the issuer typically establishes a special purpose vehicle (SPV) responsible for managing the bond issuance and the project. The SPV may be a separate legal entity or issuer subsidiary.
5. Select Service Providers: The issuer must select service providers to implement the project, such as a nonprofit organization or a social enterprise. The service providers are responsible for delivering the services to the target population and achieving the project goals.
6. Raise Capital: The social impact bond is then offered to investors to raise capital for the project. The investors may include foundations, impact investors, or other socially-minded investors. The bond offering may be structured as a private placement, sold to a small group of investors, or as a public offering, sold to a broader group of investors.
7. Implement the Project: Once the capital has been raised, the service providers implement the project according to the project plan. The issuer and the SPV monitor the project's progress and measure the outcomes based on the metrics established in the project plan.
8. Repay Investors: If the project achieves the targeted outcomes, the investors are repaid based on the payment structure established for the bond. If the project does not achieve the targeted outcomes, the investors may not receive any repayment.
9. Report on Outcomes: The issuer must report the project's outcomes to the investors and other stakeholders. This report may include detailed data on the project's impact and any challenges or lessons learned.

As we can see in this detailed overview of how a social impact bond is typically issued, the process involves more organizations and steps than a regular bond issuance. Of course, the market for this type of financial instrument is not mature, so it is possible that, as markets evolve, disintermediation will occur.

There are other similar instruments in the social finance sphere. Development Impact Bonds (DIBs) are similar to SIBs but typically used to finance social programs in developing countries. DIBs are structured so investors are repaid based on predefined development outcomes, such as improving access to clean water or reducing infant mortality rates. The difference is that multilateral organizations coordinate them instead of local governments, but the idea is similar to SIBs.

Community Development Financial Institutions (CDFIs) are specialized financial institutions that provide capital and financial services to underserved communities. They are typically structured as nonprofit organizations and may receive funding from both public and private sources. CDFIs offer a range of financial products and services, including loans, investments, and technical assistance to support community development projects.

Finally, Pay for Success (PFS) Programs are similar to SIBs, but government agencies typically fund them. PFS Programs use private funding to pay for social programs, with returns tied to achieving predefined social outcomes. PFS Programs have been used to fund various social programs, such as reducing homelessness and improving healthcare outcomes for low-income populations. The difference between PFS and SIBs is that no financial instrument is issued in the former, with the government directly funding a social initiative.

4.9 Fintechs

Fintech is a broad term that refers to companies that incorporate innovative solutions to improve financial services to customers. They can specialize in disintermediation, universalization, and customized credit scores, among other areas. Investors' demands are a powerful force for organizational change, complementing regulators' pressure in forcing banks' hands regarding their social and environmental commitments.

For our purposes, Fintechs are no different than standard banks concerning green operations. Some may be regulated as commercial banks and face similar dilemmas. Take, for instance, the rise of virtual banks without physical branches, such as Nubank in the Americas and Revolut and Monzo in Europe. If licensed as banks, they are subject to regulations similar to those of other financial institutions. When they operate as credit intermediaries in the non-banking space, they face similar constraints to other non-bank retailers. Here, we concentrate on banking fintechs and argue that although they can be more agile than established institutions, their greening challenges are comparable. For example, in the United Kingdom, regulators do not differentiate between brick-and-mortar and online-only banks, a widespread attitude among international supervisory agencies (Multilaw, 2024).

Table 4.12 describes the basics of green banking. Fintech companies can be involved in all dimensions of greening financial markets.

Table 4.12 Green financing

Retail banking	*Investment banking*	*Asset management*
Green Mortgages Green Home Equity Loans Green Commercial Building Loans Green Car Loans Green Cards	Green Project Finance Green Securitization Green Venture Capital & Private Equity Green Indices Carbon Commodities Green Project Finance	Green Fiscal Funds Green Investment Funds Carbon Funds

*Source*UNEP Finance Initiative (2007)

Most of the time, fintech companies compete with banks to get customers. However, the term has lost its original meaning, and today, it encompasses relatively new firms with a digital focus that services the financial industry in some capacity.

Regarding fintech companies that compete directly with traditional institutions, companies such as Bunq, Aspiration, and Oxbury have launched several sustainability-related initiatives. Bunq, a Dutch online bank, has created eco-friendly online subscriptions that have resulted, among other things, in over 3 million trees being planted. Aspiration, an online financial firm that offers cash management accounts, funnels money into green projects (the company, similarly to Bunq, also sponsors planting trees).

More critical to the present context are the companies that provide complementary services to commercial banks. Among these companies, NetZero helps customers determine the carbon footprint of their purchases, Nori is developing a marketplace for carbon removals, and OpenInvest helps advisors offer their clients ESG investing that aligns with their values (Muhn, 2021).

It is impossible to cover all the ways fintech companies and sustainability intersect. There is also no theoretical framework that provides a unique roadmap to analyzing the potential impact of fintech in the greening of commercial and investment banks. Thus, we offer a basic overview of all the areas in which fintech companies can help improve the sustainability outcomes of financial markets.

Regarding operations, fintech companies can help banks better integrate ESG considerations into their operations. For example, fintech companies can offer data analytics tools that enable banks to collect, analyze, and report ESG data more efficiently and accurately. Fintech companies can also provide digital platforms and marketplaces that connect banks with ESG-conscious investors and borrowers, enabling them to access a broader range of sustainable finance opportunities.

Fintech companies can also help banks to improve their customer engagement and education on sustainable finance. Many customers, especially younger generations, are increasingly concerned about sustainability and seek financial products and services that align with their values.

Regarding credit score systems (see Chapter 3), fintech companies can help banks better integrate ESG considerations into their operations by providing data analytics tools that enable banks to collect and analyze ESG data more effectively. This can help banks identify and manage ESG risks and opportunities more efficiently and make informed investment decisions. These analytics tools include, other than rating systems:

- Carbon footprint analysis: This quantitative assessment of a company's greenhouse gas (GHG) emissions can be used to identify and manage carbon risks and opportunities. Fintech companies can provide banks with carbon footprint analysis tools that calculate a company's GHG emissions across its entire value chain, including direct and indirect emissions from operations, supply chain, and products and services.
- Climate risk assessment: This is a quantitative assessment of a company's exposure to physical and transition risks associated with climate change, such as extreme weather events, resource scarcity, and policy changes. Climate risk assessment tools combine environmental data, financial data, and scenario analysis to assess a company's exposure to climate risks and opportunities.

Fintech companies may also develop marketplaces that connect banks with ESG-conscious investors and borrowers. These platforms can help banks access a broader range of sustainable finance opportunities and enable them to offer their customers more sustainable financial products and services. Some examples of digital platforms and marketplaces include:

Green bonds platforms: These platforms connect issuers of green bonds (see a previous section) with investors looking to invest in sustainable assets. Green bond platforms can give banks access to a range of green bond issuers and enable them to offer green bonds to their customers.

Crowdfunding platforms: these enable individuals and organizations to raise funds for sustainable projects and businesses from many investors.

Sustainability marketplaces: These platforms connect buyers and sellers of sustainable products and services, such as renewable energy certificates, carbon credits, and sustainable commodities. Sustainability marketplaces can give banks access to a range of sustainable products and enable them to offer sustainability-focused supply chain finance to their customers. For instance, Raise Green provides a marketplace where users can invest in local, impactful projects (Muhn, 2021). Trine uses a peer-to-peer (P2P) loan platform to power solar energy projects from thousands of individual investors who can add to the pool as little as $25 (Ściślak, 2022).

Fintech companies can use machine learning algorithms to identify and classify ESG-related risks and opportunities associated with different industries and companies based on their financial and nonfinancial performance. For instance, these firms can help design systems that incorporate ESG factors into VaR models. They can use ESG ratings from third-party data providers, such as MSCI ESG, Sustainalytics, or Refinitiv ESG. Such algorithms can also simulate the impact of different ESG-related shocks and stresses on their portfolios and estimate their potential losses.

Regarding ESG investing, fintechs can use natural language processing (NLP) algorithms to extract useful information. For example, fintech companies can use NLP algorithms to analyze news articles and social media posts related to climate change, energy transition, or social justice issues and identify the sentiment and tone of the discourse. They can also use network analysis to map the relationships between companies and industries and identify potential sources of systemic risk related to ESG issues. Carbon Collective offers roboadvisory services for users that want to divest from fossil fuels and invest in low-carbon stock market funds. Meanwhile, Tumelo helps institutional investors to vote on ESG issues (Muhn, 2021).

Finally, fintech companies can help banks reduce their carbon footprint and improve their operational efficiency by offering digital solutions for payments, lending, and other banking services. For example, they can provide digital wallets and mobile payment solutions that reduce the need for physical cash and paper-based transactions. They can also offer digital lending platforms that automate the loan application process and reduce the need for manual, paper-based workflows. Joro analyzes users' payment cards to determine the biggest drivers of their carbon footprint (Muhn, 2021).

References

Acharya, V. V., & Pedersen, L. H. (2005). Asset Pricing with Liquidity Risk. *Journal of FinaNcial Economics, 77*(2), 375–410.

Acharya, V. V., Johnson, T., Sundaresan, S., & Tomunen, T. (2022). *Is Physical Climate Risk Priced? Evidence from Regional Variation in Exposure to Heat Stress* (No. w30445). National Bureau of Economic Research.

Avramov, D., Cheng, S., Lioui, A., & Tarelli, A. (2022). Sustainable Investing with ESG Rating Uncertainty. *Journal of Financial Economics, 145*(2), 642–664.

Baldini, M., Dal Maso, L., Liberatore, G., Mazzi, F., & Terzani, S. (2018). Role of country-and firm-level determinants in environmental, social, and governance disclosure. *Journal of Business Ethics*, *150*(1), 79–98.

BBVA. (2021). How Does a Bank's Green Bond Contribute to Protecting the Environment? BBVA Communications. https://www.bbva.com/en/sustainability/how-does-a-banks-green-bond-contribute-to-protect-the-environment/

Berg, F., Koelbel, J. F., & Rigobon, R. (2022a). Aggregate Confusion: The Divergence of ESG Ratings. *Review of Finance, 26*(6), 1315–1344.

Berg, F., Koelbel, J. F., Pavlova, A., & Rigobon, R. (2022b). *ESG Confusion and Stock Returns: Tackling the Problem of Noise* (No. w30562). National Bureau of Economic Research.

BlackRock. (2020). A Systematic Approach. https://www.blackrock.com/corporate/insights/blackrock-investment-institute/publications/sustainability-in-portfolio-construction#a-systematic-approach

BlackRock. (2022). How to Invest in the Net Zero Transition. https://www.BlackRock.com/ch/individual/en/transition-investing

BlackRock. (2023). Sustainable Investing at BlackRock. https://www.BlackRock.com/ch/individual/en/themes/sustainable-investing/esg-integration

BlackRock Institute. (2022a). 2023 Global Outlook Our New Investment Playbook—In Charts. https://www.blackrock.com/corporate/literature/whitepaper/bii-global-outlook-in-charts.pdf

BlackRock Institute. (2022b). 2023 Global Outlook A New Investment Playbook. https://www.blackrock.com/corporate/literature/whitepaper/bii-global-outlook-2023.pdf

Bolton, P., & Kacperczyk, M. (2021). Do Investors Care About Carbon Risk? *Journal of Financial Economics, 142*(2), 517–549.

Bos, B. (2023). Green Bonds: Connecting Fixed Income Capital to the Global Climate Transition, Goldman Sachs Asset Management. https://www.gsam.com/content/gsam/dk/en/advisers/market-insights/gsam-insights/perspectives/2022/green-bonds-fixed-income-capital.html

Branch, M., Goldberg, L. R., & Hand, P. (2019). A Guide to ESG Portfolio Construction. *The Journal of Portfolio Management, 45*(4), 61–66.

Busch, T., van Hoorn, V., Stapelfeldt, M., & Pruessner, E. (2022). Classification Scheme for Sustainable Investments. White Paper.

Campiglio, E., Daumas, L., Monnin, P., & von Jagow, A. (2022). Climate-Related Risks in Financial Assets. *Journal of Economic Surveys.*

Cass, G., Jhavar, A., Jones, W., & Shah, K. (2022). Sustainability-Linked Bonds: Flexibility Drives Growth, Barclay's Corporate and Investment Bank. https://www.cib.barclays/our-insights/3-point-perspective/sustainability-linked-bonds-flexibility-drives-growth.html

Clark, P. (2023). A War for Climate Talent is Hotting Up. *Financial Times.* https://www.ft.com/content/8412db41-dce1-44a7-9417-25a3a534ee54

Cremers, M., Riley, T. B., & Zambrana, R. (2023). *The Complex Materiality of ESG ratings: Evidence from Actively Managed ESG Funds* (Working Paper). https://papers.ssrn.com/sol3/papers.cfm?abstract_id=4335688

Curtis, Q., Weidemaier, M. C., & Gulati, M. (2023). Green Bonds, Empty Promises. https://papers.ssrn.com/sol3/papers.cfm?abstract_id=4350209

Damodaran, A. (2012). Investment valuation: Tools and techniques for determining the value of any asset. John Wiley & Sons.

Davis, T., & Lescott, B. (2019). ESG as a value-creation tool for active investors: A profile of Inherent Group. *Journal of Applied Corporate Finance, 31*(2), 42–49.

De Angelis, T., Tankov, P., & Zerbib, O. D. (2022). Climate Impact Investing. *Management Science, 69*(12), 7669–7692.

De Jong, F., & de Roon, F. A. (2005). Time-Varying Market Integration and Expected Returns in Emerging Markets. *Journal of Financial Economics, 78*, 583–613.

Drempetic, S., Klein, C., & Zwergel, B. (2019). The influence of firm size on the ESG score: Corporate sustainability ratings under review. *Journal of Business Ethics*, 1–28.

Duan, T., Li, F. W., & Wen, Q. (2021). Is Carbon Risk Priced in the Cross-Section of Corporate Bond Returns? SSRN 3709572.

Dunn, J., Hernandez, M., & Palazzolo, C. (2020). Clearing the Air: Responsible Investment. *The Journal of Portfolio Management, 46*(3), 36–41.

Economist, The. (2020). The proliferation of sustainability accounting standards comes with costs, October 3, https://www.economist.com/business/2020/10/03/the-proliferation-of-sustainability-accountingstandards-comes-with-costs

Edmans, A. (2023). The end of ESG. *Financial Management*, *52*(1), 3–17.

EU Sustainable Finance & SFDR: Making the Framework Fit for Purpose. https://www.eurosif.org/wp-content/uploads/2022/06/Eurosif-Report-June-22-SFDR-Policy-Recommendations.pdf

European Commission. (2018). Action Plan: Financing Sustainable Growth, European Commission, Document 52018DC0097, COM/2018/097. https://eur-lex.europa.eu/legal-content/EN/TXT/?uri=CELEX%3A52018DC0097

European Commission. (2023) Platform on Sustainable Finance. https://finance.ec.europa.eu/sustainable-finance/overview-sustainable-finance/platform-sustainable-finance_en; https://capitalmonitor.ai/regions/europe/explainer-what-are-the-sfdr-regulations/

European Parliament. (2009). Directive 2009/65/EC of the European Parliament and of the Council. *Official Journal of the European Union L, 302*, 33. https://eur-lex.europa.eu/LexUriServ/LexUriServ.do?uri=OJ:L:2009:302:0032:0096:en:PDF

European Parliament. (2019). Regulation (EU) 2019/2088 of the European Parliament and of the Council of 27 November 2019 on Sustainability-Related Disclosures in the Financial Services Sector. *Official Journal of the European Union L, 317*, 1. https://eur-lex.europa.eu/legal-content/EN/TXT/PDF/?uri=CELEX:32019R2088&from=EN

Gibson, R., Krueger, P., & Schmidt, P. S. (2021). ESG Rating Disagreement and Stock Returns. *Financial Analysts Journal, 77*(4), 104–127.

Goldstein, I., Kopytov, A., Shen, L., & Xiang, H. (2022). *On ESG Investing: Heterogeneous Preferences, Information, and Asset Prices* (No. w29839). National Bureau of Economic Research.

Grewal, J., Hauptmann, C., and Serafeim, G. (2020). Material sustainability information and stock price informativeness. *Journal of Business Ethics*, 1–32.

Gustaffson-Wright, E., & Painter, E. (2023). Social and Development Impact Bonds by the Numbers, April 2023 snapshot, Brookings Institute. https://www.brookings.edu/research/social-and-development-impact-bonds-by-the-numbers/

HSBC. (2021). *We're Phasing Out Coal Financing*. HSBC. https://www.hsbc.com/news-and-media/hsbc-news/were-phasing-out-coal-financing

HSBC. (2022). *HSBC Thermal Coal Phase-Out Policy*. HSBC. https://www.hsbc.com/-/files/hsbc/our-approach/risk-and-responsibility/pdfs/221214-hsbc-thermal-coal-phase-out-policy.pdf

IISD (The International Institute for Sustainable Development). (2015). Climate Bonds Initiative. https://www.iisd.org/publications/report/how-issue-green-bond-china

Juvyns, V. (2023). *Green Bonds: Is Doing Good Compatible with Doing Well in Fixed Income?* J.P.Morgan Asset Management. https://am.jpmorgan.com/fi/en/asset-management/institutional/insights/market-insights/market-updates/on-the-minds-of-investors/green-bond-market/

Kotsantonis, S., & Serafeim, G. (2019). Four Things No One Will Tell You About ESG Data. *Journal of Applied Corporate Finance*, *31*(2), 50–58.

Lioui, A., & Tarelli, A. (2022). Chasing the ESG Factor. *Journal of Banking & Finance, 139*, 106498.

Maples Group. (2022). Guide to the EU Sustainable Finance Disclosure Regulation—Regulatory Technical Standards, The Alternative Investment Management Association Ltd and the Maples Group. https://maples.com/en/knowledge-centre/2022/6/guide-to-the-eu-sustainable-finance-disclosure-regulation

Muhn, J. (2021). *25 Fintechs Going Green*. Finovate. https://finovate.com/20-fintechs-going-green/

Multilaw. (2024). *Online Banking Services*. Multilaw. https://multilaw.com/Multilaw/ZENTSO/BusinessGuides/Presentation/Section_Home.aspx?GuideId=2&GuideCountry=United+Kingdom&GuideSection=778

Oehmke, M., & Opp, M. M. (2022). A Theory of Socially Responsible Investment. Swedish House of Finance Research Paper (20-2).

Oliveira, E. M., de Souza Cunha, F. A. F., Palazzi, R. B., Klotzle, M. C., & Maçaira, P. M. (2020). On the effects of uncertainty measures on sustainability indices: An empirical investigation in a nonlinear framework. *International Review of Financial Analysis*, *70*, 101505.

Papadopoullos, C. (2022). Long Read: How the Biggest Banks are Adding ESG into CEO Pay. Capital Monitor. https://capitalmonitor.ai/institution/banks/long-read-how-the-biggest-banks-are-adding-esg-into-ceo-pay/

Pástor, Ľ, Stambaugh, R. F., & Taylor, L. A. (2021). Sustainable Investing in Equilibrium. *Journal of Financial Economics, 142*(2), 550–571.

Pástor, Ľ, Stambaugh, R. F., & Taylor, L. A. (2022). Dissecting Green Returns. *Journal of Financial Economics, 146*(2), 403–424.

Pedersen, L. H., Fitzgibbons, S., & Pomorski, L. (2021). Responsible Investing: The ESG-Efficient Frontier. *Journal of Financial Economics, 142*(2), 572–597.

Pellegrino, S. (2022). Explainer: What are the SFDR Regulations? Capital Monitor. https://capitalmonitor.ai/regions/europe/explainer-what-are-the-sfdr-regulations/

Pietsch, A., & Salakhova, D. (2022). Pricing of Green Bonds: Drivers and Dynamics of the Greenium.

Reboredo, J. C., Ugolini, A., & Aiube, F. A. L. (2020). Network Connectedness of Green Bonds and Asset Classes. *Energy Economics, 86*, 104629.

Ritchie, G. (2023). Bankers Whose Job Title Includes 'ESG' Are Dodging Wave of Cuts. *Bloomberg News.* https://www.bnnbloomberg.ca/bankers-whose-job-title-includes-esg-are-dodging-wave-of-cuts-1.1885331

Schanzenbach, M. M., & Sitkoff, R. H. (2020). Reconciling Fiduciary Duty and Social Conscience: The Law and Economics of ESG Investing by a Trustee. *Stanford Law Review, 72*, 381.

S&P. (2022). Global Sustainable Bond Issuance to Surpass U$1.5 Trillion in 2022. S&P Global Ratings. https://www.spglobal.com/ratings/en/research/articles/220207-global-sustainable-bond-issuance-to-surpass-1-5-trillion-in-2022-12262243

Ściślak, J. (2022). Top 13 Green FinTech Companies—Sustainable FinTech Firms, Code&Pepper. https://codeandpepper.com/13-top-green-fintech-companies/

Tang, D. Y., & Zhang, Y. (2020). Do Shareholders Benefit from Green Bonds? *Journal of Corporate Finance, 61*, 101427.

Tolliver, C., Keeley, A. R., & Managi, S. (2020). Drivers of Green Bond Market Growth: The Importance of Nationally Determined Contributions to the Paris Agreement and Implications for Sustainability. *Journal of Cleaner Production, 244*, 118643.

UNEP Finance Initiative. (2007). CEO Briefing. https://www.unepfi.org/fileadmin/documents/ceo_briefing_green.pdf

Utz, S., Wimmer, M., Hirschberger, M., & Steuer, R. E. (2014). Tri-criterion Inverse Portfolio Optimization with Application to Socially Responsible Mutual Funds. *European Journal of Operational Research, 234*(2), 491–498.

Van Duuren, E., Plantinga, A., and Scholtens, B. (2016). ESG integration and the investment management process: Fundamental investing reinvented. *Journal of Business Ethics, 138*(3), 525–533.

Whelan, T., Zappa, B., Zeidan, R., & Fishbein, G. (2017). How to Quantify Sustainability's Impact on Your Bottom Line. *Harvard Business Review, 23.*

Xiao, Y., Faff, R., Gharghori, P., & Lee, D. (2013). An empirical study of the world price of sustainability. *Journal of Business Ethics, 114*(2), 297–310.

Zaremba, A., Umutlu, M., & Maydybura, A. (2020). Where have the profits gone? Market efficiency and the disappearing equity anomalies in country and industry returns. *Journal of Banking and Finance, 121*, 105966.

Zeidan, R. (2022a). Obstacles to Sustainable Finance and the Covid19 Crisis. *Journal of Sustainable Finance & Investment, 12*(2), 525–528.

Zeidan, R. (2022b). Why Don't Asset Managers Accelerate ESG Investing? A Sentiment Analysis based on 13,000 Messages from Finance Professionals. *Business Strategy and the Environment, 31*(7), 3028–3039.

Zeidan, R., & Spitzeck, H. (2015). The Sustainability Delta: Considering Sustainability Opportunities in Firm Valuation. *Sustainable Development, 23*(6), 329–342.

Zerbib, O. D. (2022). A Sustainable Capital Asset Pricing Model (S-CAPM): Evidence from Environmental Integration and Sin Stock Exclusion. *Review of Finance, 26*(6), 1345–1388.

CHAPTER 5

"Green" Central Banking, from Stress Test Models to Beyond

In this chapter, we invert the order of a linear approach in which "green" central banking is discussed, and then the most essential tools are described. As the main focus is on presenting a manual for green banking, highlighting the tools and then discussing the pros and cons of central bank "green" activism seems warranted. As in the previous chapters, we start with the regular framework banks use and then describe how to incorporate nonfinancial indicators into standard models.

The general central steps for stress test models include building scenarios that impact the evolution of assets and liabilities, incorporating econometric tools to disentangle the consequences of distinct shocks, and using Monte Carlo simulations to investigate under which conditions banks can fail. Figure 5.1 illustrates the modeling steps in a solvency stress test.

Solvency stress tests are standard, but so are liquidity stress tests or, for non-regulatory purposes, profit stress tests. The main difference between stress tests for financial and nonfinancial institutions is the interconnectedness in financial systems. Financial institutions must report the results of stress tests for regulators, which is not the case for most other companies. Generally, stress tests are used by public authorities for macroprudential (surveillance), microprudential (supervisory), and crisis management purposes, and internally, by financial institutions as an internal risk management tool (Oura & Schumacher, 2012).

R. Zeidan, *The Green Banking Transition Manual*,
https://doi.org/10.1007/978-981-96-2852-0_5

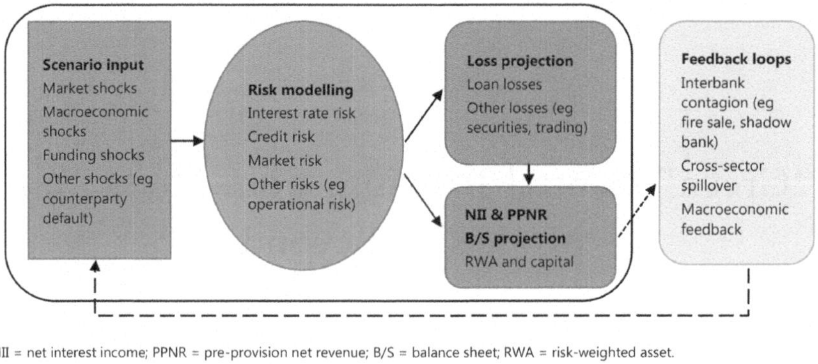

Fig. 5.1 Significant modeling steps in a solvency stress test (*Source* ESI staff)

Microprudential use includes validating the Internal Capital Adequacy Assessment Process (ICAAP) of banks and their liquidity adequacy assessments and setting up capital add-ons for banks by using rules-based methods that sometimes are based solely on stress tests (e.g., by benchmarking against formal hurdle rates). Macroprudential stress tests allow supervisors to calibrate policy changes and allow early warning exercises to identify potential weaknesses in the financial system. Macroprudential stress tests allow for a more direct assessment of feedback loops, amplification mechanisms, and spillovers of external shocks (BIS, 2017).

For developing stress test models, the additional regulatory requirements for Basel III in comparison with earlier versions are, among others:

The introduction of stricter capital requirements;

More details on the incorporation of market risk and credit risk;

New measures of liquidity risk, such as the liquidity coverage ratio (LCR) and net stable funding ratio (NSFR);

New guidelines for counterparty credit risk and credit valuation adjustment (CVA).

These additional regulatory requirements emerged after the global financial crisis. As Anderson et al. (2022) observe, the global financial crisis has coalesced the regulatory lessons in five ingredients:

i. Setting comprehensive stress scenarios that represent tail events;
ii. Regular evaluation of the impact of everyday stress scenarios;

iii. Assessing the impact of second-round effects: contagion and spillover effects;
iv. Integrating stress testing into firms' risk management frameworks and their capital and liquidity planning, and;
v. Disclosure of stress testing frameworks, results, and their link to regulatory actions.

Banks usually must segregate risks to build the models for liquidity and solvency stress tests. Table 5.1 illustrates this segregation based on the template the Bank of England shares with the banks under its supervision. It allows us to check the primary sources of systemic risks for financial institutions. Credit risk is segregated into its components, but other risks, such as operational risk and misconduct, are not even bundled. Table 5.1 also separates projections from actuals and, regarding the former, explicitly requires banks to inform how they arrive at specific risk weights.

Not all data must be reported annually. Table 5.2 shows the core data that must be reported quarterly.

The BoE (2022) also describes how the information must be filled out. For instance, there is a straightforward example regarding counterparty exposure data on "Actuals" and "Traded Risk Stress Scenarios." Assume that the bank is exposed to a counterparty called "AZ Bank." This exposure comes from nettings sets against AZ Bank's legal entities, as shown in the table. As we can see from the example, the bank may have one or more exposures to AZBank for each legal entity. Regarding AZBank London, there are three outstanding transactions. Their uncollateralized values are, respectively, £80 million for uncollateralized derivatives and £150 million for collateralized derivatives that, when taken into account collaterals, become £80 million for uncollateralized derivatives, £50 million for collateralized derivatives and £5 million for security financing transactions (SFTs).

SFTs allow banks to post assets as collateral to secure funding for their activities, so there are no values for uncollateralized current exposures (European Commission, 2023). If banks hold the assets without posting them as collateral, they are not at risk of being seized by the counterparty.

Given the values in Table 5.3, the bank reported values on AZ Bank as a counterparty group in the final stress test report are presented in Table 5.4 (Bank of England, 2022):

Table 5.1 Templates by risk area, Bank of England (2022a)

Projections	Risk area	Capital	Net interest income (NII)	Fees and costs	Op risk/ Misconduct	Credit risk Structured Finance	Credit risk Wholesale	Credit risk Retail	Pension	Traded risk	Other
	Capital resources	Capital projections	Net interest income projections	Fees and costs projections	Capital projections (Op risk projections are part of profit or loss)	Structured finance projections	Credit risk projections	Credit risk projections	Pensions projections	Counterparty credit risk losses projections	UK capital impact projections
		Capital transitional projections	Liquidity projections		Material misconduct cost projections		Leveraged loans projections			Investment Bank Profit or Loss Projections	Intra-group positions projections
										Market risk stressed profit or loss projections	Scenario specific projections
										Other fair valued items projections	

							Stressed PVA projections Stressed XVA projections	
	RWA	Capital projections (Op risk projections are part of capital req's worksheet)	Structured finance projections	Credit risk projections	Credit risk projections		Counterparty credit risk RWA	
							Market risk and CVA RWA	
Actuals		Material misconduct costs actuals	Structured finance actuals	Corporate sovereign and financial institution credit risk actuals	Retail excluding mortgage credit risk actuals	Pensions actuals		Granular securities funding and financial exposures actuals

(continued)

Table 5.1 (continued)

	Operational risk actuals	Corporate exposures actuals	Retail mortgage credit risk actuals
		Leveraged loans actuals	
		Credit risk lending actuals	Credit risk lending actuals

Bank of England (2022a). https://www.bankofengland.co.uk/-/media/boe/files/stress-testing/2022/stdf-manual-2022.pdf

Table 5.2 Reporting Periods from Template Risk Categories, Selected Areas

Cat	*Area*	*Core*	*Period*
013	Retail_mortgage_credit_risk_actuals	Core	Quarterly
014	Retail_excluding_mortgage_credit_risk_actuals	Core	Quarterly
018	Corporate_sovereign_and_financial_institution_credit_risk_actuals	Core	Quarterly
026	Reconciliations	Core	Quarterly
057	Corporate_exposures_actuals	Core	Quarterly
088	Leveraged_loans_actuals	Core	Quarterly
091	Credit_risk_lending_actuals	Core	Quarterly
022	AssetLiabilityManagement	Nonstress testing	Quarterly

Bank of England (2022a). https://www.bankofengland.co.uk/-/media/boe/files/stress-testing/2022/stdf-manual-2022.pdf

Table 5.3 Counterparty exposures data example (GBP Millions)

Legal entity	*Netting set*	*Feature*	*Uncollateralized current exposure*	*Collateralized current exposure*
AZBank London	NS1	Uncollateralized derivative	80	**80**
	NS2	Collateralized derivative	150	**50**
	NS3	SFT	N/A	**5**
AZ Bank NY	NS4	Uncollateralized derivative	110	**110**
	NS5	Collateralized derivative	272	**72**
AZBank Japan	**NS6**	**SFT**	**N/A**	3

Bank of England (2022a). https://www.bankofengland.co.uk/-/media/boe/files/stress-testing/2022/stdf-manual-2022.pdf

Each exposure is then aggregated into the respective category, with the calculation shown in Table 5.4. Aggregating risk exposure is an accounting exercise, in a way. Of course, the difficult part is that banks have millions of operations concurrently. Another reason regulators require up-to-date information is to limit the chances of relevant exposures falling between the cracks or becoming problematic before supervisors are alerted. As described in Tables 5.3 and 5.4, reporting

Table 5.4 Counterparty exposures reporting data example (GBP Millions)

Reported values	*Value*	*Calculation*
UCE for collateralized derivative netting sets	422	(150 of NS2 + 272 of NS5)
UCE for uncollateralized derivative netting sets	190	(80 of NS1 + 110 of NS4)
Total UCE for derivative netting sets	612	
CCE for SFT netting sets	8	(5 of NS3 + 3 of NS6)
CCE for collateralized derivative net settings	122	(50 of NS2 + 72 of NS5)
CCE for uncollateralized derivative netting sets	190	(80 of NS1 + 110 of NS4)
Total CCE	320	

Bank of England (2022a). https://www.bankofengland.co.uk/-/media/boe/files/stress-testing/2022/stdf-manual-2022.pdf

is straightforward, with aggregate exposures as the sum of individual exposures to individual entities.

It is the details of valuing each exposure and classifying them that make the job of preparing the data for stress test simulations challenging. Take, as observed before, hedging. CVA, CVA hedges, FVA, and FVA hedges should be stripped out and reported in the 058 Stressed XVA template (Bank of England, 2022a). However, mark-to-market hedging is far from simple, as banks might follow some predetermined hedging strategies but might not.

Ultimately, the goal is for banks to input values that reflect their operations that are robust enough so that the simulations can capture the dynamics of the banks' balance sheets correctly, even if not precisely (Baudino and Svoronos, 2021). Below, we describe how banks incorporate macroeconomic shocks, the modeling aspects, the simulation process, and the other steps required for liquidity and solvency stress tests.

5.1 Modeling.

An idealized macroprudential capital regulatory framework would estimate the joint distribution of banks' equity ratios and then ensure, through appropriate regulations, that the probability that banks will jointly become undercapitalized remains low.

Modeling stress tests is both a science and an art. Paradoxically, robust stress tests require creativity, as the process is much more than button-pushing. At first glance, we should be concerned that financial systems' health is based on modelers' creativity in setting up robust stress tests. However, stress tests aim to uncover under which conditions banks could go bankrupt. If it were only about rehashing past scenarios, stress tests would use information from past events and project it forward, for instance, the idea behind Value-at-Risk models. Such models work fine in estimating the frequency of trading days in which losses will be larger than some predetermined value. However, they can't tell how considerable those losses will be.

The newer generation of stress tests must deal with unknown but quantifiable risks and be validated with out-of-sample data. The basic structure of stress test models is straightforward: what matters is what affects banks' balance sheets and can lead to liquidity and solvency issues. Can we summarize the goal of stress tests as the answer to a simple question: are the banks' capital buffers enough to guarantee that there won't be a financial crisis soon? For a single bank, stress tests aim to estimate if capital buffers are enough to keep the bank solvent during crises. Are systemic capital buffers enough for the financial system to contain any issue that may arise? Fig. 5.2 illustrates the overview of the modeling framework for stress tests suggested by the Federal Reserve.

Projections are based on elementary financial data. The Federal Reserve calculates projected pretax net income for the firms subject to the supervisory stress test by combining revenue projections, expenses, provisions for credit losses, and other losses (Board of Governors of the Federal Reserve System, 2022c).

The classes of stress tests can be divided into internal and standardized approaches. In the internal ratings-based approach (IRB), banks develop internal models for estimating unexpected losses (UL) and expected losses (EL).

In the IRB approach, banks determine, for each asset class, the risk components, risk-weight functions, and the minimum capital requirements associated with potential losses. IRBs can be further divided into the foundation internal ratings-based (FIRB) approach and the advanced internal ratings-based (AIRB) approach (Bank of Israel, 2015). Notably, the main difference between the IRB approach in Basel II and Basel III is that the latter indicates an "asset class-based" approach instead of the

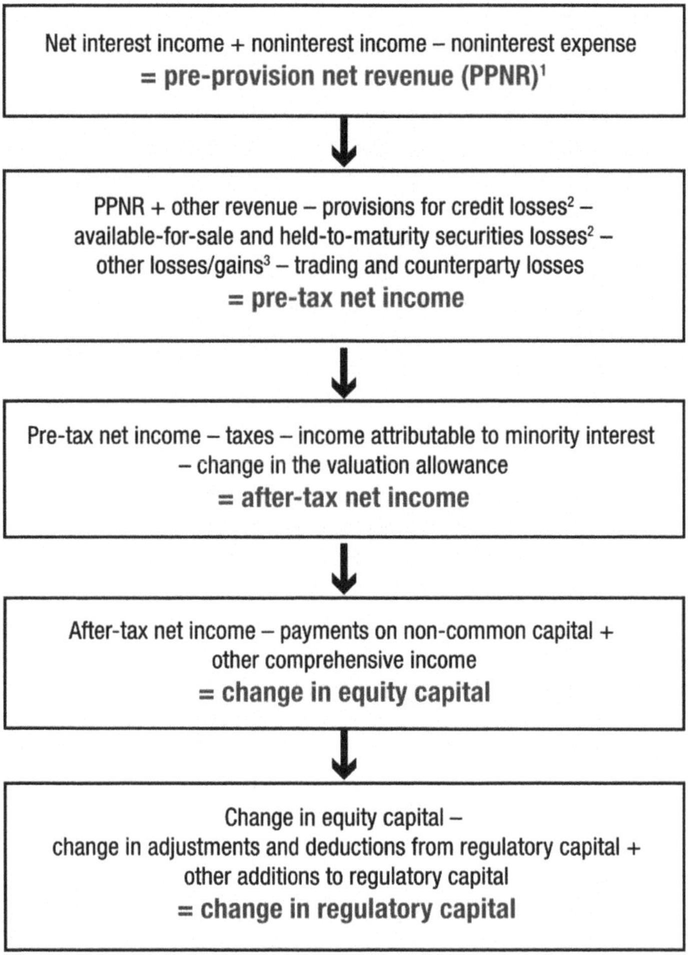

Fig. 5.2 Modeling framework for stress tests in the United States (*Source* Board of governors of the federal reserve system (2022c). https://www.federalreserve.gov/publications/2022-supervisory-stress-test-methodology-overview-modeling-framework.htm)

"wholesale" approach of the former (Hong Kong Monetary Authority, 2020).

In the foundation approach, banks only estimate the probability of default. In contrast, on the advanced approach, they model the probability of default (PD), the loss given default (LGD), and the exposure at default (EAD), subject to meeting minimum standards. For both approaches, banks rely on the risk-weight functions described in the central bank directives, usually adapted from the original ones by the BIS.

Alongside IRBs, approaches related to the standardized approach for credit risk ("SACR") for quantifying risks (e.g., CRR, VaR, and sVaR) are calculated as the 99th percentile, one-tailed confidence interval that must accurately capture all material price risks (European Central Bank, 2019). Moreover, the percentile estimation method used to obtain the 99th percentile should be based on reasonable statistical properties; they should be statistically unbiased, distribution-free, and assume that the probability of experiencing a P&L lower than the lowest simulated value is strictly greater than zero (European Central Bank, 2019).

Krebs and Nippel (2021) illustrate a traditional method for the calculation of economic capital that is based on the probability distribution of losses in the exposure at default (EaD) of a loan portfolio (Fig. 5.3).

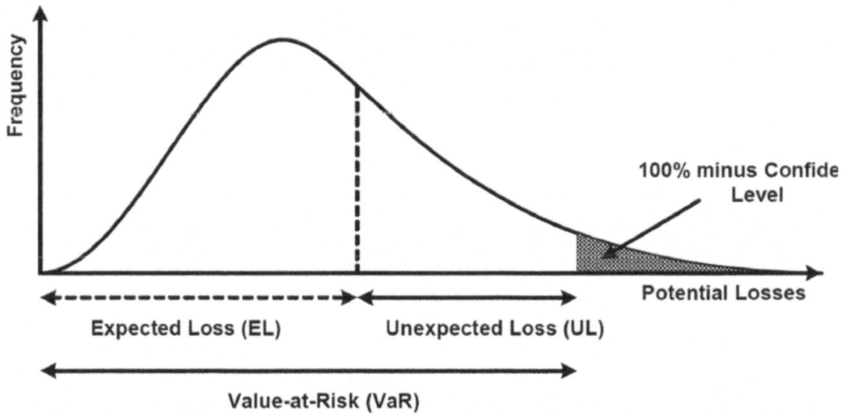

Fig. 5.3 The loss frequency of a credit portfolio (*Source* Krebs and Nippel [2021])

All approaches are supposed to allow regulators to monitor banks effectively. The quantitative thresholds should be set up so analysts can perform (European Central Bank, 2019):

(a) backtesting;
(b) discriminatory power;
(c) analyses of overrides;
(d) stability analyses of the internal ratings and risk parameters over time.

Take the analyses of override conditions, for instance. Institutions must document each case where human judgment overrides a model's inputs or outputs and the personnel responsible for approving these overrides (European Central Bank, 2019).

Stress tests don't serve only to help banks estimate required capital buffers. They may even help unearth a bank's most prominent counterpart by estimating net stressed losses (in the US, by applying the global market shock to revalue securities financing transactions and derivatives, including collateral posted or received) (Board of Governors of the Federal Reserve System, 2022c).

Methodologically, stress tests incorporate diverse ways that shocks propagate through the financial system, impacting banks' liquidity and solvency. For instance, the Board of Governors of the Federal Reserve System (2022b) indicates that the models used to project various components of banks' net revenue should include autoregressive models; aggregate and nonparametric models; and structural models.

Autoregressive models estimate future realizations of revenue and expenses depending linearly on their previous values and stochastic terms. A simple autoregressive model can be represented as:

$$y_t = \varphi_1 y_{t-1} + \varepsilon_t$$

where φ_1 is the main parameter of the model, and ε is noise. In this case, the estimated revenue (or expense, y_t) depends only on its value in the last period (y_{t-1}), which characterizes it as a first-order autoregressive process, AR(1). Autoregressive models of order *n* include *n* terms $\varphi_i y_{t-i}$.

Aggregate models take the general form (Hale et al., 2015):

$$y_t = \theta_0 + X_t\beta + \varepsilon_t,$$

in which the outcome of interest y_t is regressed on a matrix X_t that contains the macroeconomic risk covariates (and their lags, if necessary); ε_t is an error term. Such models are usually taken to data via ordinary least squares (OLS).

As the name implies, nonparametric models don't impose predefined model specifications. They usually assess possible solvency and liquidity indicators changes from simultaneous shocks on dozens or hundreds of variables.

5.2 A Bayesian Model Approach with a Stress Test Perspective.

This subsection summarizes Henry et al. (2013), who describe a former general top-down satellite model applied in the European Central Bank solvency analysis framework. The satellite equation translates an assumed scenario (baseline or adverse) into a path for the dependent variable representing some risk on a bank's balance sheet. The procedure is Bayesian in nature, reflecting the uncertainty regarding the models' parameters and risks. Bayesian methods are probabilistic and consist of three steps: specifying a prior probability distribution on the unknown parameter based on how it is expected to behave; matching the observed data to this prior distribution through a likelihood function; updating our knowledge about the unknown parameter given how likely the parameter is to act according to that or other probability distribution. In other words, Bayesian inference is supposed to represent how we all process information: we form beliefs about the world, confront those beliefs with data, and update our beliefs.

The satellite equation procedure starts with an Autoregressive Distributed Lag (ADL) model structure:

$$Y_t = \alpha + p_1 Y_{t-1} + \ldots + p_p Y_{t-p} + \sum_{k=1}^{k_i} (\beta_0^k X_t^k + \ldots + \beta_{q^k}^k X_{t-q^k}^k)$$

where Y is the dependent variable, and X^k are independent variables from a set of K predictors. The ADL model structure is flexible, allowing contemporaneous and lagged dependencies with predictor variables.

The authors evaluate all conceivable combinations of K predictor variables given the lags. The relevant individual posterior coefficient estimates from all equations are combined into the following general model for the dependent variable Y:

$$h(\beta|y) = \sum_{i=1}^{I} P(M_i|y) \frac{f(y|\beta)h(\beta|M_i)}{f(y|M_i)}$$

The formula seems complex, but it is a modified Bayes rule, which describes an event's probability based on prior knowledge. Bayes rule can be generally understood as posterior probability = likelihood * prior ÷ evidence. In the present instance, Henry et al. (2013) write that the posterior model probabilities $P(M_i|y)$ are used to compute a weighted average of the individual equations where $f(y|\beta)$ is the density function of the dependent variable, y, conditional on the predictor coefficient (β); $f(y|M_i)$ is the density function of y conditional on the model; and $h(\beta|M_i)$ is the density function of β conditional on the model.

The authors describe two central ways to compute the posterior model probabilities (weights) $P(M_i|y)$. The first refers to in-sample measures such as a Bayesian Information Criterion (BIC), which addresses the trade-off between model size and fit by penalizing larger models). The second refers to some measure of out-of-sample performance, to which the posterior model weights would be made proportional.

The authors present the outputs of the Bayesian model routine in Fig. 5.4. The dependent variable is aggregate non-performing loans (in the first differences of logarithmic levels) for a representative European banking system. We can see that the priors are straightforward: around 10% for every variable. Figure 5.4 shows that some variables have a posterior probability above 10% while six others have a lower probability. Interestingly, only one variable seems almost irrelevant in explaining the variation in aggregate non-performing loans: the unemployment rate.

The authors also present the results of normalized long-run multipliers, showing that inflation, investments, and the exchange rate between the euro and the US dollar are the most relevant for explaining the dependent variable in the long run. Simply put, a one-standard-deviation decrease in investment is associated with about one-tenth of a standard deviation increase in non-performing loans growth quarter on quarter. The variables with negative coefficients indicate they are particularly relevant in modeling adverse scenarios, as they imply that non-performing loans rise conditional upon an unfavorable scenario.

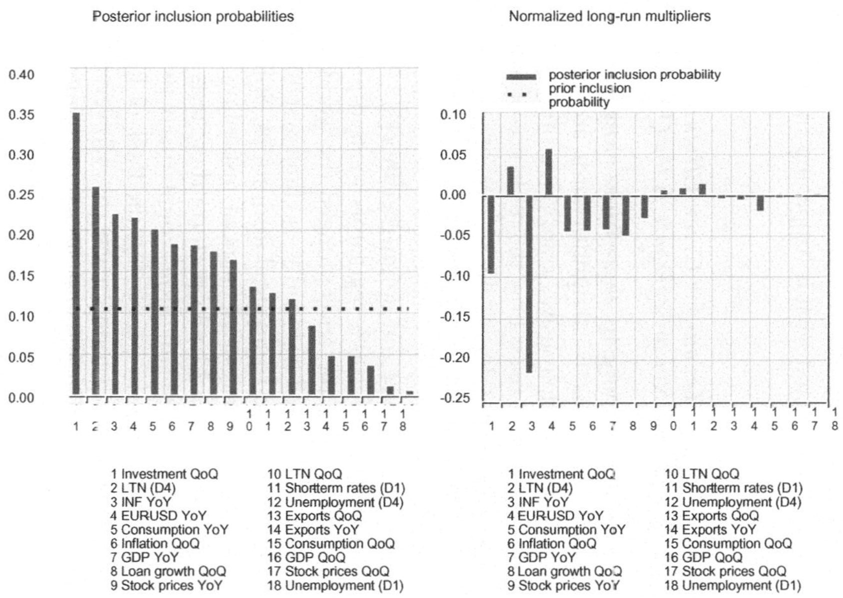

Fig. 5.4 Posterior inclusion probabilities and normalized long-run multipliers (*Source* ECB calculations. *Abbreviated variables* Long-term interest rates (LTN), price inflation (INF). Overall, 37 model variables were allowed as potential predictors; the first 18 appear in the charts. At most, The maximum size of the model equations was constrained to four, and the maximum number of lags to two. Therefore, the total number of equations of the Bayesian model searches was 74,518)

Over 74,000 equations are considered in the procedure by Henry et al. (2013). Bayesian modeling can help identify variables of interest, checking for their impact on banks' liquidity and solvency indicators. We can't stress it enough: there is no single way to perform stress tests. However, one shouldn't choose a method for its complexity. At face value, one could conclude that a procedure that analyzes dozens of thousands of equations would be more robust and "scientific," but that is a mistake. Models are only so good as our ability to understand what is happening and interpret the outputs correctly.

5.2.1 *Stress Testing CVA and Lessons for Green Climate Stress Testing: To Segregate or Not to Segregate Is the Question.*

Stress tests are forward-looking, aiming to align banks' loss-absorbing resources with actual risks. The idea is straightforward: are banks at risk of insolvency if markets fall precipitously, or are there other adverse scenarios? Stress tests are exercises to assess how the resilience of financial institutions would fare under serious but realistic unfavorable circumstances (Baudino et al., 2018). As the name indicates, these tests aim to estimate the resiliency of individual financial institutions and the whole financial system to simultaneous market and nonmarket shocks.

Before the great financial crisis of 2008, regulators focused primarily on individual banks' resiliency. After the crisis plunged the world into a recession, the goal of stress tests shifted to identify and limit systemic risk. Stress tests don't need to be confined to financial institutions. Still, since financial regulators are mandated to restrict financial instability, central banks regularly require that commercial banks perform these tests.

CVA stress testing establishes which conditions counterparty risks may lead to solvency issues. We have seen the parameters the Bank of England set for how banks should report data on counterparty risk. However, there is much more than filling out Excel templates. Banks are requested to provide the current exposure (market value) of CCR exposures, current exposure (market value) of CCR exposures net of collateral and other eligible credit risk mitigation, CVA impact on P&L, the jump-to-default exposures, the external and internal PDs (numerical values between 0 and 1), the share of cash collateral, as well as stressed current exposure and stressed LGDs (European Banking Authority, 2022a, 2022b).

Table 5.5 describes the methodologies for estimating risk-weighted assets in market and counterparty credit risks. As we can see, there are several methods for projecting RWAs. Detailing each methodology is beyond the scope of the book. However, establishing the trade-offs between these approaches provides relevant insights into incorporating climate change into stress tests.

Fundamentally, CVA RWAs include the impact of changes in credit spreads but not any changes in other financial variables.

Regarding the assumed default of a sizeable uncollateralized counterparty, the potential decrease in CVA should be captured as a strategic management action but not reflected on the "Market Risk and CVA RWA" template.

Table 5.6 describes the Bank of England's allocation of potential losses for stress tests.

For us, what matters is the implications of institutions usually segregating CCR stress test results instead of aggregating them with loan portfolios or trading position stress tests (Bank of England, 2022). Although there are solid reasons for such procedures, introducing climate risks into such procedures is trickier. Regarding these reasons, one is the non-linearity of aggregated risks. Even for bucketed CCR risks, institutions need delta sensitivities to estimate RWAs. For instance, Table 5.7 presents the sensitivities banks use to assess specific risks, as in the manual of the Bank of England.

The aggregate impact of the reported sensitivities for each tenor after bucketing should be equivalent to the impact obtained from the actual sensitivity of the cash flows to the related shocks (Bank of England, 2022).

Incorporating climate risks on banks' balance sheets requires answering one central question: should these risks be segregated or not? For insurance companies, one can potentially link climate change to organizations' balance sheets. For instance, if an internal model shows that the payouts from flooding are rising more than what usual variables capture, institutions could estimate climate change's impacts as the difference between historically calibrated models and current realizations.

For counterparty risks and other parts of stress test models, methodological challenges go beyond a simple mandate that banks incorporate damages from the change in the world's climate. The question remains: how? In the following sections, we detail the basics of stress testing in the United States and present some case studies before describing "green" stress testing.

Table 5.5 RWA projections methodology

Risk type	*Capital component*	*Expectations regarding RWA projections*
Market risk	Standardized approach	RWAs calculated under standard rules approaches are expected to increase in line with projected growth in business
	Value-at-Risk (VaR) and Stressed VaR (SVaR)	Projected combined (VaR and SVaR) capital components should change in line with projected growth in the business
	Risk Not in VaR (RNIV)	Banks should project RNIVs in line with any changes to the business volumes
	Incremental Risk Charge (IRC)	Banks should project IRC in line with any changes to the business volumes
	Comprehensive risk measure (CRM)	There is no expectation that modeled CRM-derived RWAs should increase due to the stress scenario if the standardized credit risk floor is binding
	Trading Book securitizations	RWAs related to securitizations held in the trading book are considered as part of the structured finance stress test, not the traded risk RWA stress test. If the market risk RWA submission includes trading book securitizations, this should be made clear and quantified in order to avoid double counting
CVA risk	Overall	CVA RWAs should be modeled to include the impact of changes in credit spreads but not any changes in other financial variables Regarding defaulted counterparties, there should be no corresponding reduction in CVA RWAs submitted in the "Market Risk and CVA RWA" templates, as it should be assumed that the defaulted positions are replaced on a like-for-like basis. Regarding a highly material counterparty default (for example, the assumed default of a large uncollateralized counterparty), the potential decrease in CVA should be captured as a strategic management action but not reflected on the "Market Risk and CVA RWA" template The high-level expectation is that the bank maintains its current hedging policies when projecting CVA risk capital requirements. Changes to how CVA risk is managed under stressed conditions may be considered under strategic management actions but should not be reflected as part of the "Market Risk and CVA RWA" template submission
	Standardized method	Increases in RWAs due to downward credit migration are expected to be reflected in the weights used to calculate CVA RWAs using the standardized method

(continued)

Table 5.5 (continued)

Risk type	*Capital component*	*Expectations regarding RWA projections*
	Advanced method	Where the scenario impacts credit spreads, this impact should be reflected in a change in the level of CVA RWAs
Counterparty credit risk	Overall	Where the bank has assumed counterparty defaults, no corresponding reduction in CCR RWAs submitted in the "Counterparty Credit Risk, RWAs" template is expected as the defaulted positions are assumed to be replaced on a like-for-like basis of projections. Where the impact is significant and counterparty specific (e.g., the assumed default of a large uncollateralized counterparty), the potential decrease in RWAs may be addressed as a strategic management action. Securities financing transactions are considered repurchase transactions, securities or commodities lending or borrowing transactions, and margin lending transactions
	Collateralized counterparties	Exposures should not change due to changes in financial variables in the scenario For the purpose of RWA calculation, it is assumed that margin agreements with non-defaulting counterparties will perform and collateral is received accordingly. It is also assumed that the extended margin period of risk criteria beyond those identified is not triggered. Risk weights are expected to be adjusted to the credit risk RWA calculation
	Uncollateralized counterparties	For exposures calculated using the counterparty credit risk mark-to-market (MtM) method, projected increases in position MtM should be incorporated into the exposure For exposures calculated using the IMM method, projected increases in position MtM should be incorporated into the exposure Since IMM exposure is a function of market volatility, exposures are expected to increase if sustained market volatilities in the scenario are larger under the scenario than those used to calibrate the risk measures used for regulatory purposes Risk weights are expected to be adjusted per the credit risk RWA calculation

(continued)

Table 5.5 (continued)

Risk type	*Capital component*	*Expectations regarding RWA projections*
	Treatment of unilateral accounting CVA under CRR Article 273(6)	Projected accounting unilateral CVA deducted from exposures should be consistent with the projected accounting unilateral CVA losses at the end-of-year reporting dates and correspond to accounting unilateral CVA utilized for exposure at default (EAD) offset The Bank permits banks that calculate counterparty level projected unilateral accounting CVAs to reduce EAD for calculating projected RWAs under the scenarios Increased projected CVAs can provide RWA relief if the bank calculates projected accounting CVA on a counterparty-specific basis. Otherwise, for the RWA projection, the RWA mitigating impact of increased projected accounting CVA would not be expected to be reflected in the projected RWAs

Source Bank of England (2021)

Table 5.6 Allocation of losses in the 2022 ACS traded risk stress

Losses	*Y1*	*Y2*	*Y3*	*Y4*	*Y5*
Market risk	100%	0%	0%	0%	0%
Counterparty credit risk losses	100%	0%	0%	0%	0%
Stressed CVA	100%	0%	0%	0%	0%
Stressed PVA (Trading book)	100%	0%	0%	0%	0%
Stressed PVA (Banking book)		Gains/losses will be calculated each year of the stress scenario			
Other Fair Valued Items		Gains/losses will be calculated each year of the stress scenario			
Revenues and Costs		Gains/losses will be calculated each year of the stress scenario			

Source Bank of England (2022b)

5.3 The Basics of Stress Tests in the United States.

In the US, the process of stress testing is relatively transparent. The Federal Reserve publishes four documents annually (Board of Governors of the Federal Reserve System, 2022a, 2022b, 2022c):

Table 5.7 Definition of sensitivities

Risk factor category	*Current Value*	*Greek letter*	*Greek value*
Equity, FX	X_0	DELTA	*FX'(X0) × 1%*
Interest rate, credit spread, inflation	r_0	DELTA	*Fr'(r0) × 1 bp*
Equity	X_0	GAMMA	*FX''(X0) × 1%*
Interest rate	r_0	GAMMA	*Fr''(r0) × 1 bp*
Equity and Interest rate	θ_0	VEGA	*F θ'(θ 0) × 1%*

Source European Banking Authority (2022a, 2022b)

- Stress test scenarios. This document describes the hypothetical recessions used in the supervisory stress test.
- Supervisory stress test methodology. It provides comprehensive details about the models and methods used in the supervisory stress test.
- Supervisory Stress Test Results. It reports the aggregate and individual bank results of the supervisory stress test, assessing whether banks are sufficiently capitalized to absorb losses during a severe recession.
- Large Bank Capital Requirements. It announces the individual capital requirement for all large banks, partially determined by the stress test results. More importantly, the methodology is described publicly, which allows us to explain each relevant step directly from original sources. We base this subsection on the reports for 2022, including the Excel files that describe the data banks should use to build their scenarios (Board of Governors of the Federal Reserve System, 2022a). In the report for 2022, "The scenarios start in the first quarter of 2022 and extend through the first quarter of 2025." Each scenario includes 28 variables; this set of variables is the same as the set provided in last year's supervisory scenarios. The variables describing economic developments within the United States include:
- Six measures of economic activity and prices: quarterly percent changes (at an annual rate) in real and nominal gross domestic product (GDP), real and nominal disposable personal income, the Consumer Price Index for all urban consumers (CPI), and the level of the unemployment rate of the civilian non-institutional population aged 16 years and over.

- Four aggregate measures of asset prices or financial conditions: indexes of house prices, commercial real estate prices, equity prices, and stock market volatility.
- Six measures of interest rates: the rate on 3-month Treasury securities; the yield on 5-year Treasury securities; the yield on 10-year Treasury securities; the yield on 10-year BBB-rated corporate securities; the interest rate associated with conforming, conventional, 30-year fixed-rate mortgages; and the prime rate.
- The variables describing international economic conditions in each scenario include three variables in four countries or country blocs:
- The three variables for each country or country bloc: quarterly percent changes (at an annual rate) in real GDP and in consumer price indexes or local equivalent, and the level of the US dollar exchange rate.
- Four countries or country blocs: the euro area (the 19 European Union member states that have adopted the euro as their common currency); the United Kingdom; developing Asia (the nominal GDP-weighted aggregate of China, India, South Korea, Hong Kong Special Administrative Region, and Taiwan); and Japan."

Table 5.8 brings data for each of the 28 variables that comprise the baseline scenario for the stress test models. In the original file, data stretches back to 1976 (although not for all variables). In Table 5.8, there are only projections, as, at the time of publication, the most updated actual data was for the last quarter of 2021.

From this baseline, the Fed establishes the severely adverse scenario. For that report (Board of Governors of the Federal Reserve System, 2022a), this scenario is characterized by stagflation (a sharp recession with higher inflation), higher interest rates (alongside a tightening of financial conditions), worse supply chain disruptions, and an increase in the risk premia required by investors to hold Treasury bonds. A global market shock also impacts exchange rates and other economic conditions. However, the global market shock component only applies to a firm with aggregate trading assets and liabilities of $50 billion or more (or one of the other two additional criteria). Notably, for the banks to which the global market shock applies, profits and losses from trading and counterparty credit are measured in mark-to-market terms. In contrast, revenues and losses from traditional banking are estimated using the accrual method.

Table 5.8 Macroeconomic variables used for stress test in the United States

OBS	*Q1 2022*	*Q2 2022*	*Q3 2022*	*Q4 2022*	*Q1 2023*	*Q2 2023*	*Q3 2023*	*Q4 2023*	*Q1 2024*	*Q2 2024*	*Q3 2024*	*Q4 2024*	*Q1 2025*
Real GDP growth	3.3	3.9	3.3	2.7	2.5	2.3	2.2	2.2	2.1	2.1	2.0	2.0	2.0
Nominal GDP growth	7.0	6.8	6.0	5.2	5.0	4.7	4.6	4.6	4.5	4.0	4.0	3.9	4.0
Real disposable income growth	0.2	2.3	2.5	2.3	2.5	2.6	2.6	2.5	2.3	2.2	2.2	2.1	2.2
Nominal disposable income growth	3.8	5.1	4.8	4.5	4.6	4.6	4.7	4.6	4.3	4.1	4.0	4.0	4.1
Unemployment rate	4.0	3.8	3.7	3.6	3.5	3.5	3.5	3.5	3.5	3.5	3.6	3.6	3.6
CPI inflation rate	3.9	3.0	2.5	2.4	2.4	2.3	2.3	2.4	2.3	2.2	2.2	2.1	2.2
3-month Treasury yield	0.1	0.3	0.5	0.7	0.9	1.1	1.3	1.4	1.5	1.5	1.5	1.5	1.5
5-year Treasury yield	1.3	1.4	1.6	1.7	1.8	1.9	1.9	1.9	2.0	2.0	2.0	2.0	2.0
10-year Treasury yield	1.7	1.8	2.0	2.1	2.2	2.3	2.4	2.5	2.5	2.5	2.5	2.5	2.6
BBB corporate yield	2.9	3.0	3.2	3.4	3.5	3.8	4.0	4.1	4.2	4.2	4.3	4.3	4.4
Mortgage rate	3.2	3.3	3.5	3.6	3.7	3.8	3.9	4.0	4.0	4.0	4.0	4.0	4.1
Prime rate	3.3	3.4	3.6	3.8	4.0	4.2	4.3	4.5	4.5	4.5	4.5	4.6	4.6
Dow Jones Total Stock Market Index	48,634	48,634	48,634	48,634	48,634	48,634	48,634	48,634	48,634	48,634	48,634	48,634	48,634
House Price Index	270	272	274	276	278	280	282	284	286	289	291	293	295
Commercial Real Estate Price Index	340	342	345	348	350	353	355	358	361	364	366	369	372
Market Volatility Index (VIX)	28.1	25.8	25.2	25.3	24.7	26.5	27.1	27.4	27.5	27.5	27.6	27.7	27.8
Euro Area Real GDP Growth	3.6	3.4	3.2	2.9	2.3	1.9	1.7	1.6	1.6	1.5	1.5	1.5	1.5
Euro Area Inflation	2.8	2.2	1.8	1.5	1.5	1.5	1.6	1.8	2.0	2.2	2.3	2.3	2.2

(continued)

Table 5.8 (continued)

OBS	*Q1 2022*	*Q2 2022*	*Q3 2022*	*Q4 2022*	*Q1 2023*	*Q2 2023*	*Q3 2023*	*Q4 2023*	*Q1 2024*	*Q2 2024*	*Q3 2024*	*Q4 2024*	*Q1 2025*
Euro Area Bilateral Dollar Exchange Rate (USD/Euro)	1.134	1.136	1.137	1.139	1.149	1.158	1.167	1.177	1.177	1.177	1.177	1.177	1.177
Developing Asia Real GDP Growth	5.2	6.2	6.6	6.4	5.5	4.8	4.4	4.4	4.8	5.1	5.3	5.1	4.8
Developing Asia Inflation	2.8	2.8	2.8	2.7	2.7	2.6	2.5	2.5	2.5	2.5	2.5	2.5	2.5
Developing Asia Bilateral Dollar Exchange Rate (Index, Base = 2000 Q1)	92.4	92.7	93.0	93.4	93.3	93.2	93.1	93.0	93.0	93.0	93.0	93.0	93.0
Japan Real GDP Growth	3.9	3.3	2.7	2.1	1.3	0.9	0.7	0.7	0.7	0.7	0.6	0.6	0.4
Japan Inflation	0.8	0.9	0.8	0.8	0.8	0.8	0.8	0.8	0.9	1.0	1.0	1.0	1.0
Japan Bilateral Dollar Exchange Rate (Yen/USD)	115.2	115.1	115.1	115.1	114.7	114.2	113.8	113.4	113.4	113.4	113.4	113.4	113.4
UK Real GDP Growth	3.4	3.6	3.7	3.2	2.3	1.6	1.4	1.4	1.6	1.7	1.7	1.6	1.5
UK Inflation	4.2	3.8	3.3	2.7	2.3	2.0	1.9	2.1	2.5	2.7	2.8	2.8	2.7
UK Bilateral Dollar Exchange Rate (USD/Pound)	1.349	1.348	1.348	1.347	1.359	1.371	1.383	1.394	1.394	1.394	1.394	1.394	1.394

Source Board of Governors of the Federal Reserve System (2022a)

Finally, large banks with substantial trading or custodial operations must incorporate a counterparty default scenario component. This last measure is a clear admission that (a) financial systems are interconnected in a manner unlike other markets, and (b) some banks are likely "too large to fail." Counterparty risk is not the only source of banks' interconnectedness. Still, it is significant. For instance, counterparty risk is why the Fed lent U$85 billion to AIG, an insurer, on September 16, 2008. At the height of the global financial crisis, AIG had over U$450 billion in open positions on credit default swaps. In effect, the company acted as a financial intermediary, using its AAA credit rating to borrow money at better rates than it got from its counterparties in derivatives markets. The Fed's concern is that if the company were to go under, it would leave such a hole in the balance sheet of its counterparties that it would bring down the entire financial system. On September 29, 2017, the Financial Stability Oversight Council, created by the Dodd-Frank Wall Street Reform Act to increase the regulations of financial firms, voted to remove AIG's designation as too big to fail (Amadeo, 2020).

In the European Union, the EU-wide stress test exercise is carried out on a sample of banks covering broadly 70% of the banking sector. Banks must have a minimum of EUR 30 billion in assets to be included in the sample (European Banking Authority, 2022). This precondition is another clear sign that "too big to fail" is more than an abstract concept; it is used operationally by central banks globally.

5.4 Case Study: The Pandemic and Financial Vulnerabilities in Norway

The Norwegian case illustrates how central banks operate to ensure financial stability when financial markets are volatile. Its central bank publishes annual financial stability reports. We are interested in the 2021 outlook report because it deals with some of the fallout of the covid pandemic. The Norwegian case is also interesting because Norges Bank was given decision-making responsibility for the countercyclical capital buffer and formal advisory responsibility for the systemic risk buffer in 2021. That means we can trace the changes in financial regulation due to this shift in responsibility for financial regulation in the country. Of course, the central bank was the principal advisor of the Ministry of Finance of the Kingdom of Norway on setting up the countercyclical capital buffer before. Thus, we shouldn't expect momentous changes from this formal change in regulatory oversight. The decision coincided with the creation of a committee analyzing whether to separate the Norwegian sovereign wealth fund from Norges Bank (Mendez-Barreira, 2021).

The Financial Supervisory Authority of Norway (FSAN), the Norges Bank (Central Bank), and the Ministry of Finance regulate the Norwegian financial system. FSAN has historically been responsible for prudential and market conduct supervision. The Norges Bank bears the authority for macroprudential oversight, while the regulatory framework is within the responsibility of the Norwegian Ministry of Finance (Rogdaberg & Wiese-Hansen, 2019).

The analysis of the effects of the pandemic reveals significant insights about central banks' regular operations. While the pandemic caused significant life and economic loss, the supervisory goal was limiting the possibility of a financial crisis. At the pandemic's beginning, the main vulnerability to financial markets was the increase in non-performing loans. Still, that risk diminished as the central bank expanded liquidity, acting as the lender of last resort. By 2021, the systemic risks were almost back to their normal dynamics. Norway's primary financial system vulnerability returned to high household debt, with leverage historically high compared to other countries. Two other significant sources of risk were banks' high commercial real estate exposures and interconnectedness, partly due to their cross-exposures that can propagate and amplify shocks (Norges Bank, 2021).

During the pandemic, one measure the central bank undertook was limiting the distribution of dividends so banks could boost their ability to absorb losses. Another measure was raising the systemic risk buffer from 3% to 4.5%, effective from end-2020 (later reduced to 1% in 2022). To limit the impact of asking banks for more capital buffers, the central bank made extraordinary loans to banks during the market stress in the spring of 2020. Other actions are represented in Fig. 5.5, including requirements for the systemic risk buffer, risk-weighting and the leverage ratio, and a minimum requirement for own funds and eligible liabilities (MREL) (Norges Bank, 2021). Norwegian banks comfortably fulfilled capital requirements at the beginning of market stress in early 2020, with a distance to the risk-weighted capital requirements of 1–1.5 percentage points to the leverage ratio. Still, capital requirements may have constrained individual banks on certain days (Norges Bank, 2021).

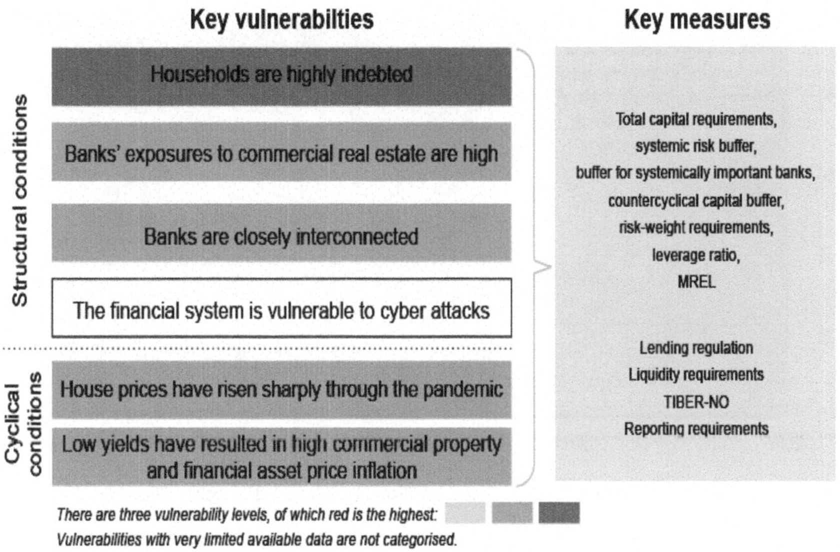

Fig. 5.5 Financial system vulnerabilities in Norway and measures implemented (*Source* Norges Bank [2021])

Also, the central bank illustrates systemic risk through a chart detailing banks' covered bond funding (Fig. 5.6). Covered bonds account for two-thirds of banks' wholesale funding. Banks own approximately 60% of covered bonds issued in Norwegian Krone, acting as issuers and investors in this market. Banks use these to satisfy liquidity requirements and as collateral for loans from the central bank. Banks' share of covered bond holdings rose after Liquidity Coverage Ratio (LCR) became a supervisory target during the Basel reforms (Norges Bank, 2021).

Given the pandemic and its new responsibilities, the Norwegian central bank published the results of the stress tests alongside considerations about financial stability in their 2021 report (Norges Bank, 2021). Interestingly, the results do not show adverse economic scenarios' impact on financial stability. The stress test shows that banks may reduce lending due to weaker commercial real estate and other sector-specific shocks, amplifying an economic downturn (Norges Bank, 2021). In this instance, these results complement the stability stress results to inform monetary policy.

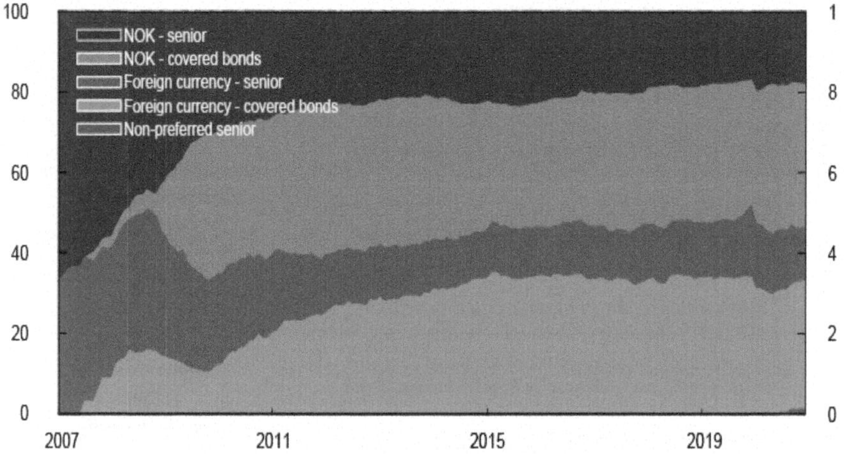

Fig. 5.6 Breakdown of bond funding outstanding. Percent (*Source* Norges Bank [2021])

For example, the central bank could reduce the countercyclical buffers to limit the amplification effect of a downturn due to specific shocks.

Also of note is that the Norges Bank investigated the possibility of cyberattacks among the stress test results. The institution concluded that cyberattacks potentially threaten financial stability due to extensive digitalization and the financial system's interconnectedness.

As for the stress testing process, the Norges Bank (2021) assumed that possible falls in GDP are measured at the 5th percentile, which means that five out of 100 cases of potential GDP growth are expected to be lower than this. Table 5.9 and Fig. 5.7 show the numbers behind the estimations and the distribution of possible outcomes for the main variables.

As we can see, the Norwegian stress test exercise has focused primarily on real state prices and a severe downturn captured by a recession. The assumption of steep declines of almost 20% per year for three straight years on prices for commercial properties and more than 12% on rents is stringent, even if the stressed GDP scenario is not particularly severe (Fig. 5.8). Still, Fig. 5.8 shows that the cyclical indicators, while negatively correlated with economic activity, as expected, do not fall drastically, revealing systemic weaknesses.

Table 5.9 Macroeconomic aggregates in the stress scenario; percentage changes from the previous year

	2021	*2022*	*2023*	*2024*	*2025*
GDP	3.9	−1.6	−1.9	2.0	1.6
Private consumption	4.0	−1.2	−0.6	1.1	1.6
Registered unemployment (rate, level)	3.1	5.2	6.9	6.5	6.4
Three-month Nibor (level)	0.5	1.0	0.8	0.7	0.5
Weighted premium above Nibor for covered bonds and senior bonds (level)	0.5	0.8	0.9	0.8	0.8
House prices	9.2	– 15.0	−13.2	0.0	2.9
Selling prices for commercial property	8.9	– 27.9	−20.8	−9.5	2.8
Rents for commercial property		– 16.4	−17.1	−6.4	3.2
Credit (C2) to households	4.8	−0.8	−0.4	– 0.9	1.4
Credit (C2) to mainland NFCs	4.9	−4.7	– 0.4	– 0.9	1.9
Credit losses (rate, level)	0.0	1.5	2.0	1.5	1.2
Oil price (USD/barrel, level)	69	58	51	54	56

Source NorgesBank (2021)

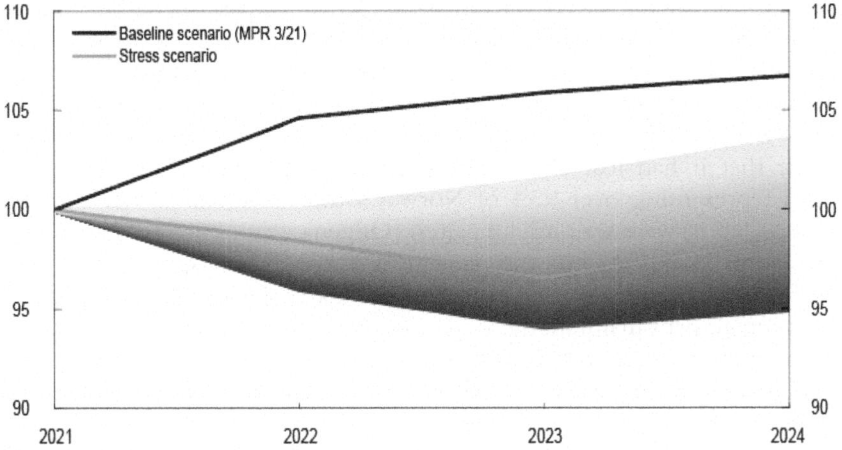

Fig. 5.7 GDP in the stress scenario and baseline scenario. Index. 2021 = 100 (*Source* Norges Bank [2021])

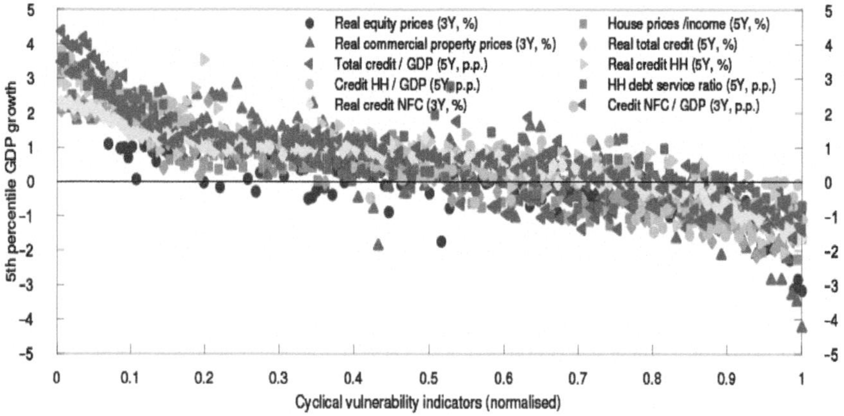

Fig. 5.8 Linkages between cyclical vulnerabilities and GDP growth: Cyclical vulnerability indicators (normalized) on the horizontal scale and 5th percentile projections for GDP growth on the vertical scale (*Source* Norges Bank [2021])

The final impact on banks' credit losses is captured in Fig. 5.9, which illustrates possible losses due to the stress scenarios described above.

Interestingly, the highest possible loss, as captured in the stress test simulation, is similar to the losses of the last financial crisis in the country, the 1988–1992 banking crisis. That crisis started on March 18, 1988, when Sunnmørsbanken, a small commercial bank, issued an earnings report that it had lost all its equity. In the subsequent four years, 13 banks representing over 95% of Norway's total commercial bank assets either failed or were seriously impaired (Ongena et al., 2003). Many weak firms went bankrupt, but the damage was not as widespread as in the case of other financial crises like in Argentina or Japan (Zeidan, 2018). The average firm maintaining a relationship with a distressed bank faced only minor and temporary downward revisions to its stock price. (Ongena et al., 2013). To highlight the welfare losses of financial crises, estimations of the fiscal cost and welfare losses from the Norwegian banking crisis range from 0.9%-2% of GDP for the former and 9.8%-27% for the latter (Moe et al., 2004).

However, even credit losses approximate that of the early 1990s crisis, banks' capital buffer wouldn't be exhausted, according to the estimates from the stress test simulations. Banks retain loss-absorbing capacity

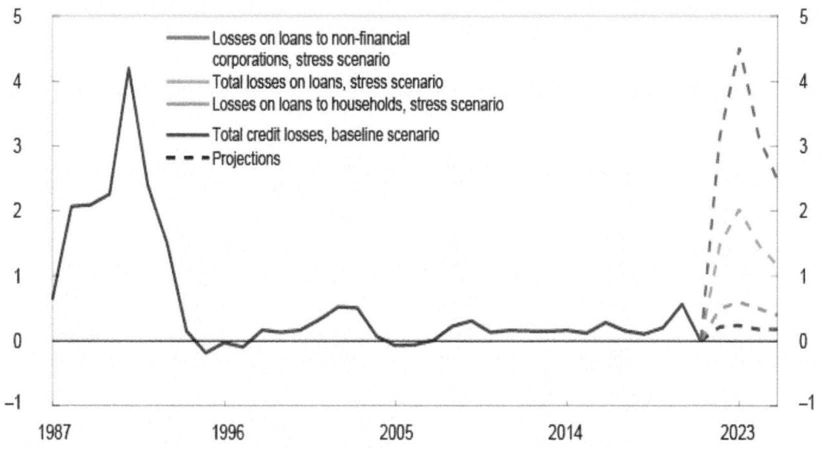

Fig. 5.9 Losses as a percentage of loans, total and by sector: Stress and baseline scenarios (*Source* Norges Bank [2021])

above what is needed in the unlikely scenario of mounting losses. Paradoxically, extraordinary government measures during the pandemic have reduced banks' credit losses, and dividend restrictions have contributed to lifting capital ratios. Banks would lose capital margin above total requirements but not bite deeply into the primary capital buffers, as shown in Fig. 5.10 (Norges Bank, 2021).

Notably, the stress test results assume that the central bank will manage the countercyclical buffer by reducing it during a downturn. If it does not do so, banks refrain from lending to maintain capital adequacy ratios, making the recession worse. Capital buffers should be reduced when other sources of capital are enough to allow banks to weather the downturn without threatening solvency (Norges Bank, 2021).

Finally, the Norges Bank (2021) report has unambiguous and robust discussions on the evolution of financial regulation. It discusses liquidity policy tools aimed explicitly at securities markets and non-bank market participants, with the central bank acting as the market-maker (and not only lender) of last resort. There are full considerations of the potential benefits and costs, such as the possibility of significant moral hazard. Table 5.10 describes the timeline of regulatory changes for Norwegian banks to comply with Basel indicators. We can see that interest rate stress

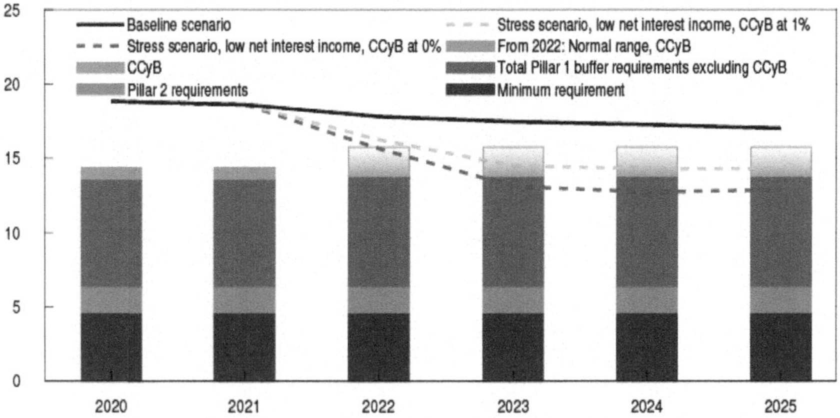

Fig. 5.10 Macro bank's capital requirements and CET1 ratio, baseline scenario, and stress scenario with lower net interest income. Percent (*Source* Norges Bank [2021])

tests were introduced in 2015 and the debt-to-income ratio in 2017. Such transparent reporting should be the norm in central banks globally.

The Norwegian case study details how central banks approach stress tests and updating regulations. With the timeline of regulatory changes at our disposal and the analysis from Norges Bank, we can see that the institution seems correct in identifying exposure to real estate as the primary source of known systemic risk. It is fascinating to notice how conservative central banks can be, as even under highly adverse scenarios, Norwegian banks are not expected to dig into their capital buffers. And still, there is no discussion of limiting the accumulation of loss-absorbing capital, except for the countercyclical buffer, which is intrinsically transient.

Finally, such a comprehensive process can be extended to ecological and other nonfinancial risks. However, that would require robust estimates of short-term shocks from these indicators and not long-term assumptions about climate impacts. In section 5.6, we discuss in more depth the requirements for "green" stress testing.

Table 5.10 Timeline of regulatory changes for Norwegian Banks

Category	*Instrument*	*Introduced*	*Current level*
Credit standards requirements for mortgages	Tolerate higher interest rates (stress test)	2015	5 percentage points
	Loan-to-value (LTV) ratio	2015	85% (60% for loans secured on secondary homes in Oslo)
	Principal repayment requirement	2015	2.5% a year with LTV above 60%
	Debt-to-income (DTI) ratio	2017	5 times gross income
	Flexibility quota (speed limit)	2015	10% (8% or up to NOK 10 m for loans on dwellings in Oslo)
Credit standards requirements for consumer credit	Tolerate higher interest rates (stress test)	2019	5 percentage points
	Principal repayment requirement	2019	Monthly principal repayment, maximum term 5 years
	Debt-to-income (DTI) ratio	2019	5 times gross income
	Flexibility quota (speed limit)	2019	5%
Risk-based capital requirements (share of risk-weighted assets)	Pillar 1 Minimum CET1 requirement	2013	4.5%
	Pillar 1 Minimum Tier 1 requirement	1991	6%
	Pillar 1 Minimum regulatory capital	1991	8%
	Pillar 1 Combined buffer requirements:		
	Capital conservation buffer	2013	2.5%
	Systemic risk buffer	2013	4.5%
	Buffer for systemically important financial institutions (SIFIs)	2015	1% for Kommunalbanken AS and 2% for DNB ASA
	Countercyclical capital buffer	2015	1%
	Pillar 2 requirements	2007	Varies across banks

(continued)

Table 5.10 (continued)

Category	*Instrument*	*Introduced*	*Current level*
Risk weighting for risk-based capital requirements	Minimum requirement for loss given default (LGD) in IRB banks' mortgage models	2014	20%
	Calibration requirement for IRB banks' mortgage models for PD and LGD	2015	
	Floor for average risk weights for mortgages	2020	20%
	Floor for average risk weights for commercial property mortgages	2020	35%
Leverage-based capital requirements	Leverage ratio	2017	3% minimum requirement + 2% buffer requirement + 1% buffer requirement for systemically important banks
Liquidity requirements	Liquidity Coverage Ratio (LCR)	2015	100%
	LCR in individual currencies	2017	100%
	LCR in NOK	2017	50% (for banks with EUR/USD as significant currencies)
Minimum requirement for own funds and eligible liabilities (MREL)	Loss absorption amount	2019	Minimum requirement for regulatory capital + Pillar 2 requirements + combined buffer requirements
	Amount necessary for recapitalization	2019	Minimum requirement for regulatory capital + Pillar 2 requirements + combined buffer requirements excluding countercyclical capital buffer requirement

Source Norges Bank (2021)

5.5 Case Study: LIBOR Transition

This case study explores a country-specific stress test requirement to illustrate how climate-related stress tests could be customized for different regions. Incorporating the LIBOR transition for UK banks in 2021 is a clear-cut instance of a regulator adapting stress tests for local conditions.

The London Interbank Offered Rate (LIBOR) was a staple of global financial markets, serving as the benchmark for the offshore Eurodollar market since it was officially created in 1986. Offshore Eurodollar accounts are dollar-denominated accounts in countries other than the United States. The offshore Eurodollar markets surged quickly after the Bretton Woods system of multilateral fixed exchange rates was abandoned in the early 1970s. For many reasons, including geopolitical, companies and governments wanted to hold and trade dollars without going through the American financial system (think of a state-owned company in the former USSR.) In addition, companies and families in oil-rich countries became immensely wealthy due to the oil crises in the 1970s, recycling petrodollars through London's financial system.

Given the robust rule of law in the United Kingdom, global agents confidently traded with banks in the City of London. Adding to that the "Big Bang," Margaret Thatcher's swift deregulation of financial markets in the 1980s that also sped up the transition to electronic trading, and London cemented itself as the largest offshore market in the world (at least, until Brexit took away some of the city's advantages).

LIBOR was an average of the interest rates on uncollateralized loans made between banks rated AA in London (thus, it was more a set of rates than a single value, with distinct values for loans of different maturities.) It was determined by the British Bankers' Association, which would poll a panel of banks on their respective borrowing costs daily. It was also the basis for many non-banking financial transactions, including residential mortgages. By 2008, nearly all subprime mortgages and half of the prime mortgage loans in the United States were indexed to LIBOR. (Schweitzer & Venkatu, 2009).

However, LIBOR was phased out due to a scandal in which several banks colluded to influence it, leading to over U$9 billion in fines by regulators in the United States and Europe. The final date for using LIBOR was December 31, 2021, for most currencies, and June 2023, for LIBOR denominated in USD. LIBOR was replaced by the Secured

Overnight Financing Rate (SOFR) in the United States and the Sterling Overnight Index Average (SONIA) in the United Kingdom.

Because of LIBOR's importance for benchmarking financial products, the Bank of England (2021) established guidelines for solvency tests that incorporated the LIBOR phasing out process. Even though it is understandable that such an important benchmark is being replaced, it does not seem that banks would be vulnerable to its well-coordinated replacement. Still, the Bank of England (2021) noted that: "for the avoidance of doubt, this does not apply to EURIBOR or HIBOR, which the Bank assumes continue over the full five-year projection period. This approach is intended to complement the Bank's ongoing interactions with participating banks in preparing for the LIBOR transition, as well as the data banks provide through other channels. By 'orderly transition,' the Bank means that participating banks have: (1) stopped entering into all new LIBOR-linked contracts by end-2021; (2) as far as possible, moved their existing LIBOR-linked contracts (where these contracts extend beyond the proposed cessation dates) to alternative reference rates by mutual agreement with counterparties; and (3) incorporated ISDA or other robust fallbacks into contracts to transition those remaining when the relevant trigger events occur. The Bank is explicitly not seeking to stress participating banks against disorderly LIBOR transition outcomes. For example, uncertainty on the legal position of remaining LIBOR-referencing contracts should LIBOR become unavailable or extreme market illiquidity for LIBOR-linked contracts. Authorities have recognized that banks may have some exposures to LIBOR, which do not have robust fallbacks and may be particularly difficult to renegotiate before the proposed cessation dates and are actively working with market participants to identify and understand these. In line with the overall assumption of an orderly transition, for the purposes of the 2021 solvency stress test, banks should make the simplifying assumption that all contracts not renegotiated before the proposed cessation dates can be transitioned through fallback arrangements."

Interestingly, the worst-case scenario for British banks would be a disorderly transition from Libor and not the orderly scenario embedded in the stress tests overseen by the Bank of England. Explicitly, the Bank of England's recommended assumptions for the stress tests conducted by the banks were (Bank of England, 2021), among others:

- LIBOR ceases to be published on 4 January 2022.

- Banks may assume that ISDA credit spreads are fixed in Q1 2021.
- Banks should assume market developments, pricing assumptions, and timing profiles over 2021 per the expectations set out by the Bank, FCA, and the Working Group on Sterling Risk-Free Reference Rates.
- Banks should assume that fallback provisions are adequate, i.e., contracts that have not been renegotiated to refer directly to alternative reference rates.
- Banks should not use different timing profiles by asset class to optimize their solvency stress test results (i.e., no cheating).
- Banks should not assume they will profit from the contracts' transitions unless solid evidence supports this.

Compellingly, these assumptions are not highly conservative, as is usually the case with solvency stress tests. Banks are dissuaded from assuming they are required to offer counterparties incentives to transition away from Libor-denominated contracts. A disorderly transition was ruled out by design in the stress test rounds of 2021. This likely would include significant transaction costs for both the Bank of England and the banks when designing worst-case scenarios that would be discarded once the transition was complete. Then again, the rules by the Bank of England regarding stress tests tend to state clearly that only measurable regulation changes should be accounted for in solvency stress tests. For instance, Fig. 5.11 establishes clear guidelines for including the effects of regulatory, legal, and accounting changes in such tests.

For our purposes, the main lessons are similar to those of SVB. When faced with specific risks entangled in financial systems, we can see how regulators design highly detailed and customized procedures to ensure that banks are not undercapitalized. The LIBOR example illustrates that the regulatory framework is already established, and banks are well-versed in stress testing their portfolios to specific risks. Arguments such as "climate change impacts are too diffuse," "we can't measure all impacts on our portfolios," and "the quality of climate-related data is too low," while all arguably true, are not obstacles per se. They make stress testing less reliable, increasing the error intervals in such estimates. Still, there is no fundamental reason for banks not to create aggressive and conservative estimates of climate change impact on their portfolios. If banks can stress test the transition of a simple (albeit relevant) reference lending rate, they can estimate, even if imprecisely, how changes in the world's climate can

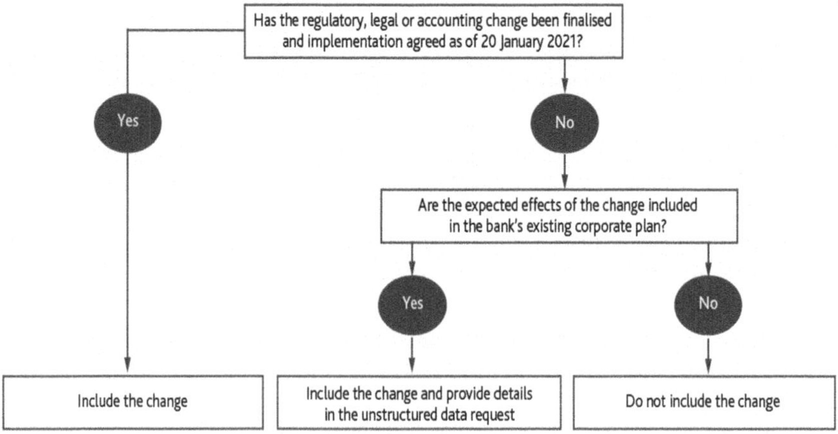

Fig. 5.11 Stylized guidance for including the effects of regulatory, legal, and accounting changes in banks' submissions of test results (*Source* Bank of England [2021])

affect their operations. We now turn to the conditions for "green" stress testing.

5.6 "Green" Stress Testing

Stress tests investigate how bank liquidity and capital can be affected by severe—but plausible—scenarios of potential adverse future events. Climate stress tests have a similar target: testing the resilience of financial institutions from different climate scenarios (Alogoskoufis et al., 2021). Regulators seek to understand if climate events might generate systemic financial risks. As with regular stress tests, there are different rules for regular and globally systemic banks.

Climate stress testing is not methodologically as challenging as "green" value-at-risk (see Sect. 3.10). While attaching climate to daily market movements is almost impossible, estimating how banks' balance sheets are affected by climate shocks over a longer period is much more straightforward, although still challenging. Many central banks have explored this type of supervisory screening, with the Bank of England planning to have biannual climate stress tests moving forward.

There are three significant sources of climate-related risks: physical, transition, and litigation (Neves, 2021). Physical risks arise from extreme weather events and gradual changes in climate. Transition risks point to the economic and social changes to meet climate goals such as those outlined in the Paris Climate Agreement. Finally, litigation risks are related to the risks associated with lending to less sustainable companies or even direct litigation from banks' customers.

Regarding the transition process, the Network for Greening the Financial System, in its first comprehensive report, has neatly divided the process into a 2×2 matrix that relates societies' strength of response (that could potentially reduce physical risks) with transition pathways that characterize the transition risks (Fig. 5.12).

The transition pathway is orderly or disorderly, while the response strength depends on whether or not climate targets are met. Interestingly, the matrix allows transition risks to evolve disorderly but without impeding societies from meeting climate targets. Still, it also allows the "too little, too late" scenario in which societies don't do enough to meet climate goals and physical risks spur a disorderly transition.

The NGFS has developed a comprehensive National Institute Global Econometric Model (NIGEM), which ties fiscal and monetary policy to climate change. The sequence for translating climate scenarios into the NIGEM is represented in Fig. 5.13.

Similar scenario building comes from the stress test by the Bank of Canada (Bank of Canada, 2022). The published results are based on four climate scenarios over a 30-year horizon from 2020 to 2050:

- Baseline scenario: A scenario with global climate policies in place at the end of 2019.
- Below 2° C immediate: An immediate policy action toward limiting average global warming to below 2° C.
- Below 2° C delayed: a delayed policy action toward limiting average global warming to below 2° C.
- Net-zero 2050 (1.5° C): a more ambitious immediate policy action scenario to limit average global warming to 1.5° C that includes current net zero commitments by some countries.

Running such scenarios has four broad steps (Richters et al., 2022):

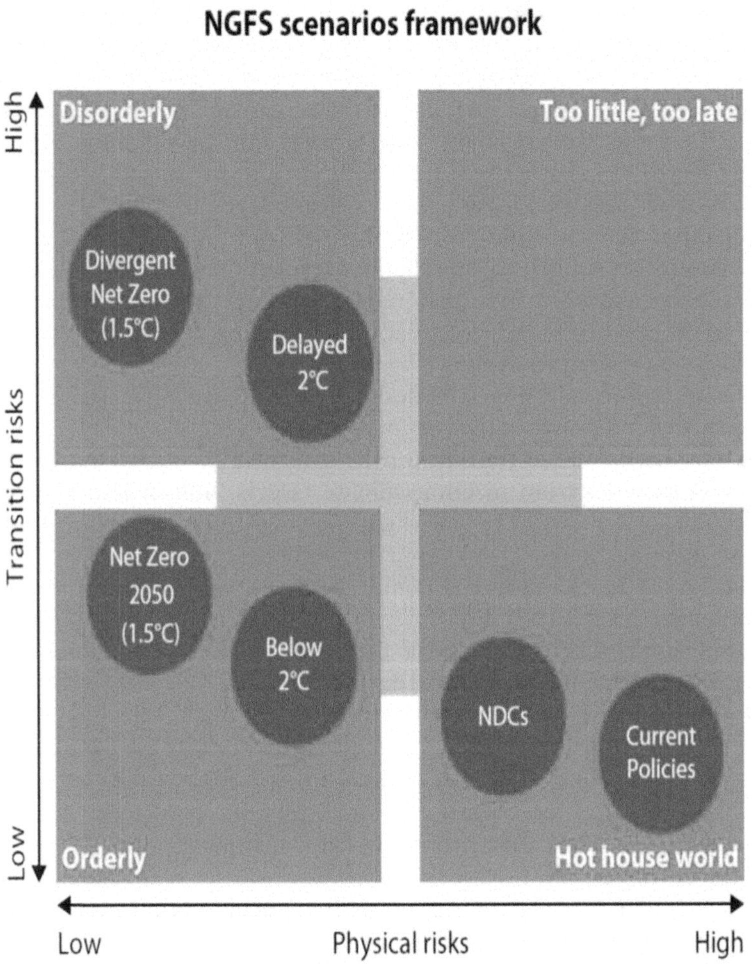

Fig. 5.12 NGFS Scenarios Framework. Positioning of scenarios is approximate, based on an assessment of physical and transition risks out to 2100 (*Source* Network for Greening the Financial System [2019])

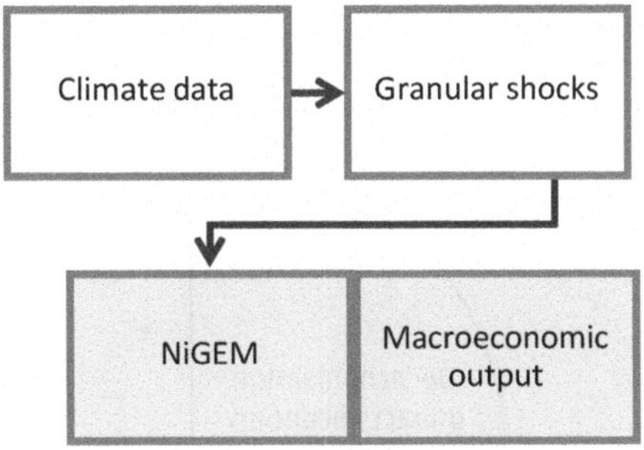

Category	Scenario	Policy ambition	Policy reaction	Technology change	Carbon dioxide removal	Regional policy variation
Orderly	Net Zero 2050	1.4°C	Immediate and smooth	Fast change	Medium-high use	Medium variation
	Below 2°C	1.6°C	Immediate and smooth	Moderate change	Medium-high use	Low variation
Disorderly	Divergent Net Zero	1.4°C	Immediate but divergent across sectors	Fast change	Low-medium use	Medium variation
	Delayed Transition	1.6°C	Delayed	Slow/Fast change	Low-medium use	High variation
Hot House World	Nationally Determined Contributions (NDCs)	2.6°C	NDCs	Slow change	Low-medium use	Medium variation
	Current Policies	3°C+	None - current policies	Slow change	Low use	Low variation

Fig. 5.13 Sequence for translating climate scenarios into NIGEM (*Source* Richters et al. [2022])

- Narrative: What are the source of the shock and underlying premise and/or target variables?
- Channels: How does the shock propagate?
- Shocks: Determine size and shock profile.
- Policy: How do agents respond? Are expectations rational or adaptive? Are the shocks anticipated or unanticipated?

One can't manage what can't be measured, which is no different for climate-related risks. The interaction between physical and economic variables can be represented in Fig. 5.14. The interaction of physical and economic variables in climate modeling. Figures 5.14 and 5.15, which describe two different approaches for modeling such connections.

The next step is materiality. Climate-related stress testing requires material hypotheses about how climate change impacts the economy in

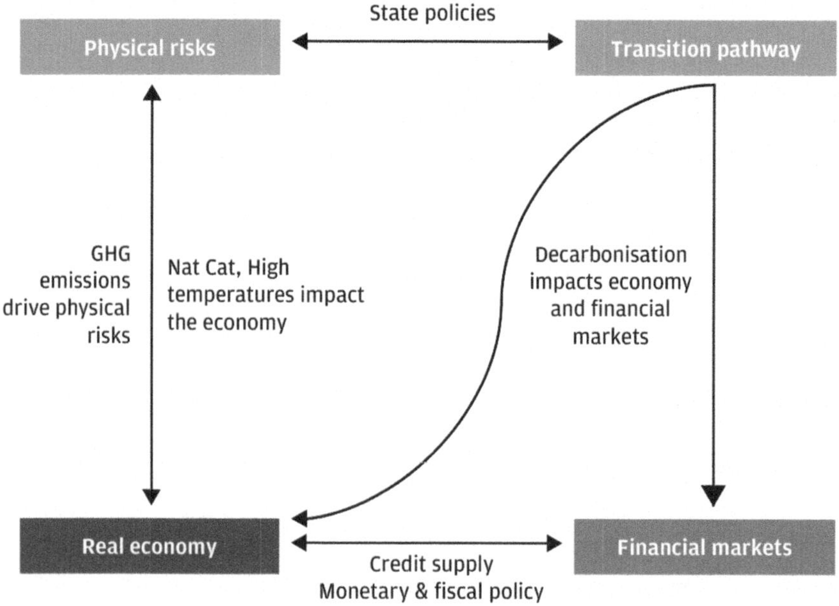

Fig. 5.14 The interaction of physical and economic variables in climate modeling (*Source* J.P. Morgan Assent Management. For illustrative purposes only)

the long run. Like the IPCC and the IEA, the NGFS uses Integrated Assessment Models (IAMs). One example of outputs from the type of models run by the NGFS is in Fig. 5.16.

The modeling of acute physical risk is described in Fig. 5.17. NGFS uses historical damage data to modulate the impact of higher frequency and magnitude of climate shocks on the broader economy.

Specifically, concerning the financial system, Fig. 5.18 illustrates the transmission channels between climate shocks and financial risks.

Risks flow to financial risks through micro and macroeconomic channels. The explicit connection between climate and impacts on credit, market, underwriting, operational, and liquidity risks allows researchers to develop relatively straightforward stress test procedures.

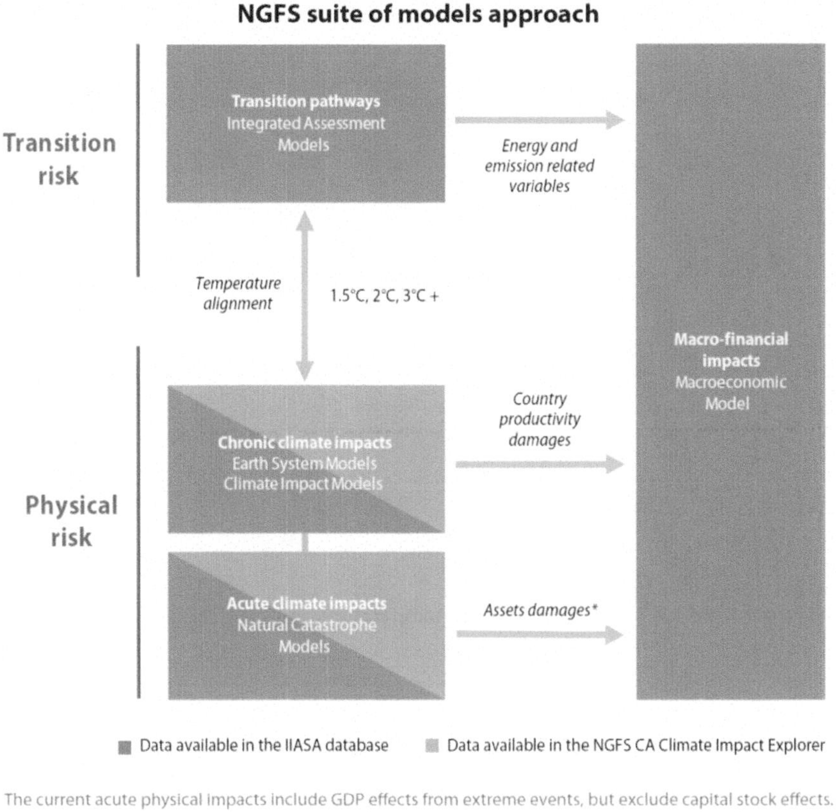

Fig. 5.15 NGFS Suite of Models Approach (*Source* Richters et al. [2022])

These procedures have been described by the European Bank Authority, which published the methodology for the 2021 EU-wide stress test (Alogoskoufis et al., 2021).

Many of the inputs are similar to those of NGFS. The European exercise considered a 30-year window. The stress test was conducted by tying the climate shocks to approximately 2,400 banks and their networks. For instance, counterparty risks dependent on financials, emissions, and physical risk scores were estimated on around 4 million firms worldwide (Alogoskoufis et al., 2021). Novel climate-specific models incorporated the potential damage to physical capital, the impact of energy prices/

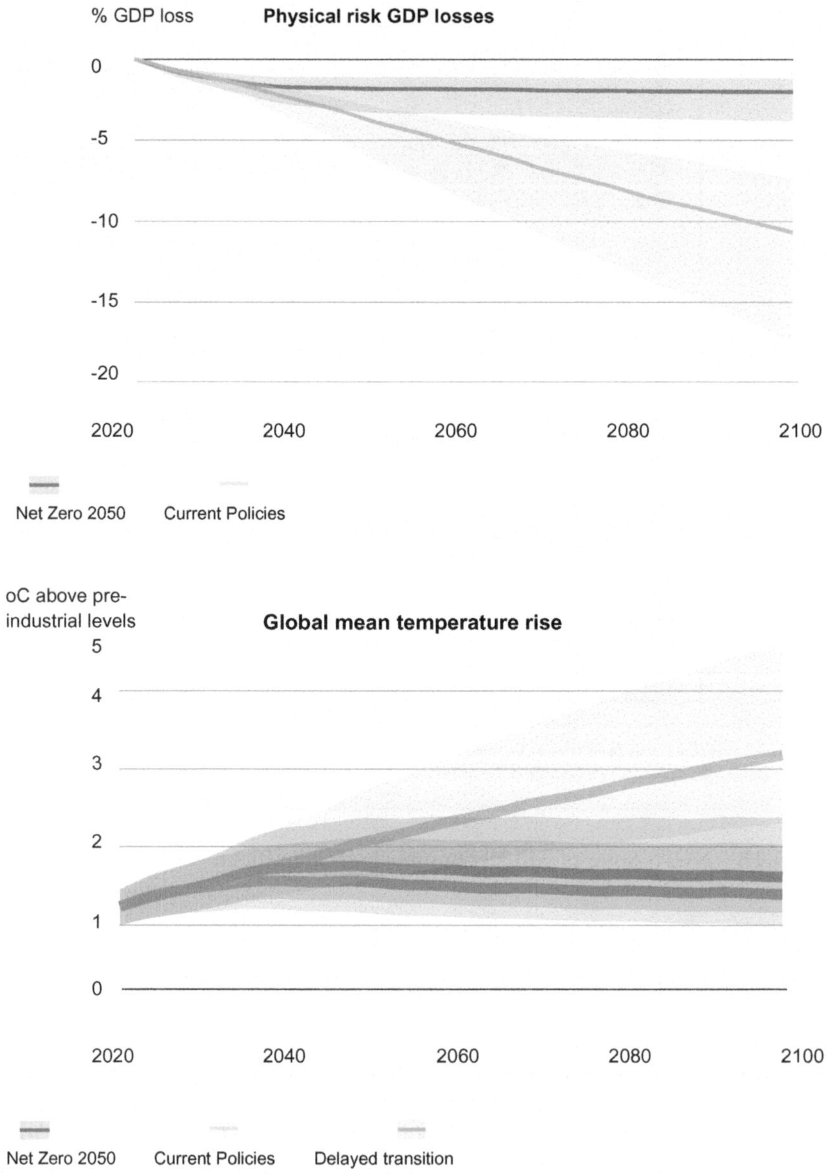

Fig. 5.16 Physical risk GDP losses and global mean temperature rise (*Source* Richters et al. [2022])

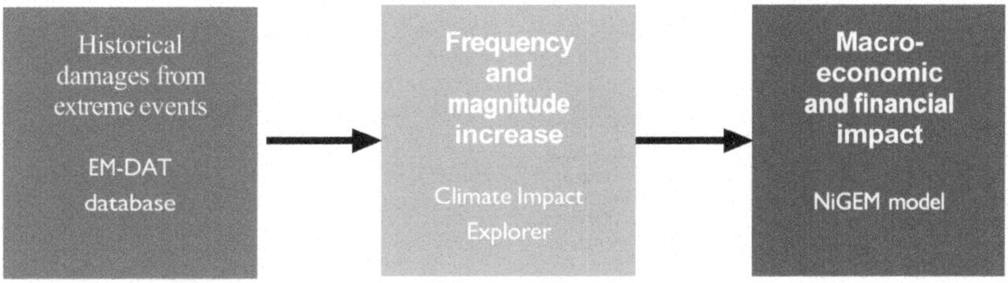

Fig. 5.17 Modeling of acute physical risk (*Source* Richters et al. [2022])

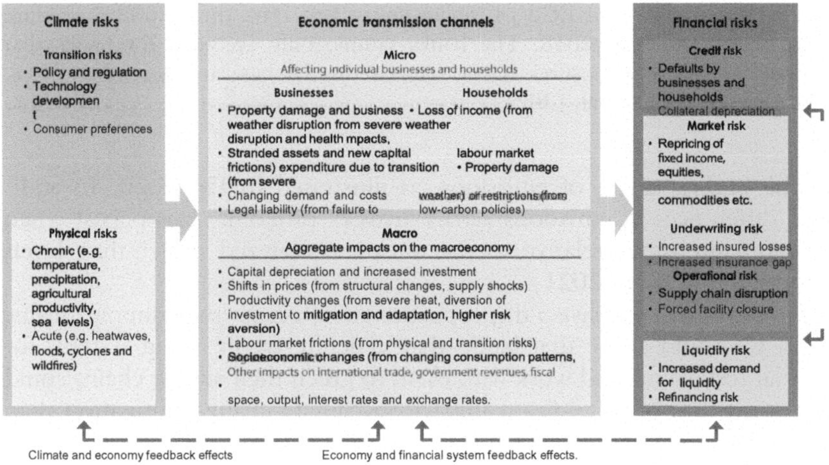

Fig. 5.18 Transmission channels: climate risks to financial risks (*Source* Richters et al. [2022])

efficiency and technology substitution, and both mitigants and amplifiers, such as insurance premiums (Alogoskoufis et al., 2021).

The European Bank Authority, given the detailed data at its disposal, could accurately map banks' counterparties together with their carbon footprint, physical risk exposure, and financial information. Figure 5.19 shows an overview of the data integration procedure.

Some of the results from the stress tests are entirely predictable, although others reveal fascinating insights. The most extensive exposures for euro area banks are to large firms. However, concerning how exposures interact with carbon emissions, indirect emissions, scope 3, make

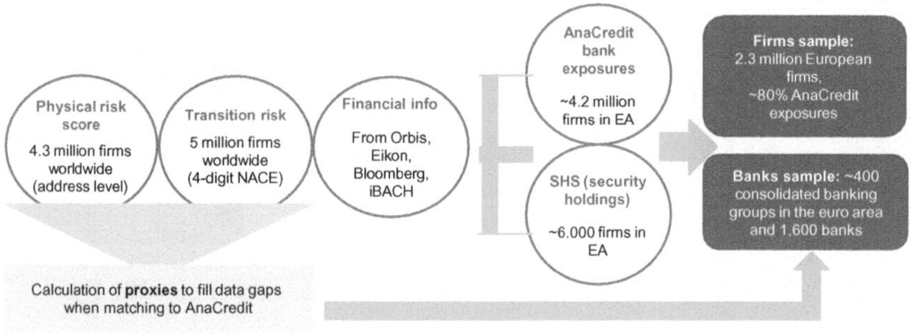

Fig. 5.19 Overview of ECB's Climate Stress Test Data Integration Procedure (*Notes* Data are from 2018. The banks sample only accounts for banks that reported non-zero exposures in the AnaCredit database in December 2018. *Source* Alogoskoufis et al. [2021])

up the highest share of emissions, as illustrated in Fig. 5.20. In addition, differences in emissions across firms of different sizes persist when emission intensities relative to revenues are analyzed rather than levels (Alogoskoufis et al., 2021).

Large focal firms have a disproportionate effect on their supply chains. Thus, we could argue that banks that generate credit rating systems for their largest clients and work with them to green their supply chains could have a much more significant impact on climate change mitigation than alternative strategies.

Another expected result is that mining, electricity and gas, and agriculture are the most emission-intense sectors. However, in absolute terms, the largest contributors to overall absolute emissions are manufacturing, electricity and gas, transport, and wholesale and retail activities. Also, 30% of European banks' portfolios are concentrated in just two of the highest emitter sectors, manufacturing, and wholesale retail, even though the distribution of scope 1, scope 2, and scope 3 emissions are heterogeneous across industries. Finally, heterogeneity across countries isn't pronounced (Alogoskoufis et al., 2021).

In absolute terms, climate change risks in the short run do not translate into systemic risk. The European Central Bank's first major climate stress test shows banks face a potential 70 billion euro hit from climate change in the short run, which pales compared to available regulatory capital (Comfort et al., 2022). Still, while stress tests shouldn't be expected

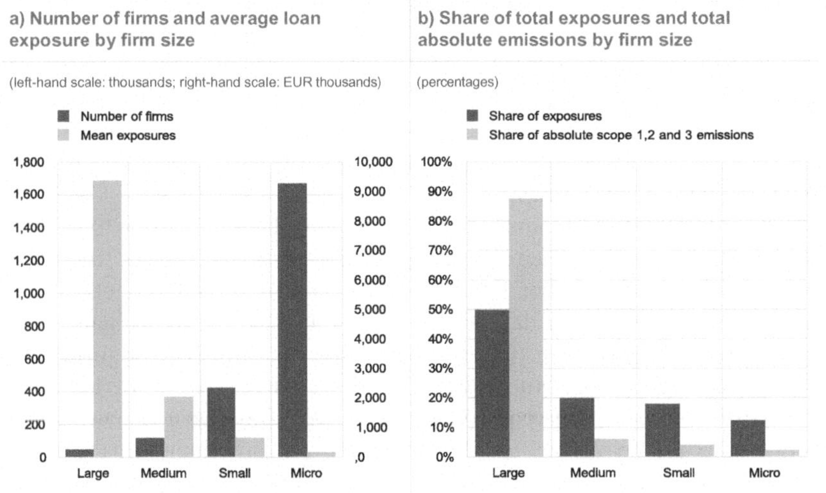

Fig. 5.20 Firm-level transmission of financial and climate risks, estimates for Europe (*Notes* Total absolute emissions refer to total absolute Scope 1, 2, and 3 emissions. Firms are categorized as large, medium, small, and micro based on total assets. The thresholds for this categorization are based on the European Commission's definition of SMEs. *Source* ECB calculations based on AnaCredit et al. [2018])

to impact capital requirements directly soon, lenders were faulted for inadequate management of climate risks (Comfort et al., 2022).

Of course, such estimates have a wide confidence interval. Hosseini et al. (2022), in their methodological report for the Bank of Canada's climate stress test exercise, argue that just one step, the borrower-level calibration, requires significant investment and expertise by financial institutions. After all, the economic impacts associated with the climate transition scenarios are spread over a long time horizon, and historical credit outcomes to inform the borrower-level assessments are less reliable because of the distinct features associated with climate-related risks (Hosseini et al., 2022).

Green stress tests are still in their infancy. The methodologies for such tests are not so different from regular stress testing that they must be described in detail in this section. We don't know all the channels through which climate change can affect financial stability (Giuzio et al., 2019). Still, the main barrier is similar to credit rating systems: sustainability-related data are not standardized. We should expect better procedures following better data availability and comparability and the development of forward-looking frameworks for risk assessments (Giuzio et al., 2019). As robust standards emerge, green stress testing should become routine for most financial institutions.

Still, regulators and financial institutions have little incentive for robust climate stress testing. Regulators use such tests to answer to stakeholders' pressures, whether from the government or civil society. Banks should comply with regulators' requests but have little to gain from being genuinely proactive. Courts may force the supervisory authorities or financial institutions, but other types of pressures have limited chances of success. Green capital requirements (Chapter 2.6) have an even lower likely chance of being successfully implemented, but their impact would be immediate. Still, internal dynamics from engaged employees in these institutions may engender meaningful change. If that is the case, the model set by the Bank of England in the following section could be adapted and expanded. We discuss the limits of greening central banks in Sect. 5.7.

5.6.1 *Bank of England's climate stress test, a short case study*

Since 2019, the Bank of England has required banks to perform climate stress tests every two years. In 2021, the three key objectives of the exercise were to improve banks' climate risk management, estimate the size of the risks that banks face, and improve the understanding of the potential responses of banks to climate-related risks (Bank of England, 2022).

Methodologically, banks modeled risks at a granular level, including their largest counterparties. However, the focus was credit books, without other risks, including nonlinear interactions between credit and asset prices.

The base scenario uses a methodology similar to the NGFS Climate Scenario Database (Ritchters et al., 2022), with three scenarios related to how society will invest in climate change mitigation: early, late, and no additional actions (Fig. 5.21).

In addition, assumptions about carbon emissions are such that stringent climate policies successfully reduce carbon emissions to net zero

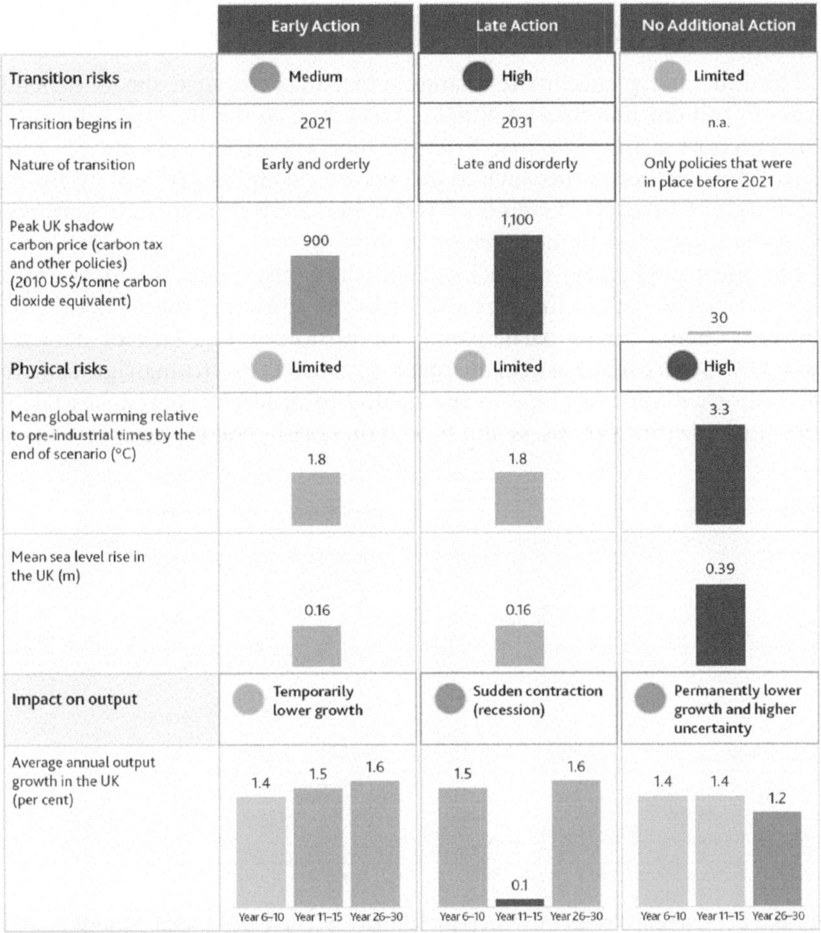

Fig. 5.21 NGFS climate scenarios *Source* Bank of England [2022])

in the United Kingdom and the EU in the first scenarios, with emissions falling moderately in the No Additional Action scenario (Bank of England, 2022).

Notably, the Bank of England's climate stress exercise makes explicit assumptions about carbon prices in the United Kingdom and EU (Fig. 5.22). In the No Additional Action scenario, carbon prices remain the same as today, rising to more than U$1000 per ton in the Late Action scenario.

The links between climate change and banks' balance sheets depend on acute and chronic risk definitions. According to the Bank of England's (2022) report, acute risks arise from the increasing frequency and severity of extreme weather events such as heatwaves, droughts, tropical cyclones, and floods. Chronic risks emerge from increased average temperatures, rising sea levels, and higher precipitation.

The most engrossing result from the stress test exercise is that banks seem to lack the data to measure such risks. As written in the report: "One recurrent theme across participants' submissions was a lack of data on many key factors that participants need to understand to manage climate risks. Another was the range in the quality of different approaches taken across organizations to assess and model these risks. All participating firms

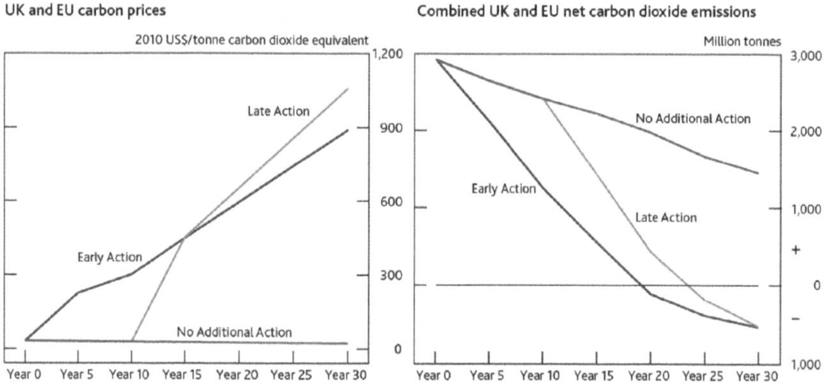

Fig. 5.22 Carbon Prices in Different Climate Scenarios, United Kingdom and Europe. (a) Carbon price depicts a shadow price of greenhouse gas emissions, i.e., the marginal abatement cost of an incremental ton of emissions. This is a simplification intended to capture a range of policies to reduce greenhouse gas emissions, including, for example, carbon taxes, cap-and-trade schemes, green subsidies, and environmental regulations. (b) As the No Additional Action scenario is calibrated based on temperature outcomes that might be observed in the period 2050–80, emissions over that later period are also relevant. The calibration of the No Additional Action scenario is consistent with the combined United Kingdom and EU net carbon dioxide emissions of 922 megatonnes per year by 2080 *Source* Bank of England [2022])

have more work to improve their climate risk management capabilities. The Bank will engage with firms individually and collectively to help them target their efforts and share good practices identified in this exercise." (Bank of England, 2022).

Most central banks have never run such exercises. For those like the Bank of England, who do, the results are predictable and unsurprising: banks are not good at bringing materiality to climate risks (Fagan et al., 2022). Such risks are indeed diffuse, but if one thing is in modern banks' DNA, it is risk management. What can't be measured can't be managed, the saying goes.

One counterintuitive result relates to the dangers of UK banks and insurers moving too quickly to remove their exposure to specific sectors. The BoE referred to banks and insurers "gradually" reducing exposures where counterparties have credible transition plans. In other words, banks should balance reductions in exposure to carbon-intensive counterparties and investments in sustainable energy solutions (Fagan et al., 2022). As we can see, a central bank's concern with financial stability trumps almost everything, including the need for climate change mitigation in a climate stress test simulation.

The next evolutionary step is for climate stress testing to coalesce into standardized procedures with high-quality data and better confidence intervals. In addition, adequate sectoral assumptions are a must. We discuss such assumptions in the following section.

5.6.2 *Sectoral Decomposition*

Mapping climate risks to central bank action or other forms of changing lending practices by commercial banks requires assumptions about industries' externalities. Of course, classifying coal production as a polluting industry is straightforward. However, determining the impact of distinct economic sectors is challenging for climate stress tests and other prudential regulations regarding nonfinancial indicators. Hosseini et al. (2022) classify industries and their segments related to direct emission costs, indirect costs, low-carbon capital expenditures, and revenues (Table 5.11).

Such classifications are relevant as a first approximation to materiality. In climate stress test exercises, central banks can be concerned with banks moving too quickly to remove their exposure to certain sectors. Ideally, we would have detailed connections between banks' operations and environmental outcomes, but that is not happening quickly enough. Thus,

Table 5.11 Sectoral Segmentation and Heat Map Tool

Sectors	*Segments*	*Direct emissions cost*	*Indirect costs*	*Low-carbon capital expenditures*	*Revenues*
1) Livestock	1) Livestock	**Moderate**			
2) Forestry	2) Forestry				
3) Crops	3) Crops				
4) Coal	4) Coal				
5) Refined oil products	5) Refined oil products				
6) Oil and gas	6) Oil and gas extraction (except oil sands)	Moderately high	Moderately low	Moderate	Moderate
	7) Oil sands extraction	High	Moderately high	Moderately high	High
	8) Crude petroleum from oil shale	Moderately high	Moderately high	Moderately high	Moderately high
	9) Contract drilling and services to oil and gas Extraction	Moderately low	Moderate	Moderately low	Moderately high
	10) Pipeline transportation	Moderate	Moderately high	Moderate	Moderately low
	11) Natural gas distribution	Low	Low	Moderately low	Moderately low
7) Electricity	12) Fossil-fuel electric power generation	Moderately high	Moderately high	Moderately high	Negative
	13) Hydro and nuclear	Low	Low	Moderately low	Moderately low
	14) Other renewables	Low	Moderately low	Moderately low	Moderately high
	15) Electric power transmission, control and Distribution	Low	Low	Moderate	Moderate

Sectors	*Segments*	*Direct emissions cost*	*Indirect costs*	*Low-carbon capital expenditures*	*Revenues*
8) Energy-intensive industries	16) Paper manufacturing, printing, and related support activities	Moderately high	Moderately low	Moderate	Moderate
	17) Chemical manufacturing, plastics, and rubber products manufacturing	Moderate	Moderately low	Moderately high	Moderate
	18) Non-metallic mineral product manufacturing	Moderately high	Moderate	Moderately low	Moderate
	19) Primary metal manufacturing and fabricated metal product manufacturing	Moderately low	High	High	Moderate
9) Commercial transportation	20) Air transportation	High	Moderately low	High	Low
	21) Rail transportation	Moderately low	Low	Moderately low	Moderately high
	22) Water transportation	Moderately high	Moderately low	Moderately high	Moderate
	23) Truck transportation, transit and ground passenger transportation, and other transportation	Moderately low	High	Moderate	Moderate

Source Hosseini et al. (2022)

understanding which sectors pose more risks in aggregate to financial institutions is necessary for green banking strategies.

Hosseini et al. (2022) indicate that all climate-related risks for agricultural products are moderate, rising, unsurprisingly, to moderately high and high for the oil and gas and electricity industries. Also notable is the low direct emissions cost of natural gas, representing the belief that natural gas is a cleaner alternative to oil and gas. There is no consensus about that in the scientific literature, but the narrative that natural gas is a "cleaner" substitute to coal and oil in energy production seems to have taken hold.

Still, Table 5.11 is a relevant starting tool for whoever is looking to build a method for improving environmental outcomes for financial institutions.

Such sectoral decompositions likely bundle more and less sustainable companies, which would be true of any firm classification. Still, mapping companies to sustainability-related outcomes wholesale is required for many initiatives. Sectoral decompositions allow applied researchers to build stress test methods with better degrees of confidence than otherwise. As such, they are essential tools for assessing climate-related financial risks.

Hosseini et al. (2022) is not the only sectoral decomposition available but is an excellent start for practitioners modeling climate stress tests. The more granular a decomposition is, the more robust the results overall, but data requirements rise in tandem. In addition, transparency declines as databases become more complex. As such, there is a trade-off between simplicity, data requirements, and transparency. The simpler a sectoral decomposition, the more intuitive the estimation is, and the easier it is to check the results.

5.7 Walking a Tightrope and Evolving Central Bank Mandates to Incorporate Climate Goals

The title of this subsection is partly inspired by the work of Demekas and Grippa (2022), who title their article "Walking a tightrope: Financial regulation, climate change, and the transition to a low-carbon economy." Today, the most relevant debate regarding central banks and climate-related financial supervision is fundamental: should supervisory authorities get involved? In some ways, we already have the answer. The

ECB has introduced climate disclosure for the companies issuing corporate bonds eligible for inclusion in the ECB's quantitative easing programs (Danmarks Nationalbank, 2021). Thus, we could argue that central banks already incorporate climate goals in their operations. But that is more of an exception than the rule.

We won't get a definitive answer to the question of central banks genuinely incorporating climate change into their mandates anytime soon. However, that does not mean the current equilibrium will remain the same. The tightrope becomes harder to thread when central banks commit to introducing concrete measures.

We have a working framework of an ideal model for climate change solutions involving the financial system. Pedersen (2023) developed a model that unifies carbon taxation with green finance. He jointly models carbon pricing mechanisms and green finance for a multi-pronged climate approach evolving globally. The results are straightforward. Carbon taxes, allowance prices, and offset prices dominate climate finance. In other words, as Pedersen put it, "the social optimum can be achieved when carbon taxes, carbon allowance prices, and carbon offset prices are identical and equal to the social cost of carbon, and when green finance is not used simultaneously." However, green finance is functional when the carbon tax is too low. In the model, carbon emissions are of type 1,2,3, the former directly tied to a firm's emissions and the others including indirect emissions from energy use or all upstream and downstream emissions in the supply chain.

If banks don't want to invest in ESG-related initiatives, they may lobby their representatives for efficient carbon emissions taxes. However, as that is also unlikely, Demekas and Grippa (2022) are probably correct: banks' supervisory authorities must walk a tightrope. In some sense, central banks seem to want to eat their cake and have them too. On the one hand, there are many preliminary initiatives regarding climate change. Several central banks have performed climate stress tests. Some directors are calling for action (BIS, 2023). European Central Bank board members claim the institution must become more climate-friendly (Smith, 2023). The European Central Bank has released a climate report card for the Eurosystem, while the Danish Central Bank explicitly stated that it "shares the ECB's assessment that climate change and the carbon transition may impact price and financial stability." (Danmarks Nationalbank, 2021).

On the other hand, other executives argue that different parts of the government should tackle climate change, leaving central banks to act on their narrow mandates. For instance, in 2023, both the National Bank of Belgium Governor Pierre Wunsch and the Federal Reserve's Chairman Jerome Powell made similar arguments that governments should combat climate change and monetary policy financing the green transition was a "misunderstanding of central banks' roles." (Smialek, 2023; Smith, 2023).

However, as we have seen in previous sections, central banks hold inordinate sway over the banking system; if they adopt green climate mandates, banks must follow. Even without explicit mandates, central banks can steer financial institutions toward greener practices; the threat of strong green regulations can induce banks' reactions.

Some authors contend that there are several reasons why central banks must consider climate change in their supervisory activities. Boneva et al. (2022) list three considerations. First, climate change risks both price and financial stability (broadly divided into physical and transition risks). Eventually, such risks should affect the transmission mechanisms of monetary policy. Second, climate change could impact central banks' balance sheets. Finally, they argue that the mandate of various central banks obliges them to support the general economic policies of their respective governments, in some cases subject to the requirement that such actions do not prejudice the price stability mandate. They argue that, at a minimum, central banks must avoid inadvertently obstructing or acting counter to these policy objectives by favoring polluting sectors or industries. That is a fair enough request, but central banks are not in the business of favoring specific industries. In 2023, Jerome Powell, then Chair of the Fed, was categoric: "While the central bank is working on better monitoring climate-related risks at financial institutions, the Fed should not try to incentivize banks to lend to green projects or discourage them from lending to carbon-producing ones." (Smialek, 2023).

Powell's argument is more subtle than a simple reluctance to tackle climate change. He argues that combating climate change has significant impacts on income distribution. And that is not the job of the Federal Reserve to subsidize, indirectly or not, renewable energies or funnel resources away from specific sectors. It is not that this is not a worthwhile endeavor, but it would not fall under the remit of a central bank to solve distributional conflicts that fall under the purview of elected officials.

Forni and Kiarsi (2023) codify much of the current orthodoxy in a framework that describes the Ramsey-optimal long-run and dynamic policy interactions between climate and fiscal-monetary policies in a climate-monetary DSGE model under sticky prices. Dynamic stochastic general equilibrium models aim to describe the effects of economic policies that may percolate through different macroeconomic markets. In particular, Forni and Kiarsi's (2023) model aims to investigate the long-run and dynamic implications of the interactions between optimal climate policy (optimal carbon taxation) and optimal fiscal-monetary policy from a type of "Integrated Assessment Model" (IAM) as is standard in climate science. In particular, their model has standard fiat money demand, sticky prices, and autonomous fiscal policy, introducing (i) a carbon circulation system that specifies how emissions over time translate into a path of CO2 concentration; (ii) a climate system that specifies the link between the atmospheric CO2 concentration and the global average atmospheric temperature near the surface; and (iii) a damage function that models the economic losses from climate change as a function of the global mean temperature. One notable but expected result from the model is that the carbon tax policy sharply reduces the fall in key macroeconomic variables such as output, consumption, and welfare. In addition, policymakers sharply increase abatement efforts in response to an unexpected increase in CO2 circulation.

The authors also model a tipping point shock in the climate system. Notably, monetary and fiscal policies move in opposite directions in this case. Fiscal policy would aim to boost employment and GDP through lower labor tax rates, while monetary policy should cool the economy through higher nominal interest rates. Still, monetary policy is not qualitatively different than in the situation without climate change shocks. Its goal remains to limit inflation volatility and not much else. Finally, the authors argue that whether a carbon taxation policy is in place matters significantly to the macroeconomic implications of unexpected climate shocks.

Forni and Kiarsi (2023) complement Pedersen (2023) and Hansen (2022), describing an orthodoxy in the approach to climate finance. Fiscal policy should be preferred to monetary policy, with economists strongly favoring carbon taxes (and other mechanisms). And that view may indeed be correct from a theoretical, first-best point of view. However, there is no indication that carbon taxes, emissions caps, or other mechanisms will soon become commonplace globally. Thus, we shouldn't expect central banks to refrain from climate action. We are already seeing this happening, and monetary authorities will likely move toward more activism, not less, despite what economic theory posits.

Moreover, we should also consider organizational inertia (see Section 5.8) as an explanation for central bank inertia. Institutions are incentivized to disregard any new threat to their operation if a change is costly. For central banks, the costs of introducing climate change financial regulations would be enormous, both directly and indirectly. Politically, anti-ESG regulation is already sprawling in the United States and several other countries. Even if these regulations are boneheaded, central banks would have to contend with them if their mandate were to include climate finance supervision. Operationally, institutions must build teams and design specific regulations to address these issues. Central banks would have to find resources to hire more people, resulting in more labor for the existing workforce.

Dafermos (2022) summarizes the dilemma faced by central banks in two propositions. Proposition 1: Financial markets and institutions have not adequately assessed their exposure to climate-related financial risks. Proposition 2: Climate risks are exogenous to the actions of central banks and financial supervisors.

Ultimately, we will not see a coordinated, unique path by the world's most important central banks. The European Central Bank and other European authorities are expected to lead the way, as the region tends to be the most proactive (or least reactive) to climate change. It may be that central banks in other regions, such as the People's Bank of China, lead the way, owning to climate change's impact on these economies.

However, for this book, the main lesson for commercial banks is: does it pay to be reactive? Financial institutions also answer to shareholders and other stakeholders. Does it really pay to be reactive? If so, then there is not much use for this book, but this won't be the first tome to be quickly lost to the whims of publishing history.

Green central banks may never come to pass, but whatever the future brings, it will require change. And for one of the biggest obstacles to greening banks, we turn to organizational inertia.

5.8 Organizational Inertia and Coordination Failures

"Organizational inertia is one hell of a drug." Human beings usually don't welcome change. And organizations are no different. Even if there is internal agreement that climate action is warranted, institutions will be slow to act. Some authors, such as Weber (2005), argue that financial institutions are inherently reactive, only changing their culture after a traumatic risk event.

Promoting change requires overcoming organizational inertia. In this section, we summarize the main framework of Zeidan et al. (2020). In that article, the authors analyze coordination problems, first enhancing theoretical models and then applying them to a case study about the beef industry.

Coordination problems lead to low-value equilibria, a suboptimal result of a technology choice—in this case, sustainability actions—by companies in a particular industry. More specifically, low-value equilibrium is a stable competitive market equilibrium that maximizes all firms' profits but falls short of maximizing the social welfare function that integrates environmental sustainability as an externality to companies' actions.

Low-value equilibrium refers to producing existing economically feasible goods and services that are still underutilized. The intuition behind the concept is simple: markets may be caught in a competitive equilibrium that maximizes a narrowly defined definition of social welfare. Thus, low-value equilibria allow us to investigate how we should move from a purely economic market equilibrium to a more sustainable future; in this scenario, the competitive market equilibrium would not be Pareto optimal. Companies would increase their profit while improving environmental outcomes, or, simply, cleaner production would come at a profit. Such a win–win scenario would be in line with calls for sustainable production. Companies can increase their profits and reduce GHG emissions to a degree, ascribing to the sustainability or the eco-imperative business scenario.

We know that for an n-player game, $G = \{A_1,\ldots, A_n; \pi_1,\ldots \pi_n\}$ of the chosen technology space $A_1,\ldots, A_n$ and related profits $\pi_1,\ldots \pi_n$, there is always a Nash equilibrium (in mixed strategies). The strategies $A^*_1,\ldots A^*_n$ are a Nash equilibrium if, for each player i, A^*_i is at least tied for player i''s best response to the other players' strategies (Gibbons, 1997).

Nevertheless, such Nash equilibrium might not maximize social welfare, including environmental sustainability $w_1, \ldots w_n$ related to the choice of technology. This static version of a choice of technology guarantees a unique equilibrium. However, nothing relates profits π to environmental sustainability. To address this, we include a Shapley value (Shapley, 1953), specifying that the differences in marginal benefits and costs for green investments contribute to low-value equilibria.

The surplus value (θ) is the source of the Shapley value distributed throughout the supply chain. The innovation lies in relating this surplus value to the cost of creating it, complementing models like that of Dai et al. (2017), and creating a bridge between green supply chain coordination literature and companies' praxis.

Next, we assume a stable industry with no structural break; companies may leave the market, and new firms may emerge. If we take a cost (C) for the creation of surplus value (sv), separable in firm (c_i) and part ρ of industry cost (C_j), and $\vartheta_i(\pi)$ represents the Shapley value of firm i, then the surplus value for firm i is the discount cash flow at the cost of capital (k). This formula is as follows:

$$\theta = \sum_{i=0} \frac{(\vartheta(\pi)_t - c_{it} - \rho C_{jt})}{(1+k)^t}$$

Sustainable investments happen whenever $E(\theta) > 0$. However, there is a catch: if there is asymmetric information regarding other companies incurring (C_j), the profit function of company i is:

$$\begin{cases} \sum_{i=0} \frac{(\vartheta(\pi)_t - c_{it} - \rho C_{jt})}{(1+k)^t} if\ enough\ companies\ incur\ in\ C_j, and \\ -(c_i + pC_j) otherwise \end{cases}$$

This equation illustrates the coordination failure of green investments. Companies benefit from sustainable investments only if there is coordination, meaning that most companies in the supply chain commit to green investments. In this model, commitment is simultaneous but does not need to be. If we relax simultaneity, companies can observe commitments by other companies, enhancing the probability that the surplus value θ will be created.

Even though the Shapley value is challenging to compute, this formal definition of the surplus value allows us to establish important insights to consider, including that it depends on the entire industry rather than any one firm.

Regarding generalizable knowledge, uncertainty about marginal benefits may impede green investment, even when companies are willing to invest in projects that aggregate output while reducing negative externalities. The concept of the Shapley value—which incorporates marginal contributions and benefits into coordinated supply chain efforts for improving environmental outcomes—can describe the efficiency, symmetry, and monotonicity of green investments.

Pure competitive markets fail to yield socially efficient outcomes if private and social marginal costs differ. In most markets, regulation or private coordination mechanisms are necessary to combine competitive incentives with social benefits. It is, therefore, important to highlight how the distinct appropriation of benefits related to green investments keeps companies from pursuing such investments fully.

There are significant complements to these points by Albert (2019), Chen et al. (2020), and Hestad et al. (2020). These authors argue that transformations toward more sustainable production cannot necessarily be achieved through existing management rationales and practices and require changes in industry-wide behavior. That, of course, assumes that sustainability actions bring value to the industry through tangible and intangible benefits (Ortiz-de-Mandojana & Bansal, 2016).

We assume that potential financial benefits would go to all industry stakeholders. Still, sustainability-related investments by financial firms would be dampened by coordination failures. Such failures cannot quickly be resolved, although we know that cost-sharing contracts can Pareto-dominate buyback contracts under financial constraints (Kouvalis & Zhao, 2015). Central banks could potentially coordinate industry-wide investments, so focusing on financial regulation comes hand-in-hand with greening commercial and investment banks.

5.8.1 Criticizing the Critics: Central Banking Challenges Posed by Uncertain Climate Change, Natural Disasters, and Inaction

The most cogent scientific article about green central banking is likely the one by Hansen (2022). Lars Peter Hansen is a recipient of the Nobel Prize in Economics and one of the top economists of the last 50 years, with a broad research agenda on monetary and macroeconomics. As one of the most prominent researchers, his article on central banking and climate change will likely drive the debate on green central banking moving forward.

Thus, we must analyze his article and understand the ramifications of his arguments. Broadly speaking, Hansen (2022) criticizes green central banking three-fold (Hansen, 2022, p. 2):

(i) hastily devised policy rules unsupported by empirically grounded quantitative modeling could backfire if or when climate policy targets are missed, harming the reputations of central banks and weakening their ability to act in the future on a variety of fronts;
(ii) attempts to take on a broader mission without formal and well-defined mandates could compromise central bank independence in the longer run;
(iii) climate change mitigation targets added to currently well-defined mandates may generate excessive expectations and unwarranted confidence in the abilities of central banks to address this critical social and economic problem while diverting the attention away from fiscal policy.

He then describes five potential policy pitfalls (Hansen, 2022, p. 2):

- Modeling systemic risk and climate change in support of rules-based policy for financial stability
- Quantifying the exposure of financial institutions and businesses that receive their loans to uncertain climate change outcomes
- Stress testing banks based on long-term possibilities of climate change
- Slanting central bank portfolios toward green technologies
- Comparing climate change challenges of central banks to those connected with other natural disasters.

The thing about Hansen's points is not if they are right or wrong. They are correct insofar as the technical aspects of his arguments. The main issue is: is delineating solely the costs of changing the status quo the way forward in the green central banking debate?

Take, for instance, the risk of compromising central bank independence. Societies' pressure on central banks to help with climate change mitigation, with politicians leading the drive, would likely compromise monetary authorities' independence (if significantly, that is another matter). However, central bank independence is a means to an end, not an end in itself. Central banks' goals include financial stability, stable inflation rates, and preventing currency crises. It does not include being independent. Of course, central bank employees prefer independence to the alternative, but that does not necessarily mean that this is a social optimum, even if there is a weak consensus that protecting monetary authorities from the worst political pressure is advisable.

Here is a thought experiment. Assume an independent central bank is failing to stave off inflation because it is incompetent. Should society refrain from establishing rules that constrain the institution's behavior in the name of independence? Positively not. In addition, central banks are never wholly independent; at best, they are operationally independent, with their remits being decided by the political process. The original Federal Reserve Act of 1913 was reformed in 1977 due to, among other things, economic shocks that the original legislation could not have predicted.

Changing central banks' mandates while keeping their independence intact is also feasible. Politicians could simply reform central banks' mandates to include climate change, a shock of similar or higher magnitude than the stagflation of the 1970s. Monetary institutions would remain independent to meet those new targets as if their mandates had otherwise evolved.

Regarding Hansen's first argument, that hastily devised policy rules unsupported by empirically grounded quantitative modeling could backfire, again, he is correct. However, what are the alternatives? Couldn't inaction also backfire? Why is the risk of hastily devised policy rules higher (or lower) than central banks doing nothing? As economists, we are trained to present counterfactual scenarios. Simply stating that there is a downside to a policy prescription is not enough to invalidate it. Would the benefits of the policy outweigh its costs? Are there other reasonable options? Is that policy dominated by a better design?

Hansen (2022) advocates for "an investment in building better quantitative models that explore how climate change might challenge financial stability." Such models already exist, although not all are highly robust. Here is another counterpoint. Climate science is neither embryonic nor models that relate economic output to climate change. Would better quantitative models convince climate skeptics or proponents of business as usual? Organizational inertia thrives on stalling tactics of the type: "We need better models," "We need more studies," "The data is not good enough for us to do anything, so we shouldn't rock the boat." Hansen (2022) is yet again correct that we need more investment and better models, but that cannot preclude action; the current climate science is unquestionably precise that early action is preferable.

Hansen's (2022) final argument that central bank climate mandates can crowd out fiscal policy is another example of a risk that exists but cannot justify inaction. Societies will likely benefit from more unambiguous green central bank mandates if such is warranted rather than relying on fiscal policy to do the same job. In addition, fiscal policy is notoriously slower than monetary policy. Macroeconomics textbooks (such as Zeidan, 2018) routinely describe fiscal and monetary policies as having distinct inside time lags. The usual definition of inside lag is the time it takes policymakers to enact a public policy, usually as a response to an economic shock. Fiscal policy usually has a much longer inside lag than monetary policy. Take some of the major crises of the last 20 years, the great financial crisis of 2007/08, and the pandemic that started in 2020. In both instances, US policymakers acted swiftly to cushion the economy. The American Recovery Act by President Obama and the pandemic checks by the Trump administration were passed quickly by congressional standards (they took less than six months and three months, respectively, from recognizing the magnitude of the economic shocks to the bills being signed). However, the Fed had already brought interest rates to zero in days. Central banks are designed to act swiftly when necessary.

If we had a global consensus on the broad monetary policies related to climate change mitigation, central banks would likely have implemented these policies shortly after the consensus was formed. The risk of monetary policy crowding out fiscal policy exists, but the risk that fiscal policy never goes anywhere is much higher. If timing matters, fiscal policy, having a much shorter inside lag, is preferable to fiscal policy. Still, if climate mitigation requires perfect models and a complete global consensus, then.

Another way to view the crowding risk pointed out by Hansen (2022) is to tie it down to the model by Pedersen (2023). Section 5.7 shows that the ideal prescription for climate change mitigation involves a carbon tax with no green finance. Insofar as central bank activism may derail a socially optimum Pigouvian tax, Hansen's (2022) argument is more robust. In addition, this argument can be standard in economics research; Smith Jr. (2022) reiterates it, commenting on Hansen's (2022) work. Still, that depends on the priors one has regarding the possibility of robust carbon taxes. It is unlikely that coordinated global fiscal policy will emerge soon, but there is no considerable impediment for central banks to act greener. Globally, the Bank for International Settlements coordinates central bank actions in a manner that fiscal authorities can't; the best example is the Eurozone, where the ECB is the bloc's monetary authority, but every country maintains budgetary autonomy.

Hansen's (2022) argument that central bank climate activism may generate excessive expectations is well-taken, but what is the counterfactual? Better not to expect anything? Ignore climate change, hoping fiscal authorities act before it is too late. If climate risks compound, earlier action is paramount. Or maybe as humankind drowns, we can say: "At least we have not violated central banks' independence!".

Masciandaro and Russo (2023) explicitly state the trade-offs between climate activism and other central bank functions. They develop a principal-agent model that considers the interactions between monetary and macroprudential policies and the relationship between central banks and their respective governments. They allow central banks to penalize brown debt instruments and favor green instruments, something that Hansen (2022) warns us against.

In their setting, the central bank is assigned monetary and macroprudential mandates and considers inflation and leverage as the targets, as in standard in central bank principal-agent frameworks. The model has two stages. The first is defined as "constitutional, the government, maximizing long-term social welfare, establishes the central bank, its degree of independence, mandates, and other institutional features. In the second stage, the central bank interacts with the current government, implementing policy decisions based on the framework from the constitutional stage (Masciandaro & Russo, 2023)." In the first stage, the government allows a positive degree of dependence on the incumbent's preferences, incorporating climate-related issues.

Formally, the economy's aggregate output is given by a macroprudential–augmented Lucas supply function; the central bank can account for an exogenous climate shock depending on its degree of independence and the government's climate preferences (Masciandaro & Russo, 2023). Central banks' pursued outcomes are inflation volatility and leverage, the latter defined as:

$$c = c_g + c_b,$$

with c_g and c_b corresponding to "green" and "brown" baseline leverage. According to its degree of dependence on the government's climate preferences, $\delta \geq 0$, the central bank can apply a penalty factor $B > 0$ to c_b and a forgiveness term $G > 0$ to c_g. Interestingly, if the central bank is completely independent, it disregards the government's preferences and ignores climate-related shocks.

Furthermore, the main result of the model is that for $\delta > 0$ and $B > G$, on average, inflation is above target, leverage is below baseline leverage, and output is below its natural level. The central bank tries to offset a net penalization with more extensive monetary accommodation. A similar but reverse result holds for $B < G$.

The authors' results show that central banks couldn't ultimately attain inflation, leverage, and output targets given a climate-related mandate following governments' climate preferences unless the penalty and forgiveness terms balance out. Still, accounting for a well–behaved climate shock does not affect, on average, the central bank's ability to achieve its targets. In addition, central banks' behavior depends not on governments' active influence but solely on their preferences; the central bank is free to set its instruments after the constitutional stage and does not pursue biased levels of the target variables. Deviations from the ultimate targets emerge from central banks' miscalibration of G and B.

These articles are sophisticated analyses of the dangers of green central banking. However, there is very little doubt that brown penalties or green incentives will likely be on the menu for central banks. Should central banks outsource climate policies to the fiscal authorities? In an ideal world, yes. However, we don't live in a world of first-best policies, and what seems like healthy skepticism can also be viewed as motivated reasoning for business as usual.

References

Albert, M. (2019). Sustainable Frugal Innovation-The Connection Between Frugal Innovation and Sustainability. *Journal of Cleaner Production, 237*, 177474. https://doi.org/10.1016/j.jclepro.2019.117747

Alogoskoufis, S., Dunz, N., Emambakhsh, T., Hennig, T., Kaijser, M., Kouratzoglou, C., Muñoz, M., Parisi, L. & Salleo, C. (2021). ECB Economy-Wide Climate Stress Test: Methodology and Results (No. 281). ECB Occasional Paper.

Amadeo. (2020). *AIG Bailout, Cost, Timeline, Bonuses, Causes, Effects, the Balance*. https://www.thebalancemoney.com/aig-bailout-cost-timeline-bonuses-causes-effects-3305693

Anderson, N., Brazier, A., Haldane, A., Nahai-Williamson, P., & Radia, A. (2022). Why Banks Failed the Stress Test: A Progress Report on Stress Testing 10 Years On. *Handbook of Financial Stress Testing, 47*.

Bank of Canada. (2022). *Using Scenario Analysis to Assess Climate Transition Risk, Office of the Superintendent of Financial Institutions (OSFI) and the Bank of Canada*. https://www.bankofcanada.ca/wp-content/uploads/2021/11/BoC-OSFI-Using-Scenario-Analysis-to-Assess-Climate-Transition-Risk.pdf

Bank of England. (2021). *Stress Testing the UK Banking System: Guidance on the 2021 Stress Test for Participants*. https://www.bankofengland.co.uk/stress-testing/2021/stress-testing-guidance-2021-for-participants

Bank of England. (2022a). *090—Stress Test Data Framework Manual Version 2022*. https://www.bankofengland.co.uk/-/media/boe/files/stress-testing/2022/stdf-manual-2022.pdf

Bank of England. (2022b). *Bank of England Publishes Results of the 2021 Biennial Exploratory Scenario: Financial Risks from Climate Change*, Bank of England. https://www.bankofengland.co.uk/news/2022/may/boe-publishes-results-of-the-2021-biennial-exploratory-scenario-financial-risks-from-climate-change

Bank of England. (2022c). *Stress Testing the UK Banking System: Guidance on the 2022 Stress Test for Participants*. https://www.bankofengland.co.uk/stress-testing/2022/stress-testing-guidance-2022-for-participants.

Bank of Israel. (2015). *The Internal Ratings-Based (IRB) Approach to Credit Risk*, Bank of Israel. https://www.boi.org.il/en/BankingSupervision/SupervisorsDirectives/ProperConductOfBankingBusinessRegulations/204_et.pdf

Baudino, P., & Svoronos, J. P. (2021). *Stress-Testing Banks for Climate Change: A Comparison of Practices*. Bank for International Settlements, Financial Stability Institute.

Baudino, P., Goetschmann, R., Henry, J., Taniguchi, K., & Zhu, W. (2018). *Stress-Testing Banks: A Comparative Analysis*. Bank for International Settlements, Financial Stability Institute. https://www.bis.org/fsi/publ/insights12.pdf

BIS. (2017). Supervisory and Bank Stress Testing: Range of Practices. https://www.bis.org/bcbs/publ/d427.pdf

BIS. (2023). *Sarah Breeden: Climate Action—Approaching a Tipping Point?*, Bank for International Settlements, https://www.bis.org/review/r230419d.htm

Board of Governors of the Federal Reserve System. (2022a). *2022 Stress Test Scenarios*. https://www.federalreserve.gov/newsevents/pressreleases/files/bcreg20220210a1.pdf

Board of Governors of the Federal Reserve System. (2022b, June). *Dodd-Frank Act Stress Test 2022: Supervisory Stress Test Results*. https://www.federalreserve.gov/publications/2022-june-dodd-frank-act-stress-test-preface.htm

Board of Governors of the Federal Reserve System. (2022c, March). *2022 Supervisory Stress Test Methodology*. https://www.federalreserve.gov/publications/2022-supervisory-stress-test-methodology-overview-modeling-framework.htm

Boneva, L., Ferrucci, G., & Mongelli, F. P. (2022). Climate Change and Central Banks: What Role for Monetary Policy? *Climate Policy, 22*(6), 770–787.

Chen, Y., Ma, J., Miao, C., & Ruan, X. (2020). Occurrence and Environmental Impact of Industrial Agglomeration on Regional Soil Heavy Metalloid Accumulation: A Case Study of the Zhengzhou Economic and Technological Development Zone (ZETZ). *China. J. Clean. Prod, 245*, 118676. https://doi.org/10.1016/j.jclepro.2019.118676

Comfort, N., Randow, J., & Malsch, L. (2022). *ECB's First Climate Test Sees Up to $71 Billion Hit to Banks*, Bloomberg. https://www.bloomberg.com/news/articles/2022-07-08/ecb-s-first-climate-test-sees-up-to-71-billion-hit-to-banks#xj4y7vzkg

Dafermos, Y. (2022). Climate Change, Central Banking and Financial Supervision: Beyond the Risk Exposure Approach. In *The Future of Central Banking* (pp. 175–194). Edward Elgar Publishing.

Dai, R., Zhang, J., & Tang, W. (2017). Cartelization or Cost-Sharing? Comparison of Cooperation Modes in a Green Supply Chain. *Journal of Cleaner Production, 156*, 159–173. https://doi.org/10.1016/j.jclepro.2017.04.011

Danmarks Nationalbank. (2021). *New ECB Strategy and the Danish Economy*. https://www.nationalbanken.dk/en/publications/Documents/2021/09/ANALYSIS_No.21_New%20ECB%20strategy%20and%20the%20Danish%20economy.pdf

Demekas, D., & Grippa, P. (2022). Walking a Tightrope: Financial Regulation, Climate Change, and the Transition to a Low-Carbon Economy. *Journal of Financial Regulation, 8*(2), 203–229.

European Banking Authority. (2022). *2023 EU-Wide Stress Test.* https://www.eba.europa.eu/sites/default/documents/files/document_library/Risk%20Analysis%20and%20Data/EU-wide%20Stress%20Testing/2023/Methodology/1043009/2023%20EU-wide%20stress%20test%20-%20Methodological%20Note.pdf

European Banking Authority. (2022). *2023 EU-Wide Stress Test—Methodological Note.* https://www.eba.europa.eu/risk-analysis-and-data/eu-wide-stress-testing

European Central Bank. (2019). *ECB Guide to Internal Models*, European Central Bank. https://www.bankingsupervision.europa.eu/ecb/pub/pdf/ssm.guidetointernalmodels_consolidated_201910~97fd49fb08.en.pdf

European Commission. (2023). *Securities Financing Transactions (SFTs).* https://finance.ec.europa.eu/capital-markets-union-and-financial-markets/financial-markets/post-trade-services/securities-financing-transactions-sfts_en

Fagan, P., Rybarczyk, K., Naeem, R., Hickman, V. (2022). *Results of the Bank of England's Climate Stress Test*, Linklaters. https://sustainablefutures.linklaters.com/post/102hpru/results-of-the-bank-of-englands-climate-stress-test

Forni, L., & Kiarsi, M. (2023). Optimal Climate and Monetary-Fiscal Policy in a Climate-DSGE framework.

Gibbons, R. (1997). An Introduction to Applicable Game Theory. *Journal of Economic Perspectives, 11*, 127–149. https://doi.org/10.1257/jep.11.1.127

Giuzio, M., Krušec, D., Levels, A., Melo, A. S., Mikkonen, K., & Radulova, P. (2019). Climate Change and Financial Stability. *Financial Stability Review, 1.*

Hale, G., Krainer, J., & McCarthy, E. (2015). *Aggregation Level in Stress Testing Models*. Federal Reserve Bank of San Francisco.

Hansen, L. P. (2022). Central Banking Challenges Posed by Uncertain Climate Change and Natural Disasters. *Journal of Monetary Economics, 125*, 1–15.

Henry, J., Kok, C., Amzallag, A., Baudino, P., Cabral, I., Grodzicki, M., Gross, M., Hałaj, G., Kolb, M., Leber, M., pancaro, C., Sydow, M., Voudis, A., Zimmermann, M., & Żochowski, D. (2013). A Macro Stress Testing Framework for Assessing Systemic Risks in the Banking Sector. *ECB Occasional Paper* (152).

Hestad, D., Tàbara, J. D., & Thornton, T. F. (2020). Transcending Unsustainable Dichotomies in Management: Lessons from Sustainability-Oriented Hybrid Organisations in Barcelona. *Journal of Cleaner Production, 244*, 118766. https://doi.org/10.1016/j.jclepro.2019.118766

Hong Kong Monetary Authority. (2020). *Implementation of the Basel III Final Reform Package*, Hong Kong Monetary Authority. https://www.hkma.gov.hk/media/eng/regulatory-resources/consultations/CP20_02_Implementation_of_the_Basel_III_Final_Reform_Package.pdf

Hosseini Jebeli, H., Johnston, C., Logan, C., Molico, M., Shen, X., & Tremblay, M. C. (2022). *Assessing Climate-Related Financial Risk: Guide to Implementation of Methods* (No. 120). Bank of Canada.

https://www.responsible-investor.com/ecb-releases-first-climate-report-card-for-eurosystem-central-banks/

Kouvelis, P., & Zhao, W. (2015). Supply Chain Contract Design Under Financial Constraints and Bankruptcy Costs. *Management Science, 62*, 2341–2357. https://doi.org/10.1287/mnsc.2015.2248

Krebs, M., & Nippel, P. (2021). Unexpected Loss, Expected Profit, and Economic Capital: A Note on Economic Capital for Credit Risk Incorporating Interest Income, Expenses, Losses, and ROE Target. *Finance Research Letters, 38*, 101481.

Masciandaro, D., & Russo, R. (2023). *Central Banks and Climate Policy: Unpleasant Trade–Offs? A Principal—Agent Approach*. BAFFI CAREFIN Centre Research Paper.

Mendez-Barreira, V. (2021). Norges Bank given New Macro-Prudential Responsibilities, Central Banking. https://www.centralbanking.com/central-banks/financial-stability/macro-prudential/7873531/norges-bank-given-new-macro-prudential-responsibilities

Moe, T. G., Solheim, J. A., & Vale, B. (Eds.). (2004). *The Norwegian Banking Crisis*. Norges Banks Skriftserie/Occasional Papers 33. https://www.norges-bank.no/contentassets/ed5dd397dce345338046a22c7e07f959/hele_heftet.pdf?v=03/09/2017122240&ft=.pdf

Network for Greening the Financial System. (2019). *A Call for Action: Climate Change as a Source of Financial Risk.*

Neves, P.D. (2021). *The Way Forward for EU-Wide Stress Tests*. SUERF Policy Briefs No 62. https://www.suerf.org/docx/f_da3c55e3be0a795729261bfd8776a627_22047_suerf.pdf

Norges Bank. (2021). *Financial Stability Report 2021: Vulnerabilities and Risks*. https://www.norges-bank.no/en/news-events/news-publications/Reports/Financial-Stability-report/2021-financial-stability/content/#_idTextAnchor009

Ongena, S., Smith, D. C., & Michalsen, D. (2003). Firms and their Distressed Banks: Lessons from the Norwegian Banking Crisis. *Journal of Financial Economics, 67*(1), 81–112.

Ortiz-de-Mandojana, N., & Bansal, P. (2016). The Long-Term Benefits of Organizational Resilience Through Sustainable Business Practices. *The Strategic Management, 37*, 1615–1631. https://doi.org/10.1002/smj.2410

Oura, H., & Schumacher, L. B. (2012). *Macrofinancial stress Testing—Principles and Practices*. International Monetary Fund Policy Paper.

Pedersen, L. H. (2023). *Carbon Pricing*. Available at SSRN 4382360.

Richters, O., Bertram, C., Kriegler, E., Anz, J., Beck, T., Bresch, D., Charles, M., Clarke, L., Cui, R., Edmonds, J., Hackstock, P., Hilaire, J., Holland, D., Hurst, I., Khourdajie, A., Kikstra, J., Kropf, C., Lejeune, Q., Lewis, J., Liadze, I., Meinshausen, M., Min, J., Nicholls, Z., Pfleiderer, P., Piontek, F., Rogelj, J., Sauer, I., Schwind, N., Schleussner, C.F., Schleypen, J.R., Sferra, F., Van Ruijven, B., Weigmann, P., Yu, S., Zhao, A., Zimmer, A., Zwerling, M. (2022). *NGFS Climate Scenario Database: Technical Documentation V3.1.* https://www.ngfs.net/sites/default/files/media/2022/11/21/technical_documentation_ngfs_scenarios_phase_3.pdf

Rogdaberg, B., & Wiese-Hansen, K. H. (2019). *Banking Regulation in Norway*. Schjødt. https://www.lexology.com/library/detail.aspx?g=10b31e53-f8ba-43b9-820a-57ede7d357c9

Schweitzer, M. E., & Venkatu, G. (2009). *Adjustable-Rate Mortgages and the LIBOR Surprise*. Economic Commentary. https://www.clevelandfed.org/publications/economic-commentary/2009/ec-20090109-adjustable-rate-mortgages-and-the-LIBOR-surprise

Shapley, L. S. (1953). A value for n-person games. *Contrib. Th. Gam., 2*(28), 307–317. https://doi.org/10.1515/9781400881970-018

Smialek, J. (2023). Powell Says Fed Will Not Be a 'Climate Policymaker. *The New York Times*, https://www.nytimes.com/2023/01/10/business/economy/powell-fed-climate.html

Smith, A. A., Jr. (2022). Discussion of: "Central Bank Challenges Posed by Uncertain Climate Change and Natural Disasters" by Lars Peter Hansen. *Journal of Monetary Economics, 125*, 16–17.

Smith, E. (2023). *Major Central Bankers Dispute Role in Tackling Climate Change as they Battle Inflation*. CNBC. https://www.cnbc.com/2023/01/11/major-central-bankers-dispute-role-in-tackling-climate-change-as-they-battle-inflation.html

Weber, O. (2005). Sustainability Benchmarking of European Banks and Financial Service Organizations. *Corporate Social Responsibility and Environmental Management, 12*(2), 73–87.

Zeidan, R., Van Holt, T., & Whelan, T. (2020). Existence Inductive Theory Building to Study Coordination Failures in Sustainable Beef Production. *Journal of Cleaner Production, 267*, 122137.

The manufacturer's authorised representative in the EU is Springer Nature Customer Service Centre GmbH, Europaplatz 3, 69115 Heidelberg, Germany. If you have any concerns regarding our products, please contact ProductSafety@springernature.com

Printed and bound by CPI Group (UK) Ltd, Croydon, CR0 4YY
01/10/2026
02225924-0008